Machado de Assis's *Philosopher or Dog?*
From Serial to Book Form

LEGENDA

LEGENDA, founded in 1995 by the European Humanities Research Centre of the University of Oxford, is now a joint imprint of the Modern Humanities Research Association and Maney Publishing. Titles range from medieval texts to contemporary cinema and form a widely comparative view of the modern humanities, including works on Arabic, Catalan, English, French, German, Greek, Italian, Portuguese, Russian, Spanish, and Yiddish literature. An Editorial Board of distinguished academic specialists works in collaboration with leading scholarly bodies such as the Society for French Studies and the British Comparative Literature Association.

MHRA

The Modern Humanities Research Association (MHRA) encourages and promotes advanced study and research in the field of the modern humanities, especially modern European languages and literature, including English, and also cinema. It also aims to break down the barriers between scholars working in different disciplines and to maintain the unity of humanistic scholarship in the face of increasing specialization. The Association fulfils this purpose primarily through the publication of journals, bibliographies, monographs and other aids to research.

Maney Publishing

Maney Publishing is one of the few remaining independent British academic publishers. Founded in 1900 the company has offices both in the UK, in Leeds and London, and in North America, in Boston. Since 1945 Maney Publishing has worked closely with learned societies, their editors, authors, and members, in publishing academic books and journals to the highest traditional standards of materials and production.

EDITORIAL BOARD

Chairman
Professor Colin Davis, Royal Holloway, University of London

Professor Malcolm Cook, University of Exeter (French)
Professor Robin Fiddian, Wadham College, Oxford (Spanish)
Professor Paul Garner, University of Leeds (Spanish)
Professor Andrew Hadfield, University of Sussex (English)
Professor Marian Hobson Jeanneret,
Queen Mary University of London (French)
Professor Catriona Kelly, New College, Oxford (Russian)
Professor Martin McLaughlin, Magdalen College, Oxford (Italian)
Professor Martin Maiden, Trinity College, Oxford (Linguistics)
Professor Peter Matthews, St John's College, Cambridge (Linguistics)
Dr Stephen Parkinson, Linacre College, Oxford (Portuguese)
Professor Suzanne Raitt, William and Mary College, Virginia (English)
Professor Ritchie Robertson, St John's College, Oxford (German)
Professor Lesley Sharpe, University of Exeter (German)
Professor David Shepherd, Keele University (Russian)
Professor Michael Sheringham, All Souls College, Oxford (French)
Professor Alison Sinclair, Clare College, Cambridge (Spanish)
Professor David Treece, King's College London (Portuguese)

Managing Editor
Dr Graham Nelson
41 Wellington Square, Oxford OX1 2JF, UK

legenda@mhra.org.uk
www.legenda.mhra.org.uk

Machado de Assis's *Philosopher or Dog?*

From Serial to Book Form

❖

Ana Cláudia Suriani da Silva

l

LEGENDA

Modern Humanities Research Association and Maney Publishing
2010

Published by the
Modern Humanities Research Association and Maney Publishing
1 Carlton House Terrace
London SW1Y 5AF
United Kingdom

LEGENDA is an imprint of the
Modern Humanities Research Association and Maney Publishing

Maney Publishing is the trading name of W. S. Maney & Son Ltd,
whose registered office is at Suite 1C, Joseph's Well, Hanover Walk, Leeds LS3 1AB

ISBN 978-1-906540-45-6

First published 2010

All rights reserved. No part of this publication may be reproduced or disseminated or transmitted in any form or by any means, electronic, mechanical, photocopying, recording or otherwise, or stored in any retrieval system, or otherwise used in any manner whatsoever without the express permission of the copyright owner

© Modern Humanities Research Association and W. S. Maney & Son Ltd 2010

Printed in Great Britain

Cover: 875 Design

Copy-Editor: Richard Correll

CONTENTS

❖

Acknowledgements	ix
Machado de Assis's Fiction Translated into English	xi
Conventions Adopted	xiii
Introduction	1
Purpose and Methodology	5
The Critical Edition of *Philosopher or Dog?*	6
Bibliographic Revision	8
Plan of the Book	10

PART I: THE FORMAT AND CONTEXT OF READING

1	Machado de Assis's Novels in Serial and Book Form	14
	Linguistic Versus Bibliographic Code	14
	The Mode of Production of Machado de Assis's Earlier Novels	17
	Traces of the Serial in Machado de Assis's Novels	22
	The Role of the Author in the Composition of the Book	31
2	*Philosopher or Dog?* and the Fashion Section of *A Estação*	35
	The Numbers of Subscriptions to the Magazine and of Readers of the Novel	35
	A Estação, a propos *Die Modenwelt*, an International Undertaking	38
	The Global Audience of *Die Modenwelt* and the Target Readership of *Philosopher or Dog?*	55
	The Changing Society of *Philosopher or Dog?*	59
3	*Philosopher or Dog?* and the Literary Section of *A Estação*	69
	The Diversification of the Contents of *Die Modenwelt*	69
	The Literary Section of *A Estação*	74

PART II: NARRATIVE TECHNIQUE AND THE TWO VERSIONS

4	The Kaleidoscopic Narrative of *Philosopher or Dog?*	94
	Gogol, Matrix of *Philosopher or Dog?*	94
	The Narrative Kaleidoscope	102
	Reliable or Unreliable Narrator	105
5	The First Version: Under the Sign of the Serial	112
	A Story that Remained Incomprehensible?	112
	Narrative Units of *Philosopher or Dog?*	114
	The Unfolding of the Plot	138
6	From the Magazine to the Book: The Global View of the Novel	142
	Focusing on Rubião	142
	Rubião's Progressive Madness	150

7 The Fictional Rhetoric of *Philosopher or Dog?*   161
    The Narrator and Implicit Author in *Dom Casmurro* and *Epitaph of a Small Winner*   161
    The Narrator and Implicit Author in *Philosopher or Dog?*   166
    The Novel as an Exemplification of *Humanitismo*   171

Conclusion: *Philosopher or Dog?* The Beginning of the End of the Serial?   177

Bibliography   183

Index   189

ACKNOWLEDGEMENTS

❖

This book could not have been completed without the help of many people and institutions at different stages of the research. They include Thomas Earle, Peter D. McDonald and John Gledson, who supervised my DPhil work on which this book is based. I must also thank Leslie Bethell and Julie Smith for providing for me with an ideal working environment at the University of Oxford. My thanks too to the staff and fellows of Wolfson College, especially Rajeswari Sunder Rajan and Fiona Wilkes, and the Taylor Institution Library, particularly John Wainwright. I am grateful too to Adelheid Rasche, curator of the Sammlung Modebild-Lipperheidesche Kostümbibliothek, Berlin, Cristina Antunes, curator of Biblioteca Mindlin, São Paulo, and José Luís Garaldi, from Livraria A Sereia, São Paulo, who provided me with access to materials related to the *Die Mondenwelt*, *A Estação* and nineteenth-century editions of Brazilian novels. The Bibliothèque national de Paris, the Swiss National Library and the British Library Newspapers at Colindale supplied materials from their collection of periodicals.

I am grateful as well for the generous grant from the Swiss National Science Foundation, which made it possible to develop this project at the University of Oxford. Travel grants from the Centre for Brazilian Studies, Wolfson College and the Faculty of Medieval and Modern Languages enabled me to do research outside the UK. In addition, the Brazilian Embassy in London financially supported the publication of this book.

I would also like to express thanks to Tania Pellegrini, Sandra Vasconcelos, Ana Maria Machado and José Murilo de Carvalho for their rigorous reading of early versions of chapters of this book. I must also thank Charlie Lyons, Claudia Voss, Luciana Lujan, Madeleine Brook, Milena Ribeiro Martins, Sean Linney, Richard Correll, and Graham Nelson for their help with numerous translations, the proof-reading and editing of the manuscript. Finally, my gratitude, as always, to my family.

A.C.S., February 2010

TO MY MOTHER, ADRIANA

MACHADO DE ASSIS'S
FICTION TRANSLATED INTO ENGLISH
❖

According to the *Encyclopedia of Literary Translation into English*,[1] with exception of *Ressurreição* (*Resurrection*, 1872) the other eight novels by Machado de Assis have all been translated into English:

A mão e a luva, 1874:
  The Hand and the Glove, translated by Albert I. Bagby Jr, Lexington: University Press of Kentucky, 1970
Helena, 1876:
  Helena, translated by Helen Caldwell, Berkeley: University of California Press, 1984
Iaiá Garcia, 1878:
  Iaiá Garcia, translated by Albert I. Bagby Jr, Lexington: University Press of Kentucky, 1977
  Yayá Garcia, translated by R. L. Scott-Buccleuch, London: Peter Owen, 1976
Memórias póstumas de Brás Cubas, 1881:
  Posthumous Reminiscences of Brás Cubas, translated by E. Percy Ellis, Rio de Janeiro: Instituto Nacional do Livro, 1955
  Epitaph of a Small Winner, translated by William L. Grossman, New York: Noonday Press, 1952; London: W. H. Allen, 1953
  The Posthumous Memoirs of Bras Cubas, translated by Gregory Rabassa, Oxford: Oxford University Press, 1997
Quincas Borba, 1891:
  Quincas Borba, translated by Gregory Rabassa, Oxford: Oxford University Press, 1998
  Philosopher or Dog?, translated by Clotilde Wilson, New York: Noonday Press, 1954; reissued New York: Farrar, Straus and Giroux, 1992, and London: Bloomsbury, 1997
Dom Casmurro, 1899:
  Dom Casmurro, translated by Helen Caldwell, New York: Noonday and London: W. H. Allen, 1953
  Dom Casmurro, translated by R. L. Scott-Buccleuch, London: Peter Owen, 1966
  Dom Casmurro, translated by John Gledson, Oxford: Oxford University Press, 1997
Esaú e Jacó, 1904:
  Esau and Jacob, translated by Helen Caldwell, Berkeley: University of California Press; London: Peter Owen, 1966
Memorial de Aires, 1908:
  Counselor Ayres' Memorial, translated by Helen Caldwell, Berkeley: University of California Press, 1972
  The Wager: Aires' Journal, translated by R. L. Scott-Buccleuch, London: Peter Owen, 1990

Casa velha (*Old House*, 1885), which by its size and complexity of plot has been traditionally classified as a *novela*, rather than a short story or a novel (*romance* in Portuguese), does not have a translation into English.

There are a few anthologies of Machado de Assis's short stories in English translation:

The Psychiatrist and Other Stories, translated by Helen Caldwell and William L. Grossman, Berkeley: University of California Press, 1963. It contains 'The Psychiatrist' and eleven other stories, namely 'A Woman's Arms', The Looking Glass', 'The Secret Heart', 'The Rod of Justice', 'The Animal Game', 'Midnight Mass', 'Father versus Mother', 'Education of a Stuffed Shirt', 'The Holiday', 'Admiral's Night' and 'Final request'.

The Devil's Church and Other Stories, translated by Jack Schmitt and Lorie Ishimatsu, Austin: University of Texas Press, 1977. It contains 'The Bonzo's Secret', 'Those Cousins from Sapucaia', 'Alexandrian Tale', 'The Devil's Church', 'A Strange Thing', 'Final Chapter', 'A Second Life', 'Dona Paula', 'The Diplomat', 'The Companion', 'Evolution', 'Adam and Eve', 'Eternal', 'A Celebrity', 'Mariana', 'A Canary's Idea', 'Pylades and Orestes', 'Funeral March' and 'Wallow, Swine!'.

A Chapter of Hats and Other Stories, translated by John Gledson, London: Bloomsbury, 2008. It contains 'In the Ark', 'The Mirror', 'An Alexandrian Tale', 'A Singular Occurrence', 'A Chapter of Hats', 'Those Cousins from Sapucaia!', 'Admiral's Night', 'Evolution', 'A Schoolboy's Story', 'Dona Paula', 'The Diplomat', 'The Fortune-Teller', 'The Hidden Cause', 'A Pair of Arms', 'The Cynosure of All Eyes', 'A Famous Man', 'The Cane', 'Midnight Mass', 'Pylades and Orestes' and 'Father against Mother'.

His short stories also appears in anthologies of Brazilian and Latin-American fiction, such as:

Oxford Anthology of the Brazilian Short Story, edited by K. David Jackson, Oxford: Oxford University Press, 2006. It contains 'Wedding Song', 'The Siamese Academies', 'The Fortune-Teller', 'Life', 'The Nurse', 'The Secret Heart', 'A Woman's Arms', 'Dona Paula', 'Father versus Mother' and 'Wallow, Swine!'.

Note

1. Olive Classe, *Encyclopedia of Literary Translation into English*, 2 vols (London: Fitzroy Dearborn, 2000), I, 880.

CONVENTIONS ADOPTED

❖

The Machado de Assis Committee has published critical editions of all of Machado de Assis's novels.[1] For textual quotations and the presentation of variations, I use the critical editions. Spelling has been updated in accordance with the most recent Portuguese orthographic agreement. In the case of the first version of *Quincas Borba*, I indicate the publication date in *A Estação* as well as the page on which the quotation is found in the critical edition. In order to describe the material appearance of the text, I use the first editions and the periodicals in which the author's serialized novels were originally published. To facilitate reading, chapter numbers from the novels are given in Arabic numerals,[2] rather than the Roman numerals shown in the original and critical editions. All quotations in Portuguese, French and German have been translated into English.

Quotations from the first version of *Quincas Borba*, other texts by Machado de Assis, Brazilian periodicals and secondary sources have been translated by Sean Linney. I have used Clotilde Wilson's 1954 translation in all quotations of the second version of *Quincas Borba*, from the 1992 edition republished by Farrar, Straus and Giroux in New York, which subsequently appeared in a London edition by Bloomsbury in 1997.

I have used the translated titles of Machado de Assis's novels in the titles and sections of the chapters of this book, but have kept the original title of the novel, in Portuguese, when they are mentioned in the body of the text.

Note

1. *Ressurreição, A mão e a luva, Helena, Iaiá Garcia, Memórias póstumas de Brás Cubas, Quincas Borba, Dom Casmurro, Esaú e Jacó* and *Memorial de Aires, edições críticas de obras de Machado de Assis* (Rio de Janeiro: Civilização Brasileira and Instituto Nacional do Livro, 1975). The Machado de Assis Committee was created by the Ministry of Education and Culture in 1958. It was made up of Antônio Houaiss, Antônio José Chediak, Augusto Meyer, Aurélio Buarque de Holanda Ferreira, Celso Ferreira da Cunha, Ciro dos Anjos, Eugênio Gomes, Francisco de Assis Barbosa, Hélcio Martins, José Barreto Filho, José Brito Broca, José Galante de Sousa, José Simeão Leal, Lúcia Miguel Pereira, Manuel Cavalcanti Proença, Marco Aurélio de Moura Matos, Mário Gonçalves de Matos, Raimundo Magalhães Júnior and Peregrino Júnior. The Committee was responsible for preparing fifteen volumes of critical editions of the novels, poems and short stories published in book form during the writer's lifetime.
2. A complete description of the contents of the 'Literary Part' of *A Estação* during the publication of *Quincas Borba* is available at <http://www.caminhosdoromance.iel.unicamp.br>.

INTRODUCTION

❖

The Brazilian writer, Joaquim Maria Machado de Assis (1839–1908), one of the greatest Latin American authors, is not unknown in the English-speaking world. Most of his novels and approximately fifty of his short stories have been translated into English, and he has also garnered the attention of some important English-speaking critics outside the circle of Latin Americanists and Brazilianists. Susan Sontag, for example, in an article published in the *New Yorker Magazine*, noted of Machado (as he is more often referred to) that his 'afterlife has not brought his work the recognition that it merits'.[1] More recently, Harold Bloom, in his book *Genius*, stressed the connection — already much studied, at least in Brazilian circles — between Machado de Assis and Laurence Sterne.[2]

Yet Machado de Assis's oeuvre has only caught the eyes of very few academics in departments other than Portuguese and Hispanic Studies. It is worth mentioning Franco Moretti's article, 'Conjectures on World Literature', in which the author fosters the comparison of Machado de Assis's novels to those of other peripheral authors — from India and Japan, for example. As is widely known, Moretti does not deal with individual novels. On the contrary, he suggests a different critical method to capture the vast wealth and variety of world literature, namely by *distant* rather than *close* reading — that is, by making extensive use of secondary sources, of studies by literary critics from all over the world. By doing so, he finds that they all agree that 'when a culture starts moving towards the modern novel, it's *always* as a compromise between foreign form and local materials'.[3] The current book, *Philosopher or Dog? From Serial to Book Form*, attempts to reinforce Moretti's findings, by examining whether they apply to the relationship that Machado de Assis maintained with the serial novel, as a genre and format of publication of fiction invented in Europe, and with the means of literary production available in Rio de Janeiro.[4]

The starting point of this book is a reading of *Philosopher or Dog?* (*Quincas Borba* in Portuguese). It is one of Machado de Assis's greatest novels and the one with the most problematic creative process. First published in serial form in *A Estação* (*The Season*),[5] an international women's magazine, between 1886 and 1891, it was then published by the French editor B. L. Garnier in book format, in 1891. Many fundamental differences exist between the serial and book versions, and the former involved the author in considerable difficulty — so much so that he had to interrupt publication more than once and finally abandoned the serial as the original format of publication for his future novels.

Although its point of depart is the two versions of *Quincas Borba*, the current study attempts to prove that *Quincas Borba* is a turning point in Machado de Assis's relationship with the serial. I have tried to demonstrate that, among the writers' novels published in serial format, *Quincas Borba* represents a great innovation in artistic form. The writer undertakes a totally new approach to the narrative material, which could be called the *global vision* of the novel.

As stated above, *Quincas Borba* was originally published in serial form in the magazine *A Estação*. As such, the composition of the first version results from the tension between the vision of the narrative as a continuous text, to be read as a standalone book, and the premise that it will in fact be read in sequence, but piecemeal. The initial incompatibility between the overall vision which the writer intended to give to the text and the need to publish it in slices generated a creative impasse, which subsequently resulted in interruptions in the publication of the novel and the use of temporary narrative solutions borrowed from popular literary forms such as the serialized novel and the melodrama. The serial version therefore documents the clash generated in the creative process between the conditions of publication and the narrative framework of the overall plan of the work.

In the creative process, the text of *Quincas Borba* obeys and breaches the injunctions of the serial not only in terms of its narrative structure but also with regard to the themes which it explores. The dialogue between the content of *Quincas Borba* and the ideological leanings of *A Estação* is visible because its creative, imaginative world is fed by the magazine and, in exchange, it maintains a dialogue with the themes disseminated throughout the other columns, the illustrations and even the advertisements. As such, it is necessary to become better acquainted with the magazine in order to understand the degree of attraction which the novel might have held for its subscribers, and even to understand its irony. I believe that a large part of the irony of *Quincas Borba* results from the accommodation between its theme and the cultural values transmitted by the magazine. One of the challenges of this book is therefore to prove that a complex and ironic intertextual relationship exists between *Quincas Borba* and *A Estação*.

The serial version of the novel must not be seen only as a document of the creative process, nor as an unfinished product, nor as a field of experimentation for the forms and themes of the book. The text of the serial form of *Quincas Borba* represents a unity in itself, with a beginning, a middle and an ending, and it successfully fulfilled its most immediate function: to entertain subscribers to the magazine. Although he did so by means of a series of attempts and errors, the writer had already delineated in the serial the intricate network of interpersonal relations of various types and densities which we know so well from reading the novel. The criss-crossing of the destinies of all of the characters, and at the same time the role played by each of them in determining Rubião's trajectory, had already been made very clear in the serial.

It cannot be doubted that, during the period in which it was serialized in *A Estação*, between 15 June 1886 and 15 September 1891, *Quincas Borba* reached a significant audience. In 1882, the circulation claimed by the magazine totalled 10,000 subscribers, which very probably represents just a portion of those who actually leafed through the magazine every two weeks. The number of readers of a periodical is always potentially much greater than the number of subscribers. In the specific case of *A Estação*, the editors believed that each subscriber represented 'termo médio, dez leitores, o que nos dá uma circulação de cem mil leitores, quando, aliás, nossa tiragem é apenas de dez mil assinaturas' [an average of ten readers, which gives us a circulation of 100,000 readers, when, in fact, our print-run is of just 10,000 subscriptions] (*A Estação*, 15 March 1882).

It can be supposed that, at least for a fraction of this audience, the novel had provided a kind of reading experience which differed from that of the reader of the single-volume novel. A large part of the argument of this book is based on the observation that the two versions provide different reading experiences, principally due to the format in which they were published. A crucial element in determining the involvement of the reader in the story, and the temporary suppositions that were constructed while the text was unfolding from instalment to instalment, is the fact that the novel required extended reading, over a period of more than five years, at intervals determined by its fortnightly periodicity (or broken up by interruptions in the publication of the novel).

The process of reading the magazine is embedded in its material framework, which is very different from that of the single-volume novel. Each issue, with its fashion section and literary pages, could be seen as a single text created by multiple authors. The readers had in their field of vision the continuation of the serialized narrative and other textual and pictorial elements, all bound together by the same editorial principles. I put forward the hypothesis that the predominantly female readership of the serial was more likely to make an immediate connection between the plot of *Quincas Borba* and fashion, which is the main subject of *A Estação*. It must be clarified here that the term *fashion* does not only apply to the predominant trends in clothing and accessories, which are replaced by new styles over a certain period of time, in line with a rhythm dictated at times by the changing seasons of the year. It also includes other areas of social activity, such as leisure (including reading), and the fashion of prestigious residential districts and high-class professions. In *Les lois de l'imitation*, Gabriel Tarde distinguishes fashion from costumes. Costumes are linked to tradition, and to the past, while fashion pays homage to the present and is guided by novelty.[6] We shall see that the magazine *A Estação* paid homage not only to fashion but also to the habits of the elite, including philanthropy. These habits would in turn be imitated by characters in *A Estação* that aspired to change class.

In common with every fashion magazine, *A Estação* fostered the desire to climb socially, because fashion plays a very important role in social mobility between classes. We shall see that the editorial leanings of the magazine played a part in the imaginative construction of the novel by transforming into fiction the social aspirations of its target readers. But, as was perhaps inevitable where Machado de Assis is concerned, the reader is given a jolt by the satire aimed at the imperial pomp (transmitted mainly through the German illustrations) contained in *A Estação*. I will show that the irony of *Quincas Borba* is synthesized in the imperial megalomania of Rubião, built on the maladjustment between the imperial leanings of the magazine and the decadent state of the Brazilian monarchy before the Proclamation of the Republic. The jolt actually comes in two forms because the serial drew its readers' attention to the high price which the characters, even the successful ones, end up paying for their participation in the social game.

In the second place, the experience of reading the serial and the book formats is different due to the changes made to the text by the writer. The first single-volume edition of the novel, as well as being stripped of the articles, illustrations and advertisements with which it shared space on the pages of *A Estação*, also offers the reader a profoundly revised text. Machado reworked the narrative all the way from the microscopic level, the restructuring of sentences, to the macroscopic level, the reordering of events. Nor must it be forgotten that he removed or condensed large sequences of episodes and added some sections or chapters.

I defend the thesis that the rewriting of the novel was guided by the writer's concern for the organization of the plot and the meaning that it would acquire when the book was read as a single volume. Here, we take plot as Peter Brooks has understood it, namely 'a structuring operation elicited by, and made necessary by, those meanings that develop through succession and time'.[7] According to the same author, the term 'plot' thus includes the design and the intention of the narrative, being 'the active process of *sjužet* working on *fabula*, the dynamic of its interpretive ordering'.[8]

The terms *fabula* and *sjužet* were coined by the Russian formalists in order to highlight the difference between what is told and the way in which events are presented in the narrative discourse. *Fabula* designates the abstract line of the events in chronological order, and *sjužet* the infinite ways in which these events can be organized within the discourse. As Brooks clarifies, *fabula* 'is in fact a mental construction that the reader derives from the *sjužet*, which is all that he ever directly knows'.[9] For Brooks, the distinction between *fabula* and *sjužet* 'is central to our thinking about narrative and necessary to its analysis since it allows us to juxtapose two modes of order and in the juxtaposing to see how ordering takes place' (Brooks, p. 13). While considering the plot we shall also consider the elements of the story and their ordering. The plot can therefore be defined as 'the interpretative activity elicited by the distinction between *sjužet* and *fabula*, the way we use the one against the other'.[10]

In rewriting *Quincas Borba*, Machado takes to its extreme his initial plan of constructing meaning through narrative blocks which are much longer than the instalments of the serial, and which ultimately included all of the novel, from the first to the last chapter. To do this, the novelist carried out a series of rewriting operations which were intimately connected. For didactic reasons, however, it will be necessary to examine them separately in the first instance. The order in which they are presented does not imply that one operation is more important than any other: they all have the same importance, although they reveal different techniques and greater or lesser commitment on the writer's part to realizing them.

Particularly with regard to omission, Machado eliminated the episodic and melodramatic elements which are traditionally identified as being typical of the serial genre, and which, as we shall see, were of little importance to the plot. Among those elements which he expanded, the writer developed in more detail the theory of *Humanitismo*, giving the philosophy invented by Quincas Borba a more far-reaching dimension in the book. Where textual additions are concerned, Machado also developed in more perceptible stages the process by which Rubião goes mad, which helped to maintain the focus on Rubião. The concentration of the narrative axis on Rubião is also achieved by means of some textual replacements and the reordering of events. From the first version we shall see that, as Genette points out, the sequence of events in the narrative is organized by means of temporarily demarcated links, following the criterion of the existence of significant temporal intervals.[11] When Machado rewrites the novel in order to publish it in book form, he inverts the order of the narrative units, thereby playing with the distinction between *fabula* and *sjužet*.

In a certain sense, the purpose of studying the first version of *Quincas Borba*, and comparing it with the book version, is to achieve greater knowledge of the latter, as it is this version which, after all, will continue to be read by the wider public, whether in paper or electronic editions. For this reason, I am concerned with examining not only what changed but also what remained the same, or barely changed, from one version to the next. These elements include the third-person narrator, the implicit reader and author, and the plot of the novel, i.e., the story of the supposed affair between, on the one hand, Rubião and Sofia, and on the other hand, Sofia and Carlos Maria. More specifically, I will investigate the way in which the plot is constructed, and the way in which the novelist builds around the plot a pact of reliability between the reader and the narrator, which at the same time serves as a mechanism by which to distract the reader from the more hidden meanings of the narrative. The difference between the plane of the narrator, in his positioning with respect to the reader, and the plane of the implicit author, who is juxtaposed with the former and grants a totalizing meaning to the narrated elements, comes into play here.

Purpose and Methodology

It is not by chance that the two versions of *Quincas Borba* have been chosen as the starting point and the main subject of research of this book. It is symptomatic that *Quincas Borba* should be the work which brings to an end the cycle of production of those novels of Machado's associated with publication in periodicals. With the exception of his first attempt at the genre, *Ressurreição* (1872), all of the other novels prior to *Quincas Borba* had been published in serial form, whether in daily newspapers or fortnightly magazines, before they passed into book form. *Quincas Borba* is the novel whose periodic publication lasted for the longest period of time, and it is also the only novel which Machado changed significantly for the first single-volume edition, which appeared in 1891. As such, the typographical material comprised by the instalments could not be used for the printing of *Quincas Borba* in book form, as they could, without exception, in the cases of *A mão e a luva* (1874), *Helena* (1876), *Iaiá Garcia* (1878) and *Memórias póstumas de Brás Cubas* (1881).

This information may seem irrelevant for a type of criticism which does not take into account the bibliographic code of a work in order to interpret it. However, we can find in it signs of the obstacles (the pressure of time, spatial limitations, and the participation of other agents in the physical and artistic configuration of the text) which the writer confronted in realizing the plan of the work and which would certainly have affected the final result.

The study of the bibliographic code of the first editions of the novel thereby provides several clues to the conditions under which the text was produced. As such, the comparison of the two versions cannot be limited to a mere survey and study of the variants. The challenge here is to read Machado de Assis's novel while at the same time focusing one's attention on its linguistic and bibliographic code, from the typographic font to its corresponding form and meaning. As D. F. McKenzie writes,

> the moment we are required to explain signs in a book, as distinct from describing or copying them, they assume a symbolic status. If a medium in any sense effects a message, then bibliography cannot exclude from its own proper concerns the relation between form, function, and symbolic meaning.[12]

The comparison of the two versions takes into account the differences in format and other characteristics of the publication of Machado de Assis's novels, whose characteristics are seen in this work as historical circumstances of the production of the text, and which cannot therefore be relegated to an inferior plane in the interpretation of the literary work.

The Critical Edition of *Philosopher or Dog?*

Although the magazine *A Estação* and the critical editions of *Quincas Borba* which were published during the writer's lifetime will be the primary sources of this book, the critical edition prepared by the Machado de Assis Committee proved indispensable throughout all stages of research, not least because it contains the only existing transcript of the serial version of *Quincas Borba*. As with other works by Machado edited by the Committee, the edition of *Quincas Borba* was established using the traditional methods of textual criticism. During the first stage, José Chediak established a genealogical classification of the versions of the text in accordance with the editions he possessed, defining the history of its dissemination and the bibliographic characteristics of each edition or version. The following abbreviations were adopted for the editions of *Quincas Borba* that were compared (only those which were published during the writer's lifetime are listed):

A — *A Estação, Jornal Ilustrado para a Família*, Rio de Janeiro: Lombaerts Typography, published fortnightly from 15 June 1886 to 15 September 1891;

B — Machado de Assis, *Quincas Borba*, Rio de Janeiro: B. L. Garnier, 1891;

C — Machado de Assis, *Quincas Borba*, second edition, Rio de Janeiro: H. Garnier [1896];

D — Machado de Assis, The Brazilian Academy of Letters, *Quincas Borba*, third edition, Rio de Janeiro: H. Garnier [1899].

During the second stage, the Committee chose the base text — D — and eventually proceeded to establish the text in accordance with critical principles which updated the spelling but at the same time respected the linguistic present created by the author.

As was mentioned previously, substantial modifications were introduced into *B* with regard to the form, content, ordering and numbering of the chapters. As such, the Committee chose to divide this edition of *Quincas Borba* into two volumes. In the first, the three editions of the novel in book form which were published during the writer's lifetime are compared. Although there are variations between those three editions, they do not constitute different versions of the same text. In the second volume, which is called *Apêndice*, the serial version is presented *in extenso* and compared with the book version.[13] The sections of the serial which coincide with the book version thereby appear in italics.

It will probably be very difficult to find a more efficient editorial solution than this by which to present the textual differences between the two versions. However, it must be stated here that the reader is encouraged to visualize the variations in opposition to the sections of the serial which were used for the book. The reading of the serial as a self-sufficient text is therefore hindered. As a result, the original bibliographic information and the narrative characteristics of the text which are related to the serial genre pass unnoticed or, at least, are obfuscated — this is a further reason why the type of research carried out here was felt necessary. The first version of *Quincas Borba* had to be read directly as it had been printed in the magazine *A Estação*, whether via the medium of paper or microfilm.

Even so, my research takes as a presupposition the rigorous work of the survey of the first version of *Quincas Borba*, carried out by the Machado de Assis Committee. In the critical-philological introduction we find, located by the Committee, the day, month, year, number, page and column of the 'Literary Section' of *A Estação* in which each chapter of the serialized version of *Quincas Borba* was published. In addition, the Committee took the trouble to cross-reference the chapters containing corresponding material in *A* and *B*, which certainly facilitated the work I undertook in comparing the two versions.[14]

The job of surveying the chapters of *Quincas Borba* in *A Estação*, carried out by the Machado de Assis Committee, was especially difficult due to the lack of order in the numbering and the absence of a connecting link. A further obstacle confronting the editors was the fact that the National Library in Rio de Janeiro did not possess all of the issues of the 'Literary Section' of *A Estação* published between the beginning and end of the publication of the serial. Chediak had to search private collections, bookshops and other libraries in Brazil and abroad for those supplements which had not been located or were incomplete. Of the 127 issues in which *Quincas Borba* might have been published, according to the calculations of the Committee, only four have not been located. At the time of creation of the critical edition, the missing issues were:

a. 15 January 1887, in which chapters 43 to 47 must have been published; these chapters presumably coincide with chapters 44 to 47 in *B*;

b. 15 April 1887, in which only the final part of chapter 62 had been located;

c. 31 May 1887 and 31 July 1891, in which Chediak believed that the *Quincas Borba* section was not published.

By presenting to the contemporary public for the first time some chapters which had been considered lost, my research not only uses, but also updates and complements the work carried out by the Machado de Assis Committee in surveying the chapters and variations contained in *A*. When examining the collection of *A Estação* belonging to the 'A Sereia' bookshop in São Paulo, I found three of the four issues of the 'Literary Section' listed above: the issues dated 15 April and 31 May 1887, and the issue dated 31 July 1891. I was therefore able to confirm, as had already been suspected, that *Quincas Borba* had not been published in the latter two issues. In the issue dated 15 April 1887, I found chapters 58, 59, 60, 61 and the first part of 62, which had not been transcribed in the critical edition.

With these three findings, it can now be confirmed that the serial version of the novel was published fortnightly in *A Estação* from 15 June 1886 to 15 September 1891, with the following interruptions:

1887: 31 May, 31 October;

1888: 15 March, 30 April, 15 May, 15 June to 15 October;

1889: 15 January, 15 February, 15 April, 15 and 31 May, 15 July, 15 August to 15 November;

1890: 30 April, 30 June, 15 September, 31 October, 31 December;

1891: 31 May, 15 July to 15 August.

In order to complete the serial, the issue dated 15 January 1887 still needs to be located. It must contain the enigmatic episode describing the hanging of a slave, which Rubião remembers in one of his aimless walks around the streets of Rio de Janeiro. Although it is incomplete, a new edition of the first version of *Quincas Borba* is now urgently required, in the first place because the critical edition has run out, and in the second place because the Machado de Assis Committee opted to transcribe the work without updating the spelling.

Bibliographic Revision

In the voluminous literature which has been published on Machado de Assis, the two versions of *Quincas Borba* could hardly have passed unnoticed, but the fundamental artistic innovation represented by this novel has received very little attention in its critical history. A year after the appearance of the critical edition, a pioneering article by J. C. Kinnear was published. My research owes much to Kinnear's assertion that Machado started revising the novel for the book edition *before* the serialization in the magazine had finished, opening up a path for research into the relationship between publication formats and narrative solutions. I disagree with the critic, however, with regard to the change which occurs from one version to the next in relation to the narrator. According to Kinnear, 'a conscious move towards unreliability can be seen in the writing of *Quincas Borba*'.[15] I do not see this type of change in the narrator's attitude to the reader; I believe that the reliability of the narrator is strictly linked to the way in which the plot is constructed, and this, as we shall see, does not change from one version to the next.

I shall prove that in the two versions the reader has access to the points of view of all of the characters and, I repeat, is therefore not deceived with respect to the plot. The reader is in the position of a spectator. The change is much more subtle than Kinnear suggests and is rooted in the way in which the writer presents the characters, or, more specifically, their thoughts, especially those of the protagonist, in order to communicate to us his mental confusion. This is also the way in which he succeeds in making more visible Rubião's descent into madness.

As will be seen, in considering the reliable narrator in relation to the plot of the two versions, I shall not be discarding the possibility that the novel contains meanings which are 'hidden' from the less attentive reader. As in *Memórias póstumas de Brás Cubas* and *Dom Casmurro*, Machado de Assis's choice of a certain type of narrator is part of the fictional rhetoric of each novel. His ultimate aim is to distract the attention of the reader from the hard truths which the novel reveals to them about their own class or the way in which they live in society.

The next significant contribution to the critical history of the novel was John Gledson's book *Machado de Assis: ficção e história*, which is convincing in its aim of relating the development of the writer's later prose works to his interpretation of the history of Brazil in the second half of the nineteenth century. *Quincas Borba* is fundamental to his argument, as Gledson succeeds in showing that the complexity of the novel's plot and structure is modulated by a more varied society and by the period of crisis suffered by the Empire in the late 1860s and early 1870s, which are fictionalized in the novel. The realism of *Quincas Borba* is at the same time social and political. For Gledson, the two versions prove that, while Machado did not have any difficulty in representing a changing society, the same cannot be said of the representation of his interpretation of the political crisis. Gledson's reading of the two versions aims to recover the process by which the author, through attempts and errors, constructed his political vision, until it took shape in the allegory embodied, above all (but not only), in Rubião, 'a incoerência e o conflito de uma sociedade inteira, bem como o seu distanciamento da realidade' [the incoherence and conflict of a whole society, as well as its gradual distancing from reality].[16]

Gledson's work aims to understand Machado de Assis's vision of the history of Brazil, which is in itself a great achievement, and he managed to demolish once and for all the myth that the writer was apolitical. But here lies the great difference between my research and Gledson's: above all, I aim to understand Machado the artist, or more specifically, the novelist, as a writer confronted with the task of giving form and unity to, and finally finishing, a work which was in progress. Moreover, the creative process is seen as one cog inside a large machine in which other agents also participate, such as the editor and the typographer of the magazine. The work therefore results from an accommodation between the author's intentions and the context in which the work is published.

Gledson is particularly interested in investigating the historical bases of Machado de Assis's plots. However, he does not fail to draw attention to the development of his narrative procedures: Gledson was the first to highlight the complexity of the plot and structure of *Quincas Borba*. I use as a starting point his suggestion that *Quincas Borba* represents a genuine structural innovation in relation to *Brás Cubas*.

In order to represent a changing society, Machado opts for a third-person narrator, which allows the different characters to present their own views on the events, thereby giving rise to what I call a narrative kaleidoscope. However, we shall see that we are not dealing with a polyphonic novel, in the sense used by Bakhtin to refer to Dostoevsky's work. Starting from Gledson's suggestion, I advance the discussion by drawing on the hypothesis of the connection between different publication formats and corresponding narrative techniques: the narrative model of *Quincas Borba* no longer fitted in the serial format. For this reason, the writing of the novel entered a period of crisis and the novelist subsequently abandoned the serial as a means of publishing his novels.

I cannot fail to mention here Marlyse Meyer, to whom I owe the suggestion of studying the role that the magazine *A Estação* played in constructing the novel's imaginary world. It was also Marlyse Meyer who opened up a pathway for research into the connection between the editorial leanings of *A Estação* and the German magazine *Die Modenwelt*, by highlighting the German origin of this journalistic undertaking.[17]

Plan of the Book

This book is divided into two parts. The first, which is composed of three chapters, concerns itself with the study of *Quincas Borba* in the context of Machado de Assis's novels and the magazine *A Estação*. Chapter 1 examines the author's relationship with the serial: from the evolution of his production of those novels which were originally intended to be published in instalments, to the crisis he suffered with *Quincas Borba*, the last of his novels to be published in this format. In the second and third chapters, I study the relationship between the themes of the novel and the textual and pictorial content of the magazine in which the first version was published. More specifically, in Chapter 2 I explore the relationship between *Quincas Borba* and the fashion section, and in Chapter 3 the relationship between *Quincas Borba* and the 'Literary Section' of *A Estação*.

The second part of this book, which contains four chapters, concerns itself with the narrative parameters of *Quincas Borba* and undertakes a comparison of the two versions. In Chapter 4, I show how the plot of the novel is constructed and discuss the position of the narrator in relation to the reader. In Chapter 5, I investigate the internal organization of the narrative based on an identification of the temporal units which are used to construct the plot. Here I also study the changes, particularly the omissions, made in the act of rewriting which resulted in the elimination of episodic elements and those elements which were characteristic of the periodical. The last two chapters are dedicated to a study of how Machado constructed the overall vision of the novel in the second version. Chapter 6 examines the reordering of the temporal units and the way in which the focus became centred on Rubião, mainly by means of textual additions. Chapter 7 identifies the way in which the unifying vision of the implicit author is imposed on the point of view of the narrator through the elaboration of the theory of *Humanatismo*, which, in the book version, becomes the unifying element of the plot.

Notes to the Introduction

1. Susan Sontag, 'Afterlives: The Case of Machado de Assis', *New Yorker Magazine*, 7 May 1990, p. 102
2. For example, Eugênio Gomes, *Machado de Assis: influências inglesas* (Rio de Janeiro: Pallas Editora e Distribuidora, 1976); José Guilherme Merquior, '*Gênero* e estilo das *Memórias póstumas de Brás Cubas*, *Colóquio/Letras*, 8 (1972), 12–20; Luiz Costa Lima, 'Sob a face de um bruxo', in *Dispersa demanda: ensaios sobre literatura e teoria* (Rio de Janeiro: Francisco Alves, 1981), pp. 57–123; Enylton de Sá Rego, *O calundu e a panaceia: Machado de Assis, a sátira menipeia e a tradição luciânica* (Rio de Janeiro: Forense Universitária, 1989); Sergio Paulo Rouanet, 'The Shandean Form: Laurence Sterne and Machado de Assis', in *The Author as Plagiarist, the Case of Machado de Assis*, ed. by João Cezar de Castro Rocha (Dartmouth: University of Massachusetts, 2006), pp. 81–103; Sergio Paulo Rouanet, *Riso e melancolia: a forma shandiana em Sterne, Diderot, Xavier de Maistre, Almeida Garrett e Machado de Assis* (São Paulo: Companhia das Letras, 2007).
3. Franco Moretti, 'Conjectures on World Literature', *New Left Review*, 1 (Jan/Feb 2000), pp. 55–68, p. 60.
4. The serial novel is understood to be a novel published in periodicals, newspapers or magazines, in serial form which possess a specific novelistic narrative structure: systematic cut-off points, suspense, simplified characterization etc. The serial is more generally understood to be a format used for serialized publications, in newspapers, of literary works of various sizes, which could include short stories, novellas, or novels. The serial also denotes the literary section of a newspaper which usually occupies the lower part of the page and the fragment of a novel published in a newspaper on a daily basis, arousing the interest of the reader.
5. Here *The Season* is the literal translation of the name of the Brazilian magazine. As we shall see in Chapter 1 of this book, there were different foreign editions of *A Estação*, including one in English, called *The Season*. Titles of magazines will be kept in their original language.
6. Gabriel Tarde, *Les lois de l'imitation* (Paris: Feliz Alcan, 1895), p. 267. On this subject, see also James Laver, *Taste and Fashion: From the French Revolution to the Present Day* (London: George G. Harrap, 1945); and Gilda de Mello e Souza, *O espírito das roupas: a moda no século XIX* (São Paulo: Companhia das Letras, 1987).
7. Peter Brooks, *Reading for the Plot: Design and Intention in Narrative* (Cambridge, MA: Harvard University Press, 2003), p. 12.
8. Brooks, p. 25.
9. The French structuralists, including Todorov, for example, translated the terms as *histoire* (which corresponds to *fabula*) and *discours* or *récit* (which corresponds to *sjužet*). See Tzvetan Todorov, *Introduction to Poetics,* trans. by Richard Howard (Brighton: Harvester, 1981), pp. 29–30; and Gérard Genette, *Narrative Discourse, an Essay in Method*, trans. by Jane E. Lewin (Ithaca, NY: Cornell University Press, 1980), p. 33.
10. Brooks, p. 13.
11. Genette, pp. 88–89.
12. D. F. McKenzie, *Bibliography and the Sociology of Texts* (Cambridge: Cambridge University Press, 1999), p. 10. Bibliography, according to McKenzie, 'is the discipline that studies texts as recorded forms, and the process of their transmission, including their production and reception' (p. 12). The discipline is also concerned with showing 'how forms effect meaning' (p. 13). Also, it helps us 'to describe not only the technical but the social processes of their transmission. In those quite specific ways, it accounts for non-book texts, their physical forms, textual versions, technical transmission, institutional control, their perceived meanings, and social effects' (p. 13). For McKenzie, typography has a symbolic function as an interpretive system (p. 17). Typographic signs have an expressive function in books, 'as they bear on editing, and as they relate to critical theory' (p. 18).
13. Machado de Assis, *Quincas Borba* (Rio de Janeiro: Civilização Brasileira, INL, 1975); and *Quincas Borba apêndice* (Rio de Janeiro: Civilização Brasileira, INL, 1975).
14. 'Introdução crítico-filológica', *Quincas Borba*, pp. 39–102.
15. J. C. Kinnear, 'Machado de Assis: To Believe or Not to Believe?', *Modern Language Review*, 71, 1 (1976), pp. 54–60.

16. John Gledson, *Machado de Assis: ficção e história*, 2nd rev. edn (São Paulo: Terra e Paz, 2003), p. 127.
17. Marlyse Meyer, chapter on 'Estações', in *Caminhos do imaginário no Brasil* (São Paulo: Edusp, 1993), pp. 73–107.

PART I

❖

The Format and Context of Reading

CHAPTER 1

❖

Machado de Assis's Novels in Serial and Book Form

My research into Machado de Assis's work as a novelist is based on an analysis of the relationship between his novels and the publishing practices which were prevalent in the second half of the nineteenth century. At the time, novels were essentially published in two formats: as serials, which appeared in pamphlets, daily newspapers, and fortnightly or monthly magazines; and as books. It was common for works of fiction to be published in serial form first and then reprinted in book form once changes (which may or may not have been substantial) had been made to the text. The debut novelist submitted himself to the usual operational requirements of the newspapers and publishers with which he collaborated, and this left marks on the work he produced. These marks can be identified in the numbering and size of the chapters, the temporal evolution of the story, and the presence of elements characteristic of serialized stories in the narrative. In this chapter, we shall see that Machado de Assis's relationship with the serial evolved progressively until it suffered a crisis with *Quincas Borba* [*Philosopher or Dog?*], the text which ended the cycle of novels written by Machado de Assis for serialized publication.

Linguistic versus Bibliographic Code

Machado de Assis published many of his short stories and novels in the Rio de Janeiro press, whether it was in daily newspapers such as *O Globo*, *O Cruzeiro*, and *Gazeta de Notícias*, or in illustrated fortnightly or monthly magazines such as *Jornal das Famílias*, *A Estação* and the *Revista Brasileira*. We must therefore ask ourselves if the editorial constraints of serial publication had any effect on the writing process. Marlyse Meyer has suggested that Machado de Assis invented the serialized short story in Brazil.[1] Before they appeared in a single volume, 'O segredo de Augusta', 'A parasita azul' and 'O alienista', for example, were published in the *Jornal das Famílias* or in *A Estação*. The author would have divided the longer short stories into chapters in such a way as to approximate the organization of the narrative into instalments, which were characteristic of the serial.

This chapter aims to explore the relationship between Machado de Assis's prose and the serialized mode of publication. I am taking as a starting point not only the linguistic aspects of the text but also the bibliographic characteristics of *Quincas Borba* and the other four novels which were first published by Machado de Assis in the Rio de Janeiro press and which later appeared in one volume. These are:

1. *A mão e a luva* [*The Hand and the Glove*]: O Globo, Rio de Janeiro, 1874: 26, 28, 29, 30 September; 1, 6, 7, 8, 15, 16, 19, 21, 23, 24, 27, 28, 29, 30, 31 October; 3 November.
2. *Helena*: O Globo, Rio de Janeiro, 1876: 6, 7–8, 9, 10, 11, 12, 13, 14, 15, 16–17, 18, 19, 20, 21, 22, 23, 24, 25, 26, 27, 28, 29, 30, 31 August; 1, 2, 3, 4, 5, 6, 7, 8, 10, 11 September.
3. *Iaiá Garcia* [*Iaiá Garcia*]: O Cruzeiro, Rio de Janeiro, 1878: 1, 2, 3, 4, 5, 7, 8, 9, 11, 12, 14, 15, 16, 19, 21, 22, 23, 25, 26, 28, 30 January; 4, 5, 6, 9, 11, 12, 13, 15, 16, 19, 20, 22, 25, 26, 27 February; 1, 2 March.
4. *Memórias póstumas de Brás Cubas* [*Epitaph of a Small Winner*]: Revista Brasileira, Rio de Janeiro, 1880: 15 March; 1 and 15 April; 1 and 15 May; 1 June; 1 and 15 July; 1 and 15 August; 1 and 15 September; 1 and 15 October; 1 November; 1 and 15 December.

There is no evidence that his debut novel *Ressurreição* [*Resurrection*] was published as a serial before the bookseller and publisher B. L. Garnier published it as a book in 1872.[2] The author's second novel, *A mão e a luva*, is therefore the first to appear as a serial. Although *Casa velha* [*Old House*], like *Quincas Borba*, was published in the magazine *A Estação*, it lies outside the scope of this study (*Casa velha* appeared between 15 January 1885 and 8 February 1886).[3] This is because *Casa velha* was not published as a single volume during the author's lifetime; it was Lúcia Miguel Pereira who later located the chapters in the 'Literary Section' of the magazine and brought them together in a single volume.[4] *Quincas Borba*, the last of Machado de Assis's novels to be originally published in serial form, is only the writer's seventh novel. It was followed by *Dom Casmurro*, *Esaú e Jacó* [*Esau and Jacob*] and *Memorial de Aires* [*Counselor Aires's Memoirs*].

TABLE 1.1: Novels published by Machado de Assis[5]

In serial and book form	Only in book form	Only in serial form
A mão e a luva, 1874	Ressurreição, 1872	Casa velha, 1885
Helena, 1876	Dom Casmurro, 1889	
Iaiá Garcia, 1878	Esaú e Jacó, 1904	
Memórias póstumas de Brás Cubas, 1881	Memorial de Aires, 1908	
Quincas Borba, 1891		

This chapter investigates the way in which the serialized novels were transformed into books, a process which, I believe, had some impact on the structure and meaning of the novels. My investigations will involve analysing the publishing context in which each of these five novels was published, as well as their typographic composition and some textual variants. Attention will be paid to:

1. The publication context, including the differences between the format of the book and the periodical, the space set aside for the writer every day in the newspaper or every fortnight in the magazine; the place where printing took place and the company which published the serial and the novel;
2. The typography, including the type and size of the font, the length of the line, the size of the printed area in the book and the number of columns in the newspaper;
3. The variants, which are, in the bibliographic sense, the typographical adjustments which make it possible to reuse the same newspaper matrix for the book. When the number of variations is very great, the text needs to be typeset again in order to print the book. For the purposes of this study, the bibliographic characteristics inherent in the variations are as important as the linguistic contents.

The case of 'Several Stories'

In fact, it is Machado de Assis himself who encourages us to consider both the bibliographic and the linguistic aspects of his literary texts. Let us remember, for example, the draft of his letter of 8 September 1902 to Mr Lansac, H. Garnier's representative in Rio de Janeiro.[6] In it, the writer discusses the proofs of the second edition of the short-story collection *Várias Histórias* [*Several Stories*], which was being prepared in France by the Garnier publishing house. In order to understand the case, we need to remember that *Várias Histórias* is made up of stories selected from Machado de Assis's collaboration with the *Gazeta de Notícias* between 1884 and 1891. The first edition in book form had already been published by the Laemmert publishing house in 1895.[7] The contract between Machado de Assis and Laemmert is dated 18 December 1894. Laemmert paid Machado de Assis 400,000 *réis* on the signing of the contract, article 5 of which specified that 'no caso de proceder-se a nova edição, os atuais editores terão a preferência em igualdade de condições' [in the event that a new edition is published, the current publishers will have preference under the same conditions]. In a letter to Machado de Assis dated 21 March 1902, Laemmert proposed a new edition in book form. At this stage, however, Machado de Assis had already sold 'a propriedade inteira e perfeita' [the whole and complete property] of the majority of his work to Garnier.[8] On 13 March 1902, i.e., one week after receiving Laemmert's proposal, Machado de Assis wrote to Garnier to propose the same work for 1,200,000 *réis*. The contract between Machado de Assis and H. Garnier for the reissuing of the book was finally signed on 27 May 1902. In the contract, Machado de Assis sold the whole and perpetual ownership of *Várias Histórias* for 1,000,000 *réis*.

In September 1902, when Machado de Assis wrote the draft of the letter to Mr Lansac, the book was already being produced. However, the writer was not impressed by the appearance of the typography. When he returned the first proofs to Garnier, Machado de Assis confessed that he found the typography unsuitable. The previous edition, which was published by Laemmert, consisted of 310 pages, while that of Garnier contained only 230. Machado de Assis believed that the new edition would have the appearance and value of a small book, which would harm its sales. Later in the letter, he compared the line length and print area of the two editions. The author believed that long lines, and a greater number of lines per page, would harm the overall appearance of the book:

> Comparez une page de la première avec une autre de la vôtre: la ligne de celle-ci est plus longue, et chaque page compte 38 lignes; les pages de celle-là sont formées avec 34 lignes, et vous pourrez voir la différence de longueur. Outre cela, voyez la première page de chaque nouvelle; dans l'édition Laemmert, elle ne compte que 13 lignes, au lieu que dans l'édition Garnier elle va jusqu'à 20. Voyez déjà les six premières feuilles d'épreuves; la matière de 108 pages que je vous envoie occupe dans l'édition Laemmert 132 pages. Pour la vérification et la comparaison, vous trouverez ci-jointes les deux premières pages de l'édition Laemmert.
>
> Je vous prie, Monsieur Lansac, de transmettre ces considérations à Monsieur Garnier, qui en reconnaîtra la justesse, et comprendra la convenance d'ordonner quelque chose pour éviter à temps ce que je crois préjudiciable à notre affaire.[9]

[Compare a page of the Laemmert edition with your own: the line in the latter is much longer, and each page has 38 lines; the pages of the former have 34 lines, and you can see the difference in length. Furthermore, look at the first page of each story: in the Laemmert edition, it has not more than 13 lines, whereas in the Garnier edition it has up to 20. Take a look at the first six sheets of proofs: the content of 108 pages which I am sending you takes up 132 pages in the Laemmert edition. You will find with this letter the first two pages of the Laemmert edition, so that you can verify and compare them.

I would kindly ask you, M. Lansac, to transmit my concerns to M. Garnier, who will acknowledge their pertinence, and will understand the advantage of arranging something to avoid in time what I believe to be harmful to our enterprise.]

The writer reveals himself to be very concerned with the production of his work, since *Várias Histórias* was now going to be included in the Garnier collection. For the writer, both the bibliographic appearance of the text and its linguistic accuracy were important.[10] Machado de Assis was well aware that a thinner book with a larger printed area would not conform to the publishing standard set by his other works, and that the appearance of the book might even affect readers' views of the quality of the stories themselves. The artistic value of the selected stories might have been measured in the light of the 'poor' presentation of the book, or by a presentation which would make it resemble cheap popular books.

Machado de Assis's letter makes it clear that the material appearance of a printed text carries signs of the social realities to which a particular sort of edition was targeted. This is because it contains traces of the interactions that took place between the individuals and groups that were set up when the text was being produced, transmitted and consumed.

Returning to the five novels which Machado de Assis published in serial form, we can ask ourselves what their typography reveals with respect to:

1. The public at which they were targeted, including those who subscribed to the newspaper and, subsequently, those who bought the novel in book form;
2. The commercial relations which gave rise to the text: whether the text was commissioned to be published in the press or as a book and whether, in the latter case, it had appeared in serial form before the book was launched;
3. The intentions of the writer. Did Machado de Assis manage to achieve his initial artistic intentions, or did he have to adapt or even reformulate them when confronted with the task of producing a text commissioned by a newspaper or promised in a contract to a publishing house?

In this respect, we are beginning to understand that a text's bibliographic code may help us to understand its literary meaning.

The Mode of Production of Machado de Assis's Earlier Novels

Just as we may be able to trace the evolution of Machado de Assis's novels in terms of their linguistic code, including, for example, their style, subject matter, narrative technique, use of irony, and the positioning of the narrator, we may also try to trace the trajectory of their bibliographic code, from *Ressurreição* onwards. *Ressurreição* was not published in serial form because it had already been promised to Garnier at least two years before it went on sale. On 30 September 1869, Machado de Assis signed a contract with B. L. Garnier, committing himself to publishing three works with that publishing company: *Ressurreição, O Manuscrito do licenciado Gaspar* [*The Manuscript of Gaspar the Graduate*] and *Histórias da meia noite* [*Midnight Stories*]. In the contract, the writer was selling, in advance, the complete and full ownership of not only the first edition but also all subsequent editions of these three works. Machado de Assis would receive 400,000 *réis* for each edition that B. L. Garnier produced. Payment for the first was made upon signing the contract. In exchange, Machado de Assis committed himself to delivering the original drafts of *Ressurreição* by mid-October 1869, *O Manuscrito do licenciado Gaspar* by mid-March 1870, and *Histórias da meia noite* by the end of that same year.

'Resurrection'

Ressurreição was not published until 1872. It is likely that Machado de Assis wrote the book between late 1871 and early 1872, as the date in the preface is 17 April 1872. *O Manuscrito do licenciado Gaspar*, on the other hand, was never published, and the short-story collection would not appear until 1873. Galante de Souza explains that the novelist very probably sold the publisher works which he had only planned, or which were in preparation, because he needed to meet his expenses, which included the cost of his marriage in 1869.[11]

After *Ressurreição*, Machado de Assis would publish *A mão e a luva*, *Helena* and *Iaiá Garcia* in the daily press. We will see that many similarities exist in the way that these three novels were produced and published. However, we shall also see that the differences, despite being small, reveal that the writer was slowly moving away from what he called, in the preface to *A mão e a luva*, 'um método de composição um pouco fora dos hábitos do autor' [a method of composition to which the author is somewhat unaccustomed]. *Memórias póstumas de Brás Cubas* [*Epitaph of a Small Winner*] was published in a fortnightly magazine in a format which was very close to the octavo format of the book.[12] After *Quincas Borba*, Machado de Assis definitively abandoned the serial form as a means of publishing his longer narratives.

From 'The Hand and the Glove' to 'Epitaph of a Small Winner'

Let us begin by looking at the places where the periodical and the first edition of the first four novels were printed. The serialized and single volume texts of *A mão e a luva* [*The Hand and the Glove*] and *Helena* were printed at *O Globo*'s printing plant, while *Iaiá Garcia* was printed at *O Cruzeiro*'s plant. The printing always took place at the printing plant of the newspaper itself, even though *O Globo* and *O Cruzeiro* were not the publishers of the book editions. *A mão e a luva* was published by Gomes e Oliveira & Cia; *Helena* was published by B. L. Garnier; and *Iaiá Garcia* was published by G. Vianna & C. The first edition of *Memórias póstumas de Brás Cubas* was printed by the Imprensa Nacional, while the *Revista Brasileira* was printed by J. D. de Oliveira.

The same typographic composition of serial was used by the publishers to compose all four of the novels in book form. This means that the type and size of the font, the line length and consequently the width of the column were maintained from one format to the next. However, the length of the printed area was different as the vertical column was made shorter in the book in order to adjust to the octavo format. Hallewell believes that this was the predominant format used to publish novels during the nineteenth century in Brazil.[13] This may have been true for the fiction published by prestigious publishing houses such as Garnier, but it was not necessarily true for the popular novels which flourished at the end of the nineteenth century, as Alessandra El Far reveals.[14] They appealed to the wider public not just because of their risqué subject matter but also because the large print runs and low cost of production made them more accessible than Garnier's comparatively well-finished editions. In the correspondence between Machado de Assis and Mr Lansac, quoted above, the writer may have feared that the physical appearance of the short-story collection *Várias Histórias* would cause it to be confused with second-rate literature.

Using the typographic composition of the serial to make the book certainly formed part of the commercial strategy employed by publishers to speed up the pace and reduce the costs of production, as Hallewell observed with regard to *Helena*.[15] In fact, the publication of the first editions of these four novels was announced just one month after the serialization had finished. Advertisements for *A mão e a luva* began appearing in the newspaper O Globo on 8 December 1874, and *Helena* was advertised in O Mosquito, of Rio de Janeiro, on 7 October 1876.[16] Moreover, *Iaiá Garcia* was advertised in O Cruzeiro on 3 April 1878, and *Memórias póstumas de Brás Cubas* was advertised in the Revista Brasileira on 15 January 1881.[17]

The serial section in 'O Globo' and 'O Cruzeiro'

A mão e a luva and *Helena* were published in the 'Serial' section of O Globo, and *Iaiá Garcia* appeared in the 'Serial' section of O Cruzeiro. Comparing the typographic composition of these novels with that of other texts published in the same section, I was able to establish that the publishers of both newspapers had determined which novels would subsequently appear in octavo format even before serialization had begun — by making this differentiation, the publishers were ensuring that the typographic matrix used for the newspaper could also be used for the book. The novels, which would later be reprinted in octavo format, were distributed across six columns in O Globo and four columns in O Cruzeiro so that the line length in the newspaper would exactly fit the width that the printed area would occupy in the book. By contrast, the rest of the newspaper was distributed over eight columns in O Globo and six columns in O Cruzeiro.

In common with *A mão e a luva* and *Helena*, other novels were published in the 'Serial' section across six columns. Among these were *Dr. Benignus* by Augusto Emilio Zaluar, *Marabá* by Salvador de Mendonça, *Ouro sobre azul* by Sylvio Dinarte (a pseudonym of Alfredo d'Escragnolle Taunay), and *Memórias de um sandeu*, by Eugène Noel, which was translated from the French (*Mémoires d'un imbécile*). Again, like *A mão e a luva* and *Helena*, these four novels were subsequently published in octavo format. The reprints of *A mão e a luva*, *Marabá* and *Ouro sobre azul* were included in the collection 'Biblioteca do Globo'. The same publishing standard was applied to all of them.

Among the texts which were distributed across eight columns in the 'Serial' section of *O Globo* are José de Alencar's articles in the series 'Ao correr da pena' and 'Às quintas', and Joaquim Nabuco's articles in the series 'Aos domingos'. And the texts distributed across six columns in the 'Serial' section of the *Cruzeiro* include articles such as 'Filósofos, bobos e folhetinistas', signed by the pseudonymous Rigoletto.

This does not mean that the typographic composition of narratives (principally translations) which were also published in *O Globo* across eight columns could not be reused to compose books in the future. This seems to have been the case of Alfred de Musset's short stories. 'O segredo de Javotte', for example, was published across eight columns in the 'Folhetim' of *O Globo* from 27 April to 7 May 1875, making nine instalments in total. This short story subsequently came to form part of a volume in B. L. Garnier's 'Biblioteca de Algibeira' [Pocket Library] collection, which was published in the 12to format. When prices at the same bookshop were compared, the volumes in this collection were cheaper than those in the 'Biblioteca Universal' octavo collection, of which Machado de Assis's novels formed part. A 'Biblioteca de Algibeira' paperback cost 1,000 *réis* and a hardback cost 1,500 *réis*, compared with the 'Biblioteca Universal' prices of 2,500 *réis* for a paperback and 3,000 for a hardback.

Formats, readers and profits

It is therefore clear that there is a close connection between the formats used to publish the same text in a newspaper and in book form: the width of the columns used in the serial determined the dimensions of the book and may also have affected the type of reader who would pick it up and the prestige it would later acquire. It was Machado de Assis himself, personified as Brás Cubas, who established categories of readers in accordance with the dimensions of books. The 12to readers enjoy 'pouco texto, larga margem' [sparse text, wide margins], and are mainly attracted by the visual appearance of the book, including 'o tipo elegante, corte dourado e vinhetas... principalmente vinhetas...' [the elegant type, burnished edges and vignettes... particularly vignettes...]. There is a second category of reader: the 'heavyweight' or folio reader, referring again to the format of the book for whom 'capítulos compridos quadram melhor' [long chapters are better].[18] Brás Cubas therefore writes a story which is suited to taste of a reader whom he claims to despise.

This example also makes it possible to assume that newspapers and book publishers could also establish partnerships in order to reduce production costs and thereby increase (or at least guarantee) the profits of both. No one would emerge a loser, much less literature. The serial attracted subscribers to the newspaper, and the publishing house already had its target readers in its sights: the subscribers to the periodical, who could acquire their favourite novels in durable book form. See, for example, the following advertisement for *Iaiá Garcia*:

> Este formoso romance, que tanta aceitação obteve dos leitores do *Cruzeiro*, saiu agora à luz em um nítido volume de mais de 300 páginas. Vende-se nesta tipografia, rua do Ourives n. 51 e em casa do Sr. A. J. Gomes Brandão, rua da Quitanda n. 90. (*O Cruzeiro*, 3 April 1878)

> [This beautiful novel, which was so well received by readers of *O Cruzeiro*, is now available in a single volume containing over 300 pages. It is on sale at this printing plant, rua do Ourives no. 51, and at the home of Mr A. J. Gomes Brandão, rua da Quitanda no. 90.]

There were now two ways of disseminating literature, and the number of readers is correspondingly increased. And let us not forget the writer, who could earn twice the amount for the same work, as was the case of Machado de Assis.

B. L. Garnier, publisher of 'Helena'

Helena constitutes a slightly different case from *A mão e a luva*. We have seen that, although the serial and the first edition had been printed at the *O Globo* printing plant, the publisher of the book was B. L. Garnier. When it was published as a book, *Helena* came to form part of Garnier's 'Biblioteca Universal' collection of titles. Perhaps it was for this reason that *Helena* was neither advertised in the pages of *O Globo* nor offered as a gift to readers who paid for an annual subscription to the newspaper in advance.

> Vantagens feitas aos assinantes do *Globo*: Todas as pessoas que pagarem adiantadamente a assinatura de nossa folha por um ano, receberão indistintamente, além do *Almanaque do Globo*, um exemplar de qualquer dos seguintes romances publicados pelas nossas oficinas: *Marabá* por Salvador de Mendonça; *As memórias de um sandeu*; *A mão e a luva*, por Machado de Assis; *Ouro sobre azul*, por Silvio Dinarte, e *O Dr. Benignus*, por A. E. Zaluar. (*O Globo*, for example, on 14, 15, 16, 17 and 25 December 1876)

> [Advantages enjoyed by subscribers to *O Globo*: Everyone who pays in advance for an annual subscription to our newspaper will receive, in addition to the *Almanaque do Globo*, a copy of any of the following novels published by our workshops: *Marabá* by Salvador de Mendonça; *As memórias de um Sandeu*; *A mão e a luva*, by Machado de Assis; *Ouro sobre azul*, by Silvio Dinarte, and *O Dr. Benignus*, by A. E. Zaluar.]

This peculiarity of *Helena* is explained in the contract dated 29 April 1876:

> Joaquim Maria Machado de Assis vende a B. L. Garnier a primeira edição, que vai mandar imprimir na tipografia do *Globo*, depois de ter saído em folhetim, de seu romance intitulado *Helena do Vale*, composta de Mil e quinhentos exemplares (1.500 exemplares), o qual formará um volume do formato do das *Histórias de meia noite*, e igual pouco mais ou menos em tudo a este último volume, pela quantia de Seiscentos mil réis (Rs. 600$000) pagáveis no ato da entrega da dita edição.[19]

> [Joaquim Maria Machado de Assis [hereby] sells to B. L. Garnier the first edition of his novel entitled *Helena do Vale*, which, after it has appeared as a serial, he is going to have printed at *O Globo*'s printing plant. The print run will comprise 1500 copies of a volume which will be in the same format as the *Histórias de meia noite*, and which will be like the latter book in more or less every respect, for the sum of 600,000 *réis* payable when the edition in question is delivered.]

It is evident from this last quotation that the process by which Machado de Assis's work was standardized in book form was already well under way. The format which made it possible was established by the most successful French publisher in Rio Janeiro. In fact, Garnier was responsible for standardizing not only Machado de Assis's work but also that of many other Brazilian writers who came to form part of the canon, publishing a series of collections of authors' works in octavo format. By examining advertisements placed in newspapers (in *O Globo* on 9 July 1876, for example) or catalogues appended to the publishing company's books, it is possible to appreciate the significance of the company's role in standardizing the work and canonizing the great authors of Brazilian literature.

The typographic characteristics of these novels were conserved from one format to the next for reasons which were primarily commercial. In a certain sense, the publishing mechanism of these newspaper publishing houses aimed to create books that were durable products, to be kept on the shelf, but they also took advantage of the sales guaranteed by the serial format, which came from France, to win readers' loyalty or attract new subscribers. In comparison with the periodical, the book had a much smaller print run and a much higher price. On 10 October 1876, for example, 9300 copies of *O Globo* were printed; an annual subscription cost 20,000 *réis*, and a single copy cost 40 *réis*.[20] The first book edition of *Helena*, on the other hand, consisted of 1500 copies, with the paperback going on sale for 2000 *réis*. In other words, the price of a single book corresponded to ten per cent of the price of the annual subscription to the newspaper. However, the profits of the publishing house were guaranteed since by reusing the matrix from one format to the next, it economized on the time and staff employed on the typographic composition. The cost of printing the book was little more than that of the paper — high as that was.

Traces of the Serial in Machado de Assis's Novels

I would like to draw attention to the demands made on the creative composition of the novel by the commercial operation: which side of the scales, the serial side or the book side, weighed most heavily on the writer when he faced the task of writing?

A confessed serial writer: the preface to 'The Hand and the Glove'

Once again, it is Machado de Assis himself who draws attention to the problems he faced. In a note which appears in the first book edition of *A mão e a luva* [*The Hand and the Glove*], Machado de Assis discusses the effect of the conditions under which it was written on the final artistic quality of the novel. The term 'conditions' is used by the writer himself. The obstacles he faced when writing the novel come into play here: the pressure of time and the space limitations imposed by the daily newspaper. Let us recall the novelist's own words. Despite this not being the method of composition to which he was accustomed, the text was written for publication in daily periodicals:

> Esta novela, sujeita às urgências da publicação diária, saiu das mãos do autor capítulo a capítulo, sendo natural que a narração e o estilo padecessem com esse método de composição, um pouco fora dos hábitos do autor. Se a escrevera

em outras condições, dera-lhe desenvolvimento maior, e algum colorido mais aos caracteres, que aí ficam esboçados. Convém dizer que o desenho de tais caracteres, — o de Guiomar, sobretudo, — foi o meu objeto principal, senão exclusivo, servindo-me a ação apenas de tela em que lancei os contornos dos perfis. Incompletos embora, terão eles saído naturais e verdadeiros?

Mas talvez estou eu a dar proporções muito graves a uma coisa de tão pequeno tomo. O que aí vai são umas poucas páginas que o leitor esgotará de um trago, se elas lhe aguçarem a curiosidade, ou se lhe sobrar alguma hora que absolutamente não possa empregar em outra coisa, — mais bela ou mais útil.

M. A. Novembro de 1874[21]

[This novel, which was subject to the pressures of daily publication, emerged from the author's hands chapter by chapter. As such, the narration and the style naturally suffered the effects of this method of composition, to which the author is somewhat unaccustomed. If I had written it under different conditions, I would have developed more, and given more colour to, those characters which have only been sketched. It is worth pointing out that the development of these characters, particularly Guiomar, was my main objective, if not my only one. The action served only as the screen on which to project their outlines. Despite being incomplete, have they emerged as true and natural?

But perhaps I am giving a great deal of weight to a matter of little importance. Here are a few pages which readers will swallow in one gulp, if their curiosity is piqued, or if they have an hour free which absolutely cannot be spent doing anything else that might be more beautiful or useful.

M. A. November 1874]

This is an example of a declared authorial intention. In this note, Machado de Assis leaves no one in any doubt that his main aim was to create the character Guiomar, and that the action serves only as a backdrop. It is also clear, as stated in the preface to the critical edition of the novel, that he is determined to 'fazer obra trabalhada, quanto a narração e estilo, numa espécie de zelo que não ocupava destacado lugar nas preocupações muito pouco artesanais dos românticos' [create a finished work in terms of narration and style, inspired by a sort of zeal which did not feature prominently in the concerns of the romantic writers, who were not much interested in craft] (*A mão e a luva*, p. 12). The other side of the equation, however, cannot be ignored. Machado de Assis is confessing that he subjected himself to a method of composition 'fora dos hábitos do autor' [to which he was unaccustomed] due to the conditions imposed by periodical publication. The writing of the novel was adversely affected by the pressure of time, space restrictions at the foot of the page, and the need to publish in instalments.

This method of composition brought with it a series of implications that affected the external and internal organization of the narrative: for example, it played a role in establishing the correlation between the number of chapters and instalments. *A mão e a luva* contains nineteen chapters distributed across twenty instalments. With the exception of chapter 10, which appeared in the periodical on 16 and 19 October, all of the other chapters fit into the fixed space at the foot of the first page of the newspaper (see Table 1.2). Consequently, chapter 10 apart, the size of the chapters is also very regular.

TABLE 1.2: Publication of *A mão e a luva*, *Helena* and *Iaiá Garcia* in periodicals

A mão e a luva (O Globo, 1874)

Instalment	Publication date	Chapter
1	26 Sept, p. 1	I
2	28 Sept, p. 1	II
3	29 Sept, p. 1	III
4	30 Sept, p. 1	IV
5	1 Oct, p. 1	V
6	6 Oct, p. 1	VI
7	7 Oct, p. 1	VII
8	8 Oct, p. 1	VIII
9	15 Oct, p. 1	IX
10	16 Oct, p. 1	X
11	19 Oct, p. 1	X
12	21 Oct, p. 1	XI
13	23 Oct, p. 1	XII
14	24 Oct, p. 1	XIII
15	27 Oct, p. 1	XIV
16	28 Oct, p. 1	XV
17	29 Oct, p. 1	XVI
18	30 Oct, p. 1	XVII
19	31 Oct, p. 1	XVIII
20	3 Nov, p. 1	XIX

Helena (O Globo, 1876)

Instalment	Publication date	Chapter
1	6 Aug, p. 1	I
2	7 Aug, p. 1	II
3	9 Aug, p. 1	III
4	10 Aug, p. 1	IV
5	11 Aug, p. 1	V
6	12 Aug, p. 1	VI
7	13 Aug, p. 1	VI
8	14 Aug, p. 1	VII
9	15 Aug, p. 1	VIII
10	16 Aug, p. 1	IX
11	18 Aug, p. 1	X
12	19 Aug, p. 1	XI, XII
13	20 Aug, p. 1	XII
14	21 Aug, p. 1	XIII
15	22 Aug, p. 1	XIV
16	23 Aug, p. 1	XV
17	24 Aug, p. 1	XVI
18	25 Aug, p. 1	XVI
19	26 Aug, p. 1	XVII
20	27 Aug, p. 1	XVIII
21	28 Aug, p. 1	XIX
22	29 Aug, p. 1	XX
23	30 Aug, p. 1	XXI
24	31 Aug, p. 1	XXI

25	1 Sept, p. 1	XXII
26	2 Sept, p. 1	XXIII
27	3 Sept, p. 1	XXIV
28	4 Sept, p. 1	XXIV
29	5 Sept, p. 1	XXV
30	6 Sept, p. 1	XXV, XXVI
31	7 Sept, p. 1	XXVI
32	8 Sept, p. 1	XXVII
33	10 Sept, p. 1	XXVIII
34	11 Sept, p. 1	XXVIII

Iaiá Garcia (O Cruzeiro, 1878)

Instalment[22]	Publication date	Chapter
1	1 Jan, p. 1, 2	I
2	2 Jan, p. 1, 2	I, II
3	3 Jan, p. 1, 2	II
4	4 Jan, p. 1, 2	III
5	5 Jan, p. 1, 2	III
6	7 Jan, p. 1	III
7	8 Jan, p. 1	IV
8	9 Jan, p. 1	IV
9	11 Jan, p. 1, 2	V
10	12 Jan, p. 1	VI
11	14 Jan, p. 1, 2	VI
12	15 Jan, p. 1, 2	VI, VII
13	16 Jan, p. 1, 2	VII
14	19 Jan, p. 1, 2	VII
15	21 Jan, p. 1	VIII
16	22 Jan, p. 1	IX
17	23 Jan, p. 1	IX
18	25 Jan, p. 1, 2	X
19	26 Jan, p. 1	X
20	28 Jan, p. 1, 2	XI
21	30 Jan, p. 1	XI
22	4 Feb, p. 1, 2	XII
23	5 Feb, p. 1	XII
24	6 Feb, p. 1	XIII
25	9 Feb, p. 1	XIII
26	11 Feb, p. 1	XIII
27	12 Feb, p. 1	XIII
28	13 Feb, p. 1	XIII
29	15 Feb, p. 1	XIV
30	16 Feb, p. 1	XIV
31	19 Feb, p. 1	XIV
32	20 Feb, p. 1	XV
33	22 Feb, p. 1	XV
34	25 Feb, p. 1, 2	XV
35	26 Feb, p. 1	XVI
36	27 Feb, p. 1, 2	XVI
37	1 Mar, p. 1	XVI
38	2 Mar, p. 1, 2	XVII

Salvador de Mendonça: another confessed serial writer

It is interesting to note that Salvador de Mendonça, in the preface to the first edition of *Marabá*, makes a very similar confession to that made by Machado de Assis. As we have seen, *Marabá* had also been published in the serial section of *O Globo* across six columns, and was subsequently published in octavo format in the 'Bibiloteca do Globo' collection.

> Embora delineado há três anos, foi o presente livro escrito quase à proporção que ia aparecendo no *Globo* em folhetins. Não se diz isto no só intuito de atenuar as faltas do autor, que é ele o primeiro a i-las conhecendo; mas principalmente por amor da arte e culto do belo que certo requeriam trabalho mais assentado. Enquanto os pensamentos, vestidos como Deus queria e o permitiam os recursos paternos, enfileiravam-se amparados uns com os outros nas colunas do jornal, onde sem voltar a página o leitor enfastiado tinha meio de seguir apenas o entrecho, ainda o peso da responsabilidade era minorado pela certeza da existência fugaz de qualquer produção estampada nas folhas diárias.
>
> Mas nos dias em que se tratou de reunir sob a forma de livro os capítulos dispersos, e reuni-los sem o tempo indispensável para modificá-los, ou pelo menos desbastar-lhes as asperezas, dar neste ponto mais luz, naquele mais sombra, comunicando ao todo mais harmonia e remediando os senões que afeiam uma obra que aspira aos foros de obra de arte, cresceu o receio do autor, cujo maior consolo era até hoje nada ter publicado sob esta forma de livro.[23]

> [Although outlined three years ago, this book was written almost in tandem with its appearance in *O Globo* in serial form. This is not said solely to diminish the seriousness of the faults of the author, who is the first to recognize them, but mainly out of love for the art and cult of the beautiful, which certainly called for a more considered work. As for my thoughts, which were dressed up as God wished and the family resources have permitted, they were aligned, holding each other up, in the columns of the newspaper, where, without turning the page, the weary reader was able to do no more than follow the plot. Consequently, even the weight of responsibility was reduced by the certainty that anything appearing in the daily papers has but a fleeting existence.
>
> But during the days when I attempted to unite the various chapters in the form of a book, bringing them together without the essential time required to modify them, or at least smooth away their rough edges, to shine more light on this point, cast more shade on that, imbuing the whole with more harmony and remedying the flaws which disfigured a work which aspires to the status of a work of art, the author's fear grew, and his greatest consolation was that he had not yet published anything in the form of a book.]

Machado de Assis and Salvador de Mendonça may not have planned the outlines of their novels with a view to publishing them in serial form. However, *A mão e a luva* and *Marabá* ended up being written under the pressure of daily publication and the need to divide the narrative material into instalments. One of the consequences of this is that, in Machado de Assis's text, as we have seen, there is a very close correlation between the external subdivision of the work into instalments and its internal subdivision into chapters. It is clear that we now find ourselves on the border between the bibliographic and the linguistic codes, without knowing exactly where the dividing line lies. This is because the way that a novel is organized into chapters may be reflected in its narrative pattern and techniques.

'Helena'

Let us now examine the case of *Helena*. We saw above that, although the first edition in book form was printed at *O Globo* newspaper's printing plant, its publisher was B. L. Garnier. We also saw that the publication of the book had been set down in a contract long before the serialization of the novel began. This proves that Machado de Assis was already thinking about publishing the novel in book form when he conceived it. It also suggests that he may have started writing it long before it began to be published in serial form. This is confirmed by the relationship between the number of chapters and the number of instalments. *Helena* was published in 34 instalments but contains only 28 chapters, which means that the text was internally divided in a way which differed somewhat from the external division imposed by serialized publication (see Table 1.2). For example, chapters 6, 16, 21, 24, 25 and 28 occupied two instalments, while chapter 11 and the start of chapter 12 were published together.

However, this does not prevent the novel from featuring some characteristics of popular literature in order to please subscribers to the newspaper. The introduction to the critical edition of the novel states that:

> até certa altura, quando Estácio entra a duvidar da virtude de Helena, sua suposta meia-irmã, tida como fruto de um dos amores extraconjugais de seu pai, o Conselheiro Vale, o romance é sereno e contido. Se a história tem fundo romântico, Machado de Assis já a tempera, aí, com uns laivos de sátira que viria a identificar a grande obra ficcional de sua maturidade. (*Helena*, pp. 12–13)

> [up to a certain point, when Estácio starts to doubt the virtue of Helena, his supposed half-sister and taken to be the fruit of one of his father Conselheiro Vale's extramarital affairs, the novel is serene and contained. If this story is essentially romantic in nature, Machado de Assis moderates it with a few hints of the satire that would come to identify the great fictional work of his later years.]

But from 'o instante em que a alma de Estácio, enamorado de Helena sem o saber, enche-se de suspeitas, o romance envereda pela linha do melodrama' [the moment when Estácio's soul, in love with Helena without knowing it, fills with suspicion, the novel heads down the path of melodrama] (*Helena*, p. 13). The novel probably possesses this hybrid nature because, while it was being written, it was infiltrated with characteristics typical of the serial form as publication took place. In the critical history of *Helena*, as Hélio de Seixas Guimarães describes, this sentimental and melodramatic load has not passed unnoticed. For the critics, it is a negative characteristic, one which is out of tune with Machado de Assis's mature work.[24] On the other hand, Guimarães states that

> o recurso ao melodrama não pode ser explicado como acidente ou desvio de rota, nem como ato involuntário de um escritor imaturo. Pelo contrário, trata-se de um registro não apenas reivindicado pelo público leitor contemporâneo como buscado pelo escritor, que o utiliza como estratégia para atingir o público

> leitor de folhetim, espaço para o qual a narrativa originalmente se destinava e passava a dividir com textos seriados de autores como Ponson du Terrail e Xavier de Montépin.[25]

> [the recourse to melodrama cannot be explained as an accident or a deviation, nor as an involuntary act on the part of an immature writer. On the contrary, it is a register which is not only demanded by the contemporary reading public but also sought out by the writer, who uses it as a strategy to reach readers of the serial for which the narrative was originally intended and whose pages it came to share with serialized texts by authors such as Ponson du Terrail and Xavier de Montépin.]

Therefore, as it was written to feature in the pages of a periodical, a format imported from France, Machado de Assis's novel is infiltrated by characteristics of the serial genre of fiction, likewise imported. Guimarães interprets the problem with *Helena* as arising from 'a inviabilidade da aplicação de procedimentos das narrativas populares europeias ao romance brasileiro' [the inviability of applying popular European narrative procedures to the Brazilian novel]. He identifies two reasons for this inviability. Firstly, a failure by the author to see that the bourgeois, urban and democratic values defended by popular English and French melodrama and fiction did not prevail in Brazil; this error would subsequently be corrected by Machado de Assis in his mature period. And secondly, Guimarães believes that Brazil simply did not contain a sufficiently large reading public to sustain popular fiction.

This second point requires greater investigation, since if we add the circulation of *O Globo* during the publication of *Helena* to the circulation of the first edition of the book, we have a total of 10,800 copies. It is necessary to investigate whether this figure is really much lower than the circulation figures obtained by, for example, Ponson du Terrail in France. But even if it was lower, it seems to me to indicate that the conditions under which the text was disseminated and consumed were very favourable. Within the limitations imposed by Brazilian society, at a time when the vast majority of the population were illiterate, these conditions (in conjunction with the novel's intrinsic literary characteristics) would guarantee that it achieved popularity among contemporary readers.[26] This is confirmed by the testimony of Gilberto Freyre, as quoted by Guimarães:

> Segundo Gilberto Freyre, a protagonista teria inspirado muitas mães, nos últimos decênios do Império e primeiros anos da República, a batizarem suas filhas com o nome da infeliz personagem, o que é um grande feito no Brasil onde, à exceção de Iracema, Peri e Ceci, poucas personagens literárias do século 19 foram integradas ao imaginário popular.[27]

> [According to Gilberto Freyre, during the last decades of the Empire and the first years of the Republic, the protagonist would have inspired many mothers to baptize their daughters with the unhappy character's name. In Brazil, this constitutes a great feat, since aside from Iracema, Peri and Ceci, few nineteenth-century literary characters entered the popular imagination.]

When discussing the readers of those novels of Machado de Assis's which were published in both formats, it must be borne in mind that the circulation of the periodicals was much higher than the print run of the first editions of the books, even though one can only take the number of subscriptions as indicative. It is therefore very probable that the five novels in question reached a greater number of contemporary readers when they appeared in serial form. Moreover, it is very likely that they were much more popular than the author's last three novels: *Dom Casmurro*, *Esaú e Jacó* and *Memorial de Aires*, which were only published in book form.

The contract for *Helena* also states that the narrative would appear in the same format as the other works by Machado de Assis which had been published by B. L. Garnier. The 'Biblioteca Universal' collection already contained *Americanas*, *Histórias da meia noite*, as well as the works of several other Brazilian writers (José de Alencar, Manuel Duarte Moreira de Azevedo, Visconde de Taunay, Bernardo Guimarães and Joaquim Manuel de Macedo) and works by foreign writers which had been translated into Portuguese (Jules Verne, Théophile Gautier and George Sand, for example).

'Iaiá Garcia'

Let us now pass from *A mão e a luva*, a novel written for the serial format, to *Iaiá Garcia*, whose chapters are not organized in a way that corresponds to the instalments which appeared nearly on a daily basis. *Iaiá Garcia*, the third novel published by Machado de Assis in the press, also appeared as a serial, but all of the evidence indicates that the whole text had been written before serialization began. Firstly, both the original publication in *O Cruzeiro* and the first edition in book form are dated September 1877. Secondly, Machado de Assis clearly wrote *Iaiá Garcia* without being bound by the fixed limits of that section of the newspaper. One consequence of this is that the chapters, with the exception of chapters 5 and 8, do not fit into the space set aside for them at the foot of the first page of the periodical. Rather, it is the space in the paper which varies in size in accordance with the editorial requirements of the narrative. Many of the novel's instalments extend to the foot of the second page (see Table 1.2).

Iaiá Garcia takes us one more step up the ladder which moves Machado de Assis away from the serialized method of composition. At least where the correlation between the number (and size) of the instalments and the chapters is concerned, nothing suggests that the writing of *Iaiá Garcia* had been restricted by the demands of serialized publication. According to Guimarães, there is 'um forte recuo na utilização dessas estratégias de apelo e aliciamento do leitor' [a significant retreat from the use of strategies designed to appeal to, and entice, the reader], although 'os esquemas melodramáticos e a atmosfera sentimental' [the melodramatic outlines and sentimental atmosphere] remain in place.[28]

'Epitaph of a Small Winner'

According to this trajectory, *Memórias póstumas de Brás Cubas* represents a great leap forward for Machado de Assis as its chapters and instalments no longer correspond to each other. This does not mean, however, that *Memórias póstumas de Brás Cubas* had not been adapted for serialization in a fortnightly magazine. There are two reasons why the first of the novels to be published in what constitutes Machado de

Assis's mature phase may have adapted very well to publication in instalments. The first reason concerns bibliography and lies in the nature of the magazine itself. The *Revista Brasileira* was primarily concerned with literature, science and the cultural movements of the country. The instalments were published in a format which was very close to that of a book. They also contained long texts, such as Machado de Assis's novel, which extended across several issues of the magazine. The texts were printed in small point 10 and each complete page contained a 37-line column, which meant that the printed area was predominantly vertical. In each fortnightly issue, the novel began on an odd page number, with a generous margin, allowing the readers to bind the novel in a single volume.

TABLE 1.3: *Epitaph of a Small Winner* in *Revista Brasileira*

First year

volume	publication date	pages	chapters
3	15 Mar 1880	353–72	1–9
4	1 Apr 1880	5–20	10–14
	15 Apr 1880	95–114	15–23
	1 May 1880	165–76	24–29
	15 May 1880	233–42	30–35
	1 Jun 1880	295–305	36–43

Second year

volume	publication date	pages	chapters
5	1 Jul 1880	5–20	44–53
	15 Jul 1880	125–38	54–63
	1 Aug 1880	195–210	63–71
	15 Aug 1880	253–72	72–84
	1 Sept 1880	391–401	85–91
	15 Sept 1880	451–62	92–100
6	1 Oct 1880	5–17	101–110
	15 Oct 1880	89–107	111–124
	1 Nov 1880	193–207	125–139
	1 Dec 1880	357–70	140–151
	15 Dec 1880	430–39	152–162

In order for the first edition of the book to be printed in octavo format, the only adjustment required was a reduction in the length of the printed area, which came to have 30 lines. Moreover, all of the chapters in the book begin on a fresh page, whether the page number is odd or even, which makes it possible to read each chapter as if it were independent. The composition of the page therefore reinforces a characteristic of the narrative structure of the text.

We are now ready to discuss the second, primarily literary, reason why the novel fit so well into the serial format. As a result of its anecdotal character, several chapters have an intrinsic unity, even when they are read individually. Comparing the narrative structure of *Dom Casmurro* with that of *Memórias póstumas de Brás Cubas*, John Gledson drew attention to the suitability of the latter to serialized publication:

[*Memórias póstumas de Brás Cubas*] is divided into episodes, anecdotes etc. which are to a great extent self-sufficient and are often remembered on their own account — the 'almocreve' (Ch. 21) is the most famous example, but the whole book is constructed in this fashion. Where characters from the beginning of the book reappear at the end — as do Marcela and Eugênia, for instance — the reappearance is again episodic and the moral clear enough. Originally it was published as a serial, and whether or not it was written as one, it suits that form.[30]

It is true that *Memórias póstumas de Brás Cubas*, with its changes in narrative technique and heightened irony, begins what is generally referred to as Machado de Assis's mature period. However, the novel maintains a very close relationship with narrative forms which adapted very well to serialized publication, such as the *Bildungsroman* and the *crônica*. On the one hand, *Memórias póstumas de Brás Cubas*, like *David Copperfield* and *Great Expectations*, traces the spiritual, moral and social development of the protagonist, even though the narrator is dead and has opted to begin his story at the end.[30] In this respect, it is a parody of the *Bildungsroman*. From chapter 10 onwards, however, the temporal progression of the narrative is linear, taking us from the protagonist's infancy to his death. On the other hand, Machado de Assis brought to the text a swift narrative style and the columnist's ability to change subject and speak about anything and everything at the same time, interspersing the episodes experienced by the narrator with a series of remarks. This was possible because Machado de Assis was an experienced columnist (*cronista*) who was fully aware that he was writing a novel in the meandering style of Laurence Sterne.

The Role of the Author in the Composition of the Book

The truth is that the commercial strategy used by *O Globo*, *O Cruzeiro*, and even in the reprinting of *Memórias póstumas de Brás Cubas*, to speed up and reduce the production costs limited the extent to which the writer was able to participate in the process of composing the book. Clearly, when we consider that the texts of *A mão e a luva*, *Helena*, *Iaiá Garcia* and *Memórias póstumas de Brás Cubas* had virtually been determined in the serial format, we must acknowledge that this is largely due to the rigid nature of the typography. Machado de Assis was only able to make a few changes, which, although small, were not without significance. This is the case of the epigraph to *Memórias póstumas de Brás Cubas* which appeared in the *Revista Brasileira*, and which was removed from every edition of the book. The epigraph in question is taken from act III, scene II of Shakespeare's *As You Like It*: 'I will chide no breather in the world but myself; against whom I know most faults', which the novelist translated as 'Não é meu intento criticar nenhum fôlego vivo, mas a mim somente, em que descubro muitos senões'.[31] Guimarães rightly states that the epigraph is

> indicativa do caráter autocrítico que Roberto Schwarz estuda nesse romance em que os vícios da classe dominante [...] são expostos e ridicularizados a partir de dentro, por um dos seus membros.[33]

> [indicative of the self-critical nature which Roberto Schwarz examines in the novel, in which the vices of the dominant class [...] are exposed and ridiculed from inside, by a member of the class in question.]

Machado de Assis replaced the epigraph with the dedication 'Ao verme que primeiro roeu as frias carnes do meu cadáver dedico como saudosa lembrança estas memórias póstumas' [To the worm who first gnawed on the cold flesh of my corpse, I dedicate with fond remembrance these Posthumous Memoirs].[33] The dedication makes the self-critical nature of the novel, to which the earlier epigraph drew attention, less explicit. At the same time, the added dedication accentuates the aggressiveness with which the narrator treats the reader throughout the narrative.

From the bibliographic point of view, this exclusion is a peripheral change resulting from the position which the epigraph occupies in the typographical matrix. The typeface of which it was composed could easily be removed. Machado de Assis also corrected typographic errors (spelling, punctuation, syntax) which had been identified in the act of reading the serial or reviewing the proofs. He also replaced words or divided, reformulated, added or removed paragraphs (e.g. at the end of *Helena*). However, none of these changes prevented the typographic composition used for the serial from being reused.

Returning to the note in *A mão e a luva* we see that in moving from one format to the next the writer has perhaps been prevented from rewriting all of the text in a manner to which he was more accustomed due to the work and the cost incurred by the publishing house in recomposing the typography. When these four novels were transferred to book format, the same linguistic sequence and type that were used in the serial were maintained.

'Philosopher or Dog?' breaking the cycle

This did not occur, however, with *Quincas Borba*, the last of Machado de Assis's novels to be printed in a periodical. The text of *Quincas Borba*, which was published over five years in the pages of the 'Literary Section' of *A Estação*, was thoroughly rewritten from the first chapter. Machado de Assis not only removed or added sections and whole chapters but also reformulated sentences and swapped the chronological sequence of events, making it impossible to reuse the typographic matrix of the periodical to compose the book.

It is symptomatic that *Quincas Borba* is not only the last of Machado de Assis's novels to be published in a periodical but also that which underwent the greatest number of changes for the book version. As was mentioned in the Introduction to this book, everything leads us to believe that this novel marks a sea change. *Quincas Borba* represents a change between a mode of novel writing and publication linked to the serial and another linked to the book. This is the question that will be discussed throughout this book.

The next chapter, however, will examine the thematic relationship between the novel and the magazine and the way in which the novel incorporates, absorbs, transforms and ironizes the main thematic lines of the magazine: its imperial leanings, and its depiction of fashion as an outer sign of social climbing.

To end this chapter, I would like to draw attention to the fact that the electronic or paper editions of Machado de Assis's work which are available to the public today do not generally convey the bibliographic characteristics of the first editions. However, even though the modern reader is not aware that the chapters and the instalments of *A mão e a luva* correspond almost exactly, one can still note that the size of the chapters is generally very regular, although one may not know why this is the case, namely, that the space set aside for the serial did not vary: it was always the foot of the first page of the periodical.

As such, studies of the bibliographic aspects of the periodical and the first editions published by Machado de Assis are not motivated by the researcher's fetish for old papers and rare works; nor do they uncover information which is only of interest to collectors or specialized libraries. Machado de Assis, who was very discreet both in relation to his private life as well as his work in progress, left us very few manuscripts. As such, the contracts, prefaces, notes, and the periodicals with which he collaborated, as well as the first editions, are of vital importance in helping us to get closer to the process by which his work was created. Ultimately, as Machado de Assis writes in the note contained in the third edition of *A mão e a luva*, which was published in 1907:

> Os trinta anos decorridos do aparecimento desta novela à reimpressão que ora se faz parece que explicam as diferenças de composição e de maneira do autor. Se este não lhe daria agora a mesma feição, é certo que lha deu outrora, e, ao cabo, tudo pode servir a definir a mesma pessoa.

> [The thirty years which have elapsed between the appearance of this novel and the reimpression now being made seem to explain the differences in the composition and the author's style. If he would not give it the same shape now, he certainly had given it another shape before, and, in the end, everything can serve to define the same person.]

Notes to Chapter 1

1. Marlyse Meyer, 'Machado de Assis lê *Saint-Clair das Ilhas*', in *As mil faces de um herói canalha e outros ensaios* (Rio de Janeiro: Editora da UFRJ, 1998), p. 20.
2. Galante de Sousa, *Bibliografia de Machado de Assis* (Rio de Janeiro: INL, 1955), p. 55.
3. Gledson includes *Casa velha* among the writer's novels, rejecting its classification as a short story and its inclusion in the volume II, of short stories, II of the *Obra completa*, Editora Nova Aguilar (Gledson, *Machado de Assis: ficção e história*, p. 21).
4. Machado de Assis, *Casa velha* (São Paulo: Livraria Martins Editora, 1944).
5. The date given is the publication date of the first edition of the book, except for *Casa velha*.
6. All of the contracts and letters quoted in this chapter can be found in *Exposição comemorativa do sexagésimo aniversário do falecimento de Joaquim Maria Machado de Assis: 20/IX/1908 — 29/IX/1968* (Rio de Janeiro: Biblioteca Nacional, 1968).
7. Sousa, p. 88.
8. The works listed in the deed dated 16 January 1899 are: *Páginas recolhidas, Dom Casmurro, Memórias póstumas de Brás Cubas, Quincas Borba, Iaiá Garcia, Helena, Ressurreição, A mão e a luva, Papéis avulsos, Histórias sem data, Histórias da meia noite, Contos fluminenses, Americanas, Falenas* and *Crisálidas*.
9. *Exposição*, p. 204.
10. In a draft of a letter dated 10 July 1903, Machado observes that the many errors in the edition of *Várias Histórias* harmed the work, particularly with regard to its being taken up by schools. He also remarked that, although other works by him contained printing errors, none contained so many errors as the collection in question (*Exposição*, p. 204).

11. Sousa, p. 462.
12. Different terms are used to specify the approximate size of a book. These terms derive from the number of sheets created when a leaf of standard size (during the period when paper was manufactured manually) was folded. The printed area of the book is printed on the front and back of these folded leaves. The largest size, the folio, results from folding the inner leaf once, which produces two folded leaves or four pages. The names of the other sizes indicate the fraction of the inner leaf that each folded leaf takes up. For example, the quarto or 4to size results from two folds and has four folded leaves or eight pages. Octavo or 8to results from three folds and has eight folded leaves or 16 pages.
13. Laurence Hallewell, *Books in Brazil* (London and Metuchen, NJ: Scarecrow Press, 1982), p. 108.
14. Alessandra El Far, *Páginas de sensação: literatura popular e pornográfica no Rio de Janeiro, 1870–1924* (São Paulo: Companhia das Letras, 2004). See in particular the first chapter: 'Livreiros do Oitocentos', pp. 27–76.
15. Hallewell, p. 98.
16. Sousa, p. 65.
17. Sousa, p. 73.
18. Capítulo 22: 'Volta ao Rio', *Memórias póstumas de Brás Cubas*, p. 153. For more on the readership of *Memórias póstumas de Brás Cubas* see Hélio de Seixas Guimarães, 'Brás Cubas e a textualização do leitor', *Os leitores de Machado de Assis: o romance machadiano e o público de literatura no século XIX* (São Paulo: Nankin Editorial and Editora da Universidade de São Paulo, 2004), pp. 175–93.
19. *Exposição*, pp. 178, 183.
20. Subscriptions to *O Cruzeiro* cost the same, as did individual copies. I do not have figures for its circulation.
21. *A mão e a luva*, p. 57.
22. The instalments are not numbered in *O Cruzeiro*.
23. Salvador de Mendonça, 'Ao leitor', *Marabá* (Rio de Janeiro: Editores Gomes de Oliveira & Cia, Tipografia do Globo, 1875), p. v.
24. See Guimarães, the chapter '*Helena e Iaiá Garcia*: em busca do leitor popular', pp. 149–70. For a review of the critical history of *Helena*, see in particular the sub-section 'O melodrama em *Helena*', pp. 158–62.
25. Guimarães, p. 161.
26. According to an imperial census carried out in 1876, which was the subject of an article by Machado de Assis, 70% of the population could not read: 'A nação não sabe ler. Há só 30% dos indivíduos residentes neste país que podem ler; desses uns 9% não lêem letra de mão. 70% jazem em profunda ignorância.' [The nation cannot read. Only 30% of the residents of this country can read; of these, 9% cannot read handwriting. 70% are living in profound ignorance.] ('História de 15 dias', 1 August 1876, *Obra Completa*, 3 vols (Rio de Janeiro: Editora Nova Aguilar, 1992), III, 345.)
27. Guimarães, p. 157.
28. Guimarães, p. 163.
29. John Gledson, *The Deceptive Realism of Machado de Assis* (Liverpool: Francis Cairns, 1984), p. 22.
30. *David Copperfield* was published in 19 monthly instalments from 1 May 1849 to 1 November 1850 by Bradbury and Evans, United Kingdom. *Great Expectations* was published in serial form in *All the Year Round* from December 1860 to August 1861. Chapter 7 will deal in more details with the narrators of *Memórias póstumas de Brás Cubas*, *Quincas Borba* and *Dom Casmurro*, from a comparative perspective.
31. *Memórias póstumas de Brás Cubas*, p. 111.
32. Guimarães, p. 185.
33. *Memórias póstumas de Brás Cubas*, p. 105.

CHAPTER 2

❖

Philosopher or Dog? and the Fashion Section of *A Estação*

This chapter explores the thematic relationship between *Quincas Borba* and the fashion section of *A Estação*. It reconstructs the history of the magazine, which was the Brazilian edition of *Die Modenwelt*, a German magazine which reproduced the same fashion content in thirteen different European languages, one of the first (if not the very first) of its kind. The chapter shows how the Brazilian edition was reproduced from its German original, while giving itself a French appearance — which was important for commercial reasons. The readership of *Quincas Borba* was limited to Brazil, yet the subscribers of the magazine belonged to the global audience of *Die Modenwelt*, which aspired to the same outward signs of well being, prosperity and status. The Brazilian author turns into fiction the aspirations of his readers by portraying a 'changing society' (Gledson), in which individuals crave European goods and imitate the habits of the elite, out of a desire to acquire *status*, or to climb the social ladder, or to avoid a downfall. The chapter therefore shows that the author knew his readers very well and took advantage of this fact to write a novel that would appeal to the subscribers of *A Estação*, but was also ironic.

The Numbers of Subscriptions to the Magazine and of Readers of the Novel

By publishing *Quincas Borba* in *A Estação*, Machado de Assis was providing entertainment for subscribers to the magazine, who were his first readers. As stated in the introduction to this book, the serial had probably passed through the homes of 10,000 subscribers before it was thoroughly revised and presented in book form. As we have seen, this is the circulation figure claimed by the publishers in the issue dated 15 March 1882. The publishers often complained that subscribers' were in the bad habit of lending their magazines to others, which represented a loss for Lombaerts. This sentiment is also registered in this reply to a devoted reader from Bahia:

> Se todos fossem como V. Ex. *A Estação* poderia estar mais perfeita, pois os próprios assinantes aproveitam o progresso que vai tendo o jornal. O que tem demorado a marcha progressiva da nossa folha é não ser cada leitor assinante. É infelizmente muito maior o número dos que aproveitam-se do jornal sem o pagar, do que dos que o assinam. (*A Estação*, 29 February 1888)

> [If everyone were like you, *A Estação* would be even more perfect since the subscribers themselves benefit from the progress which the periodical is making. The advancement of our paper has been hindered by the fact that not every reader is a subscriber. Unfortunately, the number of those who benefit from the periodical without paying for it is much greater than those who subscribe to it.]

Even though we may suspect that the number of subscriptions was exaggerated by the publisher (as ever, a common practice), if we compare *A Estação* to the number of subscriptions claimed by other successful periodicals from Rio, it was by comparison a very popular periodical. Furthermore it was able to survive for more than three decades and made its Brazilian editor a rich man.[1] The comment above, by the reader from Bahia, reveals not only that the actual number of readers was probably much greater than the number of subscribers, but also that *A Estação* was a successful publication among its readers. In the correspondence section, for example, we learn that previous issues had sold out. It is likely that readers (whose letters were unfortunately not transcribed within the body of the magazine) wanted to purchase them but that their orders were not met. We now have the evidence of a reader from Campos in addition to the one from Bahia: 'Campos — Não é possível pois esgotou-se totalmente a edição de todos os números desde julho' [Campos — It is not possible as all of the issues since July have been totally sold out] (*A Estação*, 15 March 1891). Later, we shall see that there were others from Sorocaba, Recreio and Coxim in Mato Grosso do Sul. The circulation of *A Estação* was not restricted to the limits of Rio de Janeiro, at that time the capital of Brazil. It was even in circulation in Minas, São Paulo, Campinas and cities located in the far north or south of the country, such as Belém, Manaus and Porto Alegre.

Such readers probably only had access to the novel within the textual and material composition of the magazine, mainly because the print run of the magazine was much greater than the thousand copies of the first edition which were printed in book form.[2] In fact, it may even be supposed, although we have no documents to prove it, that in these remote areas the novel continued to be read in serial form for some years after the publication of the first edition. Lombaerts themselves encouraged subscribers to collect the 'Literary Section' of *A Estação*, which certainly allowed the pages in which *Quincas Borba* was originally published to survive for a few more years:

> Estes suplementos reunidos no fim do ano formarão um álbum recreativo, que a par de lindas gravuras, constituirá uma escolha de artigos, sobre o nosso mundo elegante, obras literárias dos nossos mais festejados escritores, conselhos econômicos, artigos humorísticos. (*A Estação*, 31 March 1879)

> [These supplements, collected at the end of the year, will form a diverting album which, along with the attractive illustrations, will comprise a selection of articles about our elegant world, literary works by our most celebrated writers, financial advice and humorous articles.]

Whether the readers perused fortnightly periodicals or a collection of the supplements, *Quincas Borba* was originally read in the context described above: the reader's gaze would flit from one heading to another, skimming over the advertisements or lingering over the beautiful woodcuts. An interesting and as yet unexplored aspect of *A Estação* (which is touched on tangentially in Chapters 2 and 3 of this book) is the combination of text and image which produced a periodical that was at the same time both instructive and entertaining. For the reader of the serial, the other textual and pictorial elements were in a direct intertextual relationship with the instalments of the novel, which is not the case when the novel is read in book form.

As such, the effects produced by reading the serial and the book differ not only as a result of differences in the text. The extended publication time and the material context also make themselves felt in the act of reading. This is what we perceive in the note written by Artur Azevedo in his column in *A Estação* to promote the release of *Quincas Borba* in book form:

> Depois das *Aleluias*, de Raimundo Correia, formoso livro que tem passado completamente despercebido, tivemos o *Quincas Borba*, de Machado de Assis. As leitoras conhecem o romance, que durante muito tempo foi publicado nas colunas da *Estação*; mas essa leitura dosimétrica naturalmente pouco aproveitou, e eu recomendo-lhes que o leiam de novo no volume editado pelo Sr. B. L. Garnier. ('Croniqueta', *A Estação*, 31 January 1892)

> [After Raimundo Correia's *Aleluias*, a beautiful book which passed completely unnoticed, we have *Quincas Borba* by Machado de Assis. Readers will be familiar with the novel, which was published for a long time in the columns of *A Estação*, but that dosimetric reading was naturally of little benefit, and I recommend that you read it again in the volume published by Mr B. L. Garnier.]

Artur Azevedo is specifically writing to subscribers to *A Estação*, potential readers of the serial version of *Quincas Borba*. His main aim is doubtless to promote the book commercially. But the columnist is also drawing attention to the fact that readers who have read the novel in serial form will not necessarily find that the book offers the same reading experience. Unlike Artur Azevedo, I would not say that reading the serial was 'of little benefit'. The reader's engagement with the serialized text over such an extended period of time, however, was definitely very different from the reader's engagement with the book, which could be read in just a few days or weeks.

Moreover, not everything changed from the serial to book version. In order to understand what did change, it is necessary to identify the characteristics which are intrinsic to the serialized version and which were conserved in the one-volume version of the novel. As we shall see in Chapter 4 of this book, in rewriting the novel Machado de Assis managed to tone down the episodic and melodramatic elements which are so characteristic of the serial. However, the strong connection between the theme of the novel and the editorial leanings of the magazine are maintained from one version to the next. This is because Machado de Assis did not abandon his social realist and political intentions, even though, in the latter case, he may only have achieved the desired result in the second version.

This connection can be better understood only with a knowledge of the history of *A Estação*. As such, we need to deviate from our route so that we may study the nature of the magazine itself, as well as its underlying editorial concept.

A Estação, a propos *Die Modenwelt*, an International Undertaking

Where its editorial concept is concerned, *A Estação* is very much following in the footsteps of the German magazines *Die Modenwelt* and *Illustrirte Frauen-Zeitung*, which were published by Lipperheide. We find in these two periodicals the formula used by Lombaerts to join together a fashion magazine, aimed at a predominantly female public, and a literary and illustrated periodical, aimed at all the family, as the full name of the Brazilian publication indicated: *A Estação. Jornal Ilustrado para a Família* [*The Season. Illustrated Journal for the Family*].

We now need to move temporarily away from Rio de Janeiro and go back even further in time in order to unearth the history of these two Berlin-based periodicals and shed light on the cultural and commercial factors which link the Brazilian magazine to the German ones. We will then be better placed to investigate the way in which the German editorial concept was moved to Brazil and disseminated throughout the texts of the Brazilian contributors, including *Quincas Borba*. We must not fail to mention that the history of *A Estação* is still not well known in Brazil. Even in Germany, Lipperheide's publishing enterprise has not been widely studied, as Adelheid Rasche states in *Frieda Lipperheide: 1840–1896*.[3]

Primary research sources

Among the various books in German which were found in Machado de Assis's library, one in particular is useful in reconstructing the history of the magazine *A Estação*: *Zum fünfundzwanzigjährigen Bestehen der Modenwelt 1865–1890* [*Commemorative edition of 25 years of the existence of Die Modenwelt*].[4] As the title itself indicates, this is the commemorative edition of 25 years of the existence of the illustrated magazine *Die Modenwelt. Illustrirte Zeitung für Toilette und Handarbeiten* [*The World of Fashion. Illustrated Periodical of Toilette and Handicrafts*], published by Franz Lipperheide. Machado de Assis probably obtained it from the Lombaerts's printing plant, which was responsible not only for printing and distributing *A Estação* but also for selling the magazine *Die Modenwelt*, and its other foreign editions, in Rio de Janeiro, if not throughout the whole of Brazil.

My research into the joint history of *A Estação* and *Die Modenwelt* owes much to the information contained in this book, as well as perusal of the magazines themselves in libraries and archives in Brazil, Germany, England and Switzerland.[5] It is true that this work would benefit greatly from research into the nature of the commercial relations which existed between Lipperheide and the publishers of the various versions of *Die Modenwelt*, in the form of contracts and commercial correspondence exchanged between local publishers and the German headquarters. Unfortunately, it has not been possible to locate this type of documentation, either in Brazil or in Germany.

Perhaps the publishers Lipperheide and Lombaerts were not very different from the majority of publishers in the world, who, Robert Darnton explains, 'treat[ed] their archives as garbage'.[6] In fact, it is not known with any certainty whether the destruction of the archives coincides with the end of Lipperheide's publishing career (he sold the publishing house early in the twentieth century), or the start of the Second World War. The headquarters of the publishing house were situated in the centre of Berlin, on Potsdamer Strasse, a road which was partially destroyed during the war. The facade of one of the buildings which the publishing house occupied still exists today (no. 96, which was no. 38 at the time), although the interior has been completely restored.

In either case, Lipperheide's archives apparently did not survive. However, the Lipperheidesche Kostümbibliothek in Berlin now houses not only a collection of the periodicals published by Franz and Frieda Lipperheide, but also their private collection, which is made up of books, paintings, illustrations, designs, samples of fabrics, and photographs acquired by the couple with the profits from the publishing house.[7] Where Brazil is concerned, research has yet to be undertaken. Laurence Hallewell states that Lombaerts was bought by Francisco Alves and that its headquarters, at 17 Ourives Street, were demolished in 1904, the year in which the periodical ceased to exist, in order to make way for the current Avenida Rio Branco.[8] Could it be that Lombaerts's commercial archives were also lost in the modernization works that took place in Rio de Janeiro?

The loss of (or inability to find) the archives certainly makes research more difficult. However, it does not make it impossible to reconstruct the story partially. The Lipperheide publishing house combined the production of Berlin-based periodicals with a series of collaborations with other publishing houses in Europe and the Americas. Its aim was to spread Parisian fashion and European consumer goods throughout the West. In order to study the exact size of this international enterprise, it would be necessary to carry out research in various archives in Europe, Latin America and the United States in search of what survived of the twenty different periodicals that which connected with *Die Modenwelt* and published in a total of thirteen languages. Among these periodicals is *A Estação*, which was in circulation in Brazil between 1879 and 1904.

I do not intend to cover all of the editions of the magazine in the thirteen languages in which it was published, although one of my aims is to obtain a general understanding of how Lipperheide negotiated with other publishing houses or printing plants outside of Germany.

From the founding to the internationalization of the magazine

Founded in October 1865, the aim of the magazine *Die Modenwelt* was to teach housewives how to make clothes for the whole family, embroider, and decorate their houses. Initially, *Die Modenwelt* was essentially a fashion periodical, with four richly illustrated pages. Only in 1874 did Lipperheide launch the *Unterhaltungsblatt* [entertainment section]. In this chapter, we shall examine the fashion section of the magazine, whose illustrations, captions and editorial were reproduced in the foreign editions, including *A Estação*, after being translated.[9]

The title page of *Die Modenwelt* contained a large illustration of one or more well-dressed ladies, who might also be accompanied by children. The scene in the background was a park, a lake, the inside of a house, or even a festive salon. Depending on the position in which the ladies were drawn (they were sometimes shown in profile, from behind, or from the front) the illustrator explored the details of their collar, neckline, sleeves or the train of their dress (see Figure 2.1). The fashion editorial occupied the two outer columns of the first page and discussed trends in family clothing as the seasons changed in Europe. Moreover, as the majority of the readers, who were wives and daughters, were predominantly interested in family instruction, *Die Modenwelt* was also a periodical of principles, which gave particular emphasis to the moral values of the family. In a conversational tone, the editor Frieda Lipperheide also imparted lessons on the etiquette of the table and the salon. The order of the day was discreet elegance without extravagance:

> Die Mode ist nicht verantwortlich für Das, was die Einzelne thut; jede Frau muß aus der Fülle des Vorhandenen wählen, was ihren Verhältnissen, ihrem Alter, ihrer Persönlichkeit angemessen ist; sie muß mit echt weiblichem Tact das Uebertriebene, das Ungehörige zu vermeinden, mit Geschmack in Form, Farbe und Stoff das Richtige, das Passende herauszufinden und auf die richtige Weise anzuwenden wissen.[10]

> [It is not up to fashion to choose for each individual. Every woman must choose, from among the wide range of clothing available, that which is suited to her circumstances, her age, and her personality; with true feminine tact she must avoid the immoderate and the brash; displaying good taste in form, colour and fabric she must distinguish what is right and proper and know how to dress correctly.]

The inner pages of the magazine contained more illustrations. Marlyse Meyer's description of this part of the Brazilian magazine *A Estação* applies very well to *Die Modenwelt* because the fashion sections of these two periodicals, as we shall see in more detail later, were produced from the same editorial template. The wide variety of articles quoted below show that not only clothing but also general ornamentation and accessories were discussed:

> vestidos, chapéus, toucas, manteis, roupa de baixo, aventais de luxo, pelissas, saias, corpetes etc. etc. em matéria de indumentária feminina; e mais, peças de decoração, trabalhos de agulha, tamboretes, *cache-pots*, móveis diversos — todas as ilustrações com legendas explicativas externas, remetendo ao molde mensal, que também vem à parte.[11]

> [dresses, hats, bonnets, shawls, underwear, luxury aprons, pelisses, skirts, bodices, etc. in the area of feminine clothing; and decorative pieces, needle-work, stools, ornamental vases, various pieces of furniture — all of the illustrations come with external captions, referring to the monthly pattern, which also comes separately.]

In fact, the idea of publishing a magazine about Parisian fashion was not a novelty at the time — Parisian cultural authority in the fashion trade had been recognized long before.[12] In Germany, for example, magazines which were in circulation before *Die Modenwelt* included *Pariser Damenkleider-Magazin*, of Stuttgart. In Brazil, the Laemmert publishing house began publishing *Correio das Modas*, which contained illustrations and patterns printed in Paris, in 1840.

The novel aspect of Lipperheide's publishing enterprise seems to have been that

FIG. 2.1. *Die Modenwelt*, 1 October 1870
Staatliche Museen zu Berlin, Kunstbibliothek
Photograph by Dietmar Katz, 2007
Sammlung Modebild-Lipperheidesche Kostümbibliothek, Berlin

the company created a standard format for the publication of fashion magazines in international circulation in several European languages, a publishing model which was the precursor of the great women's magazines of today, such as *Burda*, *Marie Claire* and *Vogue*. Like *Pariser Damenkleider-Magazin*, *Die Modenwelt* promoted and defended French-style international fashion. It seems to me, however, that Lipperheide's periodical was the first to reach readers in a larger number of different countries, and that it also benefited from the supremacy of French culture in the business of fashion.

Lipperheide's interest in expanding his business throughout Europe, as well as on the other side of the Atlantic, might have stemmed partly from economic necessity, as the cost of producing an illustrated periodical was undoubtedly very high. Ultimately, according to Robert Gross:

> the trouble started with Gutenberg. His ingenious invention, with its interchangeable parts, was the model of the modern machine, costly to build, inexpensive to operate, demanding large scales to compensate for the heavy capital investment. In the relentless quest for market, succeeding generations of publishers pushed the dynamic logic of mass production to its limits.[13]

Lipperheide's plan to create an international fashion periodical was realized through what might be called partnerships with other existing periodicals: 'Before the launch of the first issue, connections were established with foreign publishers, so that *Die Modenwelt* could appear in three languages from the start'.[14] The other two periodicals were the French title *L'Illustrateur des Dames*, of Paris, and the English title *The Young Ladies' Journal*, of London. By the end of the 1880s, the journalistic model of *Die Modenwelt*, including its illustrations and fashion editorial, was being reproduced in thirteen different languages.

We are starting to appreciate that the creation of a Brazilian periodical in the template of the German publication became part of a wider commercial project. We now need to determine where and how the foreign editions of *Die Modenwelt* were produced and printed. The next step will be to carry out a survey of all of the publications which derived from *Die Modenwelt*. Ultimately, we will be able to assess the options chosen by Lombaerts to adapt his product to the socio-cultural situation of Brazil, options which were explored by Machado de Assis in choosing the subject of the novel *Quincas Borba*.

The different editions of 'Die Modenwelt' and their mode of production

As can be seen in Figures 2.2 to 2.5, the fashion sections of *Die Modenwelt* and its various foreign editions were identical in almost every respect, despite having been translated into the respective national languages. The main, and practically the only, difference was on the front page. That of the Brazilian edition was identical to that of *La Saison*, which entered into circulation in Brazil in 1872, i.e., before the creation of *A Estação*, as we shall see later.

Where were the captions translated, and where were the fortnightly issues published and printed? In Germany, or in the country where each foreign edition was to be distributed? As we are not in possession of the commercial documentation

FIG. 2.2. *A Estação, Jornal Ilustrado para a Família*, 31 August 1890
Zum fünfundzwanzigjährigen Bestehen der Modenwelt (1865-1890),
Berlin: Franz Lipperheide, 1890, p. 34

FIG. 2.3. *Die Modenwelt, Illlustrirte Zeitung für Toilette und Handarbeiten*, 20 July 1890
Zum fünfundzwanzigjährigen Bestehen der Modenwelt (1865-1890), p. 16

FIG. 2.4. *La Saison, Jounal Illustré des Dames*, 1 August 1890
Zum fünfundzwanzigjährigen Bestehen der Modenwelt (1865-1890), p. 28

FIG. 2.5. *The Season, Lady's Illustrated Magazine*, August 1890
Zum fünfundzwanzigjährigen Bestehen der Modenwelt (1865-1890), p. 20

exchanged between Lipperheide and the distributors or publishers in each country, I begin by studying the material composition of the magazines in themselves in order to formulate the hypothesis that the different editions of *Die Modenwelt* were produced in accordance with one of the three commercial models described below.

In the first model, the publisher Lipperheide translated, published and printed the foreign periodical, which was subsequently sent to the country in which it was circulated. This seems to have been the case of *La Estación* and *The Season* (New York). In the second model, the plates were sent to a local publisher, who was responsible for paginating and printing the magazine. This, most of the time, was the case with *A Estação* and *La Saison*.[15] In the case of the Brazilian magazine, it is very probable that Paula Candida, who became the columnist of the fashion section on 30 April 1890, translated the leading articles for the Brazilian magazine directly from Berlin. Her name appears on the third page of the book commemorating twenty-five years of the existence of the Lipperheide publishing house next to a further eleven translators, who translated that issue's epigraph into Portuguese, English, Dutch, Danish, Swedish, French, Italian, Spanish, Russian, Polish, Czech and Hungarian. The German epigraph reads:

> 'Wer Rosen nicht in Sommer bricht,
> Der bricht sie auch im Winter nicht.'[16]

It is followed by twelve translations, among which one in English:

> 'Cull roses while the summer lasts,
> Too late 't will be in winter's blasts.' (J. Bell)

The fashion section of *A Estação*, however, was printed at the Lombaerts's printing plant. This is recorded in the footnote on the last page of this section of the magazine. *The Young Ladies' Journal* represents the third model described above. The British periodical maintained an independent format but shared some of its characteristics with *Die Modenwelt*. In common with the German bi-monthly magazine, the English weekly magazine contained articles on clothing, needlework and coloured fashion plates.

Table 2.1 contains a list of the foreign editions of *Die Modenwelt*, as well as their publishers and the place of publication. The information may not be very precise as it refers to just one production period: the year 1890. The majority of these

Notes on Table 2.1 (overleaf)

This table reproduces data provided in *Zum fünfundzwanzigjährigen Bestehen der Modenwelt 1865–1890* related to the journals that were considered 'die verschieden Ausgaben' [different editions] of the *Modenwelt*. Journals, such as *Les Modes de la Saison* and *The Young Ladies' Journal*, are not listed as 'different editions' of *Die Modenwelt*; they are, rather, described as journals with which *Die Modenwelt* had connections. Many of these journals published clothes patterns, fashion illustrations, and special issues that were sold separately. They also sold luxurious editions containing more illustrations or supplements, which raised the price of subscription. The price given in the chart is always for the economic edition of the journal.

TABLE 2.1: Different issues of *Die Modenwelt* (see notes on p. 50)

Name	First issue	Date from which linked to *Die Modenwelt*	Publishing house
The Young Ladies' Journal, London	Jan 1864	Oct 1865	Harrison, London
Die Modenwelt, Berlin, Germany	Oct 1865	Oct 1865	Franz Lipperheide, Berlin
De Bazar, The Hague, Holland	5 Jan 1857	1 Jan 1866	Gebr. Belinfante, The Hague
Budapesti Bazár, Hungary	1 Jan 1860	1 Jul 1877	Johann von Király, Budapest
Dagmar, Kjobenhaun, Denmark	1 Jul 1866	1 Jul 1866	Carls Otto's Nachfolger, Copenhagen
La Saison, Germany *La Saison*, France *La Saison*, Belgium *La Saison*, Switzerland *La Saison*, Italy	1 Dec 1867	1 Dez 1867	Franz Lipperheide, Berlin J. Lebègue et Cie, Paris J. Lebègue et Cie, Brussels Nydegger & Baumgart Ufficio della Stagione (U. Hoepli), Milan
A Estação, Jornal Ilustrado para a Família. Edição para os Estados Unidos do Brasil	1 Jan 1872	1 Jan 1879	H. Lombaerts & Comp Portugal: Livraria Ernesto Chardron Lugan C. Genelioux – sucessores –, Porto
Freja, Malmö, Sweden	1 Jan 1873	1 Jan 1873	J. G. Hedberg, Malmö and Stockholm
Illustrirte Frauen-Zeitung, Germany	1 Jan 1874	1 Jan 1874	Franz Lipperheide, Berlin and Vienna
Modni Svet, Czech	1 Jan 1879	1 Jan 1879	Karl Vačlera, Jungbunzlau and Prague
The Season, Lady's Illustrated Magazine, New York *The Season, Lady's Illustrated Magazine*, London	1 Jan 1882 1 Oct 1884	1 Jan 1882 1 Oct 1884	The International News Company, New York 13 Bedford Street, Convent Garden
La Estación, Periódico para Senhoras, Spain *La Estacíon, Periódico para Senhoras*, South America (Argentina, Uruguai, Colombia, Chile, Paraguai)	1 Apr 1884	1 Apr 1884	Librería Gutenberg, Madrid Franz Lipperheide, Berlin Argentina: CM Joly y Cia, Buenos Aires
La Stagione. Giornale delle Mode, Milan	1 Oct 1882	1 Oct 1882	Ufficio della Satagione (U. Hoepli), Milan
Модный Свет и Модный Магазинъ, Russian	1 Dec 1866	1 Dec 1866	Hermann Hoppe
Tygonik Mód I Powiésci, Warsaw, Poland	1 Jan 1860	19 Jan 1867	E. Skiwskiin, Warschau

The Fashion Section of *A Estação* 49

Illustrations by	Texts printed by	Periodicity	Price
Harrison, London		weekly	9d (by post 1s)
Otto Dürr, Leipzig		fortnightly	1.25 Mark per term
Otto Dürr, Leipzig	Gebr. Belinfante, The Hague	fortnightly	f. 1.00 per term
Otto Dürr, Leipzig	Hungaria-Buchdrückerei, Budapest	fortnightly	2 Fl.
Otto Dürr, Leipzig		fortnightly	1 Kr. 60 Öre per term
Otto Dürr, Leipzig J. Bolbachm, Paris		fortnightly	1.25 Marks 2 Fr. 2 Fr. 2 Fr. 2.50 Fr.
Otto Dürr, Leipzig		fortnightly	Rio: 12$000 Provinces: 14$000 per year
Otto Dürr, Leipzig	Stenström and Bartelson, Malmö	fortnightly	2 Kronen per term
Otto Dürr, Leipzig		fortnightly (weekly 6 Mar 1887 to 1 Jan 1890)	2.50 Marks per term
Otto Dürr, Leipzig	Josef Zvikl, Jungbunzlau	fortnightly	1 Fl per term
Otto Dürr, Leipzig (cover printed by Keppler e Schwarzmann, New York)		monthly	?
Otto Dürr, Leipzig (supplement and cover printed by Hazell, Watson e Viney Ld, London Aylesbury)		monthly	1 shilling
Otto Dürr, Leipzig Otto Dürr, Leipzig		fortnighly	3.50 ptas per term 2.50 ptas per term
Tipografia Bernardoni di Rebeschini, Milan		fortnightly	L. 2.50 per term
Eduard Hoppe		fortnightly	2 Rubel (per six months)
E. Skiwskiin, Warschau		weekly	1.25 Rubel per term

periodicals were in circulation for a long time. Where the Brazilian magazine is concerned, for example, it is not true that *A Estação* was launched in 1872. In fact, the periodical which entered into circulation in Brazil in 1872 was *La Saison. Edição para o Brasil*. In this edition of the French periodical, the explanation of the illustrations came in both French and Portuguese. This is the information which we find in an advertisement published by Lombaerts on 2 August 1876 in the daily newspaper *O Globo*, in which the launch of the issue of 1 July 1876 was advertised.

'La Saison' and 'A Estação' in the Rio de Janeiro fashion magazine market

It is worth noting that in 1876, besides *Jornal das Famílias* (1863–1878), to which Machado de Assis also contributed, at least three other periodicals were competing in the growing fashion magazine market in Rio de Janeiro. In *O Globo* we also find advertisements for the *Gazeta Ilustrada dos Dous Mundos* and the *Ilustração da Moda*. According to the advertisement placed on 3 August 1876, the former periodical was a new fortnightly publication from London with a more varied range of contents and illustrations, including political issues, a literature and fine art section, and fashion plates with illustrations from Paris and London. The annual subscription cost 20,000 *réis*, with a promotional price for the first 5000 subscribers of 15,000 *réis*.

As for the *Ilustração da Moda*, the advertisement placed on 9 July 1876 proclaimed it to be not just the only Parisian fashion periodical written in Portuguese but also the best and the cheapest:

> O editor deste importantíssimo jornal, o melhor e mais barato até agora conhecido, tem a honra de participar para as Exmas. Senhoras que já tem à sua disposição dos 1º ao 5º números, com lindos figurinos coloridos, muitas gravuras, folha de moldes e bordados, e artigos variados de literatura dos autores mais célebres, Littré, L. Figuier e outros.
>
> [The publisher of this highly important newspaper, the best and cheapest known to date, has the honour of informing you that issues 1 to 5 are now available. They contain pretty coloured fashion plates, many illustrations, patterns and embroidery page, and various literary articles by the most celebrated authors, including Littré, L. Figuier and others.]

In comparison with *La Saison*, the *Ilustração da Moda* was in fact cheaper. The price of an annual subscription to *La Saison*, according to an advertisement placed on 2 August 1876, was 12,000 *réis* for the capital and 14,000 *réis* for the provinces. Despite being more expensive, *La Saison* still referred to itself as the best and cheapest fashion periodical. In a subsequent advertisement, however, Lombaerts changed strategy. Instead of reaffirming that *La Saison* was the cheapest Parisian fashion journal in the capital, he emphasized the superiority of the magazine, implying that the reader would find that it offered the best cost–benefit relationship. The cost of the subscription was in fact greater, but *La Saison* was larger and contained a greater variety of illustrations:

> A superioridade incontestável da *Saison* está hoje provada. Nenhuma outra folha de modas, guardadas as proporções de preço, é tão variada, rica e barata. Nenhuma, ainda mesmo as que são hebdomadárias, chegam a perfazer no fim de um ano o total de 2000 gravuras de modas, 24 lâminas representando cerca

de 100 toilettes cuidadosamente coloridas, mais de 400 moldes em tamanho natural e um sem número de explicações para fazer por si, não somente tudo quanto diz respeito ao vestuário de senhoras e crianças, como também todos esses artigos de fantasia e gosto que enfeitam e dão graça a uma casa de família. (*O Globo*, 10 September 1876)

[The indisputable superiority of *La Saison* has today been proven. No other fashion journal, in proportion to its price, is as rich, varied and cheap. And none, not even the weekly publications, manage to present, at the end of the year, a total of 2000 fashion illustrations, 24 carefully coloured plates representing almost 100 outfits, over 400 natural-sized patterns, and endless explanations to help readers make things themselves, not only ladies and children's clothes but also all of those fancy goods and luxury items which adorn and enliven a family home.]

Up to the end of 1878, it was the French edition of *Die Modenwelt* which was in circulation in Rio de Janeiro; the Portuguese version of the magazine was not launched until January 1879. It is not surprising that Lombaerts should consider *A Estação*, which was printed in its own workshop, as a continuation in the Portuguese language of *La Saison*, the periodical which it had been selling for seven years. However, as the publishers made clear to a reader from Coxim:

La Saison e *A Estação* são duas publicações distintas. Somos apenas proprietários da segunda e não da primeira. É conveniente que ao pedir a assinatura de qualquer delas haja o maior cuidado em indicá-las pelo próprio nome pois não podemos desfazer as assinaturas feitas. (*A Estação*, 15 April 1892)

[*La Saison* and *A Estação* are two different publications. We are the proprietors of the first but not the second. It is advisable when subscribing to either of them to take great care to specify them by name, as we cannot cancel subscriptions once taken out.]

What mattered to Lombaerts was *La Saison*'s first year of circulation in Brazil, because the two periodicals formed part of the same multinational enterprise. Moreover, by establishing a connection between *La Saison* and *A Estação*, Lombaerts was employing a commercial strategy: he was transferring the captive public of one periodical to the other. Initially, Lombaerts did not reveal the entity to which his magazine was actually affiliated, i.e., an international undertaking of German origin — his readers could therefore believe that they were reading a genuine French magazine. Only when *A Estação* was accused of being a false publication, for having presented French fashion that was produced between Leipzig and Berlin, did Lombaerts reveal the complexity of this publishing venture to his readers:

'*A Estação*, dizem, é um jornal alemão, e vós que julgais, seguindo os seus conselhos, trajar segundo os preceitos da Capital universal da moda, que é Paris, enganai-vos redondamente porquanto vestis apenas trajes ideados em Berlin.'

Para tal argumentação baseiam-se os detratores da *Estação* no fato de serem algumas das edições em diversos idiomas deste jornal impressas, em Leipzig.

O tronco da organização de que *A Estação* é um dos ramos está na verdade plantado em Berlin. Aí publica-se *Die Modenwelt*, jornal de modas que hoje, só sob este título, tem edição maior do que a de todos jornais de modas publicados em Paris reunidos.

Aí é redigida, aí são gravados os desenhos, aí é impressa e aí é traduzida em alguns dos quatorze[17] idiomas para dar à luz vinte publicações diferentes, cujo elemento artístico é o mesmo.[18]

['*A Estação*, they are saying, is a German periodical, and you who suppose that, by following its advice, you are dressing according to the precepts of the universal Capital of fashion, which is Paris, are thoroughly deceiving yourselves, since you are merely wearing clothes conceived in Berlin.'

A Estação's detractors are basing this line of argument on the fact that some editions of the periodical, in various languages, are printed in Leipzig.

The trunk of the organization, of which *A Estação* is one branch, is indeed planted in Berlin. It is there that *Die Modenwelt* is published, a fashion periodical which today, under this sole title, has a greater circulation than that of all the fashion periodicals published in Paris together.

There it is written, there the illustrations are engraved, there it is printed, and there it is translated into some of the fourteen languages needed to produce twenty different publications, whose artistic principle is the same.]

On at least two occasions after this date, Lombaerts informed readers that other editions of *A Estação* were on sale in Rio de Janeiro:

Recreio — Existe *A Estação* em idioma holandês, o preço de assinatura é o mesmo em qualquer dos 14 idiomas em que se publica. (*A Estação*, 31 March 1888)

Sorocaba — A Estação existe em francês, inglês, alemão, italiano, espanhol, português, holandês, dinamarquês, russo, sueco, boêmio, polaco, croato, húngaro e eslavo. Temos coleções de números iguais em todos esses idiomas que podem ser vistos em nosso escritório, bem como fornecemos assinatura a quem o deseje do jornal em qualquer desses idiomas. (*A Estação*, 31 July 1888)

[Recreio — *A Estação* exists in Dutch, the subscription price is the same in all of the 14 languages in which it is published.

Sorocaba — *A Estação* exists in French, English, German, Italian, Spanish, Portuguese, Dutch, Danish, Russian, Swedish, Czech, Polish, Croatian, Hungarian and Slavonic. We hold collections of the same issues in all of these languages which can be seen at our office; likewise we can supply a subscription to the journal for those who desire it in any of these languages.]

The Lipperheide professionals

Information contained in *Zum fünfundzwanzigjährigen Bestehen der Modenwelt* makes it possible to conclude that Lipperheide based the staff responsible for composing the periodical, including its writers, translators and designers, in Berlin and Leipzig. In these two cities the woodcuts and lithographs which would illustrate both the fashion section and the entertainment page (which I will examine in the next chapter) of *Die Modenwelt* were created. Among the engravers, we find the names Gustav Heuer and Kirmse and Kaspar Erhardt Oertel, among others. If they did not work exclusively for Lipperheide, the very least we can say is that these artists collaborated very closely with Lombaerts, owing to the great frequency with which we find illustrations bearing their signatures. Meanwhile, it was in Leipzig that the periodicals were proofread, printed and distributed throughout Germany, or sent to other countries in Europe and America. The typographer Otto Dürr was responsible for the printing, and K. F. Koehler for the packaging and distribution of the periodicals. In total, there were 398 employees, including writers, editors, designers, colourists, engravers, archivists, translators, proofreaders, typographers, machine operators, binders, loaders and distributors, of whom 225 were men and 173 were women. All of these professionals worked on the production of *Die Modenwelt* and *Illustrirte Frauen-Zeitung* and the foreign editions. Some were based in Berlin (99), while others were based in Leipzig (283), Erfurt (1), Konstanz (6), Vienna (4), Paris (3), London (1) and Rome (1).[19]

As the editor of *La Saison* writes in the opening editorial of the third year in which the magazine was in circulation:

> Faire un journal est une chose difficile et compliquée, dont les initiés seuls ont le secret. — Les journaux ilustrés sont plus minutieux que les autres, et les journaux de modes encore plus que les journaux ilustrés. — Ils nécessitent un personnel innombrable de rédactrices et redacteurs, de dessinateurs, des gravures, de coloristes, d'artistes de toutes sortes, qu'on ne rencontre pas dans un journal ordinaire, qui viennent grossir le bataillon des compositeurs, imprimeurs, papetiers, déjà si difficile à manœuvrer; quels efforts pour que ces travaux divers, separés, confiés à des mains étrangères, forment un ensemble homogène, un tout harmonieux, fondu, compact et correct, en un mot ce qu'on peut appeler: un journal! (*La Saison*, 1 October 1869)

> [Making a journal is something difficult and complicated, of which only the initiated know the secret. — The illustrated journals require more attention to detail than the others, and the fashion journals even more than the illustrated journals. — They demand an innumerable staff of female and male writers, draughtsmen, engravers, colourists, artists of all sorts, whom we do not find in an ordinary journal, and who swell the crowd of typesetters, printers, stationers, already so difficult to manage. What an effort is required for those different tasks, separated and entrusted to foreign hands, to form a homogenous ensemble, a harmonious whole, fused, compact and correct, in one word what one may call: a journal!]

Despite France being the country which dictated the rules of etiquette, and which launched the fashion which inspired *Die Modenwelt* to produce its illustrations, subscribers to *La Saison* were not the first to leaf through each issue of the magazine. The working time required to translate, compose and print the French periodical from *Die Modenwelt* was approximately one month. I was able to verify this by comparing the 1869 issues of the two magazines. The French issue of 1 November 1869 reproduces the same page layout and the same illustrations (accompanied by explicatory descriptions) as the issue of *Die Modenwelt* dated 1 October 1869. The leading articles, however, are not the same. In *La Saison*, the leading article has the title *Chronique de la Mode* and is signed by Mélanie. In *Die Modenwelt*, Frieda Lipperheide signs one article entitled *Neue Moden*. The French writer discusses the practical aspects of dress while Frieda Lipperheide tackles aspects of fashion in general.

Moreover, I was able to confirm that even the printing of *La Saison* did not always take place in France. The 1869 issues, for example, were printed in Leipzig by Jules Klinhardt, Impr. In the same year, *Die Modenwelt* was printed by A/U Edelmann, also in Leipzig. In 1872, *La Saison* was printed in Brussels, until 1 December, by A. N. Lebègue et Cie. From 16 December 1872 onwards, it was once more based in Leipzig, but this time the typographer in charge was A. Edelmann. Apparently, there existed more than one edition of *La Saison*, and the different editions were intended to be circulated in different countries, including Germany (where the printing was carried out in Leipzig by Otto Dürr), Belgium, and finally France (where it was printed by J. Lebègue of Paris). This is what I was able to ascertain by consulting the issues from the 1890s.

The examples above show that the Lipperheides exploited the new possibilities afforded by progress in transportation as well as innovations in the journalism industry. The couple benefited simultaneously from the development of the European rail network and the transatlantic steam lines on one hand, and on the other the professionalization of printing presses and the development of graphic art and printing techniques, enabling them to increase the number of copies and to widen the geographic area in which their periodical was circulated.

The history of the printing of these various magazines falls outside the scope of this study. By revealing some variations which occurred in their production, my intention has been to show that *Die Modenwelt* and its foreign editions functioned as a large set of interconnected cogs. I hope to have demonstrated, then, that *A Estação* must be seen as one piece inside a great mechanism, which, together with other European periodicals such as the *Revue des Deux Mondes*, helped to disseminate European cultural values in Brazil. As Friedrich Melford writes:

> Wie kein anderes Zeitungs-Unternehmen der Welt hat *Die Modenwelt* eine Verbreitung über den Erdball gefunden: vom Cap Finisterre bis zum Ural, von Malta bis Hammerfest, auf Cuba und Puerto Rico wie am Camp der guten Hoffnung, am Amazonenstrom und La Plata, auf den einsamen Farmen Nord-Amerika's und in den Harems zu Konstantinopel, allüberall findet sich *Die Modenwelt,* überall wohin europäische Cultur ihre weissen Hände streckt. Unter der heissen Aequator-Sonne oder da, wo fast ewiger Winter herrscht, es ist stets dasselbe Blatt, mit demselben Inhalt, denselben Abbildungen, ohne irgend welche besondere Auswahl oder Weglassung, in dreizehn Sprachen verkündend, was die Mode Neues schafft und was in der Kunst der weiblichen Handarbeiten es zu lehren giebt, sei es eine Schöpfung unserer Zeit, sei es, was aus alten Truhen hervorgeholt wurde.[20]

> [Like no other journalistic enterprise in the world *Die Modenwelt* has achieved a circulation around the globe: from Cape Finisterre to the Urals, from Malta to Hammerfest, in Cuba and Puerto Rico as well as in the Cape of Good Hope, on the Amazon river and La Plata, at the secluded farms of North America and in the harems of Constantinople, *Die Modenwelt* can be found everywhere, wherever European culture extends its white hands. Under the hot equatorial sun, or in the lands where winter never ends, it is always the same paper, with the same contents, the same images, without any particular selection or exclusion, advertising in thirteen languages what fashion creates anew and what the art of feminine handicraft has to teach, whether it is a creation of our time or something brought forth from old trunks.]

In the second half of the nineteenth century, we can already find evidence of the runaway trend towards homogenization in printing. As Robert Gross writes:

> The modern media shrank the globe, annihilating time and space. Millions read the same news, saw the same images, craved the same goods. Theirs was a standardized experience of mass culture, and if the content differed from nation to nation, the effects did not. Popular tastes, shaped by dominant media, transcended national boundaries.[21]

Nowadays, when we leaf through one of the big magazines aimed at women readers, such as *Vogue* and *Marie Claire*, or even a weekly news magazine such as *Focus* (*A Época*, in Brazil), our reading experience is very similar to that undergone by readers of *Die Modenwelt*, since the various editions of these magazines, circulating in different languages in more than one country, follow a single editorial concept and pattern, as did the publications derived from *Die Modenwelt*.[22]

The Global Audience of *Die Modenwelt* and the Target Readership of *Philosopher or Dog?*

I have tried to show the way in which the *Die Modenwelt* project constituted a network of periodicals whose cultural roots were French but whose aspirations were transnational. By transcending national borders, the editorial concept of *Die Modenwelt* formed an audience which shared the same consumer desires.

When they imbued the periodical with a transnational feel, the publishers were thinking not only of the readers but also of the advertisers. A concrete example of this can be found in the attempt by the British magazine to bring an international touch to the notes aimed at advertisers. The publishers of *The Young Ladies' Journal* alleged that the magazine was in circulation all around the world and was read by approximately half a million families, thereby constituting 'a most grand medium for advertisers' (see Figure 2.6).[23] Even though the actual number of subscribers was lower, half a million families represented the number of readers which the magazine hoped to reach.

We find the same aspirations in the Brazilian magazine, when *A Estação* was accused of not being an authentic French periodical. In their editorial of 15 November 1885 the publishers had revealed the complexity of the production process in order to defend the authenticity of their periodical. We also see in it the same attempt to emphasize the international character of the publication and the same number of subscriptions, which assured readers and advertisers of the high circulation figures of the periodical.

But what is most interesting about the editorial is that it provides confirmation that the *Die Modenwelt* project, which was shaped by French cultural authority, brought together readers from different countries into a single global audience aspiring to the same external signs of prosperity and well-being, which were considered to be universal. In Europe, it seems to me that the creation of women's periodicals containing recipes, patterns, sewing instructions and tips on home economics is connected to the entry of women into the labour market.[24] At least where England is concerned, Braithwaite believes that in the second half of the nineteenth century the country experienced an increase in the production of women's magazines because the lack of servants meant that middle-class women began to carry out domestic chores themselves:

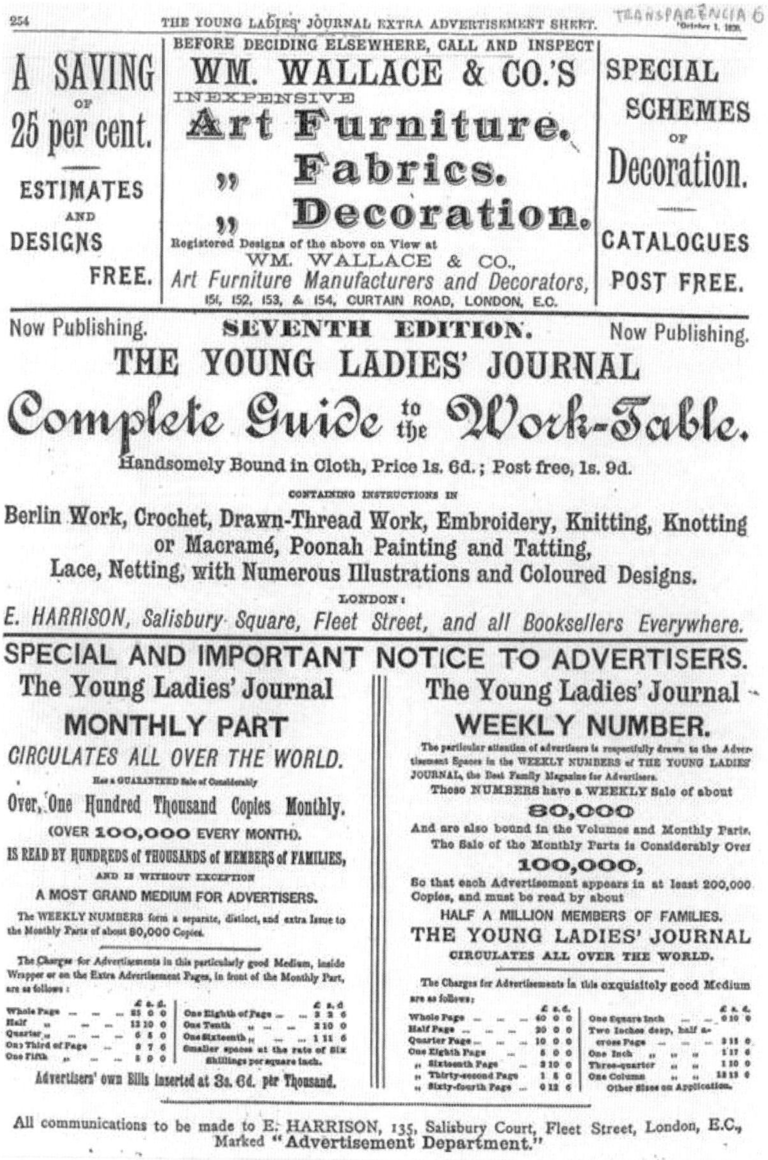

254 THE YOUNG LADIES' JOURNAL EXTRA ADVERTISEMENT SHEET. TRANSPARÊNCIA 6 October 1, 1890.

A SAVING OF 25 per cent.

ESTIMATES AND DESIGNS FREE.

BEFORE DECIDING ELSEWHERE, CALL AND INSPECT

WM. WALLACE & CO.'S

INEXPENSIVE

Art Furniture.
" Fabrics.
" Decoration.

Registered Designs of the above on View at
WM. WALLACE & CO.,
Art Furniture Manufacturers and Decorators,
151, 152, 153, & 154, CURTAIN ROAD, LONDON, E.C.

SPECIAL SCHEMES OF Decoration.

CATALOGUES POST FREE.

Now Publishing. SEVENTH EDITION. Now Publishing.

THE YOUNG LADIES' JOURNAL

Complete Guide to the Work-Table.

Handsomely Bound in Cloth, Price 1s. 6d.; Post free, 1s. 9d.

CONTAINING INSTRUCTIONS IN

Berlin Work, Crochet, Drawn-Thread Work, Embroidery, Knitting, Knotting or Macramé, Poonah Painting and Tatting, Lace, Netting, with Numerous Illustrations and Coloured Designs.

LONDON:

E. HARRISON, Salisbury Square, Fleet Street, and all Booksellers Everywhere.

SPECIAL AND IMPORTANT NOTICE TO ADVERTISERS.

The Young Ladies' Journal

MONTHLY PART

CIRCULATES ALL OVER THE WORLD.

Has a GUARANTEED Sale of Considerably

Over, One Hundred Thousand Copies Monthly.

(OVER 100,000 EVERY MONTH).

IS READ BY HUNDREDS of THOUSANDS of MEMBERS of FAMILIES,

AND IS WITHOUT EXCEPTION

A MOST GRAND MEDIUM FOR ADVERTISERS.

The WEEKLY NUMBERS form a separate, distinct, and extra Issue to the Monthly Parts of about 80,000 Copies.

The Charges for Advertisements in this particularly good Medium, inside Wrapper or on the Extra Advertisement Pages, in front of the Monthly Part, are as follows:

	£ s. d.		£ s. d.
Whole Page	25 0 0	One Eighth of Page	3 2 6
Half "	12 10 0	One Tenth "	2 10 0
Quarter "	6 5 0	One Sixteenth "	1 11 6
One Third of Page ...	8 7 6	Smaller spaces at the rate of Six Shillings per square inch.	
One Fifth "	5 0 0		

Advertisers' own Bills inserted at 3s. 6d. per Thousand.

The Young Ladies' Journal

WEEKLY NUMBER.

The particular attention of advertisers is respectfully drawn to the Advertisement Spaces in the WEEKLY NUMBERS of THE YOUNG LADIES' JOURNAL, the Best Family Magazine for Advertisers.

These NUMBERS have a WEEKLY Sale of about

80,000

And are also bound in the Volumes and Monthly Parts. The Sale of the Monthly Parts is Considerably Over

100,000,

So that each Advertisement appears in at least 200,000 Copies, and must be read by about

HALF A MILLION MEMBERS OF FAMILIES.

THE YOUNG LADIES' JOURNAL

CIRCULATES ALL OVER THE WORLD.

The Charges for Advertisements in this exquisitely good Medium are as follows:

	£ s. d.		£ s. d.
Whole Page	40 0 0	One Square Inch	0 10 0
Half Page	20 0 0	Two Inches deep, half across Page	3 11 0
Quarter Page	10 0 0	One Inch " " "	1 17 6
One Eighth Page ...	5 0 0	Three-quarter " "	1 10 0
" Sixteenth Page ...	2 10 0	One Column " "	13 13 0
" Thirty-second Page	1 5 0	Other Sizes on Application.	
" Sixty-fourth Page ...	0 12 6		

All communications to be made to E. HARRISON, 135, Salisbury Court, Fleet Street, London, E.C., Marked "Advertisement Department."

FIG. 2.6. *The Young Ladies' Journal*, 1 October 1890
British Library Newspapers, Colindale

The growth of industrialization brought new opportunities to thousands of young women who deserted the traditional role of domestic service and found clerical jobs and work in the bustling distribution and retail trades. The shortage of servants meant that the middle classes, in particular, were often confronted with their own domestic chores. This brought a demand for household hints and information, recipes, dressmaking tips and other domestic necessities.[25]

Die Modenwelt was created to serve the same growing market. Likewise in Germany, as Adelheid Rasche points out, *Die Modenwelt* 'wendet sich an Leserinnen des bürgerlichen Mittelstandes, wo Frauen vor allem für den geschmackvollen Wohn- und Kleidungsstil der Familie zuständig sind' [was aimed at women readers who belonged to the German middle classes, where women were above all responsible for decorating the home and clothing the family].[26]

Fashion and social ascent

It should not be forgotten, however, that fashion magazines in general, including those of today, promote the desire to climb the social ladder. In fact, from the nineteenth century onwards, fashion magazines became the ultimate camouflage guide for the lower levels of society, as they disseminated the ideals of fashion and were usually launched by a prestigious group. As Gilda de Mello e Souza observes, nineteenth-century society no longer erected insurmountable barriers, not even between the bourgeois and the nobility. In the nineteenth century, the possibility of 'comunicação entre os grupos substitui a antiga rigidez, ou melhor, a fixidez relativa da estrutura social, por uma constante mobilidade' [communication between the groups replaced the old rigidity; or rather, the relative inflexibility of the social structure was replaced by constant mobility].[27] And fashion played a crucial role in bringing the classes together as, according to Souza, it is

> um dos instrumentos mais poderosos de integração e desempenha uma função niveladora importante, ao permitir que o indivíduo se confunda com o grupo e desapareça num todo maior que lhe dá apoio e segurança. E como as modas vigentes são sempre as da classe dominante, os grupos mais próximos estão, a cada momento, identificando-se aos imediatamente superiores através da imitação da vestimenta.[28]
>
> [one of the most powerful instruments of integration; it plays an important levelling function as it allows the individual to blend into the group and disappear into a larger whole which gives him support and security. And as the prevailing fashions are always those of the dominant class, the groups nearest to them are continually identifying themselves with their immediate superiors by imitating their dress.]

In common with fashion magazines of today, which teach their readers to imitate (on a reduced budget) the items worn by the celebrities of the moment and the habits of the elite, *Die Modenwelt* and its different editions were a very useful tool for middle-class women in the various European countries in which they circulated.

In Brazil, when Lombaerts published the first issue of *A Estação*, the editorial contained the same promise made by the German magazine to provide readers with the means to flaunt an elegant but economical lifestyle:

> Acabamos de folhear a coleção completa dos números publicados sob o título *La Saison. Edição para o Brasil*, e não é sem experimentarmos um intenso sentimento de satisfação que vimos as provas do pouco que temos feito, mas que muito foi, para atingirmos ao alvo que almejamos. Às nossas amáveis leitoras, aquelas principalmente que nos acompanham desde 1872 perguntaremos: cumprimos nós fielmente o nosso programa, auxiliando e aconselhando as senhoras mais econômicas, fornecendo-lhes os meios de reduzirem a sua despesa, sem diminuição alguma do grau de elegância a que as obrigava a respectiva posição na boa sociedade, incutindo ou fortificando-lhes o gosto para o trabalho e moralizando a família a que, por seu turno, saberão incutir sentimentos iguais?... O jornal de modas brasileiro pois, que outrora seria uma impossibilidade, é possível hoje. *A Estação* será o primeiro jornal nesse gênero. (*A Estação*, 15 January 1879)
>
> [We have just leafed through the complete collection of the issues published under the title *La Saison. Edição para o Brasil*, and it is not without an intense feeling of satisfaction that we have seen proof that the little we have been able to do has gone a long way towards reaching our desired goal. To our kind readers, particularly those who have been with us since 1872, we ask: have we faithfully fulfilled our programme, helping and advising the most economy-conscious women, providing them with the means to reduce their expenses without any reduction in the degree of elegance which their position in good society obliges them to display, imbuing them with the taste for work or strengthening this taste in them, and raising the morals of their families, in whom, in turn, they will know how to instil similar sentiments? The Brazilian fashion magazine, which formerly would have been an impossibility, is now possible. *A Estação* will be the first periodical of this kind.]

We must not, however, take *A Estação*'s opening article literally and hastily conclude that the Brazilian magazine was aimed only at the middle classes. It is also perfectly possible that *A Estação* could have been of interest to ladies belonging to the wealthy classes, as the magazine promoted the cultural values which were prized by the Rio de Janeiro elite, who were seeking legitimacy by identifying themselves with traditional culture and European aristocracy.[29] For members of the elite, therefore, *A Estação* expressed the fantasy of cultural identification with Europe. Where the middle classes are concerned, *A Estação* fed their desire to climb the social ladder to the level of the elite.

It is worth at this point quoting a comment printed in the periodical — despite the fact that we are encroaching on the contents of the 'Literary Section' of *A Estação*, which is the subject of the next chapter — which makes it clear that the Brazilian edition actually took the most distinctive families in Rio de Janeiro society as models. It is a bibliographic note concerning the novel *A família Medeiros* by Júlia Lopes de Almeida, who also wrote for *A Estação*. Its author, Valentim Magalhães, clearly indicates the nature of the reading public which the magazine envisages: it is not necessarily those who belong to the elite, but rather those who have access to that privileged group, despite not belonging to it, like Sophia at the start of *Quincas Borba*. This note also makes it clear that acquiring a fortune or being born into the aristocracy were not the only ways to obtain social distinction: it could also acquired through education and elegance, which could be *learnt*:

Suas excelências contam, bem sei, entre as suas relações as famílias mais distintas da sociedade fluminense, quer pela educação, quer pela elegância, quer pela fortuna. Não quis acrescentar pela aristocracia, porque tal distinção não se compadece com o igualitarismo do regime democrático que felizmente nos rege.

Mas podia fazê-lo, tomando o desterrado vocábulo na acepção de nata ou escol social.

Acostumadas, assim, ao trato com essas famílias que povoam os bairros caros e fazem a fortuna dos empresários de ópera lírica, porque delas fazem parte, venho, como procurador oficioso de D. Júlia Lopes de Almeida, pedir-lhes a gentileza de se relacionarem com a família Medeiros.

Oh! não a procurem por Botafogo ou Laranjeiras.

Seria inútil: essa família é paulista e mora no interior do próspero e rico estado de S. Paulo. (*A Estação*, 31 March 1893)

[I know very well that Your Excellencies count among your acquaintances families which are among the most distinguished in Rio de Janeiro society, whether due to their education, their elegance, or their fortune. I have chosen not to add their aristocracy, because this distinction is not compatible with the egalitarianism of the democratic regime which fortunately governs us.

But it could be included, if the banished word is taken to mean the cream or the best of society.

Therefore, as you are accustomed to dealing with the families who inhabit the wealthy neighbourhoods and make the fortunes of the impresarios of the lyrical opera, because you belong to them, I come as the unofficial proxy of D. Júlia Lopes de Almeida to ask if you would be so kind as to become acquainted with the Medeiros family.

Oh, do not seek them in Botafogo or Laranjeiras!

It would be futile: that family are *paulistas* and live in the interior of the rich and prosperous state of São Paulo.]

The Changing Society of *Philosopher or Dog?*

As has been observed by Gilda de Mello e Souza and John Gledson, the characters who feature in *Quincas Borba* are, without exception, continually rising and falling in a society in which it is now possible to pass from one class to another. It must be pointed out that in a slave-owning society, such as Brazil in the period fictionalized in the novel, the barriers only stopped being insurmountable for a limited group of free and educated men, who were in fact a minority. According to Gilda de Mello e Souza, as Brazilian society was only recently formed, the possession of wealth came to represent 'a grande modificadora da estrutura social' [the great modifier of the social structure] for this privileged group, which was not the case for the castes in more traditional societies. From the Romantic period, Souza adds, the Brazilian novel, such as *Senhora* by José de Alencar was 'rico em observações sobre o poder do dinheiro' [rich in observations on the power of money].[30]

In *Quincas Borba*, money is not only an agent which modifies the society represented but is also, in structural terms, one of the elements which unifies the plot. It offers as a whole a dynamic vision of the change in the position of individuals, who are valued for what they have in relation to each other. According to Gledson, the novel represents a changing society. It is also innovative in this respect in relation to *Brás Cubas*:

> Estamos agora em 1867 (o romance começa nesse ano e termina no final de 1871), e numa sociedade muito mais variada. O mais significativo, agora, é a possibilidade de passagem de uma classe para outra; a principal escada utilizada com esse objetivo são os negócios, e Cristiano Palha, ex-seminarista, junto com sua esposa Sofia, filha de um funcionário público, são mostrados com cuidadosos detalhes, em sua suave e cínica ascensão através dos escalões sociais. A mudança de uma sociedade estável para outra (relativamente) fluida é obviamente muito importante e representa uma mudança, claro, não apenas com relação a *Casa Velha*, mas a *Brás Cubas* também.[31]
>
> [It is now 1867 (the novel starts in that year and finishes at the end of 1871), and we are in a much more varied society. The most significant point is that it is now possible to pass from one class to another, and the ladder which is most often used to achieve this end is business. Cristiano Palha, an ex-seminarist, together with his wife Sophia, the daughter of a civil servant, are depicted in painstaking detail in their smooth and cynical rise up the social ladder. The move from a stable society to another which is (relatively) fluid is obviously very important and represents a change not only with respect to *Casa velha* but also [*Memórias póstumas de*] *Brás Cubas*.]

The structural complexity of the novel and the narrative elements employed by Machado de Assis to represent that changing society will be the subject of Chapter 4 of this book. For the time being I will limit myself to showing that a close connection existed between the social realism of the novel and the magazine. Whether intentionally or not, the novelist adapted his aims to the fashion contents of *A Estação*, revealing a profound knowledge of his public.

Female readers who flicked through the serial, or read it among patterns and sewing tips, might have been most curious to learn what the female characters would wear and what their fates would be. At its most superficial level, *Quincas Borba* explores the concerns and ambitions of the magazine's target readers by presenting characters who are based on the average reader. The subscribers are women such as Sophia, who enjoy being confused with high society and therefore try to dress and behave like high-society ladies. Even the reading of novels (by Feuillet, published in serials in the *Revue des Deux Mondes*), the acquisition of a coupé and the philanthropic initiative undertaken by the Alagoas Committee are imitations of the habits of the *high-life*, to use the term employed by Artur Azevedo in his *Croniqueta*. In fact, all of the novel's female characters, who are all so different from each other (Sophia, Dona Tonica, Maria Benedicta, Dona Fernanda, and even those who are not named but who form part of the social circles in which Sophia moves) represent a wide range of flesh and blood readers, from the richest, who would have been able to pay for a subscription, to those about whom Lombaerts frequently complained because they read, but did not subscribe to, the periodical.

As *Quincas Borba*'s social realism is undisputed in the critical history of the novel, it remains for us to verify the form in which the novel engages most closely with the fashion contents of the magazine. We can then see what the characters' wardrobes tell us about their social positions.

What the female characters wear

As Gilda de Mello e Souza has pointed out, descriptions of any kind, including those related to clothing, are scarce in Machado de Assis's work in comparison with the novels of Joaquim Manuel de Macedo, for example.[32] However, clothing, accessories and decorative objects for the home are not completely absent from *Quincas Borba*. The descriptions are in fact infrequent and in the rewritten version become progressively more succinct, as we shall see in the examples below, but even so they are very effective as exterior signs of the social position that each character occupies at a given point in the story. In fact, bearing in mind the context in which the novel was originally published, among innumerable patterns and captions, the detailed description of a dress within the body of a novel could even be considered superfluous, or repetitive. Moreover, as we shall also see in this chapter, descriptions of clothing are just one among several elements which mark the stage at which a character is to be considered in their journey up or down the social ladder.

Where female characters are concerned, new stages in a character's rise or fall in that constantly changing society are very often marked by references to what the character is wearing or would like to wear. Dona Tonica, for example, avoids buying a dress which has been promised to her so that she can use the money to buy tinned food and offer Rubião a slightly better dinner then usual:

> — Sabe de uma coisa, papai? Papai compra amanhã latas de conserva, ervilha, peixe, etc., e ficam guardadas. No dia em que ele aparecer para jantar, põe-se no fogo, é só aquecer, e daremos um jantarzinho melhor.
> — Mas eu só tenho o dinheiro do teu vestido.
> — O meu vestido? Compra-se no mês que vem, ou no outro. Eu espero.
> — Mas não ficou ajustado?
> — Desajusta-se; eu espero.
> — E se não houver outro do mesmo preço?
> — Há de haver; eu espero, papai.[33]

> [— Do you know something, Papa? You buy some canned goods, tomorrow, peas, fish, etc; and we'll put them aside. Then the day he comes for dinner, we'll put it on the fire, and it'll only have to be warmed up. We'll have a better dinner that way.
> — But I have just enough money for your dress.
> — My dress? That can be bought next month or the month after. I'll wait.
> — But wasn't it ordered?
> — It can be countermanded. I'll wait.
> — And what if there's no other of the same price?
> — There will be. I'll wait, Papa.][34]

There are also the inconsistencies in Maria Benedicta's clothes:

> Em verdade, não era uma beleza; não lhe pedissem olhos que fascinam, nem dessas bocas que segregam alguma coisa, ainda caladas; era natural, sem acanho de roceira; e tinha um donaire particular, que corrigia as incoerências do vestido.[35]

> [In truth, she was not a beauty; she did not have eyes that fascinate, nor one of those mouths that, though still, always seem to be whispering a secret; she was

natural, without any rustic shyness, and she had a peculiar grace that made up for the lack of elegance in her dress!]³⁶

Carelessness in dress, as Machado de Assis prefers to call it in the first version, does not belie the country origins of Palha's cousin, even though Sophia has done her utmost to accustom her to 'as distrações da cidade; teatros, visitas, passeios, reuniões em casa, vestidos novos, chapéus lindos, jóias'³⁷ [the distractions of the city: theatres, calls, drives, household gatherings, new dresses, pretty hats, jewellery].³⁸

Let us spend more time on Sophia. As descriptions of her clothes are more numerous and occur throughout the novel, they provide an emblematic picture of the social rise of this civil servant's daughter. We will limit ourselves, however, to descriptions of her clothes and physical appearance as described on three occasions. The first is the social gathering which takes place at her house in Santa Thereza, right at the start of the novel, which the narrator describes in chapters 34 to 42.³⁹ The lady nips in her waist and bust in a simple chestnut-coloured bodice of fine wool. The character also wears real pearl earrings:

> Traja bem; comprime a cintura e o tronco no corpinho de lã fina cor de castanha, obra simples, e traz nas orelhas duas pérolas verdadeiras, mimo que o nosso Rubião lhe deu pela Páscoa.⁴⁰
>
> [She dresses well; she nips in her waist, and moulds her bust in a simple chestnut coloured bodice of fine wool, and wears two genuine pearl earrings — an Easter gift from our Rubião.]⁴¹

Later, the narrator explains to us that it was Palha who enjoyed dressing his wife in low-cut dresses, 'sempre que podia, e até onde não podia, para mostrar aos outros as suas venturas particulares'⁴² [in order to reveal his personal good fortune to others... wherever it was possible, and even where it was not].⁴³

This short but precise description is sufficient to highlight the contrast between the dress, which has been bought or sewn, and the luxury of the pearls, which, as their narrator points out, were a present from Rubião. The pearls, which Palha was probably unable to afford, therefore symbolize a change in the Palha's circle of friends as they start to mix with people above their social level. Rubião, the rich and recent arrival to the city, will act as a trampoline to facilitate their social rise.

At the birthday ball held for Camargo's daughter, which the narrator describes from the end of chapter 68 to chapter 72, the dress is once again low-cut, which emphasizes Sofia's figure and lightly browned arms.⁴⁴ The genuine pearl earrings are now matched with a diadem of artificial pearls:

> Sofia estava magnífica. Trajava de azul escuro, mui decotada, — pelas razões ditas no capítulo 35; os braços nus, cheios, com uns tons de ouro claro, ajustavam-se às espáduas e aos seios, tão acostumados ao gás do salão. Diadema de pérolas feitiças, tão bem acabadas, que iam de par com as duas pérolas naturais, que lhe ornavam as orelhas, e que Rubião lhe dera um dia.⁴⁵
>
> [Sophia was magnificent. She was wearing dark blue, very low-necked — for the reasons stated in chapter 35; her plump bare arms of a pale golden tint formed a graceful line with her back and bosom, so used to being seen in the gas-light. She was wearing also a diadem of artificial pearls so well finished that

they matched the real pearls that adorned her ears, and that Rubião had given her one day.][46]

The addition of a further accessory to the character's visual make-up once again has the effect of creating a contrast, this time between the imitation and the original. Sofia is not content to display only a pair of pearls. She wants a diadem full of them in order to appear richer than she really is. As she cannot afford them, however, she resorts to a good imitation — a trick which would certainly have pleased readers of *A Estação*. In fact, imitation was the subject of a newspaper article by Júlia Lopes de Almeida which was published on 15 March 1890. The columnist discussed falsification in art, and made a very precise distinction between the taste of an aristocrat and that of an *arriviste*. Moreover, by saying that Sophia was used to the gas-light, the narrator is revealing that the couple had a hectic social life.

Finally, at the ball which inaugurated their mansion in Botafogo, in chapter 192 at the end of the novel, the narrator reveals that the lady was wearing not just one but several very expensive jewels. These included not the pair of pearls but the necklace which Rubião had given her on her birthday in chapter 115 of both versions.[47]

> Em outubro, Sofia inaugurou os seus salões de Botafogo, com um baile, que foi o mais célebre do tempo. Estava deslumbrante. Ostentava, sem orgulho, todos os seus braços e espáduas. Ricas jóias; o colar era ainda um dos primeiros presentes do Rubião, tão certo é que, neste gênero de atavios, as modas conservam-se mais.[48]

> [In October, Sophia inaugurated her Botafogo salon with a ball that was the most famous of the time. It was dazzling. For the occasion she modestly displayed her arms and shoulder blades. Her jewellery was costly; she was still wearing the necklace that had been one of Rubião's first gifts, for truly, in that sort of adornment, fashion is most enduring.][49]

In order to compose a more complete and detailed picture of the Palhas' social rise, Machado de Assis also informs us of the various businesses which the husband enters and the districts of Rio de Janeiro in which the couple live. At the start of the novel, we know that both come from the middle classes: Palha is an ex-seminarist, and Sofia the daughter of a civil servant. Sofia and Palha's outstanding qualities are beauty in the case of the lady and business acumen in the case of the *zangão* [salesman] of the marketplace:

> O marido ganhava dinheiro, era jeitoso, ativo, e tinha o faro dos negócios e das situações. Em 1864, apesar de recente no ofício, adivinhou, — não se pode empregar outro termo, — adivinhou as falências bancárias.[50]

> [Her husband was successful, clever and enterprising, and he had a flair for doing business and for sensing situations. In 1864, though he had not held his position long at that time, he had a foreboding — one cannot call it anything else — he had a foreboding of the bank failures.][51]

These are gifts which complement each other, and which certainly make them fitter — to borrow a term from Darwin — for the process of social selection. His talents for commerce and her physical gifts compensate for the fact that they do not have a patron who favours them, are not public employees, and have not married above their station — the other three routes to social mobility during the Second Reign.[52]

By the time of the second ball, Palha is already Rubião's partner in an import company.[53] And finally, in chapter 129, we learn that his career is going swimmingly as the narrator explains the reasons why he dissolved the company he had formed with Rubião:

> A carreira daquele homem era cada vez mais próspera e vistosa. O negócio corria-lhe largo; um dos motivos da separação era justamente não ter que dividir com outros os lucros futuros. Palha, além do mais, possuía ações de toda a parte, apólices de ouro do empréstimo Itaboraí, e fizera uns dois fornecimentos para a guerra, de sociedade com um poderoso, nos quais ganhou muito. Já trazia apalavrado um arquiteto para lhe construir um palacete. Vagamente pensava em baronia.[54]

> [The man's career was becoming more and more prosperous and striking. His business was expanding; indeed, one of his reasons for severing relations with Rubião was to avoid having to divide future profits with him. Furthermore, Palha owned shares from all over and stock in the Itaborahy loan, and, together with a person of influence, he had furnished some of the war supplies, which were highly profitable. He had already engaged an architect to build him a mansion, and he was thinking vaguely of baronage.][55]

As we have seen, each new social level reached by the married couple is very well described, even though Machado de Assis does not spend long on descriptions, whether these might be of Palha's commercial investments, jewellery, literary tastes, circles of friends, hobbies, furniture, or the decorative objects which Sofia acquires, abandons, exchanges or keeps throughout the development of the narrative. It cannot be overlooked that the Palhas change address three times throughout the course of the novel, moving ever southwards: from the house in Santa Thereza they install themselves firstly on Flamengo Beach, then move to a mansion built for them in Botafogo, arriving finally in the Zona Sul, even further from the centre. The fashions launched by the prestigious groups include decoration, architecture, neighbourhoods, authors and magazines, social and leisure activities, in addition to the clothing and accessories with which they are most frequently associated. There are also the activities or habits which are traditionally linked to some classes, such as philanthropy, which in the novel is practised by the female character who occupies the position at the top of the social pyramid, Dona Fernanda. The high-society lady is allowed to carry out acts of charity and is even expected to be kind and concerned for others. Altruism is not necessarily one of the character's natural gifts; rather, it is a quality which can also be acquired through imitation. As such, Sophia's idea of setting up the Alagoas Committee is also an indication of the character's ambition to increase the pace at which she enters the circles and acquires the habits of high-society ladies.[56]

However, the story told by the novel does not consist only of successes. We have only to recall Dona Tonica, Freitas, Camacho, Maria Benedicta's mother, and Rubião himself. Even the success enjoyed by the victorious characters, such as Dona Fernanda, Sophia and Maria Benedicta, is always accompanied by frustrations. In a certain sense the novel, as printed in the pages of *A Estação*, warned subscribers of the high price paid by those who undertake social climbing at all costs. Sophia, for example, represses her amorous fantasies about Carlos Maria in order not to frustrate her husband's plans, and by doing so she avoids becoming a sort of Emma Bovary, but for reasons of social propriety. The successful, Palha included, are subservient when necessary and give up their fantasies (which are adulterous fantasies, in Sofia's case) in order not to break with decorum. And the ambitions of the losers are frustrated, as in the case of Dona Tonica, who continues to be vain, even though she has no resources, clinging to the habit of polishing her nails. She wants to marry a rich man, but the opposite fate befalls her: she ends up becoming a poor, forty-something spinster.

So far, we have examined just one aspect of the relationship between the contents of *A Estação* and the social realism of *Quincas Borba*. In Chapter 3 we shall see that the political realism of the novel is also reflected in the 'Literary Section' of the periodical. However, we shall have to cross the Atlantic once again, because this second editorial turn taken by the magazine was also imported from Germany. In the first place, I shall show how *Die Modenwelt* transformed itself from a magazine which was strictly about fashion into an illustrated and literary magazine. Subsequently, I shall investigate the presence in *Die Modenwelt* of illustrations which exalt the institution of the empire. This new diversion is necessary because it was through these imported illustrations that the editorial leanings of the German magazine were transferred to the Brazilian publication.

Notes to Chapter 2

1. The press run of the daily newspaper *Gazeta de Notícias* was 24,000 copies in 1881, and of *O Paiz* was 15,000 copies in 1885. See Leonarno Affonso de Miranda Pereira, *O carnaval das letras: literatura e folia no Rio de Janeiro do século XIX* (Campinas, Ed. da UNICAMP, 2004), p. 54. See also El Far for Lombaerts, p. 34, 35.
2. 'Joaquim Maria Machado de Assis vende a B. L. Garnier a 1ª edição constando de (1000) mil exemplares, já impressos, de sua novela intitulada *Quincas Borba*, pela quantia de seiscentos mil réis, obrigando-se o mesmo a não reimprimir nova edição sem estar esgotada esta primeira. Em fé do que passaram dois contratos de igual teor por ambos assinados. Capital Federal, 17 de Outubro de 1891' [Joaquim Maria Machado de Assis [hereby] sells to B. L. Garnier the first edition comprising (1000) one thousand copies, already printed, of his novel entitled *Quincas Borba*, for the sum of six hundred thousand *réis*, and agrees not to print a new edition until this first edition is sold out. In witness whereof, two contracts are issued of equal tenor, signed by both parties. Federal Capital, 17 October 1891] (*Exposição*, p. 183).
3. Adelheid Rasche, *Frieda Lipperheide: 1840–1896. Ein Leben für Textilkunst und Mode im 19. Jahrhundert* (Berlin: SMPK, Kunstbibliothek, 1999), p. 84.
4. *Zum fünfundzwanzigjährigen Bestehen der Modenwelt, 1865–1890*, intro. by Friedrich Melford (Berlin: Lipperheide, 1890).
5. The following periodicals were consulted, followed by the years chosen as a sample: 1. at the Lipperheidesche Kostümbibliothek, Berlin: *Die Modenwelt*, Berlin (1865–67, 1886–91); *Illustrirte Frauen-Zeitung*, Berlin (1874, 1886–91); *La Stagione*, Milan (1892); *La Saison*, Paris (1868–73); *Les Modes de la Saison,* Paris (1881–85); *The Young Ladies' Journal*, London (1874); *La Estación*, Madrid and Buenos Aires, 1886; 2. at the National Library, Rio de Janeiro, Historical and Geographical Institute of São Paulo, 'A Sereia' Bookshop and the José Mindlin Library (both in São Paulo), and CECULT, Campinas: *A Estação*, Rio/Porto, (1879–1904); 3. at the National Swiss Library: *La Saison*, Paris (1887–91); 4. at the British Library: *The Season*, London (1886); *The Young Ladies' Journal*, London (1864, 1886–91).
6. Robert Darnton, *The Kiss of Lamourette* (London: Faber and Faber, 1990), p 127.

7. This collection was donated to the city of Berlin before the couple died: Franz Joseph Lipperheide (1838–1906) and Wilhelmine Amalie Friederike Lipperheide (1840–1896).
8. Hallewell, pp. 113, 153.
9. The Literary Section of *A Estação* and its thematic relationship with *Quincas Borba* will be the subject of Chapter 3.
10. *Die Modenwelt*, 1 September 1870, quoted by Rasche, p. 19.
11. Meyer, *Caminhos do imaginário no Brasil*, p. 81.
12. On this subject see Dulcilia Buitoni, *Mulher de papel* (São Paulo: Editora Loyola, 1981). In chapter 2, 'Origens da representação: século XIX', we find a brief history of the women's press and the names of the first periodicals in Germany, England, France and Brazil. See also Brian Braithwaite, *Women's Magazines* (London: Peter Owen, 1995), pp. 9–28; and Evelyne Sullerot, *La Presse féminine* (Paris: A. Colin, 1963), pp. 5–13.
13. Robert Gross, 'Books, Nationalism, and History', *Papers of the Bibliographical Society of Canada* 36, 2 (1998), 107–23 (p. 109).
14. *Zum fünfundzwangzigjährigen Bestehen der Modenwelt, 1865–1890*, pp. 5, 6.
15. We shall subsequently see that the first issues of *La Saison* were printed in Germany.
16. Verses from Christophorus Lehmann, *Florilegium politicum*, 1630. *Zum fünfundzwangzigjährigen Bestehen der Modenwelt, 1865–1890*, p. iii.
17. In *Zum fünfundzwangzigjährigen Bestehen der Modenwelt, 1865–1890*, we find the information that *Die Modenwelt* was published in thirteen languages. I was unable to ascertain why, in this editorial, and in some notes in the 'Correspondence' section, the publishers of *A Estação* stated that their magazine was published in fourteen or even fifteen different languages. It may simply be a lapse on the part of the publisher.
18. Marlyse Meyer, who first confirmed the connection between *A Estação* and *Die Modenwelt*, also quotes this article and registers it as having been published on 15 December 1885 (Meyer, *Caminhos do imaginário no Brasil*, p. 93). The actual date was 15 January 1885, and this small correction is noted here.
19. *Zum fünfundzwangzigjährigen Bestehen der Modenwelt, 1865–1890*, pp. 47, 49.
20. Friedrich Melford, 'Die Modenwelt von 1865–1890', *Zum fünfundzwangzigjährigen Bestehen der Modenwelt, 1865–1890*, p. 13.
21. Gross, p. 109.
22. The magazine *Época* 'tem um acordo de colaboração com a revista *Focus*, editada por Focus Magazin — Verlag GmbH, para utilização de material fotográfico e editorial com exclusividade no Brasil' [has a partnership agreement with the magazine *Focus*, published by Focus Magazin — Verlag GmbH, for the exclusive use of photographic and editorial material in Brazil]. See the website <http://epoca.globo.com/edic/523/epoca_edicao_especial_2_anos.pdf> [accessed 18 January 2010].
23. *The Young Ladies' Journal*, 1 October 1890, p. 254.
24. According to Sullerot, the paper pattern first appeared in France in the periodical *Souvenir* (1849–55) and was called 'modes vrais, travail en famille' (Sullerot, p. 7). In England, Braithwaite attributed the invention of the paper pattern, as well as that of the popular magazine, to Samuel Beeton, who began publishing *The Englishwoman's Domestic Magazine* in 1852 (Braithwaite, p. 12).
25. Braithwaite, p. 14.
26. Rasche, pp. 17, 19
27. Souza, *O espírito das roupas*, p. 112.
28. Souza, *O espírito das roupas*, p. 130.
29. See Jeffrey D. Needell, *A Tropical Belle Époque: Elite Culture and Society in Turn-of-the Century Rio de Janeiro* (Cambridge: Cambridge University Press, 1987), especially chapter 5: 'The rise of consumer fetishism', pp. 156–77.
30. Souza, *O espírito das roupas*, pp. 113, 114.
31. Gledson, *Machado de Assis: ficção e história*, p. 74.
32. Gilda de Mello e Souza, 'Macedo, Alencar, Machado e as roupas', *Novos Estudos Cebrap*, 41 (1995), 111–19.
33. *Quincas Borba*, p. 273–74; *A Estação*, 31 March 1890, chap. 132; *Quincas Borba apêndice*, p. 167. The quotations are taken from the third edition of the book. The variants between *A*, *B*, *C* and *D* in

this section of the novel are: *A, B:* conserva, petit-pois, peixe; *A:* fogo, aquilo cozinha depressa, e daremos.
34. *Philosopher or Dog?*, trans. by Clotilde Wilson (London: Bloomsbury, 1997), pp. 191–92. Variants: *A, B:* canned goods, tomorrow, petits pois, fish; *A:* fire, it cooks quickly, and we'll have a better dinner that way.
35. *Quincas Borba*, p. 184; *A Estação*, 15 May 1887, chap. 64 (Continuation); *Quincas Borba apêndice*, p. 63. Variants: *A:* não era uma formosura; não; *B:* não era bonita; não era uma formosura; não; *A:* caladas. Altinha, mãos grandes, grandes olhos atônitos quando escutavam somente, mas que sabiam rir e conversar, se a boca falava também, — aí fica o principal das feições da moça. Era natural; *B:* caladas. Altinha, mãos grandes, grandes olhos atônitos quando escutavam somente, mas que sabiam falar, se a boca falava também, — aí fica o principal das feições da moça. Era natural; *A:* corrigia os descuidos do.
36. *Philosopher or Dog?*, p. 91. Variants: *A:* she was not a belle; she did not have eyes that fascinate; *B:* she was not pretty; she wasn't a belle; she did not have eyes that fascinate; *A:* to be whispering a secret. Quite tall, big hands, big astonished eyes when they were only listening, but which knew how to laugh and converse, if the mouth was speaking too, — that's the main thing about the girl's features. She was natural; *B:* to be whispering a secret. Quite tall, big hands, big astonished eyes when they were only listening, but which knew how to laugh and converse, if her mouth was speaking too, — that's the main thing about the girl's features. She was natural; *A:* she had a peculiar grace that made up for the carelessness of.
37. *Quincas Borba*, p. 191; *A Estação*, 30 June 1887, chap. 68 (continuation); *Quincas Borba apêndice*, p. 68. Variants: *A:* vestidos novos e bem talhados, chapéus lindos e graciosos, jóias.
38. *Philosopher or Dog?*, p. 99. Variants: *A:* new dresses and well tailored, dainty, pretty hats, jewellery.
39. *Quincas Borba*, p. 142–53; *A Estação*, 15 November to 31 December 1886, chaps. 32 to 41 (continuation); *Quincas Borba apêndice*, p. 35–44; *Philosopher or Dog?*, pp. 43–56.
40. *Quincas Borba*, chap. 35, p. 143; *A Estação*, chap. 33; *Quincas Borba apêndice*, p. 36. Variants: *A, B:* cintura e os seios no corpinho.
41. *Philosopher or Dog?*, p. 46. Variants: *A, B:* waist and breasts in a simple chestnut coloured bodice.
42. *Quincas Borba*, chap. 35, p. 144; *A Estação*, chap. 34; *Quincas Borba apêndice*, p. 37. Variants: *A:* até quando não podia.
43. *Philosopher or Dog?*, p. 46. Variants: *A:* whenever it was possible, and even when it was not.
44. *Quincas Borba*, pp. 192–98; *A Estação*, chaps. 68 (continuation) to 70, of 30 June to 31 July 1887; *Quincas Borba apêndice*, pp. 69–74; *Philosopher or Dog?*, pp. 91–109.
45. *Quincas Borba*, chap. 69, p. 194; *A Estação*, chap. 69; *Quincas Borba apêndice*, p. 69–70. Variants: *A:* ditas no capítulo 38; os braços.
46. *Philosopher or Dog?*, p. 103. Variants: *A:* for the reasons stated in chapter 38; her plump bare arms.
47. 'Era o terceiro presente do dia; a criada esperou que ela o abrisse para ver também o que era. Sofia ficou deslumbrada, quando abriu a caixa e deu com a rica jóia, — uma bela pedra, no centro de um colar. Esperava alguma coisa bonita; mas, depois dos últimos sucessos, mal podia crer que ele fosse tão generoso. Batia-lhe o coração.' (*Quincas Borba*, chap. 115, p. 247; *A Estação*, 31 December 1889; *Quincas Borba apêndice*, p. 146) [It was the third gift she had received that day; the maid waited for her to open it, so that she, too, might see what it was. Sophia was startled when she opened the box and saw the costly jewel, a beautiful stone, in the centre of a necklace. She was expecting something nice, but after what had happened recently, she could scarcely believe that he would be so generous. Her heart was all aflutter.] (*Philosopher or Dog?*, p. 162).
48. *Quincas Borba*, p. 341; *A Estação*, 31 August 1891, chap. 193; *Quincas Borba apêndice*, p. 244.
49. *Philosopher or Dog?*, p. 265.
50. *Quincas Borba*, cap. 35, p. 144; *A Estação*, 15 November 1886, chap. 34; *Quincas Borba apêndice*, p. 37.
51. *Philosopher or Dog?*, p. 46.
52. See José Murilo de Carvalho, *A construção da ordem: a elite política brasileira* (Rio de Janeiro: Civilização Brasileira, 2003).

53. *Quincas Borba*, chap. 69, p. 193; *A Estação*, 15 July 1887, chap. 69; *Quincas Borba apêndice*, p. 69.
54. *Quincas Borba*, chap. 129, p. 270; *A Estação*, 15 March 1890, chap. 130; *Quincas Borba apêndice*, p. 165. Variants: *A:* era agora, mais do que nunca, próspera e vistosa; *A:* dividir com outro os lucros; *A:* pensava em baronato.
55. *Philosopher or Dog?*, p. 188. Variants: *A:* becoming now more prosperous than ever; *A:* to avoid sharing his profits with others; *A:* he was thinking of baronage.
56. Philanthropy is the subject of Artur Azevedo's *Croniqueta*, *A Estação*, 15 May 1889: 'Ainda uma vez a nossa população provou que não mente o quase provérbio: a caridade naturalizou-se fluminense. O banco precatório organizado pela Imprensa em benefício das vítimas da epidemia de Campinas, teve o melhor resultado, e outro não poderia ter. Nunca ninguém recorreu debalde aos sentimentos filantrópicos deste excelente povo do Rio de Janeiro' [Once again, our people have demonstrated the truth of that almost proverbial statement: charity has settled in Rio. The benefit fund organized by the Press for victims of the Campinas epidemic has had excellent results, as it could not fail to do. No one has ever appealed in vain to the philanthropic sentiments of the fine people of Rio de Janeiro'.]

CHAPTER 3

❖

Philosopher or Dog? and the Literary Section of *A Estação*

When it was launched in Brazil, *A Estação* was intended to be a periodical about fashion, literature and the arts, containing material which would either be imported or produced by Brazilians. To solve the problem of accommodating illustrations, texts and advertisements from different countries in the same magazine, a supplement to the main fashion section was created. It was in this supplement, which was published and printed in Brazil, that *Quincas Borba* appeared. This chapter proves that, whereas the fashion part of the magazine was edited in Germany, its literary part was a truly Brazilian product, since it was not only printed but also edited in Brazil. The first version of *Quincas Borba* was therefore not edited in Germany, nor in France, as previously believed. The plates of the German illustrations for this part of the magazine were sent to Rio and fitted among the texts written or translated by the Brazilian collaborators.

Continuing the investigation into the intertextual relations between the novel and the magazine, this chapter is based on a study of the iconographic material surrounding Machado de Assis's text in this section of the magazine. It investigates the choice of illustrations in the literary part of *A Estação* and argues that Machado de Assis uses the magazine's interest in the royal families of Europe and Brazil in the novel itself. This mocks the magazine's ideology (in a time when Brazil's political regime was changing to a Republic) not only with its social-climbing heroine, Sofia, but also with its anti-hero Rubião, who in his madness believes himself to be Napoleon III. The novel establishes an ironic relationship between the historical and political situation of Brazil at the end of the Second Reign and the material context in which the narrative was being published. Besides the irony aimed at the imperial pomp of the magazine, it also calls into question the usefulness of fashion, in the widest sense, as a camouflage or disguise which allows the *nouveaux riche*, such as Sophia and Palha, to pass for aristocrats.

The Diversification of the Contents of *Die Modenwelt*

Die Modenwelt was intentionally conceived as a fashion magazine which was devoid of artistic content in order to reduce production costs and to differentiate it from the other fashion periodicals in circulation in Germany before 1865, such as *Bazar*, the *Allgemeine Musterzeitung*, and the *Hamburger Zeitschriften Jahrzeiten*.[1] In 1874, however, Lipperheide launched an extended edition — the *Illustrirte Frauen-Zeitung* [*Illustrated Women's Journal*] — which consisted of the same fashion section with the addition of a supplement, entitled 'Ausgabe der *Modenwelt* mit Unterhaltungsblatt' [*Modenwelt* Edition with Entertainment Section].[2] *Die Modenwelt* therefore stopped being a periodical which confined itself to meeting the domestic needs of mainly middle-class housewives to transform itself into a more varied magazine, which, every fortnight, provided recreational and practical reading for a predominantly female public.

The magazine generally began with an instalment of a serialized story. Then came sections entitled 'The Feminine World', 'New Handicraft', 'Fashion', 'Decoration', 'Literary Novelties', 'Home Economics' and 'Correspondence'. In addition to texts which were of specific interest to women readers, the *Illustrirte Frauen-Zeitung* contained many illustrations which were not restricted to fashion, furniture, or decoration in general. Accompanied by long explicatory captions, these images brought more diverse material to the heart of an essentially female publication. In fact, they seem to have made a significant contribution to the success of the magazine, in addition to the fact that every increase in the number of illustrations was a sign that the magazine was prospering.

There was even an attempt to change the name of this extended edition of *Die Modenwelt* to *Die Illustrirte Zeit* [*The Illustrated Times*], thereby reflecting the publisher's desire to capture male readers. The change in the periodical's name, which was announced in the issue dated 6 March 1887, was accompanied by a change in its periodicity, as it began to be published weekly:

> Mit allen Kräften sind wir von jedem bestrebt gewesen, unser Blatt immer vollkommener zu gestalten. Seit halb einem viertel Jahrhundert ist das Modenblatt der Gegenstand emsigster Mühe und Arbeit, und nicht vergebens: 352,000 Abonnenten, weit mehr, als irgendein anderes deutsches Blatt zählt, beweisen, in welchem Maße es uns gelungen ist, das Vertrauen des Publikums zu gewinnen.
>
> Nicht minder lebhaft haben wir unserer Sorgfalt dem Unterhaltungsblatte zugewendet. Die mehr als dreizehn Jahre seines Bestehens bilden eine Kette von Verbesserungen und Erweiterungen, ohne dass wir dem anfänglichen Preis irgendwie erhebt hätten. Dies geschieht auch heute nicht, wo wir abermals den Umfang wesentlich ausdehnen.
>
> Wir lassen die *Illustrirte Frauen-Zeitung* von jetzt ab jeden Sonntag erscheinen, geben also jährlich 52 Nummern und vermehren den Inhalt, indem wir, außerdem bisher Gebotenem, jeder dieser 52 Nummern noch drei bis vier Seiten Illustrationen beifügen: Bilder aus der Geschichte unserer Zeit, Darstellungen aus dem öffentlichen Leben der Gegenwart, und nicht bloß Deutschlands, sondern allen Ländern der Welt.
>
> Der Titel *Frauen-Zeitung* will indessen diese Vielseitigkeit des Inhaltes nicht mehr umspannen, und es erscheint deshalb wohl gerechtfertig, wenn wir statt *Illustrirte Frauen-Zeitung* den Titel *Die Illustrirte Zeit* an die Spitze des Blattes setzen. [...]
>
> Nicht weniger als jährlich 164 Seiten Bilder sind es, die wir unseren Lesern in Zukunft mehr bieten, als bisher. Durch diese Fülle der Abbildungen wird aber der Text in seiner Weise beeinträchtigt, viel mehr bleibt der bisherige Inhalt der *Illustrirte Frauen-Zeitung* völlig unverändert. Neben spannenden Novellen,

wie sie für die Lektüre in der Familie geeignet sind, bringt *Die Illustrirte Zeit* auch in Zukunft ihre Künste-Holzschnitte, ein auserlesenes Feuilleton und ein mannigfaches Allerlei, in welchem besonders das Interesse der Frauen und der Familie, namentlich auch die praktischen Bedürfnisse des Haushaltes, ihre eingehende Berücksichtigung finden, während wir uns, wie bisher, von der Erörterung aller kirchlichen und politischen Streitfragen fernhalten.

[We have always done our utmost to continually improve the design of our journal. For half a quarter century the fashion journal has been the object of strenuous effort and work, and not without success: 352,000 subscribers (far more than any other German journal can count) prove the extent of our success in winning the trust of the public.

We have been no less active in turning our concern towards the entertainment journal. The publication of the journal over more than 13 years demonstrates a string of improvements and expansions without increasing the initial price whatsoever. Neither does this take place today, when we are once again substantially expanding the range of our content.

From now on the *Illustrirte Frauen-Zeitung* will be published every Sunday, making 52 issues in all, and its content will be increased through including, in addition to what has been offered to date, three to four more pages of illustrations in each of these 52 issues: pictures taken from the history of our times and images of contemporary daily life not only in Germany but also from all other countries in the world.

The title *Illustrirte Frauen-Zeitung*, however, is no longer suitable to the diversity of its contents. As such, it seems justifiable to put the title *Die Illustrirte Zeit* at the top of the page instead of *Illustrirte Frauen-Zeitung*. [...]

We are offering no fewer than 164 pages of pictures per year to our readers, much more than has been offered until now. Due to the abundance of images, the nature of the texts themselves will be affected, however the contents of the *Illustrirte Frauen-Zeitung* will remain completely unchanged. In addition to thrilling novels suitable for family reading, *Die Illustrirte Zeit* will in the future continue to feature artistic woodcuttings, a feuilleton containing the best selections and a varied range of articles which particularly satisfy the interests of women and the family. In particular, the practical needs of the home will be considered in detail. Meanwhile, we will refrain, as before, from engaging in religious or political disputes.]

This strategy did not prove very successful, however, because seven months later, on 9 October 1887, the magazine returned to its original title. Although Lipperheide's decision to change the name of the magazine was not a success with its readers, this episode reveals his intention to change the direction of the periodical by introducing greater diversity in its contents in order to reach a wider public. As the publishers themselves pointed out, even after the periodical had gone back to being called *Illustrirte Frauen-Zeitung*, neither the number nor the diversity of the illustrations was initially reduced. Three years later, however, mainly as a result of tax burdens, the *Illustrirte Frauen-Zeitung* went back to being published on a fortnightly basis and contained fewer pages (*Illustrirte Frauen-Zeitung*, 1 January 1890).

The imperial leanings of 'Die Modenwelt'

Among the variety of features on offer, one theme repeatedly emerged from the pages of the nineteenth-century magazine, namely great admiration for the aristocracy and matters relating to royalty or the empire, regardless of the coat of arms in question. In this respect, if I may make the comparison, the *Illustrirte Frauen-Zeitung* was a precursor of magazines such as the British *Hello!* (*Hola!* in Spanish), with its illustrators and columnists occupying the roles of the modern paparazzi and duty reporters. The bulky issues of 1886 and 1887, for example, all of which contained sixteen pages, systematically featured a portrait on the cover, such as a woodcut reproduction of the bust of an artist or, more frequently, of members of the aristocracy, royal families, or emperors from around the world. These figures included King Wilhelm I of Prussia and his family; Grand Duchess Elizabeth von Mecklenburg-Strelitz of Germany; Princess Stephanie of Austria and her daughter; and even Princess Isabel of Brazil.

Among the artists, we find the illustrator, painter and draughtsman Adolf von Menzel.[3] The issue dated 1 March 1886 was entirely devoted to his work in order to commemorate the artist's seventieth birthday — in fact, this was the only issue of *Illustrirte Frauen-Zeitung* which was exclusively dedicated to one theme, as I was able to confirm in the corpus which I consulted. The magazine therefore made an exception in order to pay homage to the greatest living illustrator in Berlin, a man who was recognized for his illustrations and paintings related to events in the recent history of Prussia.

A further example of this fascination with imperial aristocracy occurs in the issue dated 1 January 1886, in which we find a portrait of the writer Marie von Ebner-Eschenbach, a friend of Frieda Lipperheide, who very probably met her during the periods which the publishing couple spent in the Tyrol. Born Countess Dubsky, she married the officer, engineer and teacher Moritz Ebner-Eschenbach in 1840. In 1870, when she began to write fiction, she held the title of Baroness.[4] This once again confirms the tendency of the publishers of *Illustrirte Frauen-Zeitung* to reproduce portraits of the aristocracy in their periodical.

The illustrations inside the magazine followed two trends. The first trend could include illustrations of monuments, objects, palaces, salons, edifying or exotic scenes linked to contemporary or ancient empires, or even pictures of expansionist European expeditions around the African continent. In the issue dated 1 January 1886, the gardens of the Palace of Nymphenburg in Munich are reproduced on a double page. In the issue dated 13 March 1887, the magazine features a map of sub-Saharan Africa, an illustration of black soldiers from the Egyptian equatorial province, another of slave trafficking in the province of Bahr-El-Ghazal, Sudan, and finally, a portrait of Emin Bey, an Austrian who was appointed governor of the Equatorial Provinces by the General Governor of the Sudan, General Gordon Pasha, in 1878. Among the illustrations inside the magazine, we find more portraits of imperial figures, such as that of the Empress Haru-ko of Japan, dressed in European costume. And in the issue dated 2 February 1890 — several months after the Proclamation of the Republic in Brazil, that is — there is a reproduction of a photo of the Brazilian royal family, taken 'one year beforehand' in Petrópolis. This is a version of Otto Hees's photo of 1899, which, according to Lília Moritz Schwarcz, became famous for being the last image of the family in Brazil.[5] The long caption introduces the eight individuals in the group photograph: Dona Teresa and Dom Pedro II, the ex-emperors of Brazil; dom Pedro Augusto de Sachsen-Coburg-Gotha, nephew of the emperors and eldest son of Princess Leopoldina; and Princess Isabel, the Count D'Eu and their three sons — Pedro, Luiz and Antônio. The heading mentions the recent proclamation of the Republic and praises the achievements of Princess Isabel, who on 13 May of the previous year had signed the slave liberation law on behalf of her sick father.

The second trend was for reproductions of paintings, which brought the fine arts to the inside pages of the magazine: landscapes, customs or scenes of family or country life, as well as images of ports or busy city centres. We find reproductions of pictures by Franz Skarbina, Friedrich Kallmorgen, Ewald Thiel and Richard Knötel.[6] Music scores can also be found, such as the Louis XV Minuet for piano, accompanied by explanatory illustrations of the dance steps (*Illustrirte Frauen-Zeitung*, 1 January 1886).

'Die Modenwelt', 'Die Gartenlaube' and the Second German Empire

In fact, *Die Illustrirte Frauen-Zeitung* was following a tradition which had been established, for example, in *Die Gartenlaube* (1853–1943), the most popular German family magazine during the second half of the nineteenth century.

According to Ernest K. Bramsted, *Die Gartenlaube* was the most representative and widely circulated periodical of the German liberal bourgeois between 1850 and 1900.[7] Conceived within the context of disappointment and de-politicization which arose from the 1848/49 revolution, its founder Ernst Keil, rapidly achieved great success with it among the middle classes. Keil opted for the *in-quarto* size in order to provide more space for the material, thereby creating the classic format of the German family newspaper during the nineteenth century — one that was certainly imitated by Lipperheide when he created the *Illustrirte Frauen-Zeitung*. The result was a combination of text and images to produce a newspaper which was at once instructive and entertaining. The contents of *Die Gartenlaube* between the years 1866 and 1888, Bramsted writes, 'taken as whole, reflect characteristically the intellectual and political changes within this class'.[8] Examining and comparing the contents of the volumes published in 1866 (the year of the Austro-Prussian War), 1871 (the year of German unification), and 1887 (the year of Wilhelm I's ninetieth birthday), Bramsted states that class consciousness (the liberal attitude, Enlightenment fervour and bourgeois pride) gradually adapted itself to the national sentiment as the middle classes came to identify themselves with the victorious governing caste. In the 1871 volume,

> the old democratic burgher pride was still alive, but an adjustment to the victorious Prussian monarchy and to the new prestige of the feudal stratum was found to be absolutely necessary if the sales of the periodical within a bourgeoisie fast becoming nationalist were to be maintained.[9]

In turn, the 1888 volume, 'reflects with astonishing clarity how large sections of the middle class have accepted their due place within the social order of the imperialistic Reich'.[10]

In the wake of *Die Gartenlaube*, when Lipperheide launched *Illustrirte Frauen-Zeitung* and tried to rename it *Die Illustrirte Zeit*, he attempted to adapt its ideological leanings to the middle class's recent identification with the Prussian monarchy. The difference is that, unlike *Die Gartenlaube*, Lipperheide's periodical did not openly advocate nationalism. Its policy of distancing itself from religious and political disputes had already been expressed in the leading article quoted above, when the magazine announced its change of name. Indeed, the Lipperheide publishing house had a great interest in ridding itself of an image defined by narrow nationalism. It is significant that, in an 1870 editorial, Frieda Lipperheide reinforced the international character of her periodical by stating that it was a magazine which promoted French fashion and was in circulation in several countries.[11]

Mention must be made of the fact that Germany was at war with France in 1870. When Friedrich Melford calculated the increase in the number of subscribers to *Die Modenwelt* between the years 1865 and 1890, he also emphasized that the publication of the periodical had never been threatened by the Franco-Prussian war. There had been a considerable decrease in the number of subscribers registered between June 1870 (98,928) and October 1870 (82,110). However, the number of subscribers would quickly recover, to reach the 100,000 mark the following year.[12]

In spite of the risks involved, Lipperheide's publishing venture was very successful because he located a global audience for fashion magazines and at the same time knew how to satisfy the particular interests of the German public. In the fashion section he promoted the fashion of the capital of France, the country which Germany was fighting for hegemony in Europe. In the second section, the magazine valued and defended aristocratic culture and Germany's expansionist activities.

The Literary Section of *A Estação*

Die Modenwelt therefore serves as a good example of how an international commercial undertaking adapts its product to conquer space in national markets. Just as Fanta, Coca-Cola and Nestlé yoghurts are much sweeter in Brazil than they are in Switzerland, and the style of the items sold by Zara in Spain differs from those sold in England (because they have been adapted to the taste of the consumers in each of these countries), the German edition of *Die Modenwelt* also acquired a local bias when its literary supplement was launched.

In fact, the same occurred with the Brazilian magazine during the first months of its existence. In common with *Illustrirte Frauen-Zeitung*, the main fashion section of *A Estação* was accompanied by a Literary Section, which, as we shall see later, was prepared in Brazil. Thus, in the same issue of the magazine, the Brazilian reader might find not only markedly exotic elements — such as patterns which were unsuitable for the inverted seasons of the tropics or landscapes depicting winter or spring in Europe — but also articles on Rio de Janeiro cultural movements, a few society columns, political news and news from other regions of the country, a correspondence section, educational articles and beauty tips by Brazilian writers, and, in Machado de Assis's novels and short stories, characters who inhabited the streets of Rio and adapted European fashion to the local taste and climate. Nevertheless, even the Literary Section of *A Estação* featured some imported material: the advertisements occupying the foot of the page were mainly French, and the illustrations in the inner pages of the supplement were German.

Illustrations originating from Germany

It is these illustrations which enter into a direct intertextual relationship with *Quincas Borba*. For comparison it is worth noting here that, of the entertainment sections consulted in the foreign editions of *Die Modenwelt*, the Brazilian version was the only one which reinforced the connection with Germany by importing this artistic material into the Literary Section. This was not the case in the other editions examined, namely *The Young Ladies' Journal*, *La Saison* and *La Estación*, all of which contained literary supplements. The French and Spanish magazines did not contain illustrations, and the English magazine published locally produced illustrations to illustrate the instalments of the popular novels serialized every week.

Often, the column set aside on the first page for *Quincas Borba* continued onto the top and foot of the inner pages, where the illustrations traditionally appeared. Subscribers who read the novel would inevitably have passed their eyes over these illustrations (see Figures 3.1 and 3.2). In order to understand the effect of reading the serial in the context of the magazine, as well as the motivations which led the novelist to define Rubião's madness as imperial megalomania, we need to devote a few pages of this book to the illustrations themselves. Firstly, let us demonstrate that the great majority of them did actually come from Germany.

In the publication dated 31 March 1879, Lombaerts announced that

> o suplemento literário do nosso jornal, deste número em diante, sairá também ilustrado, trazendo gravuras de atualidade ou sobre belas-artes, sempre escolhidas entre as obras primas dos abridores em madeira de França, Inglaterra, ou Alemanha.
>
> [the literary supplement of our newspaper, from this issue onwards, will also be illustrated, featuring pictures of current events or fine arts, always chosen from among the masterpieces created by the wood engravers of France, England or Germany.]

It can be stated with certainty that the illustrations came predominantly from the German magazine. At least during the years in which *Quincas Borba* was published (1886–1891), almost every issue of *A Estação* featured artistic pictures or portraits of aristocrats and imperial figures which had originally been published in the *Illustrirte Frauen-Zeitung*. Among the illustrations found are the following: 'Orsini Palace in Nemi' (15 April 1885); 'A ball at the Berlin court' (15 June 1887: see Fig. 3.3); 'The diamonds of the French crown — valuation (30 June 1887); 'Birthday of Emperor Guilherme — Student demonstration' (30 June 1887); 'The tower at Spandau, fortress of the Treasure of the German Empire' (30 November 1887); 'Dances at the court of Frederick the Great' (15 June 1885), 'The great pool of Versailles' (31 July 1885), 'The enchanted castle' (31 December 1885); 'Portrait of Emperor

76　The Literary Section of *A Estação*

Fig. 3.1. *A Estação, Jornal Ilustrado para a Família*, 30 June 1886
Biblioteca Nacional do Rio de Janeiro

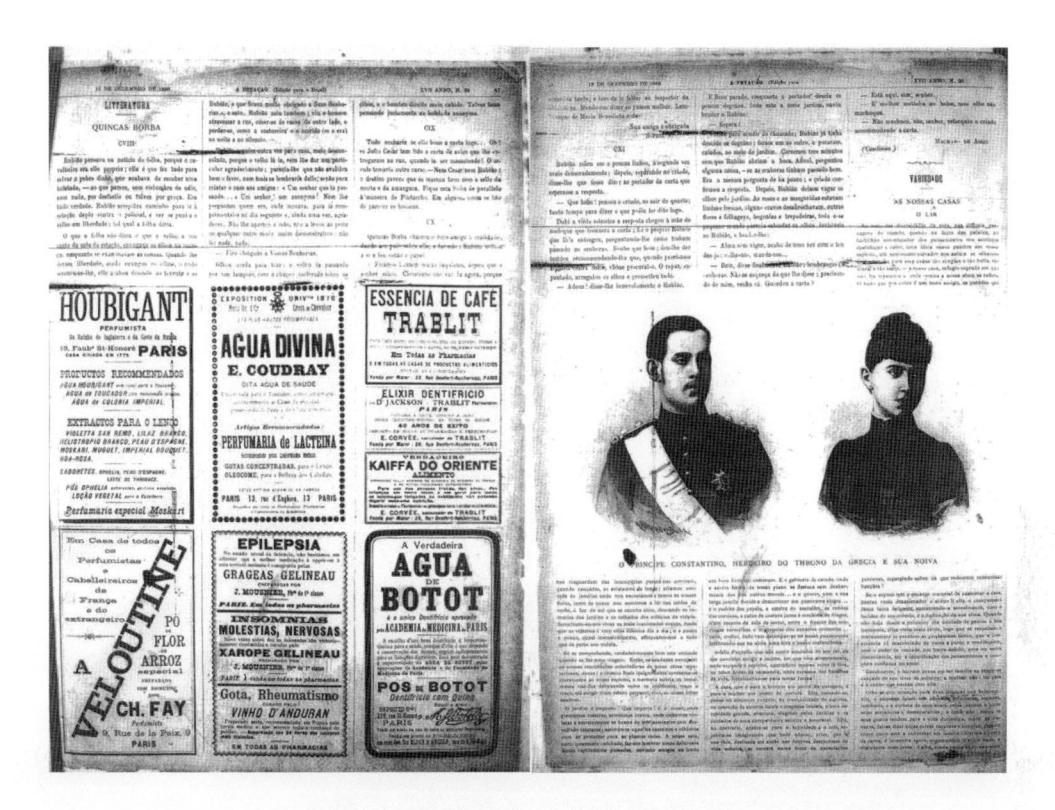

FIG. 3.2. *A Estação, Jornal Ilustrado para a Família*, 15 December 1888
Biblioteca Nacional do Rio de Janeiro

FIG. 3.3. *Illustrirte Frauen-Zeitung, Zeitung für Toilette und Handarbeiten*, 15 November 1886
Reproduced in *A Estação*, 15 July 1887: 'Um baile na corte de Berlim'
[A ball in the court of Berlin] Staatliche Museen zu Berlin, Kunstbibliothek

Frederick III, Emperor of Germany' (15 September 1888); 'The monument of Maria Theresa in Vienna' (30 September 1888); 'Prince Constantine, heir to the throne of Greece and his bride' (15 December 1888); 'Empress Augusta Vitória' (28 February 1889); 'The future Queen of Holland, Wilhelmina, heir to the throne of the Low Countries, daughter of Willem III, King of Holland, and Queen Emma, his wife' (15 September 1889); 'Marie, widow Queen of Bavaria, died on 17 May last' (30 September 1889); 'The officers of Napoleon I in Italy' (30 September 1889); 'The betrothed princes of Austria-Hungary: Archduchess Marie Valerie and Archduke Franz Salvator' (30 April 1889); 'The house in which Marie Louise, Queen of Prussia, was born' (31 December 1889); 'Kronborg Castle, current residence of the widow of Emperor Frederick of Germany' (15 January 1890).[13]

I was only able to find one issue of the magazine which contained illustrations originating from another periodical. This is the case of the drawings of 'Passepied de la Reine', which, as the publishers inform us, were taken from the Parisian newspaper *L'Illustration* and published in the issue dated 15 November 1890. On very rare occasions the woodcuts featured in the magazine were produced by local artists. When a picture was published of Madame Lebrun and her daughter, created by Brazilian engravers, the publishers did not allow this fact to pass unremarked:

> e muito nos alegramos em poder apresentar às leitoras da *Estação* uma obra prima de uma mulher, reproduzida talentosamente por gravadores brasileiros. Oxalá possa essa prova do que se pode fazer entre nós demonstrar que a xilogravura no Brasil não está tão atrasada como geralmente se supõe. (*A Estação*, 16 March 1886)
>
> [and we are very pleased to be able to present to the [lady] readers of *A Estação* a masterpiece depicting a woman, which has been skilfully reproduced by Brazilian engravers. Let us hope that this proof of what we can do demonstrates that woodcutting in Brazil is not so behind the times as is generally supposed.]

We do not know exactly which technique Lombaerts used to reproduce the illustrations. We cannot disregard the hypothesis that the reproduction was created from a printed copy of the German periodical. This was the technique used to print the drawings of the 'Passepied de la Reine' from the French newspaper *L'Illustration*. Moreover, as the publishers tell us in the correspondence section of 31 July 1888, quoted in Chapter 2, their archives very probably contained copies of the German magazine. However, the most likely hypothesis is that Lombaerts reproduced the illustrations from the die, which was produced in Berlin. This is what can be concluded from several notes published in the magazine to justify the delay in the distribution of the periodical on certain occasions. For example, printing had to be delayed for the issue dated 15 March 1880 due to a change in the timetable of the transatlantic steamships. The publishers specifically referred to the artistic components of the periodical which were transported to the capital city by sea:

> Os últimos números do jornal têm sido distribuídos com alguns dias de atraso, que foram causados por circunstâncias fora do nosso alcance. O inverno rigoroso na Europa e as quarentenas no Sul alteraram o cronograma dos vapores que trazem os elementos artísticos do jornal.

[The last few issues of the periodical have been distributed several days late due to circumstances outside of our control. The harsh winter in Europe and the quarantines in the south altered the timetable of the steamships which bring us the artistic components of the newspaper.]

This short note tells us that Lombaerts depended on imported material to compose not only the fashion section but also the literary section of his periodical. The Portuguese text could only be typeset once the illustrations had been chosen. The most emblematic proof of this may have been provided by the shipwreck of the steamship *Buenos Aires*. As Artur Azevedo reported in his 'Croniqueta' column of 15 August 1890, the crew was saved from the shipwreck but the merchandise which the steamship was carrying was not:

> Rio, 07 de agosto de 1890: Fatalidade dos nomes! Quase ao mesmo tempo que o vapor alemão *Buenos Aires* naufragava ao entrar na barra do Rio de Janeiro, a cidade de Buenos Aires revolucionava-se. Graças a Deus no naufrágio não pereceu ninguém, e a revolução terminou depois de três dias, não por falta de combatentes, como no Cid, mas por falta de munições.'

> [Rio, 7 August 1890: The destiny of names! Almost at the same time as the German steamship *Buenos Aires* was being shipwrecked on entering the bar of Rio de Janeiro, the city of Buenos Aires was in revolt. Thanks to God no one perished in the shipwreck, and the revolution ended after three days, not through a lack of combatants, as in the case of El Cid, but due to a lack of munitions.]

As can be concluded from the following note, the merchandise included the plates for an entire issue of the fashion section of *A Estação*:

> Com o presente número distribuímos a parte de modas do número de 31 de julho próximo passado, cuja entrega teve de ser adiada em consequência do naufrágio do vapor *Buenos Aires*. (*A Estação*, 15 September 1890)

> [With this issue we are distributing the fashion section of the issue dated 31 July last, the distribution of which had to be postponed due to the shipwreck of the steamship *Buenos Aires*.]

Perhaps the shipwreck resulted in the loss of some plates of artistic illustrations with which *Quincas Borba* shared the Literary Section of the magazine until the end of 1890. The issue dated 31 October 1890 contains an indication that the publishers had to replace lost illustrations with other available material:

> Por motivos inteiramente estranhos à nossa vontade, deixamos hoje de oferecer às nossas inteligentes e amáveis leitoras as gravuras com que costumamos enriquecer o suplemento literário da *Estação*. Esperamos, no próximo número, preencher a falta de que se ressente o atual. Não é, entretanto, tão sensível a falta, porque, em compensação, temos o prazer de substituir aquelas gravuras por um primor musical — a polca inédita *Onde está ela?* composição do jovem e bastante conhecido pianista Miguel A. de Vasconcellos.

> [For reasons wholly beyond our control, we cannot today offer our kind and intelligent [lady] readers the illustrations which usually enrich the literary supplement of *A Estação*. In the next issue we hope to make good the deficiency from which the current one suffers. The deficiency, however, it is not very

considerable because, as compensation, we have the pleasure of replacing those illustrations with a musical delight, the unpublished polka *Onde está ela?* by the young and highly renowned pianist Miguel A. de Vasconcellos.]

Lombaerts had to turn to locally produced material to fill the gap reserved in the magazine for the publication of German illustrations. It can even be surmised that his motivation for taking the drawings from the French newspaper *L'Illustration* had also been a temporary lack of German artistic material, since the French drawings were published just one month after the publication of Miguel de Vasconcellos's polka.

Printing site

The combination in the Literary Section of *A Estação* of imported and locally produced material raises questions over who was responsible for publishing and printing it. Laurence Hallewell and the Machado de Assis Committee affirm that *A Estação* as a whole (and, consequently, the serialized version of *Quincas Borba*) was printed in France.[14] And Marlyse Meyer, the first scholar to mention the connection between *A Estação* and *Die Modenwelt*, neither reiterates nor contests this view.[15]

However, an examination of Artur Azevedo's column makes it possible to conclude that the publishing and printing in fact took place in Lombaerts's own workshops in Rio de Janeiro. It is sufficient to note the publication date of the 'Croniquetas' of 15 May 1888 and 30 November 1889, in which Artur Azevedo mentions, respectively, the promulgation of the *Lei Áurea* abolishing slavery (13 May 1888) and the Proclamation of the Republic (15 November 1889). As the interval between these two historic events and the publication of each of the articles is at most fifteen days, even the use of the telegraph would not have allowed enough time for the texts to be sent to Europe and for the magazine to be typeset, printed and finally sent out to Rio de Janeiro for distribution.[16] Artur Azevedo's value to the researcher is such that we even learn the identity of the typographer of the magazine, at least during the year 1889. This proves that the magazine was not only printed but also edited in Rio de Janeiro:

> Não porei o ponto final sem recomendar às leitoras um livro de versos, que ultimamente apareceu, intitulado *Musgos*. O poeta, Alfredo Leite, é o paginador da *Estação*, — um artista cujo trabalho obscuro Suas Exas. estão fartas de apreciar, sem conhecer o autor. ('Croniqueta', *A Estação*, 31 January 1889)

> [I will not bid you farewell without recommending to our [lady] readers a book of verse, entitled *Musgos*, which appeared recently. The poet, Alfredo Leite, is the typographer of *A Estação*, an artist whose unheralded work you have had ample opportunity to appreciate without knowing the author.]

The typographer will again be the subject of this book in Chapter 5, in which we will discuss more specifically the typesetting of the instalments of *Quincas Borba*, for which he was responsible. Once the text has left the writer's hands, other agents, such as the typographer, become involved in producing it at a later stage, when it is adapted to the type case of each fortnightly issue of the magazine.

Comparing the entertainment page of *Die Modenwelt* with the Literary Section of *A Estação*, it can be concluded that the interval between the publication of an illustration in Germany and its reproduction in Brazil was at least six weeks. Limiting ourselves to just a few examples, E. Thiel's picture 'Train delayed by snow' and the illustration 'A factory in the Black Forest', published in Germany on 16 January 1887, were reproduced in *A Estação* on 31 March 1887. Two pictures by Adolph von Menzel, which were published in the aforementioned issue commemorating the illustrator's seventieth birthday (1 March 1886), were published in two different issues of *A Estação*: 'Blacksmith's workshop', on 15 August 1886, and 'Market scene in Italy', on 15 October 1886. Curiously, a portrait of D. Pedro's daughter, Princess Isabel, did not feature in the pages of the Brazilian magazine until long after its first publication in Germany, on 15 November 1886 (see Figure 3.4). It finally appeared in the Brazilian edition on 31 May 1888, in connection with her role in the abolition of slavery earlier that month.

Reading 'Philosopher or Dog?' among the illustrations

The illustrations featured in the Literary Section brought to *A Estação* the same ideological leanings as were found in the German magazine: the same admiration for aristocratic life and the same interest in subjects related to royalty or empire. In fact, the tendency stamped on the imported artistic component was disseminated throughout the entire contents of the magazine, from advertisements for French perfume or cloth (the imperial label enhanced the value of the merchandise), to the articles, narrative texts for the casual reader, and that most noble product of the network built on the artistic possibilities of the magazine. *Quincas Borba* was created by a writer who was already acclaimed at the time, and the presence of his name in the list of collaborators brought prestige to the magazine. The imperial leaning of the journal did not prevent Machado de Assis from forming part of that great wheel, even if he did so in order to remove it from the axle. Once again, it will be necessary to read between the lines to avoid falling into his trap. Only thus will we be able to understand that while Machado de Assis may, at first glance, appear to be adapting his work to the editorial programme of the magazine (as his novel deals with social aspirations) the overall hidden meaning of, for example, Rubião's madness in relation to that backdrop may lead us to a better understanding of the novel's salient irony.

In the Brazilian context, the German illustrations depicting the riches and refinement of other empires were in contrast to the decadent state of the Brazilian royal family at the time of Dom Pedro's return from his second trip to Europe (26 September 1877). Lília Schwarcz writes that

> When he came back from his second journey abroad in 1876, a Te-Deum welcomed his return, but the emperor seemed like a foreigner in his own land. Almost like a spectator, he watched his country's new political movements — especially. [...] As if from a box in the theater, Dom Pedro witnessed the removal and the return of the Liberals, who had been out of power for ten years. Serious problems affecting the whole country, such as the rebellion in Paraíba and Pernambuco in 1874 — the so-called 'Quebra-Quilos' or 'smash-kilos' — or the terrible drought of 1877 seemed not to affect him. And he also abandoned some of his old rituals. The symbol he chose for himself — a capital P in blue, tied with a ribbon — all but made explicit his distance from

FIG. 3.4. *Illustrirte Frauen-Zeitung, Zeitung für Toilette und Handarbeiten*, 15 November 1886
Reproduced in *A Estação*, 31 May 1888:
'A Sua Alteza, a Princesa Imperial Regente, D. Isabel, a Redentora'
[Her Highness, the Imperial Princess Regent Isabel the Redeemer]
(Staatliche Museen zu Berlin, Kunstbibliothek)

the people; the ceremony of kissing his hand had been abolished, and for some time now he used his gala-robes only on the most solemn occasions, like the obligatory Speech from the Throne that began and ended each legislative session.[17]

The lack of pomp and the decadent state of the royal family were recorded in the testimony of a contemporary, in the description of an imperial procession by the German journalist Karl von Koseritz:

> Seltsames Schauspiel das! Auf schnaubenden Rossen jagte erst eine Abteilung Kavallerie in Gala-Uniform daher, die jungfräulichen Säbel in entblösstem Zustande schwingend, und gleich nach ihm kamen vier Hofwagen mit den dienstthuenden Hofmarschällen, Kammerherren und Ehrendamen. Hofwagen, sage ich, aber was für welche!... Alle stamen aus dem vorigen Jahrhundert und zeigen mehr oder weniger die Form des Wagens, in dem Maria Antoniette einstens ihren Einzug in Paris heilt; die Vergoldung ist längst Schwarz geworden, die Stoffe sind verblichen, Alles ist im traurigsten Zustande. [...] Eine nach der andern hielten die vier alten Staatskarossen vor dem Eingang und entluden sich ihrer Last: Eine Ehrendame (Baronesse Suruhy), alt und hässlich, aber stark decolliert, und fünf oder sechs Hofbedienstete in ehemals glänzender grüner Uniform, mit Gold bordirt, den Dreimaster unter dem Arm, den Galanteriedegen an der Seite und die wadenlosen Beine in Kniehosen und seidene Strümpfe gesteckt, — so krochen sie aus ihren Karossen heraus und erinnerten lebhaft — an den Carneval. [...]
>
> Nunmehr kam die ehrwürdige Kaiserin heran: Ihr Train war etwas besser, aber noch immer verschossen und verblichen. [...] Sie trug ein schweres, decolletirtes Kleid, welches förmlich mit Brillanten besäet war, und in ihrem vollständigen ergrauten Haare das berühmte Diamanten-Collier zierte, welches ihren grössten Schatz bildet. [...] Nun erschien endlich — last not least — der Kaiser; vier Vorreiter in neuen Livreen, ein Train schöner Pferde mit reichem Geschirr und ein wenn nicht neuer so doch vollständig restaurirter Stattswagen mit Beschlägen und Ornamenten von getriebenem Silber und der Kaiserkrone über dem Schlage, zeichneten sein Erscheinen aus. Kein Zuruf begrüsste ihn, kein einziges Hoch. Ihm selbst schien das aufzufallen, den nachdem er aus dem Wagen gestiegen war, richtete er sich in seiner ganzen Höhe auf und warf einen langen, scharfen Blick auf das ihn umgebende Volk. Majestätisch konnte ich ihn nicht finden mit seinen Schnallenschuhen, seidenen Strümpfen, Kniehosen, Federkragen und grünem Sammetmantel, der von goldenen Sternen funkelt. Hauptsächlich der eigenartige Federschmuck (papos de tucano) macht einen fast carnevalartigen Eindruck. Der Kaiser geht leicht gebeugt und ist in lezter Zeit stark gealtert, auch wird er zusehends kahl, und schwere Sorgen, vielleicht auch physisches Leiden haben tiefe Runzeln in sein Gesicht gegraben. [...]
>
> Fasse ich den Totaleindruck der Feier zusammen, so war derselbe mehr komischer als Respekt einflössender Natur. Wenn die Monarchie Luxus entfaltet, so muss derselbe auch grossartig und imponirend sein, was hier nicht der Fall ist. Wohl weiss ich, dass der Kaiser keinen glänzenden Hofstaat hat, weil er seine Civilliste für Zwecke der Wohlthätigkeit verausgabt; aber so edel dieses ist, so entschuldigt es nicht die Taktlosigkeit, alten Plunder, wie die ganze Geschichte ist, als keiserlichen Luxus vorzuführen. Erscheine der Kaiser in seiner Generalfeldmarschallsuniform, die ihm so gut steht, und in einem eleganten modernen Wagen, würde die Eindruck unbedingt ein besserer sein, als in dem verblichenen Krönungs-Ornat und den noch verblicheneren

Staatskarossen aus dem 17. und 18. Jahrhundert. Einen grossartigen Eindruck macht die ganze Geschichte nicht, und die stumme Haltung des Volks trug auch nicht dazu bei, die Weihe der Stunde zu erhöben. [...] (Rio, 4. Mai 1883)[18]

[Strange spectacle! First, mounted on snorting horses, a cavalry unit wearing gala uniforms raced past, brandishing new and unsheathed sabres, and they were followed by four court carriages, with noblemen, chamberlains and ladies of honour on duty. Court carriages, I have said, but of an extraordinary kind! They all date from the previous century and have more or less the same shape as Marie Antoniette's carriage on her first visit to Paris; the gilding had turned black long ago, the upholstery faded, and everything is in the sorriest state. [...] One after another, the old state carriages stopped in front of the entrance and emptied their load: one lady of honour (the Baroness of Suruí), aged and ugly, but wearing a very low-cut dress, and five or six members of the court, dressed in once green and brilliant uniforms with gold edging, their tricorn hats under their arms, their swords in their belts, and their thin legs encased in silk breeches and stockings – thus they emerged from their carriages, putting one in mind of a carnival. [...]

Next the honourable Empress arrived. Her carriage was a little better, but still worn and blemished. [...] She wore a heavy, low-cut dress, which was ceremoniously encrusted with diamonds, and in her hair, which was completely white, there sparkled the famous set of diamonds, which constitutes her greatest treasure. [...] Finally, the Emperor appeared, his arrival heralded by four mounted escorts in new livery, a train of horses with rich harnessings and a carriage which, while not new, had at least been fully restored with silver embossed mountings and ornaments, and the imperial crown on the carriage door. Neither applause nor greetings were heard, not even a single 'hurrah'. He himself seemed upset by this because, after descending from the carriage, he raised himself to his full height and subjected the people around him to a long and penetrating look. I could find no majesty in him, with his buckled shoes, silk stockings, breeches, feather collar and robe of green velvet, on which gold medals shone. In particular, the curious feather adornment (toucan crop) created an almost carnivalesque impression. The Emperor walks with a slight stoop and has aged a lot recently. He is also visibly going bald, and his great worries, and perhaps also certain physical ailments, have left deep furrows in his face. [...]

Overall, the impression of the ceremony was more suggestive of comedy than of instilling respect. When a monarch displays his luxury, it must be done in an imposing and grandiose way, which is not the case here. I am well aware that the Emperor cannot have a brilliant court because he gives his civil list over to charitable purposes, but however noble this might be, it does not justify the lack of tact shown by passing off old junk, as all of this is, as imperial luxury. Had the Emperor appeared in his field marshal uniform, which looks so well on him, and in a modern and elegant coach, the impression would have been much better than in that faded coronation regalia and that even more faded stately caroche of the 17th and 18th century. This whole episode does not make a wonderful impression, and the public's mute attitude did not help to uplift the sanctity of the moment. [...] (Rio, 4th May 1883)]

The Emperor, as Lília Schwarcz has shown, even became the target of caricatures in the *Revista Ilustrada*, *O Mosquito* and *O Besouro*, 'noting his indifference to matters of state, and the hesitancy he was displaying in public'.[19]

The illustrations originating from *Illustrirte Frauen-Zeitung* therefore created in *A Estação* promoted an image of luxury and grandiosity which no longer existed in the Brazilian court. Among those most worthy of mention are 'A ball at the Berlin court' (*A Estação*, 15 June 1887), the carriage featured in the illustration 'Corpus Christi festival in Munich' (15 October 1887: see Figure 3.5), the military parade in 'The people in front of the Imperial Palace in Berlin', the medal-stuffed bust of Emperor Wilhelm of Germany (both dated 15 June 1880), and 'The officers of Napoleon I in Italy' (30 September 1889).

Our investigation into the intertextual relationship between these illustrations and the novel could be based on the frequent presence in the text of carriages, coaches and coupés, which are not always differentiated from each other. As fetish objects, and the cause of vanity or envy among the characters, they become symbols of the economic prosperity of those who travel in them or acquire them. Sophia's carriage, for example, which could also be a simple coupé, marks the way that she has intentionally distanced herself from old friends, thereby causing those who were considered close to the couple, such as Major Siqueira, to feel indignant:

> Antigamente: major, um brinde. Eu fazia muitos brindes, tinha certo desembaraço. Jogávamos o voltarete. Agora está nas grandezas; anda com gente fina. Ah! vaidades deste mundo! Pois não vi outro dia a mulher dele, num *coupé*, com outra? A Sofia de *coupé*! Fingiu que me não via, mas arranjou os olhos de modo que percebesse se eu a via, se a admirava. Vaidades desta vida! Quem nunca comeu azeite, quando come se lambuza.[20]

> [I used to drink many a toast to him, I had a certain knack for it. We used to play *voltarete* together. But now he has a swelled head and hobnobs with fine folk. Ah! worldly vanity! Why, the other day didn't I see his wife in a *coupé* with another woman? Sophia in a *coupé*! She pretended not to see me, but she looked out of the corner of her eye to see if I saw her and was admiring her. Worldly vanity! He who eats olive oil for the first time, spills it all over himself.][21]

A few chapters beforehand, the narrator provides confirmation of Sophia's calculating attitude, which causes her to disdain the friends who belonged to her old social circle. At first, when she was still 'on honeymoon' with grandeur, it was a question of being seen, admired and envied inside the carriage. When her position among the *nouveau riche* has been consolidated, she avoids her old friends' eyes, thereby signalling her disdain for the envy which she might cause them to feel:

> Foi assim que a nossa amiga, pouco a pouco, espanou a atmosfera. Cortou as relações antigas, familiares, algumas tão íntimas que dificilmente se poderiam dissolver; mas a arte de receber sem calor, ouvir sem interesse e despedir-se sem pesar, não era das suas menores prendas; e uma por uma, se foram indo as pobres criaturas modestas, sem maneiras, nem vestidos, amizades de pequena monta, de pagodes caseiros, de hábitos singelos e sem elevação. Com os homens fazia exatamente o que o major contara, quando eles a viam passar de carruagem, — que era sua, — entre parêntesis. A diferença é que já nem os espreitava para saber se a viam. Acabara a lua-de-mel da grandeza, agora torcia os olhos duramente para outro lado, conjurando, de um gesto definitivo, o perigo de alguma hesitação. Punha assim os velhos amigos na obrigação de lhe não tirarem o chapéu.[22]

FIG. 3.5. *A Estação, Jornal Ilustrado para a Família*, 15 October 1887
'Festa do Corpo de Deus em Munique' [Corpus Christi Festival in Munich]
Biblioteca Nacional do Rio de Janeiro

> [And so it was little by little our friend cleared the atmosphere. She severed old, familiar relations, some so intimate that they could be dissolved only with difficulty. However, the art of receiving coolly, of listening without interest, and saying goodbye without regret, was not the least of her accomplishments. One by one they were disappearing — those poor modest unpretentious women who did not have fashionable wardrobes; unimportant friends with simple diversions, and unassuming ways. Toward the men whom she passed in a carriage — which was her own, incidentally — she acted exactly as the Major had said. Only she no longer looked to see if they saw her. The honeymoon of ostentation had ended; now she would coldly turned her eyes aside, exorcising with a peremptory gesture the danger of any hesitancy on their part. It was in this way that she compelled her old friends not to raise their hats.][23]

The carriage also frequently inhabits Rubião's fantasies of grandeur. In chapter 116, for example, when he learns that Maria Benedicta and Carlos Maria are due to be married, he imagines the carriage and the horses which will take him to the ceremony:

> Casam-se, e breve... Será de estrondo o casamento? Deve ser; o Palha vive agora um pouco melhor... — e Rubião lançava os olhos aos móveis, porcelanas, cristais, reposteiros — há de ser de estrondo. E depois o noivo é rico... Rubião pensou na carruagem e nos cavalos que levaria; tinha visto uma parelha soberba, no Engenho Velho, dias antes, que estava mesmo ao pintar. Ia fazer a encomenda de outra assim, fosse por que preço; tinha também de presentear a noiva.[24]

> ['And so they're going to get married soon — I wonder if it will be a big wedding. Probably. Palha is a little better off now —' and Rubião glanced at the furniture, the porcelains and glassware, the hangings. 'It'll be big, no doubt. And the fiancé is rich.' Rubião thought about the carriage and horses that he would take. At Engenho Velho a few days before, he had seen a superb pair worthy of being painted. He was going to order another like it, whatever the price; he'd have to present one to the bride, too.][25]

Even in the second version, in an added chapter, carriages still form part of Rubião's daydreams. In the rewritten text, they can be found in the character's matrimonial delirium, which is described in detail:

> Antes de cuidar da noiva, cuidou do casamento. Naquele dia e nos outros, compôs de cabeça as pompas matrimoniais, os coches, — se ainda os houvesse antigos e ricos, quais ele via gravados nos livros de usos passados. Oh! grandes e soberbos coches! Como ele gostava de ir esperar o Imperador, nos dias de grande gala, à porta do paço da cidade, para ver chegar o préstito imperial, especialmente o coche de Sua Majestade, vastas proporções, fortes molas, finas e velhas pinturas, quatro ou cinco parelhas guiadas por um cocheiro grave e digno! Outros vinham, menores em grandeza, mas ainda assim tão grandes que enchiam os olhos.
> Um desses outros, ou ainda algum menor, podia servir-lhe às bodas, se toda a sociedade não estivesse já nivelada pelo vulgar *coupé*. Mas, enfim, iria de *coupé*; imaginava-o forrado magnificamente, de quê? De uma fazenda que não fosse comum, que ele mesmo não distinguia, por ora; mas que daria ao veículo o ar que não tinha. Parelha rara. Cocheiro fardado de ouro. Oh! mas um ouro nunca visto.[26]

[Before thinking about the bride, he thought about the wedding; he imagined all the ceremonial. There would be elegant old-fashioned coaches — if there still existed any of the sort that he saw pictured in old books. Oh! Great, proud coaches! How he liked to go on gala days and wait for the Emperor at the gate of the city palace to see the arrival of the imperial cortege, especially the coach of His Majesty, with its fine old paintings, its huge proportions and strong springs, and its four or five pairs of horses, driven by a grave and decorous coachman. It would be followed by others, smaller in size, but large enough even so to fill the eye.

One of these, or even a still smaller one, would do for his wedding, if all society were not levelled by the vulgar *coupé*. But after all, he would go in a *coupé*; he fancied it magnificently lined — with what? With a material that would not be common, which he, himself, could not make out for the moment, but which gave the vehicle the air of distinction it lacked without it. A fine pair of horses. A coachman in livery of gold. Oh! But a gold never seen before!][27]

In this quotation, we see that the narrator refers to the coach and the *coupé*, and now distinguishes between them: the first is more sumptuous and ancient and is used by the Emperor, while the second has become a vulgar object which no longer serves to differentiate people of means from others in society. Rubião obviously prefers the former and, if possible, one of those frequently seen in the imperial procession. But, in its absence, Rubião would paint his *coupé* with 'a gold never seen' to transform it into the most special *coupé* in the world. It may be added in passing that Rubião's gold is like the invisible cloth in the King's clothes in the Hans Christian Andersen story.

In the quotation above we also find an association between the carriage, the Emperor and the imperial procession. This association will subsequently be explored a great deal in the novel, when Rubião's madness acquires all of its characteristics, in other words, when the character, in the throes of madness, believes himself to be Napoleon III. Rubião's personality starts to break down in chapter 109 of both versions. It can be seen that Machado de Assis does not make an explicit link between Rubião and Dom Pedro II, despite the fact that, as Gledson argues, the character's madness allegorically represents the decline of the imperial regime in Brazil.[28] The link is first mediated by the figure of a Frenchman. Machado de Assis's choice of a foreign emperor finds parallels in the magazine, as more often than not the pictures featured busts and illustrations of riches pertaining to foreign empires. In this respect, the author could equally well have chosen Emperor Wilhelm of Germany, if his readers did not particularly identify themselves with French culture.[29]

Gledson highlights another subsidiary element in the comparison: he establishes a parallel between Sophia and Empress Eugenie because both women were beautiful and both, in a certain sense, were arrivistes who wielded great power behind the throne. Here, mention must be made of a further disguise which relates to Eugenie's political powers: just as Eugenie became powerful at the end of the Empire, when Napoleon was ill, Princess Isabel assumed the reins of power when her father was travelling around Europe in 1871. The reference to Pedro II's trips to Europe is found in the following passage, in a conversation between Rubião and Camacho: 'Rubião ouvia com seriedade; dentro de si ria à larga, pela razão de que naquele instante sentia-se incógnito, de passeio pela América, enquanto Eugênia sustinha as rédeas do governo' [Rubião listened earnestly; inside he was roaring with laughter, because at that moment he felt himself incognito, on a trip to America, while Eugenie held the reins of government].[30]

I believe that the parallel between Sophia and the French empress is also justified because Eugenie was known for her aristocratic elegance, her jewels, and the splendour of her dress. She played a very important role in the cultural and social life of the French imperial court. Moreover, she launched several fashions in Europe, such as the fashion for crinoline in the shape of a dome in 1855. At the end of the 1860s, the clothed female silhouette changed again following her abandonment of very full skirts.[31]

The character in the novel is neither an aristocrat nor a starter of fashions like Empress Eugenie, but her beauty is admired, however much her thick eyebrows spoil her overall appearance. Besides her eyebrows, the narrator observes that Sophia's manners do not come from the cradle: rather, they have been acquired, a fact which reveals her class of origin and will never allow her to pass for a true aristocrat.

Where Rubião is concerned, his imperial megalomania therefore creates an ironic link between the imported imperial pomp of the magazine and the decadent state of the Brazilian empire. As regards Sophia, the novel reveals the futility of every effort that the subscribers might make to use fashion in an attempt to pass for genuine ladies who belong to the Brazilian aristocracy, let alone the European one.

In Chapters 2 and 3 of this book, we saw the strong thematic relationship which exists between the novel and the contents of *A Estação*. The two major themes of the novel are developed on the base material which is available in the magazine itself: Machado de Assis has made use of the imperial leanings of the magazine as well as the way that fashion is used to indicate a person's rise in society. The irony of the novel is best understood when we have identified the criticism, implicit in the fate of the characters, of the way that fashion, as divulged in the pages of the magazine, acts as a camouflage for readers who wish to climb a few steps up the social ladder. Moreover, Rubião's imperial megalomania, which is personified in a foreign emperor, satirizes the fact that Rio de Janeiro society fetishizes imported products and French culture. The Brazilian writer also satirizes the distance between the reality of Brazil and Europe (a distance which the magazine itself highlights), and the distance between the grandiosity of foreign empires and the decadent state of the Brazilian court.

The first part of this book has focused on the editorial context in which *Quincas Borba* was produced, whether in comparison with other novels which the writer published in the same form (Chapter 1), or in the more specific editorial context of its publication within a magazine devoted to fashion, fine art and literature. The second part of this book will focus on narrative resources and undertakes a comparison of the two versions of the novel. It is in the second part that we will examine in depth the relationship between the structure of the novel and its mode of publication in serial and book form.

Notes to Chapter 3

1. Friedrich Melford, *Zum fünfundzwanzigjährigen Bestehen der Modenwelt, 1865–1890*, pp. 3, 5.
2. *Zum fünfundzwanzigjährigen Bestehen der Modenwelt, 1865–1890*, p. 8.
3. 1815, Breslau, Silesia [now Wroclaw, Poland] — 1903, Berlin.
4. 1830, Zdislavic, Moravia — 1916, Vienna. For more on Marie von Ebner-Eschenbach, see Henry & Mary Garland, *The Oxford Companion to German Literature* (Oxford: OUP, 1976), p. 180; and Rasche, 1999, p. 14.
5. This photograph is very similar to the two photos taken by Otto Hees which are reproduced in Lília Schwarcz, *The Emperor's Beard: Dom Pedro II and the Tropical Monarchy of Brazil*, translated by John Gledson (NY: Hill and Wang, 2004), p. 296.
6. Richard Knötel is the painter of a series of military illustrations featuring Anglo-German troops during the Battle of Waterloo and the Battles of Kulm, Leipzig and Hanau.
7. Ernest K. Bramsted, 'Popular Literature and Philistinism', in *Aristocracy and the Middle-Classes in Germany*, rev. edn (Chicago and London: The University of Chicago Press, 1964), pp. 200–27. For more on *Die Gartenlaube*, see also Kristen Belgum, *Popularizing the Nation: Audience, Representation, and the Production of Identity in 'Die Gartenlaube', 1853–1900* (Lincoln: University of Nebraska Press, 1998).
8. Bramsted, p. 203.
9. Bramsted, pp. 207–08.
10. Bramsted, p. 208.
11. Frieda Lipperheide, *Die Modenwelt*, 1 September 1870, quoted by Rasche, p. 19.
12. *Zum fünfundzwanzigjährigen Bestehen der Modenwelt, 1865–1890*, p. 6, 8.
13. The dates are those of the illustrations in the Brazilian periodical.
14. Hallewell, p. 113 and 'Introdução crítico-filológica', Machado de Assis, *Quincas Borba*, 1975, p. 39.
15. Meyer, *Caminhos do imaginário no Brasil*, p. 93.
16. Communication by telegraph, linking Brazil and Europe, began in 1874. For further information on the subject, see Diamantino Fernandes Trindade and Laís dos Santos Pinto Trindade, 'As telecomunicações no Brasil: do Segundo Reinado até o Regime Militar', online at <http://www.oswaldocruz.br/download/artigos/social14.pdf> [accessed 12 December 2009].
17. Schwarcz, p. 296.
18. Karl von Koseritz, *Bilder aus Brasilien* (Leipzig and Berlin: W. Friedrich, 1885), p. 57.
19. Schwarcz, p. 302.
20. *Quincas Borba*, chap. 130, p. 272; *A Estação*, 15 March 1890, cap. 131; *Quincas Borba apêndice*, p. 166.
21. *Philosopher or Dog?*, p. 189.
22. *Quincas Borba*, chap. 138, p. 279; *A Estação*, 15 April 1890, chap. 138; *Quincas Borba apêndice*, pp. 171–72. Variants: *A:* nossa amiga, pouco a pouco, trocou de atmosfera; *A, B:* despedir-se sem saudade, não era das suas menores prendas; *A:* Com os homens das velhas relações, fazia exatamente o que o major contara; *A:* para descobrir se a viam e se a invejavam. Acabara a lua-de-mel da grandeza.
23. *Philosopher or Dog?*, p. 198. Variants: *A:* it was little by little our friend changed the atmosphere; *A, B:* saying goodbye without missing anything no regret, was not the least of her accomplishments; *A:* Toward the men she had known a long time whom she passed in a carriage — which was her own, incidentally — she acted exactly as the Major had said; *A:* Only she no longer looked to find out if they were looking at her and envied her. The honeymoon of ostentation had ended.
24. *Quincas Borba*, chap. 116, p. 251; *A Estação*, 15 January 1890, chap. 116; *Quincas Borba apêndice*, p. 149.
25. *Philosopher or Dog?*, pp. 166–67.
26. *Quincas Borba*, chap. 81, pp. 207–08.
27. *Philosopher or Dog?*, pp. 117–18. The seed of the matrimonial delirium is found in the first version in chapter 86, of 31 October 1888; *Quincas Borba apêndice*, p. 96: 'Crê, leitor, tal foi a origem secreta e inconsciente da ideia conjugal'. In chapter 7 of this book, we shall examine the role

played by the two added chapters (81 and 82), which deal with Rubião's matrimonial delirium, in marking the progressive stages of his madness in the second version.
28. See Gledson, *Machado de Assis: ficção e história*, chapter 2, pp. 73–133, principally items VIII–XII.
29. See Gilberto Pinheiro Passos, *O Napoleão de Botafogo: presença francesa em Quincas Borba de Machado de Assis* (São Paulo: Annablume, 2000), and Needell, chap. 5.
30. *A Estação*, 31 July 1890, chap. 101; *Quincas Borba apêndice*, p. 185. This section was removed from the final version. See Gledson, *Machado de Assis: ficção e história*, p. 110.
31. For more on Empress Eugenie de Montijo, see, for example, Jasper Ridley, *Napoléon III and Eugénie* (London: Constable, 1979). For a fuller account of the history of crinoline, see Norah Waugh, *Corsets and Crinolines* (London: Batsford, 1954).

PART II

❖

Narrative Technique and the Two Versions

CHAPTER 4

❖

The Kaleidoscopic Narrative of *Philosopher or Dog?*

Machado de Assis's creative source for the writing of *Quincas Borba* cannot be limited to the themes found in *A Estação*, particularly since Eugênio Gomes has demonstrated that the novelist used elements of Gogol's short story 'Diary of a Madman' in order to define the theme and plot of *Quincas Borba*.[1] The starting point for this present chapter is a discussion of the similarities between the Brazilian novel and the Russian short story, which Gomes has already highlighted, and a comparison of the narrative resources employed by these two writers. The aim is to show that the Russian short story served as a narrative source and, at the same time, a counter-example to *Quincas Borba*. Despite being based on the same thematic substrate, Gogol and Machado de Assis used very different narrative tools in order to achieve the realist goal of depicting the interpersonal relations in the society represented in each of these two works. We shall see that the Brazilian writer opts for a third-person narrator rather than the diary form or a first-person narrator in order to depict, through various narrative prisms, a network of interpersonal relations which is much more intricate, and at the same time much less hierarchical, than that of the society represented by Gogol. This technique allows the narrator to change the angle at any time and focus on the viewpoint of not just one but several of the characters involved in the plot. The omniscient narrator occupies himself with each of the main characters in turn, seeing events through their eyes, which allows the author to build the game of suspicion around the two supposed love affairs that carry out the plot. The plot of *Quincas Borba* is in fact made up of the sum total of the different opinions and impressions that each character retains of the same event. However, in this chapter I distance myself from Kinnear's thesis that Machado de Assis deliberately moved from a reliable to an unreliable narrator when adapting the serial for its book version. From the point of view of the reader, who is in the position of spectator, the narrative offers the opportunity to observe a changing society from several angles, which definitely represents an advantage in the sense that it allows the reader to formulate her or his own version of the story.

Gogol, Matrix of *Philosopher or Dog?*

Eugênio Gomes's book *Machado de Assis* contains an article which, despite being very convincing, did not receive the attention it deserved in the critical history of

Quincas Borba.² As Gomes revealed, 'Diary of a Madman' was one of the sources which Machado de Assis used to define the theme and some elements of the plot of *Quincas Borba*:

> Exatamente como ocorre no 'Diário de um louco', no romance brasileiro à ideia fixa de caráter amoroso juntar-se pouco depois a da megalomania imperial, com Rubião transfigurado em Luís Napoleão, imperador da França, sendo interessante salientar a circunstância de que a mulher, por quem ambos suspiram tão estranhamente, tem o mesmo nome: Sofia. Coincidência?³
>
> [Exactly as occurs in 'Diary of a Madman', in the Brazilian novel the amorous character's obsession is, shortly afterwards, accompanied by imperial megalomania, with Rubião transfigured into Louis Napoleon, Emperor of France. It is worth pointing out the fact that the woman for whom they both yearn so strangely has the same name: Sophia. Coincidence?]

According to Gomes, in 'Diary of a Madman' Machado de Assis found the theme of imperial megalomania, the personification of the dog, and the name Sophia. It is as if Machado de Assis had constructed the novel around the intersection between the themes extracted from the magazine (social climbing and the imperial tendency) and the suggestions offered by the Russian short story.

Before the two works are compared, attention will be given to the editions of Gogol's short stories which were circulating in Brazil at the time of Machado de Assis, in one of which the Brazilian writer certainly read the 'Diary of a Madman'.

Translations of 'Diary of a Madman' available in Brazil in the nineteenth century

Machado de Assis possessed in his library an anthology of Gogol's short stories translated into German: *Altväterische Leute und andere Erzählungen von Nikolas W. Gogol*, Deutsch von Julius Meixner, Collection Spemann, Stuttgart, Verlag von W. Spemann, [n.d]. This volume appears in the survey of his library published by Jean-Michel Massa in the 1960s, which was recently revised by Glória Vianna.⁴ That particular copy, though, is no longer in Machado's library (which now belongs to the Academia Brasileira de Letras), and must be considered lost. However, I was able to confirm, from another copy, that 'Diary of a Madman' was in fact published in that anthology: it is the last short story and occupies pages 191–218.

It is known that Machado de Assis was able to read and write fluently in French, but the same cannot be said with complete certainty of his knowledge of German. In her short biography, *Machado de Assis na intimidade*, Francisca de Basto Cordeiro states that the writer studied German with the group comprising João Ribeiro, Capistrano de Abreu and José Veríssimo.⁵ Moreover, there are quotations in German throughout Machado de Assis's work, although they are much less numerous than those in French. One such example is found in the chronicle *Bons Dias!* of 11 May 1888, being a quotation was taken from the newspaper of the German expatriates in Rio de Janeiro, the *Rio Post*.⁶ While we may never know whether Machado de Assis read the language fluently, it cannot be doubted that he had a special interest in German language, literature and philosophy. And his library is proof of it: of a total of 718 books, twenty-seven titles are in German, either original works or translations into that language. It includes, for example, an H. Michaelis

Portuguese–German dictionary, books of poetry by Heine and Schiller, legal works by Bismarck and historical works by Alfred Klaar. Many of these were published by the same publishing house as the anthology of Gogol's short stories, Verlag von W. Spemann of Stuttgart. There are also several scientific and philosophical works, as well as German literature in translation.[7]

If Machado de Assis was unable to read the copy of 'Diary of a Madman' which was in his library, the writer certainly had access to another edition of Gogol short stories, translated into French, which was available at the time. As Eugênio Gomes clarifies:

> Não somente essa obra [*Almas Mortas*], como as demais de Gogol, já corriam, nesse tempo, pelos canais franceses. *Almas mortas*, numa tradução lançada em 1859, mas já em 1845, Louis Viardot, com o auxílio de Turgenev, havia trasladado para a sua língua as narrativas: 'Tarass Bulba', 'O diário de um louco', 'Viy' e outras, publicadas em um volume'.[8]

> [That work [*Dead Souls*], as well as others by Gogol, was already in circulation in France at the time. As well as *Dead Souls*, which was published in translation in 1859, by 1845 Louis Viardot, with the help of Turgenev, had translated into his language the narratives 'Tarass Bulba', 'Diary of a Madman' and 'Viy', among others, all published in one volume'.]

The volume referred to is the anthology *Nouvelles Choisies*, Paris, Hachette, the first edition of which was published in July 1845. In an 1853 edition with the same title, I was able to confirm that the short story 'Les Memoires d'un fou' is the first in the collection, occupying pages 3 to 42. The edition contains three narratives in total: in addition to 'Les Mémoires d'un fou', it includes 'Une ménage d'autrefois' and 'Le Roi de gnomes'. Also found in this volume is Viardot's preface, in which the choice of stories, and the circumstances in which the translation was made, are explained:

> Fait à Saint-Pétersbourg, ce travail m'appartient moins qu'à des amis qui ont bien voulu me dicter en français le texte original. Je n'ai rien fait de plus que des retouches sur les mots et les phrases; et si le style est à moi en partie, c'est à eux seuls qu'est le sens. Je puis donc promettre au moins une parfaite exactitude. Nous avons toujours suivi la règle que Cervantes donne aux traducteurs, et que je m'étais efforcé précédemment d'appliquer à ses œuvres: 'Ne rien mettre, et ne rien omettre'.[9]

> [Done in Petersburg, this work belongs less to me than to my friends who were willing to dictate to me the original text, in French. I did no more than touch up on words and phrases; and if the style is in part mine, the meaning is theirs alone. I can therefore promise at least perfect accuracy. We have always followed the rule Cervantes gives to translators, and which I previously forced myself to apply to his own works: 'Not to add or omit anything'.]

According to Helmut Stolze, those stories were translated in 1843, during Louis Viardot's stay in Russia, and the two friends were Gedeonov and the aforementioned Turgenev.[10] It is very likely that the 1845 edition contains more short stories than does the 1853 edition. For example, the narrative 'Tarass Bulba', to which Eugênio Gomes refers, was not published in the latter, as we have seen. Furthermore 'Tarass

Bulba' was described in detail by Sainte-Beuve in his review in *Revue des Deux Mondes*:

> Les autres nouvelles du volume nous offrent moins d'intérêt que celle de 'Tarass Bulba'; elles montrent la variété du talent de M. Gogol, mais je regrette que, pour un premier recueil, on n'ait pas pu choisir une suite plus homogène et plus capable de fixer tout d'abord sur les caractères généraux de l'auteur: le critique se trouve un peu en peine devant cette diversité de sujets et d'applications.[11]

> [The other stories of the volume offer us less of interest than 'Taras Bulba'; they show the variety of M. Gogol's talent, but I regret that, for a first collection, it was not possible to select a sequence that was more homogenous and more capable of identifying straight away the general characteristics of the author: the critic struggles a little in the face of this diversity of subjects and approaches.]

Gogol in the 'Revue des Deux Mondes'

Perhaps Machado de Assis's interest in Gogol had been awakened by reviews of the Russian author's work published in *Revue des Deux Mondes*, a journal which the Brazilian writer leafed through on a regular basis, and which was read by some of his characters: Sophia, for example. According to Stolze, the Sainte-Beuve article mentioned above was the first to be published in France on Gogol. And Sainte-Beuve himself makes this clear when he states that: 'avant la traduction que publie M. Viardot, il est douteux qu'aucun Français eût jamais lu quelqu'une des productions originales de M. Gogol; j'étais dans ce cas comme tout le monde' [before the translation published by M. Viardot, it is doubtful that any French national had ever read any of M. Gogol's original works; I was in this respect like everyone else].[12]

However, in Sainte-Beuve's review Machado de Assis would not have found the elements of 'Diary of a Madman' which he used to compose *Quincas Borba*. Since the French critic considers 'Tarass Bulba' to be the most interesting narrative in the collection, he devotes the greater part of the review to a description of this story. Sainte-Beuve does not cite all of the stories. In fact, the only other narrative to which he refers, because of the contrast between it and 'Tarass Boulba', is 'Un ménage d'autrefois', a story 'qui peint la vie monotone et heureuse de deux époux dans la Petite-Russie, est pourtant d'un contraste heureux avec les scènes dures et sauvages de Boulba' [that depicts the monotonous and happy life of a married couple in Little Russia, is therefore a fortunate contrast to the harsh and wild scenes of Bulba] (Sainte-Beuve, *Revue*, 1854, p. 889).

I also consulted two other articles, also published in the *Revue des Deux Mondes*, which focus on Gogol, among other Russian writers.[13] The author of the first, Charles de Saint-Julien, does not devote much space to him because his interest lies in studying the work of Solohoupe. Along with Pushkin and Lermontov, Gogol is mentioned in the introductory summary on realist Russian literature. The comments concerning Gogol deal with aspects of the work in general and of his place in Russian literature: 'Nicolas Gogol se distingue des écrivains de son pays par une puissance d'analyse et de création à laquelle la pensée moscovite s'est rarement élevée' [Nikolai Gogol distinguishes himself amongst writers in his country by a power of analysis and creation to which the Moscow thought is rarely elevated].[14] Saint-Julien mentions 'Diary of a Madman' when he quotes the Russian critic Miloukouff:

> Pouchkine abondonna la société par égoïsme, Lermontoff la maudit par désespoir, Gogol pleure sur elle et souffre. Ses souffrances sont d'autant plus vives, qu'il la dérobe sous le manteau du rire, tantôt bruyant, maladif et nerveux, tantôt calme, paisible et empreint d'une ironie serenie. Tel on voit dans la dernière partie des 'Souvenirs d'un fou'... [sic] (Saint-Julien, p. 70)

> [Pushkin abandoned society out of selfishness; Lermontov curses it out of despair; Gogol weeps over it and suffers. His sufferings are all the sharper since he cloaks it under the mantle of laughter, now rowdy, sickly and nervy, now calm, placid and marked by a serene irony. That is what we see in the last part of 'Memories of a Mad Man' [sic].

Prosper Mérimée is the author of the other article consulted. The critic recognizes the value of Gogol's work and identifies the presence of social satire in the story:

> 'L'Histoire d'un fou' [sic] est tout à la fois une satire contre la société, un conte sentimental et une histoire médico-légale sur les phénomènes que présente une tête humaine qui se détraque. Je crois l'étude bien fait et fort graphiquement dépeinte, comme dirait M. Diafoirus, mais je n'aime pas le genre: la folie est un des ces malheurs qui touchent, mais qui dégoûtent.[15]

> ['The Story of a Mad Man' [sic] is at the same time a satire against society, a sentimental tale, and a medical-legal story about the characteristics displayed by a deranged human mind. I find the study well written and most graphically depicted, as M. Diafoirus would say, but I do not like the genre: madness is one of those misfortunes which concerns us, but which disgusts us.]

Mérimée also links Gogol's work to the tradition of the English humorists, who exercise a strong influence on the Brazilian writer's later work: 'il ne lui manque peut-être qu'une langue plus répandue pour obtenir en Europe une réputation égale à celle des meuilleurs *humoristes* anglais' [he perhaps wants only for a more widely known language to obtain in Europe a reputation equal to that of the best English humorists].[16] It is possible that we have identified in this critique the origin of Machado de Assis's interest in 'Diary of a Madman', or even of his interest in Gogol's work in general.

The comments of the three critics draw attention to important aspects of Gogol's work in general, such as his use of social satire and the pessimistic nature of his writing. They also associate the Russian writer with the English humorists, who were highly esteemed by the Brazilian author. In 'Diary of a Madman', Saint-Julien and Mérimée identify representative characteristics (positive or negative) of Gogol's work, to which they had access in translation. However, neither critic examines in detail the elements of the story's plot. Mérimée highlights the dual 'sentimental' and 'medical-legal' character of the narrative, which is also found in *Quincas Borba*. While 'the suggestion originating from "Diary of a Madman" included the main theme of the novel', as Gomes reveals, it would not have been sufficient for Machado de Assis to have read the articles in the *Revue des Deux Mondes* to be able to appropriate the theme of megalomania, the personification of the dog, and the name of Sophia (Gomes, 1858, p. 118–19). The intertextuality between the two narratives is so great that it cannot be doubted that Machado de Assis had access to the text of the story in one of the translations available in his time.

For the purposes of this work, it matters little whether the Brazilian writer read Gogol in German or in French, despite the differences evident between the two translations. Among the differences which I was able to detect between these versions, in making a rapid comparison, was the choice between using a form of dialogue on the one hand and indirect speech on the other, in translations of the same passage. For this study, it is sufficient to establish that the elements of the story's plot remain unaltered from one translation to the other, as I was able to confirm, although the language of the French translation seemed to me to be a little simplified. In addition, the diary form was conserved in both. It is true that in the French the date of one diary entry, that of day 25, is missing. But this is the result of a small editorial lapse: the date is missing, but the text is not, being incorporated into the entry corresponding to the previous day, that of 'Le janvier de la même année qui est venu après le février' [January of the same year which came after February]. One significant difference between the two translations lies in the names, including those of the characters. The name 'Sophie', however, is given, in this, its French form, in both the French and German translations.

The story

As the title itself indicates, 'Diary of a Madman' is a story in diary form written by a lunatic. Poprishchin is a clerk who struggles against the rigid and impersonal bureaucracy of the oppressive regime of Nicholas I. His main obligation is to copy documents and to sharpen the pencils of the director of his department, with whose daughter he falls in love. When the diary begins (3 December), he describes the efforts that he makes to become the *fiancé* of Sophie, the director's daughter, fruitlessly since his social position does not permit him to court her. This is particularly painful since Poprishchin feels himself to be an intellectually active man, one of literary sensibility, and superior to his colleagues, whom he despises. However, he is confident that he can use his talents to reach a higher social position and thereby conquer Sophie.[17]

The first signs of madness are already becoming apparent in the character as Poprishchin discovers that Sophie's puppy, Medgi, not only speaks but also writes letters to another puppy by the name of Fidèle. His curiosity over the content of the letters leads him to steal them. He starts transcribing to his diary some excerpts which contain information about Sophie. Through the letters, the protagonist believes he is able to penetrate the private life of the young woman. Medgi writes: 'Je suis prête à te faire part de tout ce qui se passe dans notre maison. Je t'ai déjà dit quelques mots du principal personnage, que Sophie appelle papa. C'est un homme très-étrange' [I am ready to tell you everything that happens in our house. I have already told you a few words about the main character, whom Sophie call papa. He is a very strange man]. And Poprishchin's curiosity intensifies: 'Ah! Voyons, voyons, que dit-elle de Sophie. Oh! oh! rien, rien, silence. Continuons' [Oh! Let's see what she is saying about Sophie. Oh! Nothing, she says nothing. Let's go on].

Through the letters, the protagonist discovers that Sophie despises him ('Sophie ne peut jamais s'empêcher de rire quand elle le regarde' [Sophie can never stop herself from laughing when she looks at him]) and that she is set to marry a gentleman of the city: 'Sophie est folle de lui; papa très-content [...] la noce se fera bientôt, car le papa veut absolument marier sa fille à un général, ou bien à un gentilhomme de la chambre, ou bien à un colonel militaire' [Sophie is crazy about him; papa is very happy [...] the marriage will be soon, because papa wants very badly to marry his daughter to a general, or to a gentleman of the bedchamber, or to at least to an army colonel].[18]

After he suffers this last frustration, the character's madness acquires all of its characteristics. On 5 December, Poprishchin notes in his diary that he has read in the newspaper the news that the throne of Spain is vacant — Gogol is referring to the dispute over the successor to Ferdinand VII, who had died in 1833. Poprishchin is perplexed when he learns that there is no successor to the Spanish throne and believes that the true king would be living incognito in some foreign country. On April 43, 2000 (the diary dates become confused from this entry onwards), the protagonist is convinced that he himself is the successor to the throne of Spain. After definitively assuming the identity of Ferdinand VIII, Poprishchin cuts his military uniform and makes a royal robe from it, in which he can finally appear in public. The character is taken to an asylum, but he thinks he is at the Royal Spanish Palace. Poprishchin believes he has fallen into the hands of the Inquisition when he is subjected to an enquiry and cold baths. In the last diary entry, the character declares that he cannot stand the torture any longer. He begs to be saved and to be transported by a *troika* to the arms of his mother, where he will be able to free himself from persecution.

Historical context and literary recreation

If we compare *Quincas Borba* to 'Diary of a Madman' in terms of the nature of the relations between the characters, we perceive that the social network in the Brazilian novel is much more intricate and at the same time much less hierarchical than that of the society depicted by Gogol. Poprishchin struggles against the rigid and impersonal bureaucracy of the oppressive regime of Nicholas I. As we saw in Chapter 2 of this book, *Quincas Borba* in its turn depicts a changing society. According to Gilda de Mello e Sousa, Machado de Assis's novel offers as a whole a dynamic vision of change in the position of individuals who are valued in accordance to what they own in relation to others. Souza compares the social mobility in *Quincas Borba* to the symmetrical figures of the kaleidoscope, which can be continually modified or recomposed as the instrument is turned:

> [*Quincas Borba*] dá-nos uma visão preciosa desse recompor-se constante do caleidoscópio, com os afastamentos infindáveis das amizades antigas, o apego sôfrego dos mais modestos aos hábitos da classe dominante, amargura dos que se negam a aceitar a figura movediça da sociedade.[19]
>
> [[*Philosopher or Dog?*] gives us an invaluable vision of the constant rearrangement which is characteristic of the kaleidoscope, as seen in the ceaseless cooling off

of old friendships, the avid attachment of the most modest to the habits of the dominant class, and the bitterness of those who refuse to accept the changing shape of society.]

We will return later to the image of the kaleidoscope when we examine the literary resources employed by Machado de Assis to realize his plans for depicting in fiction the unending motion of the social rise and fall of a group of individuals. Even so, we cannot fail to mention here that the idea of the kaleidoscope lies at the centre of John Gledson's interpretation of *Quincas Borba*. For Gledson, the novelty of *Quincas Borba* in relation to *Memórias póstumas de Brás Cubas* resides exactly in the fact that *Quincas Borba* represents, as we saw above, a society in flux, dominated by commerce and not by the relations of the landowning bourgeois. Gledson observes that the plot of *Quincas Borba* is much more complex than that of *Memórias póstumas de Brás Cubas*, the first novel from the so-called 'later' period of Machado de Assis's work. This is because *Memórias póstumas de Brás Cubas* is made up of self-sufficient episodes and anecdotes, and also because the secondary characters do not play a significant role in the plot.[20]

In addition, Alfredo Bosi's summary of Machado de Assis's work as a whole can be applied to *Quincas Borba*: the novel offers a portrait of interpersonal relations through the 'smallest social difference.' As Alfredo Bosi writes:

> quem percorre a narrativa de Machado, que cobre a vida do Rio dos meados ao fim do século XIX, reconhece uma teia de relações sociais, quer intrafamiliais (na acepção ampla de parentesco, compadrio e agregação), quer de vizinhança, profissão e vida pública entre pares ou entre pessoas situadas em níveis distintos. E o que salta à vista no desenho dessa teia? Relações assimétricas compõem a maioria dos enredos machadianos; e levando em conta a dimensão subjetiva da assimetria, pode-se afirmar que esta se encontra em toda parte e dentro de cada personagem. A experiência do gradiente social é aqui fundamental. [...] Olhando de perto, vê-se que nesse contexto de diferenças predomina o tratamento do intervalo social menor. Daí, a presença apenas discreta do par de extremos senhor-escravo, mas a frequência significativa do par senhor-agregado, bem como a singular ocorrência do par forro-escravo, o que acusa a violência real das interações mal dissimulada pela distância aparentemente diminuída.[21]

> [whoever examines Machado de Assis's narrative, which depicts the life in Rio in the second half of the nineteenth century, recognizes a web of social relations, be they relations between family members (in the widest sense of kinship, godparents and household), neighbours, colleagues, or relations in public life between equals or people situated at different levels. And what is it that stands out in the design of this web? Asymmetrical relations make up the majority of his plots; and bearing in mind the subjective dimension of asymmetry, it can be stated that this is found everywhere, and inside each character. The experience of the social gradient is fundamental here. [...] Examining it at close hand, it can be seen that in this context of differences, the treatment of the smallest social difference predominates. As such, we see that the extreme master–slave pairing is shown only discreetly, whereas the landlord–dependent pairing occurs with significant frequency, and the freedman–slave pairing occurs just once, which reveals the real violence of interactions barely disguised through a seemingly reduced distance.]

The social gap between the characters in *Quincas Borba* is no different from the situation described above by Bosi. As we have already seen in Chapter 2, the arriviste Palha, for example, is a tradesman of middle-class origin with a good head for business. Sophia is the daughter of a civil servant and so also belongs to the expanding middle class. Rubião, on the other hand, rises at the start of the novel from the position of employee to that of sole heir to Quincas Borba's fortune, positioning himself in the category of the rich through inheritance rather than work. The social gap between Rubião and Palha is very fluid. Both have modest origins and aspire to climb socially, but the fortunes of each man continually change throughout the novel.

In comparison with 'Diary of a Madman', the social hierarchy in the Brazilian novel has been reduced to a minimum. In addition to social hierarchy, the barrier that separates private from public life has also been reduced. Rubião moves freely around the inside of Palha's house, which Poprishchin is unable to do in Gogol's story. Rubião does not have direct access to Sophia's bedroom, but he often finds himself alone with the lady in other parts of the house. Together they can gaze at the Southern Cross from the garden, or even travel by coach on their own. As mentioned in Chapter 3, the coach is another private space which, when the curtains are closed, protects the passengers from the curious gaze of the crowd on the street, as is the case in the episode towards the end of the novel.

The Narrative Kaleidoscope

In what way does Machado de Assis construct this more complex plot? Which literary resources does the writer choose from among those available in order to represent a social microcosm? The choice of a third-person narrator certainly has its advantages for the novelist who does not wish to highlight just one version of the story, as happens, for example, with the protagonist–narrator Brás Cubas, and Bento in *Dom Casmurro*.

In 'Diary of a Madman', Gogol uses the letter as a narrative device. In the absence of a third-person narrator, the letter makes it possible to access the private life of Sophie and the opinions of characters who belong to a network of social relations in which Poprishchin does not participate, due to his position in the social hierarchy. We readers therefore have access not only to the protagonist's point of view, but also to the points of view of Medgi and Sophie, even though the letters are no more than the product of Poprishchin's imagination. The opinions of Medgi and Sophie represent a doubling of the voice of the protagonist, a sign of his madness.

Unlike Gogol, Machado de Assis opted to narrate *Quincas Borba* neither in the form of a diary nor in the first person, as he did in *Memórias póstumas de Brás Cubas* and *Dom Casmurro*. He did not even choose a participating narrator, as he did in *Casa velha*, since his aim in *Quincas Borba* is not to tell a story from the point of view of just one person. Rather, the plot of the novel is constructed by revealing the impressions retained by each character of the same event, and the opinion of each character in relation to the others. As in a kaleidoscope, the novelist multiplies the narrative points of view, thus representing a changing society from not just one point of view but from the sum of the points of view of the characters.

The Kaleidoscopic Narrative

By examining two examples, we will see the way in which Machado de Assis constructs the plot of the novel. As the essential elements do not change from the first version to the second, I shall always quote from the book version, even when the numbering of the chapters does not coincide. This chapter, which is the first in which I compare the two versions of the novel, starts, in this sense, by examining what did *not* change when the novel was moved from the serial form to the book.[22]

At the start of the narrative, Machado de Assis gives prominence to two social encounters: the encounter in Palha's house, in which Rubião invites Sophia to gaze at the Southern Cross; and the ball at Camacho's house, in which Sophia dances for more than fifteen minutes with Carlos Maria. The novelist constructs the plot of the novel around these two events, i.e., around the intricate web of suspicions between the characters concerning the supposed affair between, in the first place, Sophia and Rubião and, subsequently, Sophia and Carlos Maria.

In chapters 34 to 50 of the book version, the narrator examines the encounter in Santa Thereza at Sophia's house.[23] In the garden scene, Rubião 'chamou aos olhos de Sofia as estrelas da terra, e às estrelas os olhos do céu' [called Sophia's eyes terrestrial stars, and he called the stars celestial eyes] and he asked the young woman 'que, todas as noites, às dez horas, fitasse o Cruzeiro; ele o fitaria também, e os pensamentos de ambos iriam achar-se juntos, íntimos, entre Deus e os homens' [to look at the Southern Cross every night. He would look at it too, and their thoughts would join there in intimacy between God and men].[24] Dona Tonica is the first person to feel suspicious:

> Não tardou em perceber que os olhos de Rubião e os de Sofia caminhavam uns para os outros; notou, porém, que os de Sofia eram menos frequentes e menos demorados, fenômeno que lhe pareceu explicável, pelas cautelas naturais da situação. Podia ser que se amassem.[25]
>
> [She soon perceived that Rubião's glances and Sophia's were travelling toward one another; she noticed, however, that Sophia's were less frequent and less lingering, a phenomenon that could be explained, she thought, by the caution required under the circumstances. It could be that they were in love.][26]

At home, talking to herself, the spinster swears revenge and threatens to tell all to Palha: 'Conto-lhe tudo, — ia pensando — ou de viva voz, ou por uma carta... Carta não; digo-lhe tudo um dia, em particular'[27] ['I'll tell him everything,' she thought, 'either in person or in a letter. No, not in a letter. I'll tell him everything someday, in private'].[28] Major Siqueira might also have noticed something, Rubião suspects:

> A luz do fósforo deu à cara do major uma expressão de escárnio, ou de outra coisa menos dura, mas não menos adversa. Rubião sentiu correr-lhe um frio pela espinha. Teria ouvido? visto? adivinhado? Estava ali um indiscreto, um mexeriqueiro?[29]
>
> [The light from the match gave the Major's face a look of mockery, or, if it was not quite mockery, it was something no less hostile. Rubião felt a chill run along his spine. Could he have heard, seen, guessed? Was this fellow a tattler, a meddler?][30]

Still at the party, we notice that Sophia considers Rubião's behaviour to be insulting, but she hides this feeling because her husband had told her that they must treat him with 'special consideration'. In her room, after all of the guests have left, she compares Rubião to the Devil: 'Então o diabo também é matuto, porque ele pareceu-me nada menos que o diabo. E pedir-me que a certa hora olhasse para o Cruzeiro, a fim de que as nossas almas se encontrassem?'[31] ['Then the Devil's a country bumpkin, too, because he was the very Devil. What about his asking me to look at the Southern Cross at a certain time so that our souls might meet?].[32] Palha, however, cannot break off relations with Rubião, as his wife wishes, because he owes him a lot of money:

> — Mas, meu amor, eu devo-lhe muito dinheiro.
> Sofia tapou-lhe a boca e olhou assustada para o corredor.
> — Está bom, disse, acabemos com isto. Verei como ele se comporta, e tratarei de ser mais fria... Nesse caso, tu é que não deves mudar, para que não pareça que sabes o que se deu. Verei o que posso fazer.[33]

> ['But my love, I owe him a great deal of money.'
> Sophia clapped her hand over his mouth and looked toward the corridor with alarm.
> 'Very well', she said, 'let's be done with this. I'll see how he behaves, and I'll try to be more distant — In that case, you mustn't change, so that it will not appear that you know what happened. I'll see what I can do.']][34]

Chapters 69 to 78 describe the ball on Arcos Road, at Camacho's house, in which Carlos Maria dances for more than fifteen minutes with Sophia.[35] Once again, the narrator describes in detail the impressions that the characters involved in the plot retain from the party, on the basis of which suspicion concerning the affair, this time between Sophia and Carlos Maria, is constructed. Rubião 'começava a crer possível ou real uma ideia que o atormentava desde muitos dias. Agora, a conversação dilatada, os modos dela'[36] [was beginning to believe that an idea that had tormented him for days might be a possibility or even an actuality, and now the long conversation and her manner].[37] Maria Benedicta, who secretly loves Carlos Maria, realizes that her cousin is an obstacle to her plans to win Carlos Maria's attention. The following morning, she agrees to the idea of returning to the country. Her country cousin is eaten up with jealousy, but Sophia does not notice. Maria Benedicta insinuates that her cousin enjoys dancing so that she can have a man holding her body: 'Não gosto que um homem me aperte o corpo ao seu corpo, e ande comigo, assim, à vista dos outros. Tenho vexame'[38] ['I don't like to have a man hold my body close to his and go around with me like that in front of everybody. It makes me ashamed'].[39]

The small conflict between the two characters stops when Sophia talks of Palha's plans to have her cousin married in the city. Out of pure selfishness, however, Sophia does not reveal that the much-desired fiancé is Rubião, which causes Maria Benedicta to conclude erroneously that the suitor is Carlos Maria, and that she had been the subject of the conversation between the young man and Sophia during the polka. The truth, however, is that no one at the dance, besides Sophia and Carlos Maria, could hear the conversation between the dancing couple. Carlos Maria made a flattering remark to Sophia: 'O mar batia com força, é verdade, mas o meu coração não batia menos rijamente; — com esta diferença que o mar é estúpido, bate sem saber por quê, e o meu coração sabe que batia pela senhora'[40] ['The sea was beating violently; to be sure, but my heart was beating even more wildly — only the sea is stupid, and doesn't know why it beats, and my heart knew that it was beating for you'].[41] The reader will later discover that Carlos Maria's story, in which Sofia piously believed, was a complete lie. The man confesses to himself that he was foolish to have invented what happened that night on the beach opposite Sophia's house: 'Quem diabo me mandou dizer semelhante coisa'[42] ['What the devil made me say such a thing?'].[43]

We see that Machado de Assis uses a third person narrator to reveal not only the events but also the impressions that each character retains of that event. In order to construct the plot, he multiplies the narrative points of view, as in a kaleidoscope, and creates a complete picture of the interaction between the characters during these two social encounters. Consequently, the different narrative prisms correspond to the symmetrical figures of the kaleidoscope, which alternate continually while the narrator changes the angle from which the same event is depicted. It is the narrator who, in this way, causes the kaleidoscope to rotate. It is a very different narrative procedure from that used in *Memórias póstumas de Brás Cubas* (and, subsequently, in *Dom Casmurro*), in which the narrator–protagonist sees everything from his point of view and narrates, in a parody of Sterne, his own life and opinions.

Reliable or Unreliable Narrator

The choice of an omniscient narrator, who provides the reader with a much broader vision than that possessed by each character individually, is part of the process of literary recreation of 'Diary of a Madman'. The omniscient narrator allows the reader to reconstruct, as in a mosaic, the actual event based on the impressions that each character retains of this event, or the opinions that each character has of the others. In this way, because the plot of the novel is built around multiple points of view, the reader is allowed to know much more than do the characters. The reader's field of vision in fact includes the narrative prism of all of the characters. With regard to the plot of the novel, I would say that the reader knows as much as the narrator.

Here we are touching on the question of the position of the reader in relation to that of the narrator of *Quincas Borba*, a subject which has been widely discussed in the critical history of the novel. In his pioneering article on the two versions, for example, Kinnear believes that in moving from the serial form to that of the book, Machado de Assis makes a conscious move towards narrative unreliability. Kinnear bases his argument on the rewriting of the episodes which make up the supposed affair between Sophia and Carlos Maria. According to Kinnear, it is very clear to the reader of the serial that Rubião is deceiving himself by imagining the affair. In the second version, the reader 'is never entirely sure that there is no affair until the new chapter 106, when he is as much the victim as is Rubião.'[44] For Kinnear, the reliability of the narrator is in this way defined as the propensity of the narrator to believe that there is only one reality which can be captured by observation. According to this view, the reliable narrator believes, and makes the reader believe, in the ability of fiction to recreate reality. Chapter 106 is central to his interpretation because the identical nature of the text and numbering in the two versions proves that Machado de Assis began rewriting before the publication of the serial had been finished. It cannot really be a coincidence, because the somewhat disorganized numbering of the chapters in the serial was already apparent in no. 121, which was published on 31 July 1889.

Machado de Assis interrupted the publication of the novel between the months of August and November 1889, a period in which, according to Kinnear's hypothesis, the novelist probably devoted his time to revision. When the publication of the novel begins again, on 30 November 1889, the serial does not continue to use the numbering employed previously. Rather than continuing with chapter 122, we have number 106. When Machado de Assis revised the material published previously in *A Estação* he was already thinking about the book, and so he ensured that the numbering of the serial and the book were the same from this point in the narrative.

Kinnear's statement needs to be discussed in stages. In the first place, it is beyond doubt that in the first version the narrator is reliable and that, consequently, the reader is not deceived with regard to the plot of the novel, as has already been proven here. The question now is to verify whether or not, in moving from the serial form to that of the book, there really was a change from a reliable to an unreliable narrator with respect to the construction of the suspicions regarding the affair. I do not believe that this actually occurs, because the reliability of the narrator is intrinsically linked to the way in which Machado de Assis constructs the plot of the novel, and this does not change between the serial and the book. In both versions the reader is placed, as in the theatre, in the position of spectator and, I repeat, is not deceived with regard to the plot of the novel. The reader is led to attune her or his opinions with those of the narrator so as not to judge the characters in accordance with traditional moral values, as we shall see in Chapter 7 of this book.

In order to make the reader believe in the story of the affair between Carlos Maria and Sophia (and, consequently, in the story of the coachman), the field of vision must be limited to that of Rubião and the various narrative prisms generated by the exposition of other characters' points of view must be ignored. Let us examine two examples which prove that, because Machado de Assis maintained or even emphasized the kaleidoscopic vision of the narrative when rewriting, the reader's point of view is not limited to that of Rubião. Before chapter 106, the reader of the second version is made aware that Sophia's concerns are no longer focused either on Carlos Maria or Rubião. This is the episode in which Rubião goes to Sophia's house on the occasion of the death of Maria Benedicta's mother. Sophia tells him of her plans to organize a women's committee to collect donations for the victims of the Alagoas epidemic. The narrator reveals everything to us: the charitable and at the same time egocentric nature of the project. Sophia now dreams of achieving social prominence through the Alagoas Committee.

> Era tudo verdade. Era também verdade que a comissão ia pôr em evidência a pessoa de Sofia, e dar-lhe um empurrão para cima. As senhoras escolhidas não eram da roda da nossa dama, e só uma a cumprimentava; mas, por intermédio de certa viúva, que brilhara entre 1840 e 1850, e conservava do seu tempo as saudades e o apuro, conseguira que todas entrassem naquela obra de caridade. Desde alguns dias não pensara em outra coisa. Às vezes, à noite, antes do chá, parecia dormir na cadeira de balanço; não dormia, fechava os olhos para considerar-se a si mesma, no meio das companheiras, pessoas de qualidade. Compreende-se que este fosse o assunto principal da conversação; mas, Sofia tornava de quando em quando ao presente amigo.[45]
>
> [It was all true. It was true too, that the committee was going to bring Sofia to the fore and give her a push upward. The women selected were not of our lady's circle; only one was a speaking acquaintance; but through the intervention of a certain widow, who had shone between 1840 and 1850 and who still preserved the nostalgia and refinement of her day, she had succeeded in getting them all to go into that charitable undertaking. For some days she had thought of nothing else. Sometimes in the evening before tea she would appear to be asleep in the rocking chair, but she was not asleep; she had her eyes closed so that she might see herself in the midst of her companions, who were all persons of quality. It's quite understandable, then, but this was the chief topic of conversation. From time to time, however, Sofia would turn to our friend.][46]

At this stage, Sofia despises neither Rubião nor Carlos Maria. She still treats the former with special attention, as her husband had asked her to do in chapter 50; and she shows similar concern for the latter because he will come to marry Maria Benedicta. But she does no more than this, because the lady is now caught up with noble dames and philanthropic enterprises in order to attain not only her monetary goals but also the status required to enter high-class society. The narrator reveals the clear distinction between appearance and hidden intentions.

The quotation above was taken from the book version. It is substantially different from the corresponding section in the serial. In the process of rewriting, Machado de Assis strengthened the kaleidoscopic vision of the narrative. Rather than focusing on Palha's participation in the scheme, in the book version the writer goes deeper into Sofia's thoughts. Let us now compare it with the same passage in the serial version:

> Era tudo verdade. Era também verdade que esta comissão ia pôr em evidência a pessoa de Sofia, e dar-lhe um empurrão para cima. Uma titular, senhora idosa e recolhida, presidiria a comissão; Sofia tinha outras senhoras em vista, pessoas mui da moda, e, por intermédio da titular alcançaria que todas aceitassem aquela obra de misericórdia. Trabalhariam juntas, pediriam juntas, comeriam juntas, às vezes; o costume traria a comunhão. Poder-se-ia crer que esta ideia nascera na cabeça do Palha; mas era dela mesma, original. Palha o que fez foi aprovar, animar e trabalhar. Não lhe faltaria com dinheiro para as despesas necessárias; pôr-lhe-ia um coupé às ordens, dar-lhe-ia os vestidos que precisasse; estimulou-a, aconselhou-a, cuidou das carteirinhas de notas, do papel, da circular que devia ter, ao alto, (ideia dele) as armas da presidente...[47]
>
> [It was all true. It was true too, that the committee was going to bring Sofia to the fore and give her a push upward. A titled noblewoman, an aged and

> withdrawn lady, would preside over the committee; Sophia had other ladies in her sights, very fashionable people, and, through the intervention of the noblewoman, she would succeed in getting them all to accept that charitable undertaking. They would work together, raise money together, sometimes eat together; the activity would bring companionship. One might have thought that this idea had come from Palha's head; but it was hers, an original one. What Palha did was approve, encourage and work. He would not lack money for the necessary expenses; he would put a coupé at her disposal, give her the dresses that she needed; he encouraged her, advised her, took care of the box of calling-cards, the paper, and the circular letter that should bear the committee president's coat of arms at the top (his idea)...]

The writer gives more space not only to the female character but also to her enterprising spirit and the independence that she retains in relation to her husband. One of the advantages of the kaleidoscopic narrative viewpoint is that the secondary characters, particularly the female ones, gain in complexity as more space is devoted to them. We have not just one complex female character, as in *Helena* and *Dom Casmurro*, but at least four: Sophia, Maria Benedicta, Dona Tonica and Dona Fernanda, who are all very different from each other.

A further example which sheds doubt on Kinnear's argument can be found in chapter 105. It is now the seventh day after the death of Maria Benedicta's mother. Rubião returns to Sofia's house, with his suspicions intensified as a result of the envelope addressed by the lady to Carlos Maria, which the messenger had dropped in Rubião's doorway and which he erroneously assumes to be a love letter. The subject of the letter carried by Rubião leads Sophia to recall her encounters with Carlos Maria, and his jokes, and to wonder why the 'adventure' resulted in nothing:

> Nunca Sofia compreendera o malogro daquela aventura. O homem parecia querer-lhe deveras, e ninguém o obrigava a declará-lo tão atrevidamente, nem a passar-lhe pelas janelas, alta noite, segundo lhe ouviu. Recordou ainda outros encontros, palavras furtadas, olhos cálidos e compridos, e não chegava a entender que toda essa paixão acabasse em nada. Provavelmente, não haveria nenhuma; puro galanteio; — quando muito, um modo de apurar as suas forças atrativas... Natureza de pelintra, de cínico, de fútil.[48]

> [Sophia had never understood why the adventure had failed. The man seemed to be truly fond of her, and no one had compelled him to declare himself so boldly, or pass by her windows late at night, as she heard him say that he did. She even recalled other meetings, stolen words, ardent glances, and she could not understand how all that passion could come to nothing. Probably there was none; probably it was pure gallantry, at most a means of perfecting his powers of attention... His was a cynical, conceited nature.][49]

Sophia finally reaches the conclusion that Carlos Maria was a cynic. The reader, however, has already been warned that the man has been lying since the morning following the ball at Camacho's house. The quotation above, which is identical in both versions, has the attribute of synthesis and reiterates that there has never been any affair between Carlos Maria and Sophia. Only the inattentive reader, to whom the narrator addresses himself in chapter 106, could really have believed in the affair:

... ou, mais propriamente, capítulo em que o leitor, desorientado, não pode combinar as tristezas de Sofia com a anedota do cocheiro. E pergunta confuso: — Então a entrevista da rua da Harmonia, Sofia, Carlos Maria, esse chocalho de rimas sonoras e delinquentes é tudo calúnia? Calúnia do leitor e do Rubião, não do pobre cocheiro, que não proferiu nomes, não chegou sequer a contar uma anedota verdadeira... É o que terias visto, se lesses com pausa. Sim, desgraçado, adverte bem que era inverossímil que um homem, indo a uma aventura daquelas, fizesse parar o tílburi diante da casa pactuada. Seria pôr uma testemunha ao crime.[50]

[... or more properly, the chapter in which the reader, disoriented, is unable to reconcile Sophia's distress with the tilbury driver's story, and asks in bewilderment: 'Then the Harmonia Street tryst, Sofia, Carlos Maria, that whole clangor of noisy, delinquent rhymes was all calumny?' Calumny on the part of the reader and on Rubião's part, not on the part of the poor driver, who did not give any names or even tell a real story. You would have seen that, had you read carefully. Yes, unhappy reader, note that it was unlikely that a man bent upon an adventure of that sort would stop the tilbury right in front of the house of assignation. That would provide a witness to the crime.][51]

As Kinnear observes, in the process of rewriting Machado de Assis makes characters disappear or become less important, and also eliminates some episodes.[52] The critic does not mention, however, that some chapters were expanded. Kinnear is even less interested in the hypothesis that by eliminating, suppressing, expanding or reordering episodes or chapters, Machado de Assis was adapting the text to be read in one volume rather than in serial form. In the last three chapters of this book we will examine the significance of these rewriting operations in terms of the redefining of the standard by which the novel is read. Machado de Assis was searching for an outcome which did not tend towards the serial form in its characteristics. However, while he could not find a solution to the conflict, the writer allowed the narrator to insist on Rubião's suspicion in order to gain time, unfolding the narrative in episodes which resort to the melodramatic and which, later on, would subsequently be eliminated or condensed. This was the resource used by the writer to ensure that the plot remained compelling before he found a solution to the narrative impasse. In rewriting the episodes which increase Rubião's suspicions, Machado de Assis changed focus, concentrating on the development of the madness of the character who is now the protagonist.

Machado's aim in constructing a narrative kaleidoscope is, above all, realist. He creates the perfect portrait of the complicated nature of the relations between individuals: there is a great abyss between what the characters actually are and think, and what they represent in society. One result of this is that the characters do not truly know each other — even those who share the intimacy of marriage, as do Palha and Sofia, or Dona Fernanda and Theophilo. Also, as the characters retain different impressions of the same event, the multiplicity of viewpoints becomes more significant than the event itself. We perceive that we are very close to *Dom Casmurro* in respect of Machado's treatment of the relationship between real and imagined events.[53]

Machado's narrative skill in *Quincas Borba* (and, consequently, the universal dimension of the novel) lies in his ability to reveal, through a multiplicity of viewpoints, the true nature of the relations between individuals: like characters in fiction, men only know each other partially. In the play of social relations, everyone is wearing a mask. Rubião might be the exception who proves the rule. His sincerity goes hand-in-hand with his madness, which leads us to conclude that, for the society depicted in the novel, sincerity is a sign of foolishness.

Notes to Chapter 4

1. Eugênio Gomes, 'Machado de Assis e Gogol', in *Machado de Assis* (Rio de Janeiro: Livraria São José, 1958), pp. 120–27.
2. Eugênio Gomes's article is not quoted in any of the studies on *Quincas Borba* listed below: Kinnear, 'Machado de Assis: To Believe or Not to Believe?'; Passos, *O Napoleão de Botafogo*; Guimarães, *Os leitores de Machado de Assis*; Flávio Loureiro Chaves, *O mundo social do Quincas Borba* (Porto Alegre: Movimento, 1974); Teresa Pires Vara, *A mascadara sublime: estudo de Quincas Borba* (São Paulo: Duas Cidades, 1976); Gledson, *Machado de Assis: ficção e história*; Ivo Barbieri (org.), *Ler e reescrever Quincas Borba* (Rio de Janeiro: EdUERJ, 2003).
3. Gomes, pp. 120–21.
4. Cf. José Luís Jobim (org.), *A Biblioteca de Machado de Assis* (Rio de Janeiro: Topbooks, Academia Brasileira de Letras, 2001).
5. '[Machado de Assis] aderira ao grupo de João Ribeiro, Capistrano de Abreu e José Veríssimo que denodamente enveredaram pelo estudo do alemão, depois de aplicar-se ao do inglês com o professor Alexander, com quem, em solteira, minha mãe e as irmãs mais velhas o haviam aprendido' [[Machado de Assis] belonged to the group comprising João Ribeiro, Capistrano de Abreu and José Veríssimo, who daringly endeavoured to study German after applying themselves to the study of English with the teacher Alexander, with whom, when unmarried, my mother and elder sisters had learnt the language] (Francisca de Basto Cordeiro, *Machado de Assis na intimidade*, 2nd edn, rev. by the author (Rio de Janeiro: Pongetti, 1965), p. 53).
6. *Bons dias! Crônicas (1888–1889)*, edition, introduction and notes by John Gledson (São Paulo: Editora da UNICAMP, Editora Hucitec, 1990), pp. 57–59. See particularly p. 58, n. 6.
7. Cf. Jean-Michel Massa, 'A biblioteca de Machado de Assis', and Glória Vianna, 'Revendo a biblioteca de Machado de Assis', both in José Luís Jobim (org.). *A biblioteca de Machado de Assis*, p. 69–75, 125, 272.
8. Eugênio Gomes, *Machado de Assis*, pp. 116–17. The full name of the short story is 'Viy ou le roi de Gnomes'.
9. Louis Viardot, 'Préface'. In: Nicolas Gogol, *Nouvelles choisies* (Paris: Hachette, 1853), pp. v–vi.
10. With regard to the quality and faithfulness of Viadort's translation of Gogol's original, see Helmut Stolze, *Die Französiche Gogolrezeption* (Vienna and Cologne: Böhlau Verlag, 1974), p. 18.
11. Sainte-Beuve, 'Revue littéraire: *Nouvelles russes*, par M. Nicolas Gogol', *La Revue des Deux Mondes*, Nouvelle série, 12 (1845), 883–89 (p. 889).
12. Ibidem, p. 883.
13. Nikolai Gogol was actually of Ukrainian origin.
14. Charles de Saint-Julien, 'La Littérature en Russie. Le Comte W. Solohoupe', *La Revue des Deux Mondes*, Nouvelle période, 12 (1851), 70–74 (p. 70).
15. Prosper Mérimée, 'La Littérature de Russie. Nicolas Gogol', *La Revue des Deux Mondes*, Nouvelle période, 12 (1851), p. 631.
16. Ibid.
17. Proper names are spelt as they are in the French translation.
18. 'Les Mémoires d'un fou', *Nouvelles choisies*, 1853, pp. 21, 22, 25, 26.
19. Souza, pp. 114–15.
20. Gledson, *Machado de Assis: ficção e história*, p. 82. See also the same critic's *The Deceptive Realism of Machado de Assis*, p. 22.
21. Alfredo Bosi, *Machado de Assis: o enigma do olhar* (São Paulo: Ática, 1999), pp. 153–54.
22. In this chapter, all quotations from *Quincas Borba* will be taken from *Quincas Borba* (1975), whose base text is the third edition of the novel in book form (1899). When there are variants in *Quincas Borba apêndice*, these will be specified in a footnote.

23. *Philosopher or Dog?*, pp. 43–73; *Quincas Borba*, pp. 142–68; *A Estação*, 15 November 1886 to 28 February 1887, chaps 32–50; *Quincas Borba apêndice*, pp. 35–52.
24. *Quincas Borba*, chaps 39 and 41, pp. 147, 149; *A Estação*, 30 November 1886, chap. 38, 15 December 1886, chap. 40; *Quincas Borba apêndice*, pp. 39, 41; *Philosopher or Dog?*, p. 50, 52.
25. *Quincas Borba*, chap. 37, p. 145; *A Estação*, 30 November 1886, chap. 36; *Quincas Borba apêndice*, p. 38.
26. *Philosopher or Dog?*, p. 48.
27. *Quincas Borba*, chap. 43, p. 153; *A Estação*, 31 December 1886, chap. 42; *Quincas Borba apêndice*, p. 45.
28. *Philosopher or Dog?*, p. 57.
29. *Quincas Borba*, chap. 42, p. 151; *A Estação*, 31 December 1886, chap. 41 (continuation); *Quincas Borba apêndice*, p. 43. Variants: *A:* um bisbilhoteiro, um denunciante?
30. *Philosopher or Dog?*, p. 55. Variants: *A:* a meddler, an accuser?
31. *Quincas Borba*, chap. 50, p. 164; *A Estação*, 15 February 1887, chap. 50; *Quincas Borba apêndice*, p. 50.
32. *Philosopher or Dog?*, p. 70.
33. *Quincas Borba*, chap. 50, pp. 167–68; *A Estação*, 15 February 1887, chap. 50 (continuation); *Quincas Borba apêndice*, p. 52. Variants: *A, B:* Está bom, disse, não falemos mais nisto. Verei como ele se comporta; *A, B:* sabes alguma coisa. Verei o que posso fazer.
34. *Philosopher or Dog?*, pp. 72–73. Variants: *A, B:* 'Very well,' she said, let's talk no more of this. I'll see how he behaves; *A, B:* it will not appear that you know something. I'll see what I can do.
35. *Philosopher or Dog?*, pp. 101–15; *Quincas Borba*, pp. 192–204; *A Estação*, 15 July to 15 October 1887, chaps 69 to 79 (continuation); *Quincas Borba apêndice*, pp. 69–83.
36. *Quincas Borba*, chap. 70, pp. 196–97; *A Estação*, 31 July 1887, chap. 70; *Quincas Borba apêndice*, p. 73.
37. *Philosopher or Dog?*, p. 105.
38. *Quincas Borba*, chap. 77, p. 203; *A Estação*, 31 August 1887, chap. 75 (continuation); *Quincas Borba apêndice*, p. 77.
39. *Philosopher or Dog?*, p. 113.
40. *Quincas Borba*, chap. 69, p. 195; *A Estação*, 31 July 1887, chap. 69 (continuation); *Quincas Borba apêndice*, p. 72.
41. *Philosopher or Dog?*, p. 104.
42. *Quincas Borba*, chap. 75, p. 202; *A Estação*, 15 October 1887, chap. 79 (continuation); *Quincas Borba apêndice*, p. 83.
43. *Philosopher or Dog?*, 111.
44. Kinnear, p. 58.
45. *Quincas Borba*, chap. 92, p. 220.
46. *Philosopher or Dog?*, p. 132.
47. *A Estação*, 31 October 1888, chap. 96; *Quincas Borba apêndice*, p. 109.
48. *Quincas Borba*, chap. 105, p. 235; *A Estação*, 31 July 1889, cap. 120; *Quincas Borba apêndice*, p. 134.
49. *Philosopher or Dog?*, p. 148.
50. *Quincas Borba*, chap. 106, p. 236; *A Estação*, 30 November 1889, chap. 106; *Quincas Borba apêndice*, p. 137.
51. *Philosopher or Dog?*, p. 150.
52. Kinnear, p. 56.
53. On this subject see Antônio Cândido, 'Esquema de Machado de Assis', in *Vários escritos*, 3ª edição revista e ampliada (São Paulo: Duas Cidades, 1995), pp. 17–39, (p. 25).

CHAPTER 5

❖

The First Version: Under the Sign of the Serial

This chapter shows that what caused the author difficulty during the writing of the serial was above all the fact that the decision to use an omniscient narrator, who occupies himself by turns with several characters, involved him in units of narrative which were too long and too lacking in suspense to fit the serial section. To compensate for this lack of suspense and the repeated narration of the same events (retold through the eyes of different characters), Machado de Assis made use of melodrama and created false suspense; it was this, along with the uncertainties of the plot, that caused him to lose his way, thereby forcing him to interrupt the serialization several times. Furthermore, the author did not have control over the edition of the magazine, which generated further problems, such as the creation of false cliffhangers at the end of instalments by Alfredo Leite, the typographer. Only in November 1889, when the chapters were renumbered and the whole novel revised, with many exclusions and few, but important, additions, and with the creation of a new character, did he solve his problems.

A Story that Remained Incomprehensible?

Whoever reads *Quincas Borba* in serial form, whether in the critical edition or in the pages of *A Estação*, will find several incongruities. The first thing that strikes us, even before we start reading, is the highly irregular numbering of the chapters.[1] Furthermore, the reader who follows the narrator's directions very closely will see that the text contains references to chapters whose numbers do not correspond to the chapter specified. In chapter 69, for example, which is dated 15 July 1887, the narrator refers to a previous chapter when describing Sophia: 'Trajava de azul escuro, mui decotada, — pelas razões ditas no capítulo 38; os braços nus, cheios, com uns tons de ouro claro, ajustavam-se às espáduas e aos seios, tão acostumados ao gás do salão' [She was wearing dark blue, very low-necked — for the reasons stated in chapter 38; her plump bare arms of a pale golden tint formed a graceful line with her back and bosom, so used to being seen in the gas-light].[2] The section specified, however, is found not in chapter 38 but in chapter 34, of 15 November 1886: Palha 'tinha essa espécie de vaidade impudica; decotava a mulher sempre que podia, e até quando não podia, para mostrar aos outros as suas venturas particulares' [had that sort of shameless vanity; he dressed his wife in low-cut dresses whenever he could, and even when he couldn't, in order to reveal his personal good fortune to others].[3]

A further, more serious, example is the reference in the serial to a chapter which in fact only exists in the book version. In chapter 137, of 15 April 1890, the narrator refers to Rubião's matrimonial delirium: 'Sentado na loja do Bernardo, gastava toda uma manhã, sem que o tempo lhe trouxesse fadiga, nem a estreiteza da rua do Ouvidor lhe tapasse o espaço. Repetiam-se as visões deliciosas, como as das bodas (cap. 81) em termos a que a grandeza não tirava a graça'. [Seated in Bernardo's shop, he would while away a whole morning, without time hanging heavy or the narrowness of Ouvidor Street hemming him in. Delightful visions, like those of the wedding (chapter 81) were repeated, and in such form that their grandiose nature did not deprive them of their charm.][4]

The wedding visions are actually found in chapter 81 of the *book* version.[5] Moreover, they do not exist in the serial, which proves that a chapter that is essential to constructing the protagonist's progressive madness was added during the rewriting process to publish the book. This example concurs with Kinnear's argument, according to which Machado de Assis started revising the text for the publication of the book before finishing the serialization in the magazine: 'There are three distinct phases of publication; from the evidence of each section, it can be assumed that the material already published was revised in the interval which occurred before the next section was put into print'.[6] I would go further still by stating that, after each interval, the continuation of the writing of the serial presupposed the already revised text and not the chapters published in *A Estação*.

Despite the inconsistencies in the serial, I do not believe that the process of reading it in small doses was affected to the extent that the text, as Kinnear believes, 'could not have been read and understood by any subscriber to *A Estação*'.[7] In the first place, due to the ephemeral nature of the periodical, the reader would hardly have been motivated to return to previous instalments in order to pick up a reference. The serial version of *Quincas Borba* was published over a period of more than five years, so even those readers who had collected the supplements would end up with a very large pile of old papers, which would be difficult to handle. Secondly, with the exception of the episode concerning the Alagoas Committee circular, the elements of the plot are coherent and remain the same from one version to the next. As we shall see, the temporal marking of the novel is already intrinsically coherent in the serial.

I therefore prefer to maintain the hypothesis that it is principally due to the publication format that the two versions provide different reading experiences. As has already been stated, a crucial element in determining the involvement of the subscriber in the story, and the temporary suppositions that were constructed while the text was unfolding from instalment to instalment, is the fact that the novel required extended reading, over a period of more than five years, at intervals determined by its fortnightly periodicity. As we saw in Chapters 2 and 3 of this book, the material framework of the two formats is very different due to the presence or absence of surrounding iconographic and textual content. Moreover, the reading experiences provided by the serial and book formats are different as a result of the rhythm at which reading takes place. Finally, the two reading experience differ due to the alterations made to the text by the writer.

Over the next three chapters we shall see that Machado de Assis takes to its extreme his initial plan of constructing meaning through narrative blocks which are much longer than the instalments of the serial, ultimately including all of the novel, from the first to the last chapter. This is precisely what, in this work, I call the global vision of the novel, and which I begin discussing here.

I will start here to investigate the fictional tools employed in the first version of *Quincas Borba*, the implications of which have not been systematically considered in any study of the variants in the novel. The aim is to study the evolution of the narrative in the material context of the magazine, based on a close reading of the text, in search of the system of conventions which allowed the serialized text to gain form and meaning: the structure of the plot and its unfolding in time, the manner in which details of various kinds were introduced, whether to generate suspense or to define or introduce (new) characters or, in short, to start, delay or conclude the story. It will be important not only to detect these narrative conventions but also to observe whether or not they were suited to the format of serialized publication. As such, my aims also include investigating the way in which the internal structure of the text was adapted to its external division into instalments. It is not my intention, however, to offer an interpretation of every incident or to decide what Machado de Assis's intentions were when he included this or that element or episode in the narrative.

The aim is to learn how the text is organized in order to highlight, if possible, the points at which Machado de Assis's narrative vision of *Quincas Borba* comes into conflict with the serialized mode of publication. In this case, by 'narrative vision' I mean the basic narrative parameters which the author established for the novel from the point when it began to be published in the magazine (and which were discussed in Chapter 4).

Narrative Units of *Philosopher or Dog?*

I believe that we will only manage to produce a systematic comparative study of the evolution of the two versions if we take as a starting point some organizing element which is intrinsic to the narrative and which has not undergone much change in both texts. Only then will we have any chance of not getting lost among inconsistently numbered chapters and the movement back and forth between one text and the other. Since the two versions do not always follow the same narrative sequence, this is a risk which is particularly hard to avoid.

The organizing elements which are intrinsic to the narrative and which are to be taken as a starting point are, as Genette points out, its demarcated temporal junctures, in accordance with the criterion that the text contains significant temporal intervals.[8] In *Quincas Borba*, as we shall see below, I was able to identify these intervals fairly quickly. This criterion proved to be effective, not only because the same narrative junctures are found in both versions, but also because Machado de Assis very probably undertook the task of rewriting while considering the temporal limits established between these junctures. By following this analytical criterion, we can proceed more safely with a step-by-step comparison of the two versions and, at the same time, delimit, within the continuous flow of the text, the point(s) at which the composition of the novel passed through periods of crisis.

In this chapter I present one by one the five temporal units into which the novel is divided, taking as a starting point the first version up to chapter 122 of 31 July 1889 (chapter 105 in the definitive version). This cut-off point is justified because between 31 July and 30 November 1889 the publication of the serial suffered its most significant interruption. According to Kinnear, this was the point at which Machado de Assis interrupted the serialization in order to revise the already published material with a view to composing the book. I have several reasons for focusing a large part of my analysis on a comparison of the two versions of this first part of the novel. Firstly, that despite not agreeing with what Kinnear says regarding the axis which guided Machado de Assis during the rewriting process, I believe to be definitive his assertion that the novelist began revising for the book edition precisely at chapter 122, published on 31 July 1889. Secondly, by that time the longest interruptions in publication had taken place, which indicates that the writing of the first half of the novel proved more problematic than that of the second. Thirdly, some narrative sequences in the chapters up to 106 were reordered to produce in the book a different reading experience from that which Artur Azevedo aptly defined as the *dosimetric* one provided by the magazine; as such, the pattern of reading of each version differs not only as a result of its specific material framework but also because of the restructuring of the first half of the novel. Finally, the first part of the novel contains the greatest number of characteristics borrowed from the serial and popular literary genres such as the melodrama, which shows that, when the writing process entered a period of crisis, the novelist made use of devices characteristic of serials in order not to interrupt publication definitively. As we shall see, he persisted with these devices until he found a resolution to the plot.

In the first narrative unit Machado de Assis follows the model of the serial very closely, making the story evolve in parallel with the passing of real time, i.e., the weeks in which the instalments were published. Thus a pattern of gradual reading was established in the novel, which was not, however, maintained in the second narrative unit. There, the writer assembles the plot on the basis of the kaleidoscope of impressions which each character retains of the same event, and which, as was seen earlier, gives rise to the first set of suspicions. This technique causes time to be dilated, which contrasts strongly with the temporal rhythm that Machado de Assis had established throughout the course of the first unit. I believe that the first maladjustment between the narrative technique and the mode of publication occurs in the second unit of the first version.

Although the serialization hinders the overall vision, in which several events compete to construct the same picture, the composition of the novel had not at this stage entered a period of crisis, because the plot — specifically the set of suspicions concerning the affair between Sophie and Rubião, and subsequently, Sophie and Carlos Maria — was already prepared, or at least delineated, before publication started. Once the plot is assembled, however, the novelist seems to lose direction as he does not know how to resolve the conflict, that is, he does not how to disassemble the set of suspicions once they have been constructed. That is the hypothesis which I put forward to explain the reasons that brought the narrative to a crisis point. This crisis is reflected in the multiplicity of melodramatic episodes which are irrelevant to the plot and, subsequently, in the interruptions in publication which start to occur more frequently.

From the narrative point of view, the solution which Machado de Assis finds to the creative impasse is also linked to the outcome of the plot. The writer finds an ending characteristic of the serial in order to resolve the conflict and fulfil the need to finish the serialization. We shall see that the solution found to the outcome of the plot was the introduction of a new character, Dona Fernanda, after chapter 106.

It must not be forgotten that Machado de Assis was actually carrying out two tasks at the same time. Before returning to the writing of the serial, he revised the previous chapters with the publication of the book in mind. As such, when he continued writing the novel from chapter 106, he began to write the serial and the novel at the same time. In order to get around the difficulty of producing continuity in a text which met the requirements of both formats, he mixes resources characteristic of the serial and also redefines the reading pattern of the novel, which, in the second version, highlights the overall vision of the narrative.

For methodological reasons, the most detailed study of the change in reading pattern has been left to the next chapter so that we may try to distinguish more clearly between two very closely linked rewriting operations: on the one hand, the omissions, which are most numerous, and which weaken the serial and episodic character of the novel and, on the other hand, the reordering and adding of scenes, which in large part are responsible for strengthening the global meaning of the novel

First Narrative Unit: We Are Reading a Serial Novel

The first five instalments of *Quincas Borba*, which were published between 15 June and 15 August 1886, correspond to that part of the narrative which takes place in the interior of Minas Gerais, in Barbacena.[9] When the novel begins we are transported into a story *in medias res*, to the dialogues between Quincas Borba and the doctor, and between the doctor and Rubião. The start of the novel places the reader in the middle of the action without any preliminary explanation: no description is provided of the geographical space in which the story is to take place, and the characters who are to participate in the action are not introduced. We discover from the outset that the character who gives his name to the novel is ill and is in fact going to die. It is true that Quincas Borba does not need to be introduced, because it is possible that he is known to the reader: the writer–narrator reminds us, a few lines later, that the philosopher has already figured in *Memórias póstumas de Brás Cubas*, which had been published four years previously.

Chapter 1 also informs us that Quincas Borba is an eccentric, the author of a certain philosophy book in which his lack of fear of death is probably explained. In chapter 2 we learn of the existence of a dog with the same name as his owner, and the instalment ends with Rubião adjusting his expression in the mirror to try to cloak behind a melancholy face his excitement at the prospect of being included in the will. Right from the *incipit*, the two series of dialogues already point to a certain disjunction between the words that the doctor addresses to Quincas Borba, on the one hand, and to Rubião, on the other, concerning the true state of the patient's health. Although the reader does not yet know who Rubião is, this image of him standing in front of the mirror, trying to adopt an expression suitable for the sickroom, provides a forewarning that pretence and self-interest, which characterize the way that one character treats another, will dominate the inter-personal relations described throughout the novel.

That, *grosso modo*, is the summary of the first instalment, which contains the first two chapters of the novel. The reader that turned the first page of issue 41 of the supplement in order to finish reading the narrative on page 44 would certainly have passed her eyes over the German illustrations, which, as we saw in Chapter 3 of this book, occupy the inside pages of this part of the magazine. The story of Rubião (or rather, of Quincas Borba, as understood thus far) continues on the third page of the supplement, sharing space with two columns by Artur Azevedo — *Croniqueta* and *Teatros* — and with several more advertisements. On the date on which the serialization of *Quincas Borba* started, the literary section of *A Estação* consisted of four pages. As had already occurred with other narratives by Machado de Assis which were also published in that periodical, the new novel gained a privileged place on the first page, occupying three full columns, which, however, were often curtailed by advertisements at the foot of the page.[10] In the issue dated 15 June 1886, *Quincas Borba* appears above advertisements for the French perfumists Veloutine and Germandrée as well as others for Chassaing wine and Falières syrup (the former claiming to act against infections of the digestive system, and the latter to alleviate ailments of the nervous system; see Fig. 4.1). When the text of the instalment did not fit into the space on the first page, it was arranged in a somewhat untidy and asymmetrical way around the German illustrations on the inner pages or at the top of the first column on the last page, as happened in the first instalment.

Having finished reading the narrative within that typographic framework, what questions does the text raise? What story, or rather, whose story is the novel going to relate? That of Rubião, or of Quincas Borba — of whom, in any case, there are two, as the title of the English translation of the book reinforces? Who is this Rubião, and what are the contents of the will? Only in fifteen days' time, when the second instalment was to be published, would the narrator be able to answer the three questions which every narrative puts to its readers (who? where? and when?), thereby satisfying their curiosity over the will and the figure of Rubião. In this way, having started in full flow, the first two chapters at the same time prepare the atmosphere for the flashback with which the next instalment begins. In chapter 3, the narrator returns to the past so that we learn who Rubião is, where and when the action is taking place — Barbacena, 1867 — and also the circumstances connecting the nurse to the philosopher.

The shape of the novel therefore seems to fit, unproblematically, into the serial model. For example, the way that time is configured in the story evolves, as we have

Figure 4.1. *A Estação, Jornal Ilustrado para a Família*, 15 June 1886
Biblioteca Nacional do Rio de Janeiro

seen, as the scenes progress. The technique used to compose the scenes is borrowed from the theatre: through it, the work is organized into scenes, in imitation of the play form. To the extent that they are required, the writer then inserts flashbacks which explain and justify the narrative present. The linking together of scenes (even when they are interspersed with flashbacks) provides a model by means of which the story can continually and gradually develop, giving the impression that it is taking place in real time. Once the flashback is over, the action of the novel returns again to the present, which in the first two instalments lasts one day. The whole episode, from the forecast of Quincas Borba's death in Barbacena to the shifting of the action to Rio de Janeiro in chapter 20, takes approximately ten weeks. The part of the action which takes place in Barbacena, which can be considered to be the first narrative unit of the serial version of *Quincas Borba*, lasts approximately thirteen weeks. As such, it is of the same duration as the period over which the six instalments in which it is narrated were published.

Characteristics of the serial

We shall see below that the start of *Quincas Borba* contains at least two more characteristics of the serial: the use of unpredictable devices in order to complicate the plot, and the creation of suspense. Let us turn our attention to the first characteristic, i.e., the resources used by the writer to make the story progress and complicate the plot. In order to change scene and effect a temporal leap, Machado de Assis uses at least three strategies. Firstly, he may introduce a new character into the action, whether secondary or otherwise, such as the notary, the doctor and the godmother Angélica, who appear in chapters 2, 8 and 18 respectively. These people always appear or are mentioned in successive scenes in connection with the illness and the clause in Quincas Borba's will. Secondly, he may use either correspondence or news in order to introduce a new fact, such as the letter sent from Rio to Rubião (chapter 9), or the obituary of Quincas Borba published in one of the city's newspapers (chapter 11). Rubião receives confirmation of Quincas Borba's madness through the former device, while it is through a newspaper that news of the philosopher's death reaches Barbacena. The third resource is the narrator himself, who is responsible for guiding or even manipulating the order of events. He plays the role of a prompter, informing us in the commentary of the total duration of a scene or the time which has elapsed between two series of events. In order to introduce the flashback, for example, chapter 3 starts with a rhetorical question: 'Mas que Rubião é este? E, antes de tudo, onde estamos nós?' [But what Rubião is this? And, above all, where are we?]. This creates a temporal cut-off point which allows the narrator to go back to the point at which Quincas Borba moves to Barbacena and falls in love with Rubião's sister. Later, the narrator sets down another temporal marker, this time when he jumps forward to the future. We learn that at most seven days elapse between the first scene and the day on which Quincas Borba agrees to the idea of going to Rio de Janeiro: 'Um dia, no princípio da outra semana, o doente levantou-se com ideia de ir à corte, voltaria no fim de um mês, tinha certos negócios.' [One day, at the start of another week, the patient got up with the idea of going to the capital city, he would return after a month, he had certain business dealings.].[11] Adding together the temporal markers left by the narrator, we arrive at the approximate total of ten weeks for the duration of this first narrative unit of the novel.

The final characteristic among those typical of the serial is also the best known: the creation of suspense. At the start of *Quincas Borba*, we also find the same technique used to arouse apprehension in the reader, even though the instalments do not necessarily end on a note of suspense. In chapter 3, when the narrator answers the question which opens the chapter, the phrase 'por ora' [for the time being] is used to create the expectation of the action moving somewhere else: 'Estamos, por ora, em Barbacena, Minas Gerais' [We are, for the time being, in Barbacena, Minas Gerais].[12] Chapter 15 anticipates the fact that Rio de Janeiro, capital of the Empire and the habitual setting for Machado de Assis's novels, will also be the setting of a large part of the action of *Quincas Borba*. Rubião reveals his intention of moving to the city:

> Tudo se baralhava na cabeça do Rubião, — e, no meio de tudo, este grave problema, — se iria viver na Corte, ou se ficaria em Barbacena. A ideia de ficar não era má; dava-lhe umas cócegas de brilhar onde escurecia, de quebrar a castanha na boca aos que se riam dele; mas a Corte, que ele conhecia, com os seus atrativos, movimento, teatros em toda a parte, mulheres na rua, muitas, com vestidos de francesa... Nada; iria para a Corte; estava cansado de viver escondido.[13]

> [Confusion reigned in Rubião's head, and, in the midst of everything, this grave problem — would he go to live in the capital city, or would he stay in Barbacena? The idea of staying wasn't a bad one; he was tempted to dazzle where he had languished in obscurity, to get his own back on those who used to laugh at him; but the capital city, which he knew well, with its charm, its bustle, theatres everywhere, women in the street, lots of them, clad in French fashions... There was no question; he would go to the capital city; he was tired of living in hiding.]

As stated in the passage above, the women would be dressed in the French style, like subscribers to *A Estação*, who sewed their dresses, or sent them to be sewed, according to patterns sold with the magazine.[14] It is also assumed that the female characters in the novel, Sophia and Dona Fernanda, for example, will also be dressed in the French style, or will at least have dressed at some point in accordance with the prevailing fashion, as is the case, most famously, of Dona Tonica. There is also Maria Benedicta, who is a sort of opposite of Dinah Piedefer, the character who features in Honoré de Balzac's *La Muse du Département* (1843). Maria Benedicta moves to the capital, receives lessons in piano and French, attends dances, and goes on walks around the shopping streets of Rio de Janeiro in the company of Sophia. As a result, she gradually becomes acclimatized to the way of life of the city, without completely abandoning her seriousness and rural spirit. In Balzac's novel, the protagonist suffers the reverse process. Having moved from Paris to the provinces, the differences in the ways of behaving, thinking and dressing that exist between the capital and countryside gradually become mixed up to form a unique combination — one which is admired by provincial women and detested by Parisians.[15]

We see here that the narrator has already begun to create expectations concerning the female characters who will inhabit the narrative, a fact which becomes even more evident in chapter 17. With the death of Quincas Borba, Rubião sees himself as freed from the obligation to look after the dog and orders a slave to take it to the godmother, Angélica. After becoming aware of the clause in the will, though, Rubião runs to the godmother's house in search of the animal. In chapter 17, which consists of a single paragraph and which was eliminated in the subsequent version, the narrator apologizes to the readers for the fact that the first woman to appear in the narrative is ugly:

> A comadre era muito feia. Peço desculpa de ser tão feia a primeira mulher que aqui aparece; mas as bonitas hão de vir. Creio até que já estão nos bastidores, impacientes de entrar em cena. Sossegai, muchachas! Não me façais cair a peça. Aqui vireis todas, em tempo idôneo... Deixai a comadre que é feia, muita feia.[16]

> [The godmother was very ugly. I apologize for the fact that the first woman to appear here is so ugly; but the pretty ones will be coming on. Indeed, I believe that they are already in the wings, impatient to come on to the stage. Calm yourselves, girls! Don't bring down the curtain on my play. You will all make your entrances here, when the time is right... Leave the godmother, since she's ugly, very ugly.]

According to the narrator (and employing the theatrical metaphor), the play will be acted by other female characters, who will come on to the stage gradually, when it is more convenient to the plot. The patient reader will see that the narrator keeps his promises. As we saw in Chapter 2 of this book, the reader of the novel will find more than one woman playing a role that is relevant to the plot: Sophia, Dona Tonica, Maria Benedicta and Dona Fernanda, in that order of appearance.

Second Narrative Unit: A Sunday Which Lasts Thirteen Instalments

One of the difficulties of relating Machado de Assis's fiction to the model of the serial lies in the myth that its composition did not require planning. According to Queffélec, however, there is no truth in the belief that serial writers wrote the following day's narrative every day in order to be able to respond to the immediate demands of the reader, the magazine and even the censors. On the contrary, works were found to be 'bel et bien planifiées dans la grande majorité des cas *avant* la parution en feuilletons' [certainly planned, in most cases, *before* the publication in serial form], which, however, did not limit the writer's freedom to extend or add episodes in order to complicate the plot or deviate from the main line of the narrative.[17] Perhaps Brito Broca means exactly this when he states that 'os autores escrevendo, geralmente, *au jour le jour* iam adaptando o desenvolvimento da intriga aos limites e às exigências do folhetim' [authors who generally wrote *day by day* adapted the development of the plot to the limits and requirements of the serial].[18] Thus, while they were in possession of a plan, novelists who wrote for the press could extend or include new episodes, thereby delaying the conclusion of the narrative.

This also seems to have applied to Machado de Assis when he was composing *Quincas Borba*. It is very probable that, before starting the serialization, the novelist had already planned those narrative units of the first version, whether individually or as a whole, upon which the construction of the plot depends. We saw that the first narrative unit, which comprises chapters 1 to 18, corresponds to that part of the action which takes place in Barbacena. In the short chapter 19, the narrator makes a geographical and temporal leap from Barbacena to the capital city, skipping over the months in which the inventory and the train trip from the province to the capital take place — all of which will subsequently be described in various flashbacks which occur throughout the second narrative unit.[19] The second narrative unit begins by showing Rubião already settled in Botafogo. It begins in chapter 20 of the same instalment — 'Aqui está o nosso Rubião no Rio de Janeiro' [Here is our Rubião in Rio de Janeiro] — and only ends at the end of chapter 50, dated 28 February 1887: 'Não, senhora minha, ainda não acabou este dia tão comprido' [No, my lady, this very long day has not finished].[20] Between chapters 20 and 50, Rubião plays with his dog, has lunch with Freitas and Carlos Maria, and receives a basket of strawberries from Sophia. At the end of the afternoon, Rubião goes to Sophia's house. There, he invites Sophia to gaze at the Southern Cross and ends up meeting Major Siqueira and Dona Tonica who, as we have seen, suspect that Rubião and Sophia are lovers. At the end of the night, the guests go down Santa Thereza hill. The narrator has us accompany Dona Tonica and her father, and subsequently Rubião, on their way home. The latter, on arriving in the lower part of the city, remembers the episode in which the slave was hanged.

Here, we cannot fail to mention that this is the only instalment in the novel which has not yet been found, either by myself or previously by the Machado de Assis Committee. There is no doubt, however, that it was included in the first version, because the narrator refers to it in chapter 49, published in the following instalment:

> Ah! tinha vivido um dia cheio de sensações diversas e contrárias, desde as recordações da manhã, e o almoço aos dois amigos, até aquela última ideia de metempsicose, passando pela lembrança do enforcado, e por uma declaração de amor não aceita, mal repelida, parece que adivinhada por outros...[21]

> [Ah! He had lived a day full of diverse and contrary sensations, from the recollections of the morning, and the lunch with his two friends, to the latest idea of metempsychosis, passing through the memory of the hanged man, and through an unaccepted, harshly rebuffed, declaration of love, which seemed to have been guessed at by others...]

Rubião is seen for the first time walking around Rio, in Constitution Square and along São Francisco, until he gets into the coach which takes him to his mansion in Botafogo. In the sequence of the text, the narrator takes us back once more to Sophia's house, this time to enter the intimacy of the couple's bedroom. Alone with her husband, the hostess speaks to Palha of Rubião's daring flirtation. For the reader, this long day finishes here.

To end this narrative unit, Machado de Assis uses two pretexts which will be used later to complicate the plot: the appearance of Carlos Maria and another letter. On the morning following the soirée, among new and old friends, Sophia sees Carlos Maria riding on horseback and then receives a letter from the country.[22]

The unexpected appearance of Carlos Maria, and the laughter provoked by the postman, make Sophia momentarily forget her headache and the annoyance caused by Rubião. The reader already knows Carlos Maria from the lunch at Rubião's house. Now he appears in another context. In this way, Machado de Assis ends this narrative unit by making possible (as in a television soap opera) the subsequent development of stories parallel to that of the protagonist, Maria Benedicta's secret love for Carlos Maria, and the attraction between Carlos Maria and Sophia. Until this point, Carlos Maria has simply been a friend of Rubião's. The young man already stands out among the other diners who frequent Rubião's house as he is held in higher esteem by the recent arrival to the city.

The secondary characters in the novel will therefore be able to interact with each other inside the different social circles to which the protagonist, acting as a kind of common denominator, has access. The letter from the country, meanwhile, brings news from Palha's aunt and cousin, Maria Augusta and Maria Benedicta, who will be introduced properly at a later stage. The construction of a substantial part of the plot will depend, as we have seen, on the countrywoman's point of view.

Throughout these thirteen instalments the narrator plants the seeds of suspicion concerning the romance between Sophia and Rubião — seeds planted not in the readers' minds, but in those of characters such as Dona Tonica and Major Siqueira. As seen in the previous chapter of this book, Machado de Assis dilates the passing of time by showing a multiplicity of view points relating to the same episode, incorporating incidents from the past which are replete with meanings used to construct the plot and the characters of the novel. This does not constitute a defect. In fact, it represents an evolution in the narrative technique used to develop the plot, involving a departure from the chronological passing of time. José de Alencar had already shown that the narrative does not need to respect a strictly linear temporal progression, but rather that it was possible to insert the past *into* the present by using flashback. Afrânio Coutinho attributes to Alencar the development in the Brazilian novel of the technique of intercalating narrative planes, 'com a ação e o tempo retroagindo até um ponto anteriormente narrado, sob outra perspectiva' [with the action and time moving back to a previously narrated point, seen from another perspective]. This is the case of *Senhora* (1870), in which 'o início da história, que vai explicar toda a primeira parte já narrada, só vai ser contado do 1º ao 8º capítulo da segunda parte' [the story, which is going to explain the whole of the already narrated first part, is only going to be told between the first and eighth chapters of the second part].[23]

Machado de Assis, however, seems to have gone very far in extending the narration of events which occurred on the same day over so many chapters, knowing that they would have to be divided up, with the whole episode taking over six months to be published. Contrary to what occurs in the first unit, in which the novelist opts for an opening which follows the passing of real time very closely (i.e., it lasts a very similar amount of time to that required to publish the instalments), from chapter 21 onwards the novelist prefers to focus on the characters' impressions of a couple of events, as we saw in Chapter 3. Therefore, if the first unit had fitted without too many problems into the space reserved for it every fortnight, the same does not occur with the second unit. This is because, when it is divided up for serial publication, damage is done to the perception that the thirteen instalments form part of the same temporal block.

Typographic composition of instalments

Let us analyse now the way in which the instalments might have been typographically composed, basing our observations on some examples, in order to examine the disjunction more closely. I believe that, from the point at which he began the creative composition of the first version of *Quincas Borba*, Machado de Assis was not tied to a pre-established limit with regard to space or words. It seems highly unlikely that the instalments left the novelist's hands one at a time, in response to the pressures of fortnightly publication. The most probable scenario is that the writer sent Lombaerts large narrative chunks, which were divided up and accommodated to the space allocated to *Quincas Borba* in each issue of the magazine. Besides the fact that meaning is constituted in long narrative units, another element which supports this hypothesis is the material composition of the periodical itself: many instalments do not respect the length of the chapters. As such, it is safer to suppose that the chapters had indeed been established by the writer. During the serialization of the novel, chapters frequently extend across two or more instalments. This first occurred in chapter 14, which is divided into two, having been started on 31 July 1886. Only the last paragraph was left out and was published on 15 August 1886. A further example is chapter 50, which, being very long, had to be distributed over three successive issues of the magazine.

The idea that Machado de Assis planned his narrative in narrative units which were longer than the space allocated to the novel in the magazine concurs with Kinnear's hypothesis that the novel was written in large blocks or stages (three, according to Kinnear).[24] Thus only one part of the text, that which fitted into the fortnight's instalment, was placed in the typographic mould. The remaining parts were left for the forthcoming instalments.

Who, then, was responsible for deciding where the cut-off point should be: Machado de Assis, or the editor? In order to answer this question, it is necessary to examine how some instalments in the second narrative unit of the novel end. As has already been noted with respect to the first narrative unit, the elements which arouse the reader's curiosity (for example, those which anticipate the movement of the action to Rio de Janeiro, and predict the appearance of beautiful women) do not coincide with the end of the instalment. Cliffhangers, which, according to Afrânio Coutinho, occur 'num momento culminante de uma cena ou sequência de cenas, para que o leitor voltasse ao romance' [at the culminating moment of a scene or series of scenes to make the reader return to the novel], cannot be found in the first narrative unit of *Quincas Borba*.[25] In the second narrative unit, however, we find some instalments whose moment of suspense coincides, at least at first sight, with their end. This occurs on 31 August 1886 and 31 January 1887. In the former case, the narrative is interrupted when Rubião says 'Lá vou' ['I'll go'], which causes the reader to expect that the protagonist is going to meet Sophia, or at least, that he will leave the room he is in order to find out why the dog is so restless. In the second version, this piece of dialogue is rewritten. In the book we read '— Lá vou soltá-lo' ['I'll go and unleash him'], which removes the ambiguity from Rubião's stated intentions.[26]

The hand of the typographer is evident in the instalment dated 31 January 1887, where he interrupts the narration before Sophia reveals to her husband the declaration of love made by her new friend:

> Sofia reclinada no canapé, riu das graças do marido. Criticaram ainda alguns episódios da tarde e da noite; depois, Sofia, acariciando os cabelos do marido, disse-lhe de repente:
> — E você ainda não sabe do melhor episódio da noite.
> — Que foi?
> — Adivinhe.
> (Continua.)[27]

> [Lying on the sofa, Sophia laughed at her husband's witticisms. They discussed some of the episodes that had taken place in the evening and at night; then, caressing her husband's hair, Sophia suddenly said to him:
> 'And you still don't know the best thing that happened at night.'
> 'What was it?'
> 'Guess.'
> (Continues)]

'I'll go' and 'Guess' are bits of dialogue which announce a change of scene or the presentation of new information which is central to the evolution of the plot. However, the next instalments to be published, which were dated 15 September 1886 and 15 February 1887 respectively, do not satisfy the reader's curiosity with regard to the suspense created at the end of the previous issue. On 15 September 1886, Rubião goes neither to the kennel nor to Santa Thereza. Rather, he remains engrossed in his thoughts and moves only to sit on the pouf, in the same room where the coffee had been served. Sophia, whom the reader is anxiously expecting, will not appear until the issue dated 15 November 1886. She appears again on 15 February 1887, when, in a now empty room lit by a small number of lamps, she whispers the news of Rubião's bold behaviour to her husband. The problem is that this news is already old for the reader. The word 'guess' could only serve to arouse Palha's curiosity. To the reader, this word is actually making the narrative repetitive, because it gives forewarning that the incident which took place in the garden will be related once again, albeit from a different point of view. For the reader of the serial, Rubião's boldness is described twice. In fact, Palha is the only person who is still unaware of the story. The next instalment, therefore, does not bring anything new to the narrative in the linear sense, despite adding some very important information. Instead of rebuking his wife's licentious attitude, Palha makes us aware that he owes a lot of money to Rubião and that the couple will therefore not be able to break off relations with him. From here onwards, Sophia must begin the complicated game of pretence and seduction, using her feminine charms without exceeding moral limits in order to keep the naive Rubião within the couple's circle of prominent friends. With one more piece of the jigsaw puzzle now added, the reader will realize that the pretence actually includes all of the interpersonal relations in the novel. It no longer applies only to Quincas Borba's treatment by his nurse, but also to the treatment of Rubião, in his position as a new capitalist, by the supposed friends that he has recently acquired in the capital.

The typographer

We therefore see that the endings of these instalments are no more than false or ironic cliffhangers as they are in opposition to an intrinsic characteristic of the serial and therefore end up undermining the genre. If Machado de Assis had been responsible for determining the place where the cut-off would be made, it is possible that he would have decided to break off these two instalments with 'I'll go' or 'Guess' precisely in order to express the opposite of the literal meaning of these words. However, we cannot reject the hypothesis that, once the text had been written, the composition of the instalments was the responsibility not of the author but of the editor, or rather, the typographer of the magazine.

As we saw in Chapter 3 of this book, which stated the place where the 'Literary Section' of *A Estação* was edited and printed, Lombaerts depended on a professional who was responsible for the more general task of paginating that supplement of the magazine. It is even possible to identify the name of the typographer (in 1889, at least): Alfredo Leite. On more than one occasion, Artur Azevedo refers to the typographer, on this occasion to apologize to the reader for the brevity of his column of 30 June 1887: 'E termino aqui, porque o paginador da *Estação* recomendou-me que escrevesse muito pouco. Eloy, o herói' [And I am finishing here, because the typographer of *A Estação* has recommended to me that I write a little less. Eloy, the hero].[28] Consequently, it was Alfredo Leite, or another typographer, who determined the length of each instalment of the novel in accordance with the other items in the magazine.

The task of composing the pages of the literary supplement of *A Estação* must have required an orchestra of different people, in different roles, which Machado de Assis was probably not conducting. The novelist was already a celebrated author and no longer concerned himself with typography, as he did at the start of his career with the periodical *Marmota*. There is a further fact which supports the hypothesis that it was the typographer rather than Machado de Assis who had the task of dividing the prepared text into instalments and arranging the somewhat disordered numbering of the chapters. If that task had been Machado de Assis's responsibility, he would have been more careful with regard to the numbering.

On 15 June 1896, when the publication of the novel began, *A Estação* did not yet seem to have many established collaborators, aside from Machado de Assis and Artur Azevedo. José Simões put his name to some serialized narratives, which were published in 1886.[29] In the first year of publication of *Quincas Borba* we also find some verses by Lúcio de Mendonça, Olavo Bilac, Carlos Coelho, Alberto de Oliveira, Raimundo Correia, Joaquim Cahn and Luís Delfino. From 1888 onwards, however, the number of regular contributors increases while the publication of serialized stories and writings, including some by Artur Azevedo, becomes more frequent.[30] The greatest novelty is constituted by those sections written by women, such as Júlia Lopes de Almeida, from December 1888 onwards,[31] and Inês Sabino Pinho Maia, from 1890 onwards.[32] As such, from around 1888, the typographer had to handle a greater number of contributors and, consequently, of texts. As part of his work, the typographer also had to fill the two inside pages with German illustrations in accordance with an editorial principle which was upheld throughout those six years. We should also mention that, from 31 March 1887 onwards, the number of advertisements on the first and last pages increased, occupying part of the space traditionally allocated to the publication of *Quincas Borba*.

These difficulties are manifested in the diverse appearance of the different copies of the literary supplement of *A Estação*. Nowadays, if we leaf through the magazine, we have the impression that we are reading a somewhat amateurish periodical. If we compare the 'Literary Section' with the entertainment page of *Die Illustrirte Frauen-Zeitung*, this impression is heightened. In the Brazilian magazine, for example, the ordering of the material and the frequency with which some sections appear is very irregular. Also, the lengths of the texts vary a great deal, and the same pattern is not always maintained with regard to the spacing between the lines. These points indicate that, with every issue, the typographer was obliged to make small adjustments to the spacing, font size and the way that the texts were distributed in the columns in order to make the space available for the texts written by the contributors, which did not have a predetermined number of words.

On 30 June 1887, Artur Azevedo apologized for being brief because the typographer had asked him not to write too much, probably because he knew in advance that there would be a lot of material to fit into the four pages which he was responsible for composing. It was easier to ask a regular contributor, such as a columnist who normally wrote his column within the fortnightly interval, to be brief. On some occasions, in order to resolve the problem of the lack of space in what was a very successful fashion magazine, the editors added two extra pages to the body of the supplement. Eventually, on 15 July 1890, Lombaerts seem to have definitively implemented what was previously a temporary solution, adding two pages to that part of the periodical.

If the novelist really did not have control over the serialization of his text, then the serial version of *Quincas Borba*, in its material configuration, could be considered as the fruit of a partnership between the writer and the magazine, represented by the figure of the typographer. Moreover, we have possibly identified the first reader of *Quincas Borba*: Alfredo Leite, together with the other typographers who may have taken turns in that role during the five years in which the novel was published. If this actually occurred, what would the motivations or limitations which guided or restricted the work of this professional have been? The typographer reads the magazine in a manner guided by the editorial need to divide it into sections. Unlike Machado de Assis, who might have seen in Rubião's 'I'll go' or Sophia's 'Guess' the possibility of being ironic once again, the typographer — who probably did not read the novel in any depth while he was composing the type — might have interrupted the instalment after those two phrases because he believed that they introduced genuine cliffhangers.

Whether they were introduced with ironic intent or not, those two cliffhangers project the serial model more explicitly onto the continuation of the plot. The typographer may have made the subscriber wish to see not only the appearance of beautiful women, dressed in the French style, and the movement of the action to the capital city, but also, subsequently, a genuine serial. It is true that when we return to these old pages in order to reread the novel (in a form which the author himself would not have wished), aware of the version which was revised and printed in one volume, the temporal distance makes us think that 'Guess' and 'I'll go' are rather a manifestation of Machado de Assis's irony. In the context in which the text was produced, we see here that these bits of dialogue may have been generated by editorial circumstances, such as the authority of the typographer over the manuscript when it was not under the novelist's control.

Third Narrative Unit: Preparing the Ground for the Second Set of Suspicions

So far we have identified the first two narrative units in the serial version of *Quincas Borba*: the part that takes place in Barbacena and the Sunday of the soirée at Sophia's house. In total, these two units correspond to the first 50 chapters of the novel, which were published, without interruption, between 15 June 1886 and 28 February 1887. The latter instalment also contains chapters 51 and 52, which, together with the erroneously numbered 54 of 15 March 1887, make up the transition from the second to third unit.

As we saw above, on the day after the social encounter at Sophia's house, the hostess wakes up with a headache, receives the letter from the country and sees Carlos Maria pass by on horseback. The third narrative unit then starts in chapter 55, dated 15 March.[33] With this change, the narrator makes a temporal leap of fifteen days, which is equivalent to the periodicity of the magazine and the time which elapses between the night of the social encounter and Palha's visit to Rubião to investigate his friend's disappearance:

> Quinze dias depois, estando Rubião em casa, apareceu-lhe o marido de Sofia. Vinha perguntar-lhe o que era feito dele? onde se tinha metido que não aparecia? estivera doente? ou já não cuidava dos pobres? Rubião mastigava as palavras, sem acabar de compor uma frase única.[34]

> [Fifteen days later, when Rubião was at home, Sophia's husband appeared. Had to come to enquire what had happened to him? Where had he hidden himself? Had he been ill? Or did he no longer look after the poor? Rubião stumbled over his words, without managing to put together a single phrase.]

On entering the room, Palha realizes that Rubião is in the company of Camacho, a character who does not form part of his social circle and who, in fact, is also new to the reader. Although he is a failure, this journalist with political ambitions has made a good impression on Rubião and, in the narrative present, amid exchanged glances, secretly joins Palha in his plan to keep him in the capital. Here, Machado de Assis finds the opportunity to include two flashbacks. In chapter 57, dated 15 March 1887, and in the following chapter (erroneously numbered 56), the narrator explains why Rubião wanted to leave them, and summarizes the feelings and events experienced by him during the fortnight. At the end of the chapter, he returns again to the narrative present only to move back in time again (in chapter 57 of 31 March 1887) to introduce this new friend of Rubião's to us more fully and to reveal the circumstances in which they met. Returning once more to the present, we see that Rubião is completely convinced that he is not returning to Minas. It is also here that the seed of the protagonist's political aspirations is sown.

From chapter 60 to 66, Rubião is left alone until the following day, when he receives the *Atalaia* and has lunch with Freitas. Motivated by the desire to subscribe to Camacho's publication, he sets out for the newspaper's headquarters. Before he gets there, however, the Deolindo incident occurs, which transforms the character into a local hero. Walking around the roads and neighbourhoods of Rio, Rubião shows us some of its popular characters and some of its horrors, such as the episode in which the slave is hanged, the scene in which Deolindo is knocked over, and Rubião's walk to Formosa beach.

After leaving Camacho, Rubião returns to the street. There, he crosses paths with Sophia, who is accompanied by her cousin and aunt from the countryside, the authors of the letter with which Machado de Assis ends the second narrative unit. In the evening, Rubião goes to Sophia's house, where Maria Benedicta and Dona Augusta meet; there he bumps into Carlos Maria who he is saying goodbye to Sophia. We then learn that Carlos Maria is a habitual guest at both Rubião's and Sophia's houses, although his reasons for visiting the latter's house are as yet unknown. It is here that all the characters who make up all of the circles of friends come together, with the exception of Freitas and the other diners. The situation is therefore set up to create the second set of suspicions concerning the supposed affair between Carlos Maria and Sophia, which will be the subject of the fourth narrative unit. The following day, on which Rubião reads the news of the Deolindo incident in *Atalaia*, can also be considered to form part of this third unit.

The third narrative unit therefore lasts three days and extends over six instalments, from 15 March to 15 June 1887. The first interruption in the publication of the novel occurs here (on 31 May), as does the first error in the numbering of the chapters, as has been noted above. Within the serial, the main objective of this unit is to introduce Camacho and reveal the interests of Rubião's friends in keeping him in the city and awakening his political ambitions. In the next chapter of this book, we shall see that in rewriting this narrative unit, Machado de Assis focuses on the characterization of Rubião in order to begin the progressive development of the protagonist's madness.

Fourth Narrative Unit: Eight Months Later

The transition between the third and fourth units is very subtle, because Machado de Assis brings it about by focusing on Maria Benedicta. In chapter 68, which runs from 15 to 30 June 1887, there is a genuine pause in the development of the action as all attention is focused on this new female character. The purpose of this pause is to effect a temporal leap of eight months, a period which allows the characters to evolve or (false) friendships and fortunes to be consolidated. In this chapter, we learn of the progress made by Maria Benedicta since she moved to the city, the reasons which, after a great deal of resistance, lead her to learn French and piano, and the fact that her beauty and talents are now starting to rival those of her cousin. In order to return to the present, the novelist skilfully concludes the chapter (in the same way in which the next chapter begins) with Maria Benedicta counting on Rubião's watch the fifteen minutes during which Carlos Maria and Sophia dance a waltz:

> Maria Benedita sorriu de um modo tão particular, que a outra não insistiu. Não foi riso de vexame, nem de despeito, nem de desdém. Desdém, por quê? Contudo, é certo que o riso parecia vir de cima. Não menos o é que Sophia polcava e valsava com ardor, e ninguém se pendurava melhor do ombro do parceiro; Carlos Maria, que era raro dançar, só valsava com Sofia, — dois ou três giros, dizia ele; — Maria Benedita contou uma noite quinze minutos.
> (Continua.)
> Capítulo 69
> Os quinze minutos foram contados no relógio do Rubião, que estava ao pé da Maria Benedita, e a quem ela perguntou duas vezes que horas eram, no princípio e no fim da valsa.[35]

> [Maria Benedicta smiled in so peculiar a way that the other did not insist. It was not a smile of humiliation or displeasure, or contempt. Contempt? Why should it be? And yet it is true that the smile appeared to be supercilious. No less true is it that Sophia waltzed and polkaed with vivacity, and no one clung more gracefully to her partner's shoulders than she. Carlos Maria, who seldom danced, waltzed only with Sophia — two or three whirls, he would say. Maria Benedicta counted fifteen minutes one evening.
> (Continues)
> Chapter 69
> The fifteen minutes were counted on Rubião's watch. He was beside Maria Benedicta, and twice she asked him what time it was, at the beginning and at the end of the waltz.]

We are thereby thrown directly into the centre of the ball scene, even before we learn, as the narrator will tell us in chapter 69, that 'decorrido oito meses desde o princípio do capítulo anterior, e muita coisa estava mudada' [eight months had elapsed since the beginning of the previous chapter, and much had changed].[36] Now, Sophia no longer lives in Santa Thereza. She has already moved to Flamengo, Palha and Rubião are now partners, and the latter's capital needs a 'regímen do bom juro' [a good interest rate].

As we saw in Chapter 4 of this book, the ball scene on Arcos Road and the characters' subsequent kaleidoscope of impressions are the subject of chapters 69 to 78 of the book form. In fact, there are not many variations between the book and the serial between chapters 69 (15 July) and 79 (15 October). As we shall see, there is just one reversal of the order in which the characters appear on the stage. This proves that when he devoted himself to the book, Machado de Assis was relatively satisfied with the construction of the plot in this narrative unit.

The same cannot be said, however, of the rest of this narrative block. From chapter 80 onwards, the serial contains many more episodes than does the definitive version, which indicates that episodes were eliminated as not having a specific function in the plot. Rather, they had been created out of the sheer pleasure, or more accurately, the displeasure, of writing. The novelist eliminated episodes and synthesized others because he was not satisfied with the final result of the already published material. The re-ordering of the focus on each of the characters involved in the plot one day after the ball forms part of the same process of omitting the episodic.

In the serial version, on the day after the ball we first of all see Sophia, who is thinking about Carlos Maria's flirtatious behaviour (chaps 71–72). Afterwards, she briefly talks to her husband, who is on his way out to work, and who asks her to dissuade her cousin from returning to the country (chaps 73–75). Sophia is going to meet Maria Benedicta and, after the conversation, the countrywoman leaves believing that her cousins are planning to marry her to Carlos Maria, as has already been discussed in Chapter 4 of this book (chaps 75–78). In fact, Palha is planning to marry her to Rubião, so that the debts remain within the family. In the serial, eight chapters in total are devoted exclusively to these two characters. In the following chapter, the narrator returns to Carlos Maria (chap. 79). This is when we learn that the young man lies to Sophia during the fifteen-minute waltz. He leaves on horseback and sees Rubião's dog, which had escaped, in Largo do Machado (chap. 80). When he returns home, Rubião is waiting for him. At this stage, the protagonist is certain that Carlos Maria is having an affair with Sophia, and wants to extract a confession from him (15 and 30 November 1887, chap. 80 continuation). The conversation between the two characters verges on the melodramatic. The revelation of Rubião's love for Sophia, and the accusation of adultery, hang by a thread. The narrator reveals the intensity of the protagonist's (contained) feelings:

> Interiormente, mordia-se; as lágrimas queriam vir-lhe aos olhos. Como as mãos lhe tremessem muito meteu-as nas algibeiras das calças; a voz saía-lhe soturna, apesar do esforço que ele fazia para alegrá-la.[37]
>
> [Inside, he was choked up; tears were prickling in his eyes. As his hands were trembling hard, he put them in his trouser pockets; his voice sounded sad, despite the effort that he was making to sound cheerful.]

In the end, the feelings and accusations are not exposed because the subject of Quincas Borba's escape diverts Rubião's attention to his obligation towards his deceased friend. When Carlos Maria reveals to Rubião that he has seen Quincas Borba roaming around the city, Rubião forgets his aim of obtaining a confession from Carlos Maria. Without the confession, the explosion of emotions does not take place and there is therefore neither a revelation nor a climax in the unfolding of the plot.

The episodes which follow (chapters 72 [sic], 82 (continuation), 83 and 83 (continuation)) are driven by the dog's escape. They reintroduce Major Siqueira and Dona Tonica, who have found and given shelter to Quincas Borba. Rubião pays the reward and takes Quincas Borba back home. Here, the narrator has the opportunity of returning to the subject of Dona Tonica's spinsterhood (she has now turned forty) and awakening in Rubião the desire to get married, in accordance with the Major's advice.

As such, if we examine the appearance of the characters, or the episodes generated after the ball on Arcos street, we have the following summary, in order of appearance:

1. Sophia (chaps 71, 72);
2. Sophia and Palha (chaps 72–74);
3. Sophia and Maria Benedicta (chaps 75–78);
4. Carlos Maria (chap. 79);
5. Carlos Maria sees Rubião's lost dog (chap. 80);
6. Rubião visits Carlos Maria (chap. 80 continuation, 15 and 30 November 1887);
7. Carlos Maria alone (chap. 81);
8. Rubião looks for Quincas Borba and publishes the advertisement regarding the reward (chap. 72 [sic])
9. The dog is at Major Siqueira's house, Rubião takes him home (chaps 72 [sic], 83)
10. Major Siqueira plants the idea of marriage in Rubião's mind (chap. 83 continuation)
11. Matrimonial delirium (chaps 84–86)

During the rewriting process, this part of the unit was worked on substantially. In particular, Machado de Assis eliminated the interspersed events which prolong the narration and, with them, the aspects characteristic of melodrama and the serial. In the final version, we find the following arrangement, in accordance with the numbering established for the order of the characters or episodes summarized above: 1, 2, 4, 3, 10, 11.

In the first place, as has already been stated, we see that the novelist changes the order in which the characters' impressions of the ball are presented. Carlos Maria's impressions come after Sophia's, and Maria Benedicta's impressions come after his. Moreover, the conversation between the two ladies is shortened. Maria Benedicta's fit, which messes up her hairdo, is left out, as is the walk the two ladies take on the beach. Machado de Assis then omits the episode describing Quincas Borba's escape. He retains only two elements from this episode, which are essential to regaining control of the plot. In chapter 78 of the book version, in a very ingenious manner, Machado de Assis includes the appearance of Major Siqueira and the idea of marriage, which he plants in the protagonist's mind. These are the essential connections, within that profusion of concatenated incidents, required to develop the theme of Rubião's madness. Let us examine the first two paragraphs:

> Rubião é que não perdeu a suspeita assim tão facilmente. Pensou em falar a Carlos Maria, interrogá-lo, e chegou a ir à rua dos Inválidos, no dia seguinte, três vezes; não o encontrando, mudou de parecer. Encerrou-se por alguns dias; o Major Siqueira arrancou-o à solidão. Ia participar-lhe que se mudara para a rua Dois de Dezembro. Gostou muito da casa do nosso amigo, das alfaias, do luxo, de todas as minúcias, ouros e bambinelas. Sobre este assunto discorreu longamente, relembrando alguns móveis antigos. Parou de repente, para dizer que o achava aborrecido; era natural, faltava-lhe ali um complemento.
> — O senhor é feliz, mas falta-lhe aqui uma coisa; falta-lhe mulher. O senhor precisa casar. Case-se, e diga que eu o engano.[38]
>
> [Rubião did not lose his suspicions so easily. He considered questioning Carlos Maria, and even went to Inválidos Street three times the next day. Not finding him in, he changed his mind and stayed behind closed doors for three

days. It was Major Siqueira, who, having gone to inform him that he had moved to Dous de Dezembro Street, drew him out of his solitude. The Major very much liked our friend's house; its decorations, its drapes, all its little accessories, and he discoursed long upon the subject, recalling some of the furnishings of an earlier day. Suddenly he paused to say that Rubião seemed bored in the house, and that was only natural, since he was without a complement.

'You are happy, but there is something you need. You need a wife. You must get married. Marry, and tell me whether I'm wrong.'][39]

In the rewritten passage above, Machado de Assis frustrates Rubião's plan to extract a confession from Carlos Maria by simply noting that the young man was not at home when Rubião went to look for him. The writer thereby manages to eliminate the whole section of dialogue between Carlos Maria and Rubião, which in fact did not play any relevant part in the plot. On the contrary, it only served to overload the narrative with serial elements, as if the novelist wished to compensate for the lack of direction with melodramatic imagination. The strategy which Machado de Assis uses here to justify the appearance of a character from an episode which has already been eliminated is to include Major Siqueira's visit to Rubião to inform the latter of his change of address.

While eliminating the melodramatic, the novelist focuses on the process of Rubião losing his mind by extending and increasing the focus on the character's matrimonial delirium. As such, in the second version, the matrimonial delirium is highlighted more and becomes the culminating point of this narrative unit. In the next chapter of this book, I shall examine as a whole all the sections added to the chain of events in which the progressive stages of Rubião's madness are better delineated. For the time being, we shall continue to present narrative units in order to highlight the work done by Machado de Assis to control the plot and eliminate, by rewriting, the features most typical of the serial narrative.

Fifth Narrative Unit: Composition in Crisis and the Appeal to the Melodramatic Imagination

The next narrative unit also has quite rigid temporal limits, being confined to the ten days which cover the death of Maria Benedicta's mother, the mass held on the seventh day, and the three days following the mass. In the first version, it runs from chapter 87, dated 15 February 1888, to chapter 122, dated 31 July 1889.[40] In the definitive version, this unit corresponds to chapters 83 to 105.[41] Note that the numbering used in the two texts moves even further apart during the development of this unit and that, once the unit has ended, the two systems converge again. Chapter 106 is the same, in terms of both number and content, in the two versions. On the basis of this coincidence, Kinnear believes that it was between the months of July and November 1889, i.e., before Machado de Assis had finished the serialized novel, that the writer revised the serial which had already been written and published in order to begin composing the book.

In fact, this is the narrative unit which suffered the most interruptions: on 15 March, 30 April, 15 May, 15 July to 15 October 1888, 15 January, 15 February, 15 April, 15 and 31 May, and finally, 15 August to 15 November 1889. This could be an indication that Machado de Assis was completely losing control, not only because of the lapses in publication but also because, as Kinnear observed, he was continuing to harp on the same subject, i.e., Rubião's suspicions. Let us examine how the unit develops step by step, as we did with the third and fourth units.

In chapter 87 of the serialized version (corresponding to chapter 83 of the book version), the narrator says: 'Um dia, indo ao armazém, achou o Palha de luto. Morrera a tia da mulher, D. Maria Augusta, na fazenda; a notícia chegara na véspera à noite' [One day, going to the warehouse, he found Palha in mourning clothes. His wife's aunt, Maria Augusta, had died on the ranch; the news had arrived the previous night.].[42] The aunt's death is a good pretext for Rubião to visit Sophia and so satisfy his desire to see the object of his love dressed in black. Before going to Sophia's house, Rubião, who, as usual, does not have much to do, wanders aimlessly along the street, totally bored, until he remembers Freitas, who is ill, in a terminal state (chaps 88–89). As can be seen, the reappearance of this character is totally episodic. It serves to occupy Rubião's time, to make him remember that he used to be poor, and to fill up a few more pages of the periodical. It also allows our hero to do a good deed by leaving in Freitas's mother's hands a bundle of six twenty-thousand-*réis* notes. Lastly, it also takes us to a more remote corner of the city, as in Eugène Sue's serial: a landscape which is very different from Ouvidor Street and the drawing room of an arriviste. We enter a simple house and walk along the semi-deserted Formosa beach, where children, barefoot and in shirt sleeves, casually play among anchored canoes.

Machado de Assis then adds a further episode in which he focuses repeatedly on the affair between Carlos Maria and Sophia. On the way back to the city from Freitas's house, the coachman again awakens suspicions in Rubião's mind by relating the story of the seamstress–procuress. The protagonist returns home, dresses in black, has dinner with the diners and finally visits the family in mourning (chaps 90–96). There, his suspicions fade only to be reawakened by the seamstress responsible for making Sophia's black dresses. By pure coincidence, and somewhat unconvincingly (as in a television soap opera) she lives on the same street as the other seamstress in the story invented by the coachman. Visibly upset, Rubião breaks off his visit to chase after the two seamstresses in an attempt to confirm the coachman's story. As one story pulls the other, Machado de Assis is obliged to put an end to the episode of the pursuit. In order to do so, he has to narrate what happened to the seamstresses and the bank manager that the protagonist bumped into on the way (chaps 97–105).

Here, the narrator shows signs of a change in his attitude. In chapter 17, dated 15 August 1886, he had aroused the reader's curiosity over the continuation of the story with the announcement that beautiful women were yet to appear, but now the narrator seems to lose patience, or at least to have little desire to continue with the story. The novelist gets bogged down in Rubião's suspicions and is hemmed in by secondary characters, such as the seamstress and the bank manager. He includes in the novel the conversation between Dondon and the seamstress and relates what happened to the couple. At the start of chapter 105, dated 30 November 1888, the weary narrator exclaims: 'O resto? Oh! O resto das coisas!' [The rest? Oh! The rest of the things!]⁴³ and causes Rubião to lose sight of the couple. In order to conclude completely the episode of the pursuit, Machado de Assis ends up having to include another event which is almost reminiscent of a detective story: Rubião witnesses an act of violence and serves as a witness at the police station. In this way, among hindrances, pursuits and police bulletins, Machado de Assis seems to allow himself to be completely dominated by the serial form.

Not everything in this unit is insignificant, however, as one of the main themes of the novel is consolidated in this narrative unit. Continuing with his aim of depicting a changing society, the writer manages here to redefine the position of the characters within the social microcosm of the novel. Freitas is seen to be completely ruined and on the verge of death, while the social rise of the Palhas continues apace. Sophia and her husband are renewing their circle of friends, which already includes bankers and high society ladies, the latter being involved in the charitable activity promoted by Sophia through the creation of the Alagoas Committee.

In accordance with the central theme of a magazine such as *A Estação*, which was principally about fashion, Sophia needs not only a coupé at her sole disposal but also mourning clothes and other made-to-measure dresses. Moreover, it is the first time that mention has been made of the Alagoas Committee. The organization is a good illustration of Sophia's social rise as charitable activity is recognized (even to this day) as being an occupation which bestows prestige on the social elite. The Alagoas Committee also has a function within the plot: it immediately gives rise to false proof of the affair between its patron and Carlos Maria, and, in chapter 106, dated 30 November 1889, it provides the device which allows the plot to be resolved: the inclusion, as in a good serial, of a new character, Dona Fernanda, and her social network. Her presence is completely coherent with the plot up to the point at which the long interruption takes place, as she joins Sophia's circle of friends through the same charitable committee.

Here, the episode in which the appeal to the melodramatic imagination reaches its climax needs to be related: Machado de Assis arms Rubião with a revolver when the latter goes to Sophia's house to drag a confession of adultery out of her. Rubião believes that definitive proof of the affair is to be found in the circular from the Alagoas Committee, addressed by Sophia to Carlos Maria, which the postman drops in front of his house. In the serial, Rubião visits Sophia twice. On the first visit (chaps 116–17), the protagonist forgets to take the letter. He mentions it but as he does not have it with him, the subject of adultery recedes. Rubião then tells her of the secret plan of his political candidature and confesses his passion again. The whole conversation is also interrupted by the coming and going of Maria Benedicta. The following day, Rubião returns to Flamengo Beach, this time with the letter in his hand and a four-shot revolver in his pocket. This is chapter 119, dated 15 June 1889, which incites the reader to imagine that the conflict will be resolved through violence: 'Pode ser que ela, uma vez de posse da carta, a guarde consigo, e eu fico sem saber nada. Neste caso ameaço-a; se tentar correr, mato-a'. ['It could be that she, once in possession of the letter, keeps it with her, and I will remain in the dark. If that's the case, I'll threaten her; if she tries to run, I'll kill her.']⁴⁴

This chapter ends on a note of suspense:

Depois que ficaram a sós, nenhum deles soube por onde começasse. Venceu a curiosidade; Sofia pediu-lhe o papel, a famosa carta; que diria ela?
— Não sei o que diz, porque não a abri, explicou Rubião; tenho-a comigo desde muitos dias, mas não lhe toque.
— Como sabe que é minha?
— A letra do sobrescrito é sua.
Rubião tirou a carta do bolso da sobrecasaca; antes de a entregar, verificou se trazia o revólver; a mão tremia-lhe.
(Continua.)[45]

[Once they had been left alone, neither of them knew where to start. Curiosity won out; Sophia asked him for the paper, the famous letter; what would it say?
'I don't know what it says, because I haven't opened it,' explained Rubião. 'I've had it with me for several days, but I haven't touched it.'
'How do you know that it is mine?'
'The address is in your handwriting.'
Rubião took the letter from the pocket of his frock coat; before handing it to her, he checked that he had the revolver; his hand was trembling.
(Continues)]

It can be seen that at a few times Machado de Assis is on the verge of resolving the impasse in the plot in a melodramatic manner, i.e., by staging a highly emotional conflict which involves the use of physical force and contains strong moral connotations. I believe that the novelist appeals to the melodramatic imagination in order to compensate for the deceleration in the pace and repetitive character of the narrative. Kinnear had already drawn attention to these signs of uncertainty regarding the direction of the narrative and the melodramatic and farcical tone that characterizes the confrontation between Sophia and Rubião.[46] In the serial, the contents of the letter are finally revealed, which destroys the possibility that the conflict will be resolved through melodrama.

In the second version, Machado de Assis will restructure that narrative unit again. In moving from the first to the second version, he uses chapters 84–86 to elaborate the matrimonial delirium in more detail (chapter 79–82 of the book). In Chapter 7 of this book, the rewriting of this section will be examined in more detail. In the meantime, let us limit ourselves to the omissions. Machado de Assis reduces to a minimum unnecessary developments such as Rubião's long conversation with Palha, Rubião's visit to Freitas and the pursuit of the seamstresses. He also removes the conversation between the seamstress and Dondon and the police incident which Rubião witnesses. In some cases, in place of dialogue, the scene is narrated. In others, sequences of dialogue are omitted, which reduces the participation of secondary characters in the action, such as Freitas's mother, the seamstress and Dondon. The focus is thereby turned on Rubião.

In the first version, to delay the revelation of the contents of the letter, Machado de Assis postpones Rubião's reading of it. Rubião first reads an item in the newspaper concerning the police incident which he witnessed and then he mulls over the news. In rewriting the novel, Machado de Assis omits the news item in the newspaper and, subsequently, chapters 107 to 110. The writer also reverses the order of the episodes. In the second version, Camacho's visit is placed before Freitas's burial. In the first version, Rubião receives three letters: one from Sophia, one from Camacho, and one from Freitas's mother. In the book, Rubião does not receive a letter from Camacho. The journalist's visit occurs after lunch and replaces the long episode, now omitted, describing Rubião's lunch with Sarmento. In the serial, Rubião visits Sophia twice, as stated above, while in the definitive version there is just one visit. In the book, the scene is composed by patching together dialogue taken from two scenes in the serial. There is still a confrontation between the characters, the revelation of feelings, some brief physical contact, and more violent bodily movement, but the novelist opts to leave the letter sealed. In addition to the disordered numbering of the chapters and references to non-existent chapters, this is another area in which the serial becomes incoherent.

Kinnear believes that this change proves that Machado de Assis was clearly dissatisfied with the way in which Rubião's suspicions are handled, or, more specifically, with the way in which the text allows the reader to grasp these suspicions, having caused both the reader and the protagonist to feel doubtful up to chapter 106. I believe, however, that Machado de Assis chooses not to destroy Rubião's suspicions during his honest face-to-face confrontation with Sophia precisely so as to reduce the emotional intensity of the episode. If Machado de Assis had insisted on resolving the conflict by melodramatic means, this could have given rise to a moral debate as the characters would have to reveal openly their true interests in maintaining the ties of friendship. As has been stated in this chapter, however, the two series of dialogues at the beginning of the novel have already drawn the reader's attention to the pretence which will govern the code of social conventions. This becomes even clearer in the conversation between Sophia and Palha on the night of that long Sunday, after all of the guests have left the soirée.[47] The room is now lit 'por poucos bicos de gás' [by a few gas jets], which suggests an intimate atmosphere; it is this intimate atmosphere which explains the reserve with which the couple tackle such delicate matters. The dialogue, however, is very direct as it omits nothing in revealing to the reader the pact signed by the couple in order to continue handling Rubião without breaking the boundaries of decorum. Remember that Palha reveals to his wife the breadth of his financial obligations to Rubião.

The element which constituted a new development in the plot was this pact, and not the repetition of the episode describing Rubião's flirtation with Sophia. Recall that chapter 50 ended with the false cliffhanger prefaced by the word 'Guess'. At that stage in the narrative, Machado de Assis was already indicating that neither immoderation nor frankness would play a part in the interpersonal relations described in the novel, except, of course, where the depiction of Rubião's madness is concerned.

The Unfolding of the Plot

The publication of *Quincas Borba* was interrupted for three and a half months between 31 July and 30 November 1889. In chapter 108, the narrator informs us: 'Durante alguns meses, Rubião deixou de ir ao Flamengo' [For several months, Rubião stopped going to Flamengo].[48] The duration of the interruption is thereby incorporated into the narrative. It roughly corresponds to the period of time during which Rubião stops visiting Sophia at her house, which is now in Flamengo. It is during the second of Rubião's disappearances that various events will unfold which are significant in starting the process by which the conflict in the novel will be resolved. They are narrated in a long flashback which is interspersed with Rubião's assertion that Carlos Maria and Maria Benedicta are about to be married: 15 January 1890 (chaps 116–18), 31 January (chap. 118–continuation), 15 February (chaps 118–continuation, 119, 120) and 28 February (chaps 121–25).

In this way, on 30 November 1889, when the publication of the novel is restarted, Machado de Assis begins to make use of two characteristics which are intrinsic to the serial. The first concerns the use of the passing of time to accentuate changes in the social and psychological situations of the characters, and the second concerns the introduction of a new character. Here, we return to the question of narrative rhythm and the reader's perception that the rise or fall of the characters is not only gradual but also irreversible. The characters take turns on the stage during the last few rounds, in which the narrator advances and finally fixes their final positions in the social microcosm. For example, the narrator reveals the speedy process by which the Palhas grow rich, either by describing exterior signs (such as the furniture in the house and, in the first version, the uniformed servants bearing the initials C. P. on their buttons, the construction of the mansion in Botafogo, and Sophia's silk dresses and accessories), or by detailing their new ambitions, among which is the vague intention of gaining a baronetcy. As for Dona Tonica, after making an attempt on her latest candidate she ends up as an old maid and is moved outside of Sophia's social circle, together with her father.

It is also in the four instalments comprising the flashback that the narrator introduces a new unexpected nucleus of characters, in which Dona Fernanda is the key figure. In addition to acting as an intermediary who serves to determine the outcome of the marriage between Carlos Maria and Maria Benedicta, Dona Fernanda also facilitates the creation of a series of other episodes which distract the reader's attention from the driving thread of the narrative. These episodes include the constitution of the new ministry, in which Theophilo, Dona Fernanda's husband, hopes to participate. Dona Fernanda will also take on an important role in diagnosing Rubião's madness and installing him in the sanatorium.

No substantial changes were made to the text during the rewriting of the second half of the novel. Machado de Assis cut or synthesized some scenes, making the narrative even less episodic. This applies to the scene describing Sophia, Rubião and Palha's horse ride, which is narrated from chapters 142 to 148, dated 31 May 1891. In the book, these chapters were summarized in chapter 143. A further example concerns Palha's suspicions that Sophia is having an affair with Rubião after the coach episode, which are described in chapters 144 to 147 of the first version, chapters which were subsequently omitted. Finally, part of the instalments dated 31 March and 15 June 1891 were eliminated. In the first, Sophia visits Maria Benedicta and Carlos Maria after the birth of the couple's daughter. In the second, Dona Fernanda discusses Rubião's treatment and internment in the sanatorium with Dr Falcão.

We see that the reason for both the occasional interruption of the serial and the solution found by the writer to his creative impasse (which subsequently results in the resumed publication of the serial) have to do with the plot. Having assembled the plot, Machado de Assis finds it difficult to dismantle it without succumbing to melodrama. By a hair's breadth the novel did not end in shots and the precocious death of its heroine, Sophia. Physical confrontation, highly charged emotional scenes and, in the end, blood, were no longer to his taste, as they had been in the times of *Helena*. While not being melodramatic, the solution which he found to conclude the plot was still very characteristic of the serial. It is with the entrance on to the stage of Dona Fernanda, who binds together all of the characters in ties of kinship or friendship, that the characters gradually find their destinies. It is she who is responsible for Maria Benedicta's marriage to Carlos Maria, which indirectly makes her a relative of Sophia's. It is she who takes Dona Tonica's place among Sophia's friends, thereby helping the latter to climb socially. And it is she who looks after Rubião.

For those who finished reading the serial, the solution to the crisis which hindered the writing of the novel was wholly characteristic of the serial form: it comes about through the introduction of a new character and her social nucleus. Through pure novelistic artifice, this character is at the same time a matchmaker, a charitable person, a relative of one character, and a friend of others. For those who read the novel in book form, the placing of Rubião at the centre of the narrative, the development of the progressive stages of his madness, and the transformation of the whole narrative into an exemplification of *Humanitismo* transforms the reading experience, even though, from chapter 106 (30 November 1889) onwards, there are few variations between the two versions. Moreover, however much the introduction of a new character might be classed as a narrative resource characteristic of the serial, we see that Dona Fernanda, the kindest and most socially stable character in the novel, has much to do with *Humanitismo*: although she stands at the top of the pyramid, as the wife of a man who aspires to the ministry, she participates in the game of social climbing in the highest sphere of the political elite. Her altruism seems on the surface to be a natural tendency or a sign of feminine liberation. In fact, she is behaving in a way that would be expected of ladies of her social standing.

The rewriting operations responsible for transforming the serial into a book shall be the subject of the next (and last) two chapters of this book.

Notes to Chapter 5

1. See 'Introdução crítico-filológica', *Quincas Borba*, 1975, pp. 39–46.
2. *Quincas Borba apêndice*, p. 70.
3. *Quincas Borba apêndice*, p. 37.
4. *Quincas Borba apêndice*, p. 170, my underlining. *Quincas Borba*, chap. 137, p. 277, *Philosopher or Dog?*, p. 196.
5. See Chapter 3 of this book.
6. Kinnear, p. 56.
7. Ibid.
8. Genette, pp. 88–89.
9. First narrative unit: chaps 1–2 (15 June), chaps 3–5 (30 June), chaps 6–9 (15 July), chaps 10–14 (31 July), 14 (continuation)–18 (15 August 1886); *Quincas Borba apêndice*, pp. 7–21.
10. Stories by Machado de Assis which were published in *A Estação* include: 'Um para o outro', 30 July to 15 October 1879; 'O caso da viúva', 15 January to 15 March 1881; 'Dona Benedita', 15 April to 31 June 1882; 'Capítulos dos chapéus', 15 August to 15 September River 1883; 'A viúva Sobral', 15 April to 30 May 1884; 'Curta história', 31 May 1886; 'Pobre Finoca', 31 December 1891 to 31 January 1892; 'A inglesinha Barcelos', 31 May to 30 June 1894; 'Relógio parado', 15 January to 31 March 1898. For a list of Machado de Assis's collaboration with *A Estação*, see Galante de Sousa, 1955, pp. 231–33.
11. *Quincas Borba apêndice*, chap. 5, p. 12.
12. *Quincas Borba apêndice*, chap. 3, p. 9.
13. *Quincas Borba apêndice*, chap. 15, p. 19.
14. The editorial dated 15 July 1890, for example, announces an increase in the number of patterns published: 'Novo melhoramento acaba de ser feito, aumentando-se o número de moldes que publicamos com mais duas folhas no correr do ano e aumentando o número de páginas da nossa parte literária' [A new improvement has just been made, increasing the number of patterns which we publish, with two more pages this year and an increase in the number of pages in the literary section]. According to the same editorial 'a norma seguida em relação a tudo quanto publicamos é colocar a assinante em condições de tudo executar de per si ou sob suas vistas' [the standard followed in relation to everything that we publish is to make it possible for everything to be made by subscribers themselves, or under their supervision].
15. See in particular chapter 10: 'Comment Dinah devient femme de province', Honoré de Balzac, *La Muse du département*, <http://fr.wikisource.org/wiki/La_Muse_du_département> [accessed 15 July 2006].
16. *Quincas Borba apêndice*, chap. 17, p. 20.
17. Lisa Queffélec, *Le romain-feuilleton français* (Paris: Presses Universitaire de France, 1989), p. 30.
18. Brito Broca, *Românticos, pré-românticos, ultra-românticos: vida literária e romantismo brasileiro* (São Paulo: Polis; Brasília: INL, 1979), p. 175.
19. *A Estação*, 31 August 1886, chap. 19; *Quincas Borba apêndice*, p. 22.
20. Second narrative unit: chaps 20–22 (31 August), chaps 22 (continuation)–25 (15 September), chaps 26–28 (30 September), chaps 28 (continuation)–29 (15 October), chaps 30–32 (31 October), chaps 31[sic]–35 (15 November), chaps 36–38 (30 November), chaps 39–41 (15 December), chaps 41 (continuation)–42 (31 December 1886), probably chaps 43–47, not located (15 January), chaps 48–50 (31 January), chaps 50 (continuation) (15 February), chap. 50 (continuation)–52 (28 February 1887); *Quincas Borba apêndice*, pp. 22–55.
21. *Quincas Borba apêndice*, p. 47.
22. *A Estação*, chaps 51–52 (28 February 1887), chaps 54 [sic] (15 March 1887); *Quincas Borba apêndice*, pp. 52–55.
23. Coutinho, p. 297.
24. Kinnear, p. 56.
25. Afrânio Coutinho, 'José de Alencar e a ficção romântica', *A literatura no Brasil*, vol. 3 (Rio de Janeiro: José Olympio e UFF, 1986), p. 295.
26. *Quincas Borba apêndice*, chap. 22, p. 24; *Quincas Borba*, chap. 3, p. 108. Note here that the order

of chapters changes from the first to the second version. This will be the subject of Chapter 6 of this book.

27. *Quincas Borba apêndice*, p. 48.
28. 'Croniqueta', *A Estação*, 30 June 1887.
29. 'Pelo telefone': 15 July, 30 August, 15 September, 30 September 1886; 'A impiedosa': 15 December 1886.
30. 'Um bilhete de loteria': 31 October 1887; 'Argos': 15 February, 15 March 1888; 'Rogério Brito': 30 April, 31 May 1888; 'Parizina': 30 June 1888; 'A toalha de crivo': 15–31 July 1888; 'E minha mãe!': 15 February 1889; '22 e 27': 28 February, 15 March 1889; 'O cão e o gato': 15 April 1890. It can be seen that Artur Azevedo published the most stories in the years in which the serialization of *Quincas Borba* suffered the greatest number of interruptions.
31. 'As nossas casas': 15–31 December 1888; 'Guiomar Torrezão': 31 March 1889: 'Nossas casas': 15 August 1889; 'Maria Amália Vaz de Carvalho': 31 October 1889; 'Belas Artes': 15 March 1890; 'Os livros': 30 June 1890; 'Higiene': 30 August 1890; 'A cozinha': 31 May 1891; 'Entre dois berços': 30 April 1891.
32. 'A tempestade' (poetry): 30 November 1889; 'Esboços e perfis': 14 April 1890; 'Esboços femininos': 30 April, 31 May, 30 June, 15 July–31 August, 31 October–30 November, 31 December 1890; 15–31 January, 28 February, 15 March, 15 April–15 September 1891; 'A cruz' (poetry): 31 May 1891.
33. Third narrative unit: chaps 55–57 (15 March), chaps 56 (continuation) [*sic*]–57 (31 March), chaps 58–60 (15 April 1887), chaps 63 [*sic*]–64 (30 April); chaps 64 (continuation)–65 (15 May), chaps 66–68 (15 June 1887); *Quincas Borba apêndice*, pp. 55–68.
34. *Quincas Borba apêndice*, chap. 55, p. 55.
35. *Quincas Borba apêndice*, caps. 68 (continuation) and 69, p. 69.
36. Fourth narrative unit: chap. 69 (15 July), chaps 69 (continuation)–71 (31 July), chaps 72–75 (15 August), chap. 75 (continuation) (31 August), chaps 75 (continuation)–77 (15 September), chaps 78–79 (30 September), chaps 79 (continuation)–80 (15 October), chap. 80 (continuation) (15 November), chaps 80 (continuation)–81 (30 November), chap. 72 [*sic*] (15 December), chaps 82 (continuation) [*sic*]–83 (31 December 1887), chap. 83 (continuation) (15 January 1888), chaps 84–86 (31 January 1888); *Quincas Borba apêndice*, pp. 69–96.
37. *Quincas Borba apêndice*, p. 87.
38. *Quincas Borba*, chap. 78, p. 205.
39. *Philosopher or Dog?*, pp. 114–15.
40. Fifth narrative unit: chap. 87 (15 February 1888), chaps. 88–89 (29 February), chap. 90 (31 March), chaps 91–93 (15 April), chaps 94–97 (31 May), chaps 96 [*sic*]–98 (31 October), chaps 99–103 (15 November), chaps 104–08 (30 November), chaps 109–11 (15 December), chaps 112–15 (31 December 1888), chaps 112 [*sic*]–113 (31 January 1889), chap. 112 [*sic*] (28 February), chap. 113 (15 March), chap. 114 (31 March), chaps 115–18 (30 April), chaps 117 (continuation) [*sic*]–119 (15 June), chap. 119 (continuation) (30 June), chaps 120–22 (31 July 1889); *Quincas Borba apêndice*, pp. 96–137.
41. *Quincas Borba*, pp. 210–36.
42. *Quincas Borba apêndice*, p. 96; *Quincas Borba*, p. 210. Book version (B, C, D): 'Um dia, como houvesse saído mais cedo de casa, e não soubesse onde passar a primeira hora, caminhou para o armazém. Desde uma semana que não ia à praia do Flamengo, por haver Sofia entrado em um dos seus períodos de sequidão. Achou o Palha de luto; morrera a tia da mulher, Dona Maria Augusta, na fazenda; a notícia chegara na antevéspera, à tarde.' [One day, as he had left home earlier and did not know where to spend the first hour, he walked to the warehouse. He hadn't been to Flamengo Beach for a week, as Sophia had entered one of her cold phases. He found Palha in mourning clothes; his wife's aunt, Maria Augusta, had died on the ranch; the news has arrived the previous day, in the evening.]
43. *Quincas Borba apêndice*, chap. 105, p. 114.
44. *Quincas Borba apêndice*, chap. 119, p. 131.
45. *Quincas Borba apêndice*, p. 132.
46. Kinnear, p. 58.
47. *Quincas Borba apêndice*, p. 52.
48. *Quincas Borba apêndice*, chap. 108, p. 138.

CHAPTER 6

❖

From the Magazine to the Book: The Global View of the Novel

The revision of the novel for book publication started before the conclusion of its serialization. Many excisions were made, eliminating secondary characters and episodes that were melodramatic, or unimportant to the construction of the plot. Machado de Assis also added a few, but important, paragraphs and chapters, and reordered some events. This chapter shows that the reordering of the first twenty chapters, the elimination of secondary material, and the small additions made gave prominence to a single main character, Rubião, and to his progressive madness.

Focusing on Rubião

Among the more significant changes made to the text when it passed from the magazine to the book form was the increased focus on Rubião. Beforehand, the focus of the novel had been more variable: in the serial, the parallel destinies of secondary characters such as Maria Benedicta, Carlos Maria, Freitas and Dona Tonica could be traced with equal enthusiasm, even though Rubião's trajectory merited greater attention in the projection of the narrative.

John Gledson, in *Machado de Assis: ficção e história*, has already highlighted the fact that the characterization of Rubião was one of the author's chief concerns when he rewrote the whole novel, and that it was with this character that the author faced his greatest difficulties.[1] Gledson interprets the characterization of Rubião, on which the author worked so patiently, as a political allegory of the nation, in accordance with a suggestion made by Araripe Júnior: 'Quem nos diz que este personagem não seja o Brasil?' ['Who would say that this character is not Brazil?'].[2] In this book, while not disregarding the implications that the variations have for the allegorical meanings of the novel (both historical and political), I am particularly interested in the part played by those changes to the narrative structure which concern Rubião, more specifically, those changes which involve the restructuring of the 'plotting' of *Quincas Borba*. Peter Brooks prefers this term to 'plot', as the gerund form emphasizes the dynamic aspect of the narrative:

> that which moves us forward as readers of the narrative text, that which makes us — like the heroes of the text often, and certainly like their authors — want and need plotting, seeking through the narrative text as it unfurls before us a precipitation of shape and meaning, some simulacrum of understanding of how meaning can be constructed over and through time.[3]

The systematic work which Machado de Assis carried out on Rubião in rewriting the serial version for the book was central to redefining the plot and, consequently, to the way we read the novel in its second version. In other words, the changes made to Rubião's character play an important role in defining a new pattern of reading for the book form. This is what I would now like to prove, starting with an example which documents the work done by the writer in reorganizing the text at the macroscopic level.

Rotation of the first twenty chapters

The process of focusing attention on Rubião begins when Machado de Assis reorders the events of the first twenty chapters of the novel. In the words of Augusto Meyer, the serial version 'começava então pelo começo' [started at the beginning] by revealing the philosopher's illness and the prognosis of his death.[4] In chapter 3, i.e., in the second instalment of the serial, the narrator explains who Rubião is and what the circumstances are which unite the two characters. All of the action up to chapter 18 takes place in Barbacena. Only in chapter 20 does Rubião rise to the position of capitalist and protagonist, with the scene in which he admires Botafogo bay from the mansion which he has inherited from his friend.

In the book version, Machado de Assis rotates the order of the events, placing what was in chapter 20 of the serial at the start of the novel. As a result, when the tale opens Rubião is already a man of means, firmly established in Rio de Janeiro, even though this situation, which at the same time is both social and spiritual, is only transitory. Thus we first meet him at the peak of his wealth and mental health — if we believe that our hero was ever sane. The events which take place in Barbacena are then presented in a flashback, as is the train journey from Minas Gerais to the capital and Rubião's subsequent encounters with the Palhas. Here, the flashback catches up with the narrative present, returning to the opening scene in which Rubião finds himself alone on the balcony of his mansion in Botafogo. The flashback is so long (it runs from chapter 4 to 27) that without the narrator's warning we might not realize that in chapter 27 the narrative returns to that same scene, in which Rubião is on the balcony of the mansion:

> Tudo isso passava agora pela cabeça do Rubião, depois do café, no mesmo lugar em que o deixamos sentado, a olhar para longe, muito longe. Continuava a bater com as borlas do chambre. Afinal lembrou-se de ir ver o Quincas Borba, e soltá-lo. Era a sua obrigação de todos os dias. Levantou-se e foi ao jardim, ao fundo.[5]

> [All of this was running through Rubião's head, after his morning cup of coffee, in the very spot where we left him sitting and gazing off into the distance. He was still drumming with the tassels of his dressing gown. Finally he remembered to go and see Quincas Borba and unleash him. That was his daily duty. He got up and went out to the back garden.][6]

Here Machado de Assis is playing with the distinction between *fabula* and *sjužet*. Despite the fact that in both versions the narrated event (*fabula*) is the same, the order in which the events are presented within the narrative discourse (*sjužet*) is different. By reordering the material contained in the twenty chapters, the writer is giving the novel a new 'dynamic shaping force', which leads to a new type of plotting in which Rubião is the main focus.[7]

When we reach chapter 27 of the book, we are able to understand Rubião's transformation that had been referred to tantalizingly in chapter 1: ' — Vejam como Deus escreve direito por linhas tortas'[8] ['See how God writes straight on crooked lines]'.[9] The same statement is not found in the serial version because the events which take place in Barbacena have been narrated before Rubião's move to Rio.

The reader is therefore inclined to see the events narrated in these twenty-seven chapters as a whole. The serial emphasizes the chronological order of the events and does not provide a very clear view of the fact that the circumstances affecting the hero in the first part of the novel form a single unit. Moreover, as we shall see in the next chapter of this book, the relationship between Quincas Borba and Rubião in the second version is more visibly that of master and disciple, even though Rubião fails to understand the workings of *Humanitismo* when the philosopher didactically explains it to him through an example.[10]

From very early on in the book version, in fact, from the opening chapter, the reader (prompted by the narrator) is able to associate Rubião's recent fortune with the theory of *Humanitismo*. At the start of the novel, however, God is responsible for the very sudden (and, let it be said in passing, very artificial) change in the character's destiny:

> — Vejam como Deus escreve direito por linhas tortas, pensa ele. Se mana Piedade tem casado com Quincas Borba, apenas me daria uma esperança colateral. Não casou; ambos morreram, e aqui está tudo comigo; de modo que o que parecia uma desgraça...[11]

> ['See how God writes straight on crooked lines. Had Sister Piedade married Quincas Borba, I could have hoped only for a collateral inheritance. She did not marry him; both died, and now everything is mine; so that what seemed a misfortune...'][12]

We cannot fail to observe that the idea of creating meaning through narrative blocks which are much longer than the instalments of the magazine was already present in embryo form in the serial. In the previous chapter we saw that, from chapters 20 to 50, Machado de Assis created a narrative unit lasting one day, which had to be divided into 13 instalments, taking over six months to be published. In the book, therefore, he simply takes to its extreme the principle of constructing longer narrative units, as chapters 1 to 50 now belong to the same continuous day.

Elimination of secondary characters

Let us examine a further, more specific, example which shows that the focus on Rubião can also be perceived at the microscopic level, where it is also possible to detect a subtle change in the positioning of the narrator in relation to the character. Here I discuss the rewriting of chapters 58 to 62, dated 15 April 1887, the serialized versions of which had not yet been located by the Machado de Assis Committee when it was editing the critical edition.

Chapters 58 to 62 of the serial version correspond to chapters 58 to 60 of the book version. Machado de Assis rewrites some sections, omits some dialogues and merges the last three chapters — these are the main changes which occur in the rewriting process. I will focus on the three groups of variations which I consider to be most significant because they reveal, at a microscopic level, the work done by Machado de Assis on the characterization of Rubião.

In chapter 59, Camacho and Palha meet at Rubião's house: 'Palha e Camacho olharam um para o outro... Oh! esse olhar foi como um bilhete de visita trocado entre as duas consciências. Nenhuma disse o seu segredo, mas viram os nomes no cartão, e cumprimentaram-se'[13] [Palha and Camacho looked at each other. Oh! that look was like a calling card exchanged between two consciences. Neither conscience told its secret, but they saw their names on the card, and they greeted each other].[14] At this stage in the narrative, Rubião is thinking of returning to Minas because he believes that he has been very stupid in declaring his love for Sophia and he feels embarrassed by the idea of remaining in Rio. Chapter 59 shows Camacho and Palha's interests in keeping Rubião in Rio. First, Palha tries to persuade Rubião to put off his plans, proposing a trip to Minas with himself and his wife: 'Sofia é companheira para estas viagens'[15] ['Sophia is a good companion for such trips'].[16]

The first rewritten section begins when Rubião tries to justify his return to Barbacena by invoking the elections. Now it is Camacho's turn to intervene. In the serialized version, the dialogue between Rubião and Camacho is presented in direct speech. In the book, the dialogue is condensed and incorporated into the narrative voice. Machado de Assis then omits another of Palha's interventions and once again incorporates Rubião's words into the narrative voice, as we see in Table 6.1 (p. 146).

The process of eliminating dialogue and incorporating it into the narrative voice gives this section a new rhythm. Machado de Assis creates a new cadence of voices, making the transition from direct speech to free indirect speech more subtle. This movement allows us to penetrate Rubião's thoughts without breaking up the dialogue, as happened in the serialized version. As Mattoso Câmara states, rather than

> apresentar o personagem no palco da narração como uma figura dramática, que fala por si (discurso direto) ou de lançá-lo aos bastidores para nos informar objetivamente sobre o que ele disse (discurso indireto estrito), o narrador associa-se ao seu personagem, transpõe-se para junto dele e fala em uníssono com ele.[18]

> [presenting the character on the narrative stage as a dramatic figure, who speaks for himself (direct speech), or placing him behind the scenes to inform us objectively of what he says (indirect speech, in the strict sense), the narrator associates himself with his character, entering the narrative with him and speaking in unison with him.]

The adoption of free indirect speech, continues Mattoso Câmara, 'conserva os traços afetivos, mas não impõe ao leitor a noção de que o personagem pensou em frases definidas e nítidas, pois as frases apresentadas são do autor, tendo apenas a coloração afetiva do personagem'[19] [conserves the emotional traces but does not impose on the reader the idea that the character thinks in defined and clear sentences, as the sentences shown are those of the author; they bear only the emotional colouring of the character].

A: A Estação, 15 April 1887

Rubião agitava-se no canapé, um pouco trêmulo. Sorria, abanava a cabeça. Camacho alegava os sucessos políticos...

— Por isso mesmo, as eleições, interrompia Rubião.

— Não, deixe lá as eleições. Cá temos muito que fazer por ora. Precisamos lutar aqui mesmo, na capital; aqui é que devemos esmagar a cabeça da cobra. Lá irá quando for tempo; irá então receber a recompensa e matar as saudades... E sabia que político não tem saudades; e o dever do cidadão é entregar-se ao seu partido, militar no ostracismo para triunfar no dia da vitória.

A recompensa era, com certeza, o diploma de deputado. Rubião entendeu bem, posto que o outro não lhe falasse em tal. Visão deliciosa, ambição que nunca teve, quando era um pobre diabo. Ei-la que o toma, que lhe aguça todos os apetites de grandezas e de glória... De outro lado, o amigo Cristiano continua a falar da necessidade de ficar, por enquanto, — mormente agora que acaba de saber da vocação política do amigo. Concorda com o outro, sem saber bem por quê, nem para quê. Tudo é que fique.

— Mas uma viagem de alguns dias, disse Rubião sem desejo de lhe aceitarem a proposta.

— Vá de alguns dias, concordou Camacho.

A lua estava então brilhante...

A

Rubião squirmed on the sofa, trembling a little. He was smiling and shaking his head. Camacho cited the political events...

'Exactly, the elections,' interrupted Rubião.

'No, forget about the elections. We have a lot to do here for the time being. We need to fight right here, in the capital; it's here that we have to crush the head of the cobra. You'll go there when it's time; you'll go there to receive your reward and allay your homesickness... Did you know that there is no homesickness in politics; and that the duty of the citizen is to devote himself to his party, to fight on in exile in order to triumph on the day of victory.

The reward would surely be the title of deputy. Rubião understood this very well, although the other had not spoken to him of it. A delicious vision, an ambition which he had never had, when he was a poor devil. An ambition that has laid a hold upon him now, whetting his appetite for greatness and glory... On the other hand, his friend Cristiano keeps talking of the need to stay, for the time being — particularly now that he has just learnt of his friend's political vocation. He agrees with the other, without really knowing why, nor for what purpose. Everything points to him staying.

'But a trip of a few days,' Rubião said, without wanting them to accept the proposal.

'Go for a few days,' Camacho agreed.

The moon was bright now...

D: Quincas Borba, p. 178

Rubião agarrou-se às eleições próximas; mas aqui interveio Camacho, afirmando que não era preciso, que a serpente devia ser esmagada cá mesmo na capital; não faltaria tempo depois para ir matar saudades e receber a recompensa... Rubião agitou-se no canapé. A recompensa era, com certeza, o diploma de deputado. Visão magnífica, ambição que nunca teve, quando era um pobre diabo... Ei-la que o toma, que lhe aguça todos os apetites de grandeza e glória... Entretanto, ainda insistiu por poucos dias de viagem, e, para ser exato, devo jurar que o fez sem desejo de que lhe aceitassem a proposta.

A lua estava então brilhante....

Philosopher or Dog, p. 84

Rubião snatched at the forthcoming elections, but here Camacho intervened, asserting that that was not necessary, that the serpent should be crushed right there in the capital, and that there would be plenty of time afterwards to allay his homesickness and receive a reward. Rubião squirmed on the couch. The reward would surely be the title of deputy. A magnificent vision, an ambition he had never had when he was a poor devil — an ambition that has laid a hold upon him now, whetting his appetite for greatness and glory. Meanwhile, he still insisted that he must go for a few days, and, to be exact, I am compelled to make it clear that he did it without any wish that they accept this proposal.

The moon was bright now...

TABLE 6.1: Chapter 59 in *A* and *D*[17]

A: A Estação, 15 April 1887

61

No dia seguinte recebeu um jornal que nunca vira antes, a *Atalaia,* sem nome de redator, artigos anônimos, várias notícias, poucos anúncios e de grandes letras. O artigo editorial desancava o ministério; a conclusão, porém estendia-se a todos os partidos e à nação inteira: — *Mergulhemos no Jordão constitucional.* Rubião achou-o excelente; tratou de ver onde se imprimia a folha para assiná-la. Freitas, que veio almoçar com ele, deu-lhe explicações sobre a *Atalaia.* Era redigido pelo Dr. Camacho, um Camacho...

— Conheço; ainda ontem esteve aqui comigo, interrompeu Rubião.

— É dele, e não é má. Que diz o número de hoje?

Freitas leu o artigo com ênfase, por modo que o Rubião ainda o achou melhor do que quando o lera na cama. Concordaram que era magnífico. Ao almoço, falaram muito do Camacho, confessando Rubião que simpatizava com ele, e pedindo ao outro a sua opinião. A opinião era a mesma. Depois indagou dos costumes da pessoa, da consideração em que o tinham, e todas as respostas foram agradáveis; era homem circunspecto, estimado, perfeito cavalheiro, um *gentleman.*

62

Nesse mesmo dia foi ao escritório de Camacho. Queria elogiar o artigo e assinar a folha. Ia andando pela rua da Ajuda, quando sucedeu dar com um menino de dois anos, se tanto, no meio da rua, e um carro que descia a trote largo, com o cocheiro distraído. A mãe, que estava à porta de uma colchoaria, deu um grito angustioso, mas não teve forças para correr a salvá-lo.

— Deolindo!...

A

61

The following day, he received a newspaper that he had never seen before: the *Atalaia,* with no editor's name, anonymous articles, several news items, few advertisements and large letters. The editorial inveighed against the ministry, though its conclusion was expanded to include all the parties and the whole nation: — *Let us plunge into the constitutional Jordan.* Rubião thought it excellent, and looked to see where the sheet was printed so that he might subscribe to it. Freitas, who had come to lunch with him, explained a few things about *Atalaia* to him. It was edited by Dr Camacho, a Camacho...

'I know him; he was here with me just yesterday,' interrupted Rubião.

'It's his, and it's not bad. What does today's issue say?'

Freitas read the article with such emphasis that Rubião found it even better than when he had read it in bed. They agreed that it was magnificent. At lunch, they spoke a lot about Camacho, and Rubião confessed that he sympathized with him, and asked the other man what he thought. His opinion was the same. Afterwards, he inquired into his habits and the consideration in which he was held, and all of the replies were full of praise; he was a serious, respected man, a perfect gentleman.

62

That same day he went to Camacho's office. He wanted to praise the article and subscribe to the paper. He was walking along Ajuda Street when he came across a boy of no more than two years of age, standing in the middle of the road, and a carriage was approaching at a quick pace, and the driver was not paying attention. His mother, who was standing in the doorway of a mattress shop, gave an anguished cry, but she lacked the strength to run to save him.

'Deolindo!'

TABLE 6.2: Chapters 61 and 62 in *A* (above); chapter 60 in *D* (opposite)

D: Quincas Borba, p. 179

No dia seguinte recebeu um jornal que nunca vira antes, a *Atalaia*. O artigo editorial desancava o ministério; a conclusão, porém estendia-se a todos os partidos e à nação inteira: — *Mergulhemos no Jordão constitucional.* Rubião achou-o excelente; tratou de ver onde se imprimia a folha para assiná-la. Era na rua da Ajuda; lá foi, logo que saiu de casa; lá soube que o redator era o Doutor Camacho. Correu ao escritório dele.

Mas, em caminho na mesma rua:
— Deolindo!...

Philosopher or Dog, p. 86

The next day he received a paper that he had never seen before, the *Atalaia*. The editorial inveighed against the ministry, though its conclusion was expanded to include all the parties and the whole nation: *Let us plunge into the constitutional Jordan.* Rubião thought it excellent, and looked to see where the sheet was printed so that he might subscribe to it. It was in Ajuda Street, and he went there first of all when he left the house. There he learned that Doctor Camacho was the editor. At once he hurried to the latter's office, but, as he reached the street on which it was located, he heard a woman's voice calling frantically from the door of a mattress shop:
'Deolindo! Deolindo!'

Moreover, six paragraphs in the magazine are condensed into just one in the book. The focus passes from game of persuasion played by Camacho and Palha (who take turns to speak) to the effects of the words spoken by the two characters on Rubião's present mental state. The hero begins to harbour political ambitions and is closer to developing his imperial megalomania.

In Table 6.2 (p. 147) we see that the omission of one passage makes the narrative more concise and also facilitates the joining of chapters 59 and 62. It is now the morning after Camacho and Palha's visit, which corresponds to the first paragraph of chapter 69 of the serial. In the book version, the section corresponds to the second paragraph of chapter 60, since, in rewriting the novel, Machado de Assis had already merged the short chapter 60 with chapter 61. Rubião receives the newspaper *Atalaia* at home and is reading Camacho's furious article. In the book version, Rubião is alone all the time, while in the first version Freitas comes for lunch. Once again, Freitas reads the article aloud. The two friends then talk about *Atalaia* and its editor. In the next chapter, Rubião sets out for Camacho's office, but on the way an incident occurs (see Table 6.2).

Firstly, Machado de Assis eliminates Freitas's participation in the action. His appearance was brief, but it contained all of the elements which make up a scene, including a change of scenario, the entrance and exit of the character, and the constituent dialogues. Once again the focus falls on Rubião, who is now alone in the scene. Rather than speaking with another character (Freitas, in this case), he is left alone with his thoughts.

The writer also omits the first paragraph of chapter 62, the aim of which was to introduce a new dramatic situation, with a new scene, new characters and new dialogues. This is the Deolindo episode, which transforms Rubião into a hero in the eyes of those who witness the incident, and which subsequently appears as a news item in a newspaper. In this case, the omission results in an intensification of the dramatic nature of the novel, as Rubião tries to prevent Deolindo from being run over by the runaway carriage. In the serial, the description of the accident is

A: A Estação, 15 April 1887; *Quincas Borba apêndice*, p. 59	*A*
— Ia quase morrendo, disse a mãe. Se não fosse este senhor, não sei o que seria do meu pobre filho. Era um acontecimento no quarteirão. Vizinhos entraram a ver o que sucedera ao pequeno; na rua,[20] crianças e moleques, espiavam pasmados. A criança tinha apenas um arranhão no ombro esquerdo, e certamente produzido pela queda, não pelos cavalos. — Ah! mas você é descuidada, Josefina! dizia o marido. Como é que você deixa sair assim o menino? — Estava aqui na calçada, redarguiu a mãe. — Qual calçada! A criança o que quer é brincar. Você é muito distraída... — E você também não é? Quero ver se você também não se distrai. — Não foi nada, interveio Rubião; em todo caso, não deixem o menino sair à rua; é muito pequenino. — Obrigado, disse o marido; mas onde está o seu chapéu?	'He was nearly killed', said the mother. Had it not been for this gentleman, I don't know what would have become of my poor boy.' It was an event in the block. Neighbours came in to see what had happened to the child; out on the street white children and little Negro boys were looking on with astonishment. The child had only a scratch on the left shoulder that was certainly caused by the fall rather than the horses. 'Ah, but you're careless, Josefina,' the husband said. 'How could you have let the child go out like that?' 'He was here on the pavement,' replied the mother. 'What pavement? What the child wants to do is play. You're very inattentive...' 'And what about you? I bet you would get distracted too!' 'It was nothing', interjected Rubião. 'In any case, don't let the child go out onto the road; he's very small.' 'Thank you' said the husband. 'But where is your hat?'
D *Quincas Borba*, p. 180.	*D* *Philosopher or Dog*, p. 86
— Ia quase morrendo, disse a mãe. Se não fosse este senhor, não sei o que seria do meu pobre filho. Era uma novidade no quarteirão. Vizinhos entravam a ver o que sucedera ao pequeno; na rua, crianças e moleques, espiavam pasmados. A criança tinha apenas um arranhão no ombro esquerdo, produzido pela queda. — Não foi nada, disse Rubião; em todo caso, não deixem o menino sair à rua; é muito pequenino. — Obrigado, acudiu o pai; mas onde está o seu chapéu?	'He was nearly killed,' said the mother. 'Had it not been for this gentleman, I don't know what would have become of my poor boy.' It was an event in the block. Neighbors came in to see what had happened to the child; out on the street white children and little Negro boys were looking on with astonishment. Actually, the child had only a scratch on the left shoulder from the fall. 'It was nothing,' said Rubião. 'In any case, don't let that little boy go out into the street; he's too small.' 'Thank you,' said the father. 'But where is your hat?'

TABLE 6.3: Chapter 62 in *A*; chapter 60 in *D*

delayed by the opening of the chapter (and also by Freitas's appearance). But in the book the scene is presented without any intervention or explanation.

In Table 6.3 (p. 149), we notice that the discussion between Deolindo's parents concerning the carriage incident has been omitted.

In cutting out these four bits of dialogue, Machado de Assis does not eliminate Deolindo's father and mother from the action, as he had done with Freitas. Their participation, however, is curtailed by the writer. The small amount of friction between Deolindo's parents had nothing to do with Rubião. It served only to bring to the narrative the familiar problems associated with minor characters. It was perhaps for this reason that Machado de Assis decided to eliminate the dialogue in question. The writer retains only the words addressed to Rubião: 'He was nearly killed,' said the mother. 'Had it not been to this gentleman, I don't know what would have become of my poor boy.'; 'Thank you,' said the father. 'But where is your hat?'

The element which unites these three rewritten excerpts is the fact that more attention is focussed on Rubião. In Table 6.1, as we saw, the focus changes from Camacho and Palha's game of persuasion to the effects that the two characters' words have on Rubião's mental state. In Table 6.2, the removal of Freitas from the action leaves Rubião alone on the balcony, talking to himself, until he is aroused from his thoughts by the urgent need to save Deolindo. In Table 6.3, Machado de Assis cut out a small family dispute which in no way concerned the hero.

As regards the positioning of the narrator in relation to Rubião, a preference for indirect free speech can be observed as a device to allow the hero's mental confusion to come to the surface more often. This device will be used again in the sections which reveal the writer's concern with marking the progressive stages of Rubião's madness, which we shall now examine.

Rubião's Progressive Madness

It is clear that Machado de Assis's careful revision of these five chapters would not have had any impact if the same principle had not been applied to the narrative in a more wide-ranging manner, as in the previously examined case of the first fifty chapters of the novel. It is as if the writer were now placing Rubião at the top of a pyramid, with the female characters placed on one side of the base and the male characters on the other. In rewriting the text, the novelist moves from depicting the parallel trajectory of the other characters to marking the development of the protagonist's madness in more distinctive stages.

Let us now examine, step by step, the main changes involving the protagonist's madness which have been made from one version to the next. The first is found at the start of the novel, i.e., in that part of the action which takes place in Barbacena. As Gledson has observed, the serial puts more emphasis on Rubião's ambitious and selfish character.[21] In the first place, the fact that part of the action now occurs in a flashback rather than in real time means that some very important sections describing Quincas Borba's treatment at the hands of Rubião — now greedy for his friend's inheritance and struggling to conceal his glee at his decline — are eliminated. As in a scene acted out on stage, the serial reveals in detail the nuances of Rubião's facial expressions, tone of voice and thoughts. In chapter 1, in a section which was subsequently eliminated, the narrator says 'que as palavras de Rubião não lhe saíam naturalmente persuasivas; mas podiam iludir a um doente, e foi o que lhe pareceu' [that Rubião's words did not sound naturally persuasive; but they were capable of deceiving an ill person, and that is what he believed].[22] And in chapter 2, the narrator reveals the extent of Rubião's calculating behaviour with respect to Quincas Borba in a section that was also left out of the second version:

> Rubião desmentia com o gesto; mas, ou porque não tivesse a força necessária para mentir bem, ou por qualquer outra razão particular, o gesto era frouxo, era quase meia confissão. Tirou-lhe o espelho, sorrindo amarelo, vexado de não poder confessar tudo. Fez alguns arranjos no quarto; depois pegou em jornais, para lê-los ao doente, como era costume: mas o doente disse-lhe que antes da leitura, mandasse chamar o tabelião; queria fazer testamento.
> — Testamento? repetiu o outro estremecendo.
> E disse-lhe que não, que se deixasse disso, mas não alcançou nada; creio que lhe faltava o talento da persuasão, creio também que as palavras já lhe saíam da alma desejosas de ser inúteis. O doente teimou, ele não teve remédio, e obedeceu; foi dentro e deu as indicações precisas ao pajem, que era o mais inteligente dos fâmulos. Voltou depois ao quarto do doente; passando por uma sala, foi a um espelho, consertar a expressão do rosto. Os músculos recusavam-se: mas uma bela perspectiva dá vontade ao ânimo, e este pôde então reagir sobre a face e compô-la. Foi assim que dali a pouco entrou no quarto uma espécie de monge compassado e tristonho, pegou dos jornais, e começou a ler melancolicamente as primeiras notícias políticas.[23]

> [Rubião gestured to indicate his disagreement; but, either because he lacked the strength required to lie properly, or for some other particular reason, the gesture was weak, almost halfway to being a confession. He took the mirror away from him, giving a sickly smile, annoyed that he wasn't able to confess everything. He tidied a few things in the room; then he picked up the newspapers to read them to the sick man, as was his custom: but the sick man told him to call the notary before reading; he wanted to make his will.
> 'Will?' the other repeated, trembling.
> And he told him no, that he should leave off that, but his words had no effect; I believe that he lacked the talent to persuade, I also believe that the words wanted to be futile as they left his soul. The sick man insisted, there was no getting out of it, and he obeyed; he went inside and gave precise instructions to the page, who was the most intelligent of the servants. Then he returned to the invalid's bedroom; passing through a room, he approached a mirror to compose his expression. His muscles refused to co-operate: but a beautiful prospect lends will to the spirit, and thus his spirit was able to fight back against his face and compose it. So it was that a short time later a sort of measured and gloomy monk returned to the bedroom, picked up the newspapers and began to read the first items of political news in a melancholy tone.]

It can be seen above that in this first version, the reader becomes aware that Rubião is happy that his friend is expected to die and that he is incapable of hiding it. It is not that Rubião is not calculating in the rewritten version, nor that he is completely lacking in analytical ability, but he does become more indecisive and is more concerned with obeying Quincas Borba's orders. Moreover, the fact that, in the book, Rubião effectively becomes Quincas Borba's disciple diverts the reader's attention away from the protagonist's premeditated attitude.

The change which occurs in the characterization of Rubião is very subtle in this first narrative unit. In the book, the writer softens Rubião's calculating side while putting more emphasis on his lack of understanding, including his failure to understand the nature and workings of *Humanitismo*. It is interesting to note here that in chapter 57 of *A* and chapter 56 of *D*, there is a reference to the episode of the letter, quoted above. The section in which the reference is found remains the same, but the effect it causes is different: in the book, it is not just a recapitulation of what was written previously but an interpretation of the episode of the letter. This interpretation is proffered not by Rubião but by the narrator and contains 'a coloração afetiva do personagem' [the emotional colouring of the character], as defined by Mattoso Câmara. Neither does the character think in definitive, clear sentences, nor is the narrator's judgement passed at a distance:

> Rubião estava arrependido, irritado, envergonhado. No cap. 10 deste livro ficou escrito que os remorsos deste homem eram fáceis, mas de pouca dura; faltou explicar a natureza das ações que os podiam fazer curtos ou compridos. Lá tratava-se daquela carta escrita pelo finado Quincas Borba, tão expressiva do estado mental do autor, e que ele ocultou do médico, podendo ser útil à ciência ou à justiça. Se entrega a carta, não teria remorsos, nem talvez legado, — o pequeno legado que então esperava do enfermo.[24]

> [Rubião was contrite, annoyed, ashamed. In chapter 10 of this book, it was written that this man's remorse came easily but that it did not last long; it was not explained what kind of acts might make it brief or protracted. There, it was a question of that letter written by the deceased Quincas Borba, so expressive of the writer's mental state, and which he, Rubião, since it could be of use to science or the law, concealed from the doctor. Had he shown the letter, he would not have had remorse — or, perhaps, any legacy, either — not even the small legacy that he was at that time expecting from the sick man.][25]

A second sign of the gradual progression of Rubião's madness can be found in the rewritten version of the end of chapter 63, shown in Table 6.4. Rubião is in Camacho's office when he learns that the Baroness wants to see him. In the serial, the narrator describes the lady and informs us only that Rubião has crossed paths with her in the corridor. It is also insinuated that Camacho treats her with more consideration than does Rubião. In the book, the Baroness's visit is not announced, which renders unnecessary a couple of dialogues which facilitate the transition from one scene to the other. Instead of it being the porter, i.e., a secondary character, who gives the cue, it is the narrator himself who undertakes to close the scene, acting, as he sometimes does, as a stage manager. In this way, the structural control over the coming and going of the characters becomes virtually imperceptible in the book. Instead, the repercussions of these small events in Rubião's mind become more important. The action which will be highlighted in the continuous stream of activity running from the farewell, when Rubião is still in the office, to the moment when he finds himself on the street, takes place in the corridor. Rubião is now seen descending the stairs. He stops on the first step to hear the warm greeting which Camacho gives the Duchess, which is taken from the first version, and continues

A: A Estação, 30 April 1887;
Quincas Borba apêndice, p. 61

— Está aí uma senhora que deseja falar a V. Ex., veio dizer o porteiro.

Rubião levantou-se.

— Mande entrar. Adeus, até breve; temos de fazer uma reunião...

Rubião despediu-se. No corredor passou por ele uma senhora alta, vestida de preto, com um arruído de seda e vidrilhos. Indo a descer a escada, ouviu a voz do Camacho, mais alta do que até então: — Oh! senhora baronesa!

64

A

'There is a lady here who wishes to speak to you', the porter came to say.

Rubião stood up.

'Send her in. Goodbye, see you soon; we must arrange a meeting...'

Rubião made his departure. In the hall a tall, black-gowned woman passed him with the sound of silk and glass-bead embroidery. As he was about to descend the stairway, he heard Camacho's voice, louder than before: 'Oh, Baroness!'

64

D
Quincas Borba, p. 183.

62

Rubião despediu-se. No corredor passou por ele uma senhora alta, vestida de preto, com um arruído de seda e vidrilhos. Indo a descer a escada, ouviu a voz do Camacho, mais alta do que até então: — Oh! senhora baronesa!

No primeiro degrau parou. A voz argentina da senhora começou a dizer as primeiras palavras; era uma demanda. Baronesa! E o nosso Rubião ia descendo a custo, de manso, para não parecer que ficara ouvindo. O ar metia-lhe pelo nariz acima um aroma fino e raro, coisa de tontear, o aroma deixado por ela. Baronesa! Chegou à porta da rua; viu parado um *coupé*; o lacaio, em pé, na calçada, o cocheiro na almofada, olhando; fardados ambos... Que novidade podia haver em tudo isso? Nenhuma. Uma senhora titular, cheirosa e rica, talvez demandista para matar o tédio. Mas o caso particular é que ele, Rubião, sem saber por quê, e apesar do seu próprio luxo, sentia-se o mesmo antigo professor de Barbacena...

63

D
Philosopher or Dog, p. 89–90

62

Rubião made his departure. In the hall a tall, black-gowned woman passed him with the sound of silk and glass-bead embroidery. As he was about to descend the stairway, he heard Camacho's voice raised in greeting: 'Oh, Baroness!'

On the first step he paused. The lady's silvery voice began to speak; the first words concerned a lawsuit. Baroness! And our Rubião continued on down the stairs falteringly and quietly so as not to seem to have been listening. The air sent up his nose a rare, delicate perfume, a thing to make you giddy, the perfume that the lady had left behind. Baroness! He reached the street door and saw a *coupé* waiting; the lackey was standing on the sidewalk and the driver sitting on the cushion, looking out, both in livery. What could be so new and startling in all that? — Nothing. A lady of title, sweet-smelling and rich, engaged in a lawsuit, for no other reason, perhaps, than to have something to do. But the fact is that Rubião, without knowing why, and despite his own wealth, felt as though he were again the teacher of Barbacena.

63

TABLE 6.4: Chapter 63 in *A* and 62 in *D*

to descend meekly, half stupefied, as if he had been suffering from vertigo, because he is imbibing the trace of perfume left by that 'cheirosa e rica' [sweet smelling and rich] lady. Down below, outside the building, he sees the coupé and the uniformed employees. However much the narrator interrupts the description to remark that Rubião still feels like a teacher from Barbacena, the sensations experienced by the protagonist propel him towards delirium.

Besides other indications of Rubião's tendency to delirium, his fear that Quincas Borba's soul has actually transmigrated into the dog can be considered as a further sign of his gradually developing madness. In chapter 4 of the first version and chapter 5 of the second, the philosopher explains to him why the dog bears his name. According to the philosopher, *Humanitas*, i.e, the principle of life 'reside em toda a parte' [resides everywhere], even in the dog, which can therefore 'receber um nome de gente' [receive a person's name].[26] By calling the dog Quincas Borba, the philosopher surmises that he will survive after his death in the name of the dog. In chapter 49 of both versions, Rubião is already shivering at the thought of the dead man being inside the dog:

> Olhou para o cão, enquanto esperava que lhe abrissem a porta. O cão olhava para ele, de tal jeito que parecia estar ali dentro o próprio e defunto Quincas Borba; era o mesmo olhar meditativo do filósofo, quando examinava negócios humanos... Novo arrepio; mas o medo, que era grande, não era tão grande que lhe atasse as mãos. Rubião estendeu-as sobre a cabeça do animal, coçando-lhe as orelhas e a nuca.[27]

> [He looked at the dog while he was waiting for the door to be opened. The dog looked at him, too, and in such a way that the deceased Quincas Borba seemed to be right there inside of him; the dog was looking with the same contemplative gaze with which the philosopher used to examine human affairs. Another shiver, but Rubião's fear, though great, was not so great that it tied his hands. He spread them out over the animal's head, scratching his ears and his neck.][28]

In chapter 69 of both versions, the narrator writes that 'a suposição de que naquele Quincas Borba podia estar a alma do outro nunca se lhe varreu inteiramente do cérebro'[29] [the supposition that within that Quincas Borba might be the soul of the other was never entirely dispelled from his mind].[30] In this way, continues the narrator, the protagonist sees a hint of disapproval in the dog's eyes, as if the dead man were condemning Rubião for his excessive spending. Rubião believes that this is all nonsense, but, just in case, he caresses the animal in an attempt to co-opt the dead men inside of him.

While this observation is found in both versions, in the book it functions as another stage in Rubião's mental degeneration, to which may be added the character's highly irrational and excessive suspicion regarding the supposed affair between Sophia and Carlos Maria. When his suspicion reaches its peak, Rubião, as seen earlier, is driven to pursue the seamstresses and also contemplates killing Sophia. If, on the one hand, the novel published in *A Estação* had become repetitive and very characteristic of a serial (see Chapter 5), on the other hand, those scenes which are episodic in nature, and which verged on the melodramatic, acquire a different outline in the rewritten version. Together with the addition of the dizziness caused by the Baroness's perfume, and Rubião's marriage-related delirium, which will be examined below, they now form part of the interlinked stages of the hero's rapidly developing insanity.

In the next large added section, Machado de Assis will make Rubião's madness evolve from that obsessive state to the point at which his personality breaks down and megalomania develops. Rubião experiences marriage-related delirium and delusions of grandeur, which are described in chapters 79 to 82, and which are largely found only in the second version. The roots of this delirium are found in chapters 84 to 86 of *A*, and the seeds are sown by Major Siqueira on his visit to apologize for his daughter's words, when the nature of the reward for picking up the dog Quincas Borba was ascertained (*A*, chap. 83). In the book, the pretext for Siqueira's visit is that he wants to inform Rubião that he has moved to Dois de Dezembro Street, as the entire episode describing the escape has been removed (*D*, chap. 78).

Chapter 84 of *A* is identical to chapter 79 of *D*. In both, the narrator establishes that it is not the dog's personality that is breaking down but Rubião's. This becomes apparent when the reader is told that the voice which the protagonist hears was coming from the depths of Rubião's own unconscious. He makes the same gesture of caressing the dog, despite, as the narrator reminds us, being fearful that the spirit of the deceased man has taken up residence in the animal:

> — E por que não? perguntou uma voz, depois que o major saiu.
> Rubião, apavorado, olhou em volta de si; viu apenas o cachorro, parado, olhando para ele. Era tão absurdo crer que a pergunta viria do próprio Quincas Borba, — ou antes do outro Quincas Borba, cujo espírito estivesse no corpo deste, que o nosso amigo sorriu com desdém; mas, ao mesmo tempo, executando o gesto do capítulo XLIX, estendeu a mão, e coçou amorosamente as orelhas e a nuca do cachorro, — ato próprio a dar satisfação ao possível espírito do finado.
> Era assim que o nosso amigo se desdobrava, sem público, diante de si mesmo.[31]
>
> ['And why not?' asked a voice, after the Major left.
> Frightened, Rubião looked around; he saw only the dog looking at him. It was so absurd to think that the question might come from Quincas Borba, or rather the other Quincas Borba, whose spirit might be within this one's body, that our friend smiled scornfully, but the same time executing a gesture we have seen in chapter 49, he put out his hand and fondly scratched the animal's ears and neck, an act calculated to please the spirit of the deceased that might be within.
> Thus it was that our friend split himself in two, with only himself for an audience.][32]

The last chapter, number 82, describing Rubião's marriage-related delirium ends with the narrator's declaration, which is absent from the first version: 'E o espírito de Rubião pairava sobre o abismo'[33] [And Rubião's mind hovering above the abyss].[34] As these chapters coincide with the end of the fourth narrative unit, as defined in Chapter 5 of this book, the focus now falls on Rubião's descent into madness.

In chapter 85 of *A*, the first substantial differences occur with respect to the meaning that the idea of marriage assumes in each of the versions and the positioning of the narrator as mediator and analyst. In the first place, the delirium described in the serial does not yet have clear outlines. It is made up only of confused reminiscences. Quoting Goethe, the narrator compares these reminiscences to a long journey which cannot be described because the hero cannot manage to gather together his memories. He only manages to distinguish, from the 'turbilhão de coisas e pessoas' [vortex of things and people], 'as mãos de padre e ombros de mulheres, ramalhetes de cravos brancos entremeados de hissope e carruagens' [the priest's hands and the wife's shoulders, bouquets of white carnations intermingled with hyssop and carriages].[35] In the first version, the conjugal idea is in fact an obscure and unconscious one. Secondly, in chapter 86 of *A*, the narrator reflects, for the benefit of the reader, on the causes underlying Rubião's desire to get married. As far as the character is concerned, the origin of the conjugal idea remains secret and unconscious. Only the narrator manages to decipher it and then share it with the 'leitor profundo' [profound reader]. At the start of the chapter, he writes: 'Sim, leitor profundo. A vida de Rubião carecia de unidade. Sem o perceber, o que ele buscava no casamento era a unidade que a vida não tinha.' [Yes, profound reader. Rubião's life lacked unity. Without realising it, what he was searching for in marriage was the unity that was absent from his life.][36] At the end of the chapter, the narrator comments:

> Crê, leitor, tal foi a origem secreta e inconsciente da ideia conjugal. As outras explicações são boas, por serem razoáveis e até honestas, mas a verdadeira e única é a que aí fica. Crê ou fecha o livro. Assim, por exemplo, se o próprio Rubião dissesse que o casamento era um modo de calafetar o capital que abria água, podes aceitar essa explicação, não como causa, mas como efeito. Em verdade, ele gastara, muito, ia gastando... Celibato não é incompatível com economia; mas Rubião não tinha força nem vontade; talvez o casamento lhe desse o segredo de viver com parcimônia, — ou tento, pelo menos.
>
> Isso, porém, era puro efeito do ato. A causa era a que ficou dita. O matrimônio enfeixaria os esforços, recolheria em si o homem disperso...[37]
>
> [Believe it, reader: this was the secret and unconscious origin of the marriage idea. The other explanations are good, being reasonable and even honest, but there is only one truth and it is this. Believe it or close the book. Thus, for example, if Rubião himself says that marriage was a way of caulking his capital, which had sprung a leak, you may accept that explanation as an effect rather than a cause. In fact, he had spent a lot, he was spending... Bachelorhood is not incompatible with frugality; but Rubião possessed neither strength nor will; perhaps marriage would reveal to him the secret of living parsimoniously, or at least with care.
>
> That, however, was purely an effect of the act. The cause was the one already noted. Marriage would bring together his strengths, gathering up the dispersed man into himself.]

The principle which guided the rewriting is also manifested in the change in the narrator's position in relation to the character through the adoption of free indirect speech, as opposed, in this case, to indirect speech. Instead of pontificating objectively on the secret origin of the conjugal idea, the narrator builds his commentary on the confused thoughts of the character. The result of this is that in the book, in the first place, Rubião has greater ability to consider the reasons which lead him to consider marriage. In the second place, however, the secret cause is only insinuated. The doubt is felt not just by Rubião but also by the narrator. What was inconclusive analysis in the serial has become just a possibility, introduced by the words 'podia ser' [it might be]:

> Sim, podia ser também um modo de restituir à vida a unidade que perdera, com a troca do meio e da fortuna; mas esta consideração não era propriamente filha do espírito nem das pernas, mas de outra causa, que ele não distinguia bem nem mal, como a aranha.[38]
>
> [Yes, it might be, too, a way to restore to his life the unity that it had lost with the change of fortune; but this consideration was not the child of his mind nor of his legs, but of something else, which he, like the spider, was unable to distinguish clearly.][39]

In the book, before adding the two chapters in which Rubião's marriage-related delirium acquires all of its contours, Machado de Assis explores, also in chapter 80, the relationship between fantasy and reality by listing the novels that Rubião is reading to fill his time: 'os históricos de Dumas pai, ou os contemporâneos de Feuillet' [the historical ones of Dumas *père*, or the contemporary ones of Feuillet]. He is attracted to these writers by

> uma sociedade fidalga e régia. [...] Aquelas cenas da corte de França, inventadas pelo maravilhoso Dumas, e os seus nobres espadachins e aventureiros, as condessas e os duques de Feuillet, metidos em estufas ricas, todos eles com palavras mui compostas polidas, altivas ou graciosas, faziam-lhe passar o tempo às carreiras.[40]
>
> [an aristocratic and Royal society. [...] Those scenes of the French court invented by the marvellous Dumas, his noble swordsmen and adventurers, Feuillet's countesses and dukes, who moved about in luxurious hothouses with considered and courteous speech, exalted and elegant, passed the time quickly for him.][41]

The visual imagery acquired from reading these novelists is mixed with the pomp of the Imperial procession, which the character often waited to see at the palace in Rio de Janeiro. Together, reality and fiction provide the outline of Rubião's matrimonial dreams. In the first version, the pomp has already been registered in his memory of the carriages. In the second, the writer again turns to the carriages, and adds the coaches and coupés lined with a special gold. Then he lingers over the guests, who are all of the first order, followed by the palace, the carpet, the satin shoes, the polkas, the internuncio, the ladies with the most beautiful necks in the city, and the ornamental objects, all of which are imported, specifically from Bohemia, Hungary and Sèvres.

Following Gledson's hypothesis that the novel symbolizes the end of the Empire, and my hypothesis concerning the close connection between the Imperial leanings of the magazine and the theme of imperial megalomania found in the novel, it can be supposed that some historical events which preceded the fall of the Empire are echoed in Machado de Assis's characterization of Rubião's delirium.

For example, on 9 November 1889, just a few days before the Proclamation of the Republic, the last great party of the monarchy, which became known as the Fiscal Island Ball, took place. The ball was a homage to the officers of the Chilean ship 'Almirante Cochrane'. It is estimated that around 5000 people took part in the ball, including the royal family, members of the government and the foreign diplomatic corps, high-ranking members of the Armed Forces, as well as the high society of the capital city. The ball was marked by excess and extravagance in terms of the decoration, music and menu (which was replete with imported dishes and drinks). Even as the ball was taking place, Republicans lead by Lieutenant Colonel Benjamin Constant were meeting at the Military Club to discuss a way out of the crisis facing the Empire.

There may be a close relationship between the actual time of writing and the time when the novel is set. The novel takes place between 1867 and 1879, but the writing of it coincides with the end of the monarchy. I believe that there is an ironic parallel between the imperial pomp of Rubião's marriage-related delirium and that last attempt to exalt the monarchy. According to Lília Schwarz, the imperial family had already lost its pomp some years previously, and were even a frequent target of cartoonists working for the Rio press.[42] Magazines such as *A Estação*, however, by showing illustrations of other empires which featured a great deal more pomp, such as that of Bismarck in Germany, were creating the illusion of royal refinement — a refinement which was no longer part of Brazil's reality. The Fiscal Island Ball can therefore be read as an attempt by the royal family to recover its refinement, but it became, in fact, the night when it said farewell: on 15 November, barely a week after the ball, the Republic was declared, and the Brazilian royal family went into exile in Europe two days later.

The possible parallel between the Ilha Fiscal Ball and Rubião's marriage ceremony is found not in a direct reference to Ilha Fiscal but in a reference to the island of Prospero, the character in Shakespeare's play *The Tempest*. The allusion occurs in the next chapter, which is also not found in the first version. At the start of the chapter, the narrator says:

> Esses sonhos iam e vinham. Que misterioso Próspero transformava assim uma ilha banal em mascarada sublime? 'Vai, Ariel, traze aqui os teus companheiros, para que eu mostre a este jovem casal alguns feitiços da minha feitiçaria.'
>
> As palavras seriam as mesmas da comédia; a ilha é que era outra, a ilha e a mascarada. Aquela era a própria cabeça do nosso amigo; esta não se compunha de deusas nem de versos, mas de gente humana e prosa de sala. Mais rica era. Não esqueçamos que o Próspero de Shakespeare era um duque de Milão; e eis aí, talvez, porque se meteu na ilha do nosso amigo.[43]
>
> [Those dreams came and went. What mysterious Prospero was thus transforming a banal island into a sublime masquerade? 'Go, Aerial, bring the rabble, here, to this place; for I must bestow upon the eyes of this young couple some vanity of mine art.'
>
> The words would be the same as those of the play; the island and the masquerade were different. The former was our friend's head, and the latter was composed, not of goddesses and verse but of human folk and drawing-room prose. But it was elegant. Let us not forget that Shakespeare's Prospero was a Duke of Milan; perhaps that's how he got to our friend's island.][44]

Here, the island signifies the mental world in which Rubião lives: a world which is only his and which is far from the mainland, or reality. Later in the chapter, the mention of Prospero is justified by Rubião's interest in noble titles, which leads him to grant himself one and scribble it repeatedly: 'Marquess of Barbacena'. The hero dreams of being as noble as the characters in the French novels which he reads, or a member of the imperial cortege of the reigning monarch of his country. At the end of chapter 82, a further sign of Rubião's developing madness can be found: the protagonist believes that Quincas Borba is barking intelligible sentences, such as ' — Case-se, e diga que eu o engano' ['Marry and tell me whether I'm wrong'], like the puppy Medgi in Gogol's story.[45]

In chapter 82 of the book, we come to the end of the fourth narrative unit. It can then be perceived that the reorganization of this narrative unit, which involved eliminating melodramatic elements and repetitive scenes (see Chapter 5 of this book), coincides with the detailing of Rubião's marriage-related delirium. The effect of this is to take the focus away from the episodic and move it on to a more secure means of driving the plot forwards: Rubião and his descent into madness, which starts with the dizziness caused by the Baroness's perfume, passes through his belief in the transmigration of the philosopher's soul and his obsession with Sofia, and evolves into delirium, megalomania and the breakdown of his personality, eventually manifesting itself in the cutting of his beard. In common with all of the other episodes which, from this point onwards, deal directly with Rubião's madness, this one is found in both versions and did not undergo any substantial modifications. After cutting off his beard, Rubião, who believes that he is Napoleon, walks incognito around the streets of the capital city. This, let it be said in passing, is an allusion to Gogol's story (chap. 152). From this point onwards, Rubião's madness becomes public. His friends and the diners come to witness the moments in which his personality breaks down into that of the French emperor. At the end of the novel, his foolishness culminates in the act of his coronation without a crown, which takes place a few minutes before he dies.

Notes to Chapter 6

1. Gledson, *Machado de Assis: ficção e história*, p. 90.
2. Araripe Júnior, 'Ideias e sandices do ignaro Rubião', *Gazeta de Notícias*, Rio de Janeiro, 5 February 1893, p. 1, in Guimarães, *Os leitores de Machado de Assis*, pp. 403–06, p. 405.
3. Brooks, *Reading for the Plot*, p. 35.
4. Augusto Meyer, *A chave e a máscara* (Rio de Janeiro: Edições Cruzeiro, 1964), p. 174.
5. *Quincas Borba*, chap. 27, p. 133; *A Estação*, 30 September 1886, chap. 27; *Quincas Borba apêndice*, p. 28. Variants: *A:* café, sentado no *pouf,* olhando para longe... muito longe... Afinal, lembrou-se de ir ver o Quincas Borba e soltá-lo... Levantou-se e.
6. *Philosopher or Dog?*, p. 33. Variants: *A:* coffee, seated on the *pouf*, looking into the distance... the far distance... In the end, he remembered to go and see Quincas Borba and unleash him... He got up and.
7. Brooks, p. 13.
8. *Quincas Borba*, p. 107.
9. *Philosopher or Dog?*, p. 3.
10. *Quincas Borba*, pp. 112–14.
11. *Quincas Borba*, chap. 1, p. 107; *A Estação*, 31 August 1886, chap. 20; *Quincas Borba apêndice*,

p. 22. Variants: *A*: Se tenho casado a mana Marica com o Quincas Borba, apenas alcançaria uma esperança colateral. Não os casei; ambos morreram.
12. *Philosopher or Dog?*, chap. 1, pp. 3–4. Variants: *A*: Had I married Sister Marica with Quincas Borba I could have hoped only for a collateral inheritance. I did not marry them; both died.
13. *Quincas Borba*, p. 177.
14. *Philosopher or Dog?*, p. 84.
15. *Quincas Borba*, p. 178.
16. *Philosopher or Dog?*, p. 84.
17. An explanation of the abbreviations is found in the Introduction, p. 6.
18. Mattoso Camara Jr., *Ensaios machadianos* (Rio de Janeiro: Livraria Acadêmica, 1962), pp. 30–31.
19. Mattoso Câmara, p. 39.
20. End of p. 28, *A Estação*, 15 April 1887.
21. See Gledson, *Machado de Assis: ficção e história*, p. 90
22. *Quincas Borba apêndice*, p. 7.
23. *Quincas Borba apêndice*, p. 9.
24. *Quincas Borba*, chap. 56, p. 173; *A Estação*, 15 March 1887, chap. 57; *Quincas Borba apêndice*: p. 57.
25. *Philosopher or Dog?*, p. 79.
26. *Quincas Borba apêndice*, p. 10; *Quincas Borba*, p. 110, *Philosopher or Dog?*, p. 10.
27. *Quincas Borba*, p. 161; *A Estação*, 31 January 1887; *Quincas Borba apêndice*, p. 47.
28. *Philosopher or Dog?*, p. 66.
29. *Quincas Borba*, p. 193; *A Estação*, 15 July 1887; *Quincas Borba apêndice*, p. 69.
30. *Philosopher or Dog?*, p. 102.
31. *Quincas Borba*, chap. 79, p. 206; *A Estação*, 31 January 1888, chap. 84; *Quincas Borba apêndice*, p. 94.
32. *Philosopher or Dog?*, p. 115–16.
33. *Quincas Borba*, p. 210.
34. *Philosopher or Dog*, p. 121.
35. *A Estação*, 31 January 1888, chap. 85; *Quincas Borba apêndice*, p. 95.
36. *A Estação*, 31 January 1888, chap. 86; *Quincas Borba apêndice*, p. 95.
37. *A Estação*, 31 January 1888, chap. 86; *Quincas Borba apêndice*, p. 96.
38. *Quincas Borba*, chap. 80, pp. 206–07.
39. *Philosopher or Dog?*, p. 116.
40. *Quincas Borba*, chap. 80, pp. 207.
41. *Philosopher or Dog?*, p. 117.
42. See Chapter 3 of this book.
43. *Quincas Borba*, chap. 82, pp. 208–09.
44. *Philosopher or Dog?*, p. 119.
45. *Quincas Borba*, chap. 87, p. 215. See Chapter 4 of this book.

CHAPTER 7

❖

The Fictional Rhetoric of *Philosopher or Dog?*

To state that the narrator of *Quincas Borba* [*Philosopher or Dog?*] is reliable in relation to the plot is not to say that there are no meanings in the novel which are hidden from the less attentive reader. One of the ways of reaching the deeper meanings of the novel is by perceiving the relationship established within the text between the implicit author and the narrator. For example, the implicit author may leave clues in order to make the reader distrust the narrator's authority over his own story. This relationship between the narrator and the implicit author has been studied by Gledson, who showed how Machado de Assis, in rewriting the novel for book publication, scattered across different parts of the narrative those elements which, taken together, convey the political meaning of the work.[1]

The relationship between the implicit author and the narrator in the second version of *Quincas Borba* is also the subject of this seventh and last chapter. I am firstly concerned, however, with understanding how Machado de Assis adapted the serialized text to be published in book form — a process which owes much to the reformulation of *Humanitismo*. In *Quincas Borba*, Machado de Assis plays with the distance between the narrator and the implicit author, not necessarily to prevent the less attentive reader from capturing the universalizing meaning conveyed by *Humanitismo*, but rather to avoid shocking her/him with the observation that the society fictionalized in the novel is moved by a new bourgeois morality, motivated by the desire to make a profit and grow rich at any cost.

As the distance between the narrator and the implicit author has received particular attention in relation to Machado de Assis's first-person novels, let us examine how these distances operate in *Memórias póstumas de Brás Cubas* [*Epitaph of a Small Winner*] and *Dom Casmurro*, according to their main critics. My aim is to show that Machado de Assis's choice of a particular type of narrator forms part of the fictional rhetoric of each work, regardless of the narrative point of view chosen.

The Narrator and Implicit Author in *Dom Casmurro* and *Epitaph of a Small Winner*

According to the American critic Wayne C. Booth, every narrative, whether it be in the first or the third person, is always presented as if it were passing through the consciousness of a storyteller or narrator. When the inexperienced reader comes across an omniscient narrator, he is less likely to perceive that the story is mediated. Conversely, if the narrator is an 'I', the reader is more aware that there is a mind placed between him and the events.

Booth believes that the reader must not make this mistake because, by placing a narrator in the story (whether it be a mere observer, a narrator–agent, or a character), the writer immediately produces some measurable effect on, for example, the course of events or the formation of the reader's judgement. The reader must know how to measure the distance between the narrator and the implicit author. According to Booth, the latter is:

> the implicit picture of an author who stands behind the scenes, whether as stage manager, as puppeteer, or as an indifferent God, silently paring his fingernails. The implied author is always distinct from the 'real man' — whatever we may take him to be — who creates a superior version of himself, a 'second self', as he creates his work.[2]

The critical history of the three main novels by Machado de Assis's — *Memórias póstumas de Brás Cubas*, *Quincas Borba* and *Dom Casmurro* — perhaps offers proof that readers are in fact more likely to perceive the partiality of an 'I' than a 'he'. The first study to cast doubt on a Machadian narrator — Bento, nicknamed Dom Casmurro — was published in 1900. One year after the publication of *Dom Casmurro*, which is narrated in the first person, José Veríssimo suspected that Bento's opinion of his wife Capitu might be biased:

> Dom Casmurro a descreve, aliás, com amor e com ódio, o que pode torná-lo suspeito. Ele procura cuidadosamente esconder estes sentimentos, sem talvez consegui-lo de todo. Ao cabo das suas memórias sente-se-lhe uma emoção que ele se empenha em refugar.[3]
>
> [Dom Casmurro describes her, moreover, with love and hate, which could make him suspect. He carefully tries to hide these feelings, perhaps without fully achieving this aim. At the end of his memoirs, one senses in him an emotion which he does his utmost to dismiss.]

Capitu, however, would have to wait sixty years before a critic would finally defend her against the accusation of adultery. Helen Caldwell's study, *The Brazilian Othello of Machado de Assis*, acquitted the female character for the first time in print. Caldwell identifies that the problem presented by the novel lies in the imposition of the authorial voice on the story. At certain points in the narrative, the implicit author warns the reader that Bento is only telling his version of the story. Up to this point, critics had failed to detect the signs left by the author which compromised the narrator's credibility. For Caldwell, the verdict in fact remains open, with the reader being charged with the task of judging whether Capitu is innocent or guilty.

The Brazilian Othello of Machado de Assis therefore opened the way for a long series of studies on the dubiousness of Bento's story. Chief among these studies is that of John Gledson, who defends the thesis that the narrator of *Dom Casmurro*, in common with the other narrators in Machado de Assis's later work, is unreliable. According to Gledson, from *Memórias póstumas de Brás Cubas* onwards, the writer creates his novels at several levels, which grants them at least a dual nature: the author highlights a plot which is superimposed onto another level, in terms of which the work must be interpreted. The reader who manages to get around the red herrings and pretence, which are so well elaborated by the Machadian narrator, can bring up, little by little, the other layers of interpretation and eventually arrive at the allegorical meaning of the novel.[4]

In the specific case of *Dom Casmurro*, Gledson believes that Bento does his utmost throughout the narrative to convince the reader of Capitu's infidelity by reconstructing impressions of the past, which, however, fail to stand up in the absence of more concrete evidence. By insisting that his version of events must prevail, the narrator, as the story narrative progresses, causes the novel to become a study of Bento's pathological obsession rather than of Capitu's adultery. Bento is therefore a deceiver who is also deceived.

From the perspective of the sociological critic, the narrator can be seen as a product of the society depicted; as such, he shares that society's limitations. Bento has a distorted view of the world because he is prejudiced by his privileged social position. As he cannot understand the world as it is, the protagonist creates his own version for himself and 'ultimately his own metaphorical plot (the adultery) which joins in sin and damnation the two characters who most threaten his world'.[5]

Dom Casmurro is not the only first-person novel by Machado de Assis which requires its readers to be wary of the resources employed by the narrator to obscure their judgement or prevent them from asking questions. According to Robert Schwarz, the narrator in *Memórias póstumas de Brás Cubas* also demythologizes himself throughout the narrative, transforming himself from a hero into a victim. The most convincing sociological criticism establishes that *Memórias póstumas de Brás Cubas*, like *Dom Casmurro*, was written against its author narrator. As if it were a case of the tables being turned, the ideological and literary resources which the narrator values most highly are those which the writer uses to criticize the group to which the narrator belongs.[6] In *Memórias póstumas de Brás Cubas*, the implicit author uses a narrator who analyses everyone on the basis of their social standing in order to reveal the defects and inconsistencies of an entire class (to which his potential readership belongs), within which progressive ideas, such as liberalism, absurdly coexist with archaic social structures such as slavery and the ownership of large estates.

We know that Machado de Assis possessed an intimate knowledge of his readership (as has already been discussed in this book in relation to the subscribers of *A Estação*), and that he used this knowledge to draw the reader into the fiction even when, as in *Memórias póstumas de Brás Cubas*, the fictitious reader is unexpectedly offended. It could be thought that there is a contradiction here, or an error of judgement on the part of the writer, who might end up disheartening readers with his constant assaults on them. The contradiction, however, is scarcely apparent and a very well thought out narrative strategy is in fact being employed. The reader of *Memórias póstumas de Brás Cubas* can continue reading because, despite being offended, the work is first and foremost an enjoyable one whose sense of humour derives from the tradition of *Tristram Shandy*. It is this humour which allows the writer to say the most absurd things (underneath which hidden meanings no doubt lie).

The original target readership of *Memórias póstumas de Brás Cubas* was the subscribers of *Revista Brasileira*, the periodical in which the novel was originally published. As Moema Vergara points out, these readers belonged to a literary elite, but one whose members were not necessarily drawn only from the dominant class.[7] The *Revista*'s readership had widened as a result of changes which took place at the end of the nineteenth century, including the development of higher educational establishments. According to Vergara, individuals who did not belong to the dominant class, such as Machado de Assis and Tobias Barreto, formed part of the literary elite. As the former was a representative of the Rio de Janeiro middle class, and Tobias Barreto was a self-taught native of Sergipe who influenced many of the authors who wrote for the *Revista*, both found 'no cultivo das letras uma forma de ascensão social' [in the cultivation of letters a way of rising socially].[8] Despite reaching the public beyond the dominant class, however, the *Revista Brasileira* was still a 'um projeto autorreferente' [self-referential project], made by and for the Brazilian literary elite. As Midosi stated in 1879, it was a magazine which aimed 'oferecer uma amostra da competência dos brasileiros distintos por suas grandes faculdades e luzes, alguns ainda pouco conhecidos neste vasto império' [to offer a sample of the ability of Brazilians distinguished for their great mental powers and knowledge, some of whom are little known in this vast empire].[9]

The *Revista Brasileira* aimed to be a vehicle for speculating about the problems facing the country, cultural changes and contemporary science. Imitating the book format, it published its long articles in fortnightly instalments, in a manner similar to *La Revue des Deux Mondes* but very different from the literary supplement of *A Estação*.[10] *Memórias póstumas de Brás Cubas* was also published in serial form, among the long articles issuing from the pens of doctors, naturalists, engineers and jurists who were responsible for popularizing contemporary science at the end of the nineteenth century and the beginning of the twentieth century in Brazil.[11] We perceive that the narrator Brás Cubas, the inventor of a patent plaster, and his friend Quincas Borba, the inventor of a philosophy, are creations which parody not only the target readers of the periodical (and, consequently, of the novel), but also the group of collaborators itself, as well as that other group composed of cultivated men who were interested in science and progress.

It seems to me that Shandian humour is used to divert, in both senses of the word. Firstly, the novel amused the reader: it entertained the mind with a text that was lighter and more humorous than the scientific and informative articles with which it shared space in the periodical. Secondly, the humour distracted the reader from the hidden meanings of the novel, some of which could require self-examination. According to Schwarz, the implicit author uses a narrator who analyses everyone on the basis of their social standing in order to reveal the defects and inconsistencies of the group to which he belongs, in which progressive ideas such as liberalism coexist, absurdly, with archaic social structures such as slavery and the ownership of large estates.

In this respect, the effect of reading *Memórias póstumas de Brás Cubas* is very different from the feelings aroused in the reader by naturalist novels such as those by Aluísio Azevedo. It is true that his work, *O Mulato*, published in 1881 (the same year as *Memórias póstumas de Brás Cubas*) denounces very strongly one of the central problems of Brazilian society at the time, namely the existence of slavery and the racial prejudice underlying it. However, regardless of the extent to which the practice of slavery in the capital of the Empire provided material for impassioned political debates for or against abolition, the Maranhão customs and people reproduced in the novel could strike the Rio de Janeiro-based reader as being as exotic and remote as the figure of the Indian, who is described romantically in the novels of Alencar.

The technical success of *Memórias póstumas de Brás Cubas* and *Dom Casmurro* was possible because Machado de Assis eliminated the moral and intellectual distance between his narrators and the target readers in order to avoid shocking them or causing them to abandon the novel in the first instalments or chapters. Moreover, Machado de Assis knew very well how to maintain his readers' attention in a way that made reading the book a pleasant and moving experience. In the case of *Dom Casmurro*, as Gledson points out, these artifices prevent the reader from realizing, as the narrative progresses, that 'the enjoyment and emotion are also part of Machado de Assis's plan and they may cloud the judgement'.[12] When he reaches the last chapter, the sensation that overwhelms the spirit of the reader is one of strong discomfort, as indicated by José Veríssimo's testimony in relation to *Dom Casmurro*. This critic, who was both a representative of the literary elite and an opinion former (and who himself wrote for the *Revista Brasileira*), does not see himself in the mirror and therefore distances himself, accusing the writer of being a sceptic and a pessimist who is disenchanted with life and disillusioned with humanity:

> Mas, quando em um escritor como ele, de uma tão alta honestidade literária, sentimos esta espécie de repugnância orgânica de um tão humano e legítimo sentimento, esta falta desnatural do amor, ao qual devem a arte e a literatura mais que as suas mais belas obras, a sua mesma existência, desperta-se-nos também a curiosidade de indagar da sua mesma obra até que ponto será qual se nos figura. Dessa obra ressumbra uma filosofia amarga, cética, pessimista, uma concepção desencantada da vida, uma desilusão completa dos móveis humanos.[13]
>
> [But when, in a writer such as he, of such great literary honesty, we sense this kind of organic repugnance towards such a human and legitimate sentiment, this unnatural lack of the love to which art and literature owe not just their most beautiful works but their very existence, there awakens in us a curiosity to discover in this work the extent to which it is we who are depicted in it. This work conveys a bitter, sceptical, pessimistic philosophy, a disenchanted view of life, a complete disillusionment with human motives.]

In order to understand the irony of the novel and to accept the invitation to lie on the couch, the flesh and blood reader will need to perceive that both the personification of the narrator as a member of his class, as well as the praise or criticism with which the narrator treats the mock reader, are no more than a rhetorical resource used to prevent him or her from realizing that, right from the outset, the attack is actually aimed at them.

The Narrator and Implicit Author in *Philosopher or Dog?*

Let us return to *Quincas Borba* [*Philosopher or Dog?*] to examine the distance between the narrator and the implicit author. *Quincas Borba* is generally seen as a return to the most traditional narrative mode, the model of the realist school. As Ivan Teixeira writes,

> Machado abandona a forma livre do romance anterior, para produzir um relato sóbrio e verossímil, bem próximo da estética realista. Dessa vez, diferentemente de *Memórias póstumas de Brás Cubas*, o narrador não participa da ação. Mantém-se distante, observando o que acontece, como se tudo fosse independente de sua voz. Preocupa-se em ordenar bem os acontecimentos para produzir a impressão de que o leitor está diante da vida e não de uma trama fictícia. É mais ou menos como num filme regular em que a estória oculta a presença do diretor.[14]

> [Machado abandons the free form of the previous novel to produce a restrained and believable story which is close to the realist aesthetic. This time, in contrast to *Memórias póstumas de Brás Cubas*, the narrator does not participate in the action. He maintains himself at a distance, observing what happens, as if everything were independent of his voice. He concerns himself with ordering events properly so as to produce the impression that the reader is looking at life and not at a fictional plot. It is more or less as in a film in which the story hides the presence of the director.]

I believe, however, that the difference between the first and third person points of view only serves to cover an underlying similarity between *Memórias póstumas de Brás Cubas, Quincas Borba* and *Dom Casmurro*. In *Quincas Borba*, the writer is also searching for the right dose with which to win the trust of the readers and at the same time launch attacks on them. Since, in *Quincas Borba*, Machado de Assis is relating a story that goes against some conventional moral principles, he opts to develop it in a way which does not shock the reader, or which prevents him or her from realizing that relations between the individuals depicted in the novel are governed by a new set of values. This new set of values, or 'a quebra de valores antigos' [the breaking up of old values], in the words of José Murilo de Carvalho, was also registered in 1891 in the play (*teatro de revista*) *O Tribofe* by another of *A Estação*'s collaborators, the same Artur Azevedo who wrote the *Croniqueta* section.[15] In *O Tribofe*, Carvalho writes:

> o engano, a sedução, a exploração, a mutreta, o tribofe, enfim, aparecem encarnados em pessoas muito reais e possuem até mesmo certo charme. Entre jogadores, cocotes, *bons vivants*, fraudadores de corridas, proprietários exploradores, perde-se a virtude da família interiorana. Primeiro, some a empregada, seduzida por um personagem que se diz lançador de mulheres, ou seja, formador de prostitutas; a seguir, vai o próprio fazendeiro nos braços de uma cocote; finalmente, desaparece o filho em agitações estudantis. Todos pegam o 'micróbio da pândega'. Se do ar da cidade medieval se dizia que tornava livre social e politicamente, do ar do Rio pode-se dizer que libertava moralmente.[16]

> [deceit, seduction, exploitation, trickery and swindling are personified in very real people and even possess a certain charm. Among gamblers, cocottes, *bon*

viveurs, racing fraudsters and exploitative landlords, a family from the interior loses its virtue. First, the maid disappears, seduced by a character who calls himself a promoter of women, in other words, a trainer of prostitutes; then, the rancher himself falls into the arms of a cocotte; and finally, the son disappears in student disturbances. They all catch the 'revelry germ'. If the air of the medieval city was said to bestow social and political freedom, the air of Rio could be said to liberate its inhabitants morally.]

In *Quincas Borba*, we also witness the fall of a character from the provinces who is undone by his failure to understand the new rules governing social relations and matters of the heart in Rio de Janeiro. As Kátia Muricy states, 'é diante dessa nova razão que Rubião se perde — ele perde a razão' [faced with the new reasoning, Rubião is lost — he loses his reason]. For Muricy, Rubião's madness is therefore a consequence of the character's inability to understand and adapt to the new (bourgeois) social rules of the city, which she calls the 'nova razão' [new reasoning].[17]

Artur Azevedo and Machado de Assis have very similar goals, but they reach them by using very different resources and literary genres, with each writer following his own temperament: one taking a more direct route which had great appeal to popular taste, and which was characteristic of the theatre, on whose stage vices and virtues are personified; and the other taking a route which is indirect and subtle and which, for that reason, leaves room for doubt and, as we shall see, compromises judgements as to whether it is right or wrong.

In order to grasp the message of the novel, the reader will need, as in *Memórias póstumas de Brás Cubas* and *Dom Casmurro*, to perceive the exact distance between the narrator who is guiding the reader through the story and the implicit author, who will establish the new rules of conviviality in a changing society. The implicit author superimposes himself on the narrator's point of view. In order to understand his position in the novel, we must turn our attention again to the narrative kaleidoscope, the process used by Machado de Assis to construct the plot of the novel. In Chapter 4 of this book we saw that it is the task of the narrator to create a picture of the interaction between the characters during two social events and, at the same time, to focus on the impressions that each character retains of this picture. The plot is therefore constructed by means of the summation of the multiple points of view in the narrative, which, as I discuss below, does not go so far as to constitute polyphony, in the sense in which Bakhtin uses the term.

It would be erroneous to conclude that Quincas Borba is a polyphonic novel in the Bakhtinian sense, since the term refers to a position adopted by the author in relation to the characters, which, according to Bakhtin, was invented by Dostoevsky. Bakhtin believes that Dostoevsky managed to free his characters from the unifying vision of the author by giving up his privileged position. Bakhtin writes that 'Dostoevsky never retains any essential "surplus" of meaning' — in other words, the author's field of vision does not cross or collide with the characters' field of vision and attitudes.[18] Until the given moment, the author does not release any essential information which is inaccessible to the protagonist, such as any foresight into his own future experiences. The author never knows more than the protagonist knows of himself or of the other characters at any particular time, because he deprives himself of the omniscient, self-enclosed field of vision.

Dostoevsky writes about people who are really represented as being free, because the author gives up the surplus information in his viewpoint and places himself on the same level as his characters. The last word does not belong to the author; nor is it based on any information which the protagonist cannot see or understand, or on anything located outside his conscience. The result is the creation of a multiplicity of conflicting voices. According to Bakhtin, in Dostoevsky's novels,

> the major characters and their worlds are not self-enclosed and deaf to one another; they intersect and are interwoven in a multitude of ways. The characters do know about each other, they exchange their 'truths', they argue or agree, they carry on dialogues with one another (including dialogues on ultimate questions of world view).[19]

In the case of Quincas Borba, however, the characters' points of view acquire meaning *dialogically* only in the unifying vision of the implicit author, which is superimposed on them. Some characters may possess a slightly wider vision and may reflect either on their position in the social network in which they participate or on the other characters. This is the case of the manipulators Palha and Camacho, who take advantage of Rubião's naivety in order to maintain their social positions or climb a step of the social ladder. But they never manage to be free in the way that Bakhtin believed that Dostoevsky's characters are. Not even the most ambitious characters realize that they form part of a huge wheel exemplified by *Humanitismo*. The philosophy is therefore the surplus information added by the implicit author onto the characters' points of view, which, according to Bakhtin, Dostoevsky manages to cast off in his novels. The only character who has heard mention of *Humanitismo* is Rubião, through the lessons given to him by Quincas Borba. At the peak of his lucidity, the protagonist shows signs of having finally understood the theory:

> — Ao vencedor as batatas! Não a compreenderia antes do testamento; ao contrário, vimos que a achou obscura e sem explicação. Tão certo é que a paisagem depende do ponto de vista, e que o melhor modo de apreciar o chicote é ter-lhe o cabo na mão.[20]
>
> ['To the victor, the potatoes!' He probably had not understood it before the will; indeed, we have seen that he found it obscure and meaningless. For it is true as can be that the landscape depends upon one's point of view, and that the best way to appreciate the whip is to be holding its handle in one's hand.][21]

Rubião, however, does not realize that the theory allows the situation to be reversed. When he goes down 'from Barbacena to pull up and eat the potatoes that grow in the capital', he does not realize that he is going to be used by people claiming to be his friends.[22] The metaphor will be repeated only at the end of the novel, when the impoverished Rubião finds himself in Barbacena once again. His mental state leaves no doubt as to the penetration and clarity with which he pronounces the phrase coined by the philosopher. Instead of showing that Rubião has profoundly understood the irony of his fate, it serves only as further proof of his insanity. The reader perceives the irony which results from the contrast between Rubião's decadent state and his imperial megalomania.

Unlike Rubião and the other characters, the reader has access not only to the various narrative prisms but also to the surplus information regarding *Humanitismo*. The reader may therefore relate the trajectory of all of the characters, as a whole, together with the theory elaborated by the philosopher who gives his name to the book. Even though the connection is not explicit, the reader, from a privileged position, can perceive that *Humanitismo* functions as a unifying element in the plot, which simultaneously explains and connects all of the episodes and the characters' fates into a single intricate network of cause and effect.

The novelist has strategically chosen an omniscient narrator in order to instil in the reader the feeling of possessing a privileged viewpoint, of being able to go beyond the superficial layer of appearances and penetrate the minds of the characters. The pact of reliability between the reader and the narrator is based on the fact that the reader is allowed to know more about the characters than they know about themselves or each other, as in the case of the impressions that the characters retain of the two social encounters, which are shared between narrator and reader, but not with the characters. The narrator keeps the reader entertained with the novelistic element of the work, namely the plot, and, more importantly, the ability which he has to distinguish between real events and imagined ones. It is certainly a way of winning the trust of reader, who is flattered and made to feel shrewd. However, it also prevents the reader from judging the characters in accordance with the prevailing moral standards.

Little by little the reader will understand that the rules of conduct have changed, and that people are governed more by the rules of *Humanitismo* than by the traditional standards of loyalty and benevolence. When it is put into practice, as it is in the novel, *Humanitismo* enters into conflict with the Christian moral values which are synthesized in three of the Ten Commandments: thou shalt not steal, thou shalt not covet thy neighbour's wife, and thou shalt not covet thy neighbour's goods.

This is why the change does not occur all at once. There are moments in which Palha thinks about Maria Benedicta's future, as in the quotation below:

> Pode acontecer, que Maria Benedita fique ao desamparo... Ao desamparo, não digo; enquanto vivermos somos todos uma só pessoa. Mas não é melhor prevenir? Podia ser até que, se lhe faltássemos todos, ela vivesse à larga, só com ensinar francês e piano. Basta que os saiba para estar em condições melhores. É bonita, como a senhora foi no seu tempo; e possui raras qualidades morais. Pode achar marido rico.[23]

> [Maria Benedicta may be left all alone — No, I'll not say all alone, because so long as we are living we're all one family. But isn't it better to look to the future? It might even be that, if we're all gone, she could live well only by teaching French and the piano. Just knowing them will put her in a better position. She's pretty, just as you were in your time, and she has a rare moral qualities. She may find a rich husband.][24]

Palha also warns Rubião that his fortune is yielding less and that his capital needs to recover strength. As trustee of Rubião's shares, policies and deeds, and the collector of the rent from three of his houses, Palha warns him not to put so much money into the cause espoused by the Alagoas Committee. Rubião's partner even tries to resist his request that 10 contos (i.e. 10 million *réis*) be released for another lost loan:

> Basta de ceder a tudo; o meu dever é resistir. Empréstimos seguros? Que empréstimos são esses? Não vê que lhe levam o dinheiro, e não lhe pagam as dívidas? Sujeitos que vão ao ponto de jantar diariamente com o próprio credor, como um tal Carneiro que lá tenho visto. Dos outros não sei se lhe devem também; é possível que sim. Vejo que é demais. Falo-lhe por ser amigo; não dirá algum dia que não foi avisado em tempo. De que há de viver, se estragar o que possui? A nossa casa pode cair.[25]

> [I have given into everything long enough; it is my duty to be firm. Safe loans? What loans are they? Don't you see that they're just taking your money away from you and not paying what they owe? Fellows who carry it to the point of having dinner every day at their creditor's house, like a certain Carneiro whom I have seen there. I don't know whether the others owe you too. Quite possibly they do. It's too much. I am speaking to you because I'm a friend; you'll not be able to say some day that you were not warned in time. What will you live on if you go through what you have? Our firm can fail.][26]

Even here, however, Palha also thinks about his own interests: he wants a husband to be found for Maria Benedicta and he might not want Rubião to spend his money, so that a large part of it will remain for him. Moreover, as the narrator is constantly turning the kaleidoscope, we see that there are characters such as Siqueira who see Palha in a negative light.[27]

The same principle which compromises our judgement is applied to the only character who can be placed above suspicion in the novel: Dona Fernanda. From this angle, even Dona Fernanda's kindness could be relative. In fact, the critical history of the novel contains a small tradition of studies on Dona Fernanda, which defend or give the lie to her immanent kindness. One member of the former team is Guilhermino César. The second team includes John Kinnear and Ingrid Stein. I believe, however, that Dona Fernanda is neither kind by nature nor acting only out of self-interest.[28] Rather, her altruism is simply a way of exercising such freedom as she has as a dependent woman (all the women in the novel are dependent, except perhaps the godmother Angélica in Barbacena). In her social position, as a sign of status, it is expected that she should concern herself with other people, the poorest and most vulnerable.

Returning to the Palhas, the fact is that the reader only perceives that their slow but continual social rise is inevitable towards the end of the novel, upon realizing that this rise actually affirms the new values which prevail in the fictionalized society of the text. Machado de Assis, however, is not starting from scratch. As the work represents a changing society and was originally aimed at a public which was observing, suffering or benefiting from the changes taking place in the real world, there is an agreement that the border between vice and virtue, generosity and greed, and kindness and brutality, is shifting. A group might even agree that, just as society is changing, the old rules are being adapted to the new ways in which people are surviving or climbing the social ladder. At the end of the book, together with the reversal in Rubião's fortune (symbolized by his coronation without a crown), the reader witnesses an about turn, an adjustment of values, or at least confirmation that the rules of survival in society are changing or have already changed.

The Novel as an Exemplification of *Humanitismo*

The elaboration of the philosophy of *Humanitismo*, and its function as a unifying element in the plot, is a late construction which in fact appears only in the book. In previous chapters we have seen that the process of rewriting *Quincas Borba* primarily involved elements being omitted. We also began to examine the additions, which, despite being few, are equally significant in defining the reading pattern of the narrative as a whole, i.e., in forming the global vision of the novel. Rubião's descent into madness, which was the subject of Chapter 6 of this book, is better understood in the second version as a result of the sections which were added, principally to the first half of the novel. The elaboration of the philosophy of *Humanitismo*, like the elements concerning the progressive stages of Rubião's madness, was added when the second version was written. As José Chediak writes in his introduction to the critical edition of *Quincas Borba*,

> com efeito, o que há sobre Humanitas na primeira redação pública do romance não vai além do que se lê em dois curtos parágrafos — 24 e 26 — , no capítulo 4 em *A* (folhetim) e V em *B* (edição de 1891), na breve referência na carta que a Rubião escreve Quincas Borba, e na lenda que refere o Autor ter-se criado em torno do Rubião (cap. 132, em *B*: 133 em *A*). A essência mesma da filosofia, exposta e exemplificada no capítulo 6 de *B* em diante, inexiste em *A*. O próprio sinete — 'Ao vencedor, as batatas' — só aparece, em *A*, no final do livro, quando Rubião, ensandecido, está de regresso a Barbacena.[29]

> [indeed, the material concerning Humanitas in the first version made available to the public consists of only two short paragraphs (24 and 26) in chapter 4 of *A* (the serial) and chapter V in *B* (1891 edition) in the brief reference contained in the letter which Quincas Borba writes to Rubião, and in the account which the author says was created about Rubião (chap. 132 in *B*, 133 in *A*). The very essence of the philosophy, which is expressed and exemplified in chapter 6 of *B* onwards, is absent from *A*. The motto itself — 'To the victor, the potatoes' — appears only at the end of the book in *A*, when the insane Rubião is back in Barbacena.]

In the book version, this metaphor 'To the victor, the potatoes!' appears in chapter 6, which brings into the narrative an example of how *Humanitismo* works in practice. Firstly, Quincas Borba (now clearly in the role of master) tells his disciple, Rubião, of the case of his grandmother being run over by a runaway carriage. Then, still attempting to explain the functioning of the theory to Rubião, he tells the story of the two starving tribes and the field of potatoes, which is only sufficient to feed one of the tribes. This chapter functions as a *mise en abîme*, which establishes a parallel between, on the one hand, the story being narrated and the didactical example and, on the other hand, the exterior story involving Rubião, Quincas Borba and the characters who are still to be introduced. Narrated by the master, these two stories, which are internal to the narrative, anticipate (albeit with little credibility) the overall meaning of all of the characters' individual stories.

In chapter 18, some sections of which we saw previously, and which was added to the second version, the formula is repeated several times by Rubião at the moment when the character associates his reversal of fortune with *Humanitismo* in action:

> — Ao vencedor, as batatas!
> Tão simples! tão claro! Olhou para as calças de brim surrado e o rodaque cerzido, e notou que até há pouco fora, por assim dizer, um exterminado, uma bolha; mas que ora não, era um vencedor.[30]
>
> ['To the victor, the potatoes!'
> It was so simple, so clear! He looked down at his patched suit and his frayed duck trousers and he realized that until just a little while before he had been, so to speak, one of the exterminated ones, a bubble, but that now he was a victor.][31]

Contrary to what happens in the first version, the reader can more easily associate *Humanitismo* with the character's trajectory and, subsequently, with the continual social rise and fall experienced by all the characters in the novel, without exception. In the serial, the cult of *Humanitas* is a satire aimed at the scientific philosophies of that era, such as Comte's Positivism and Darwin's theory of evolution. It is an invention of the character Quincas Borba, and serves to characterize his eccentric nature. In the second version, *Humanitismo* acquires a much more far-reaching dimension. It is still loaded with satire, but it goes from being a characteristic feature of an eccentric and mad character to the unifying element of the plot.[32]

The truth is that *Humanitismo*, and its relevance to the story being narrated, is not revealed openly to the characters, much less to the reader. It is the task of the reader to establish the relationship, which does not require much in the way of physical or interpretive effort. In the *in-8º* format, flicking from the back to the front of the text takes only a few seconds and requires just two fingers. If the book were resting on a table, it could even be done while holding a cup of coffee or a cigar in one hand. Nor is much interpretive effort required, as sufficient elements exist in the second version to help us to establish the relationship. Besides the characters' trajectories, there are several symbols scattered throughout the novel, such as the pair of bronze statuettes of Mephistopheles and Faust found in chapter 3, and Aesop's fable of the cicada and the ants in chapter 90.

The pair of bronze statuettes, which Rubião acquires on Palha's advice, are at the same time, as Marta de Senna explains, part of the new millionaire's luxurious decor and a forewarning of the mental decay suffered by Rubião, 'que, de certa maneira, perderá a alma, sob a tutela de Cristiano Palha, arremedo tropical da sofisticação civilizada do Mefistófeles goethiano' [who, in a certain sense, loses his soul under the protection of Cristiano Palha, who represents a tropical imitation of the civilized sophistication of the Goethian Mephistopheles].[33] The parallel which is insinuated, on the one hand, between Palha and Mephistopheles, and on the other hand, between Rubião and Faust, is not, however, found in the first version. Instead of Mephistopheles, we find a statuette of Don Quixote, which, alongside Faust, provides a second prediction of Rubião's final madness but does not suggest the organic relationship between the two characters, whose destinies are bound together from the first chapter of the second version.

In turn, the classical opposition between the cicada and the ants also appears only in the second version, in the episode in which a jealous Rubião ponders the story told by the coachman and uses a towel to kill a line of ants which is passing along the windowsill. The brutality of the action is compensated for by a cicada which starts to hum the syllables of Sophia's name. We then find the following commentary:

> Felizmente, começou a cantar uma cigarra, com tal propriedade e significação, que o nosso amigo parou no quarto botão do colete. Sôôôô.... fia, fia, fia, fia, fia, fia... Sôôôô... fia, fia, fia, fia... fia...
> Oh! precaução sublime e piedosa da natureza, que põe uma cigarra viva ao pé de vinte formigas mortas, para compensá-las. Essa reflexão é do leitor. Do Rubião não pode ser. Nem era capaz de aproximar as coisas, e concluir delas, — nem o faria agora que está a chegar ao último botão do colete, todo ouvidos, todo cigarra. Pobres formigas mortas! Ide agora ao vosso Homero gaulês, que vos pague a fama; a cigarra é que se ri, emendando o texto:
> Vous marchiez? J'en suis fort aise.
> Eh bien! mourez maintenant.[34]

> [Fortunately, a cicada began to sing, so appropriately and so meaningfully, that our friend paused at the fourth vest button. Soooo.... fia, fia, fia, fia, fia, fia... Soooo... fia, fia, fia, fia... fia..
> Oh! Sublime and compassionate precaution of Nature, that in compensation, places a live cicada by the side of twenty dead ants. That, of course, is the reader's reflection. It could not be Rubião's. He was not in a state to put things together and draw a conclusion from them — nor could he, even now that he is coming to the last vest button, all ears, all cicada — Poor ants! Go now to your Gallic Homer, that fame may reward you. The cicada is laughing, amending the text:
> Vous marchiez? J'en suis fort aise.
> Eh bien! mourez maintenant.][35]

In the first version, the cicada was in fact a little bird, a creature which is much more melodious and graceful (and also more romantic) than the cicada, with its strident song. This is the corresponding section in *A Estação*:

> Felizmente, começou a trilhar na chácara um passarinho, com tal melodia e graça que o nosso Rubião esqueceu por um instante as cogitações de outra espécie. Chegou a parar no quarto botão do colete, tão namorados eram os trilhos do animal: So, so, so... fia, fia, fia... So, so, so... fia, fia, fia.[36]

> [Fortunately, a little bird in the country property began to sing with such melody and grace that our Rubião forgot for a moment all other kinds of thoughts. He even paused at the fourth vest button, so amorous were the creature's trills: So, so, so... fia, fia, fia... So, so, so... fia, fia, fia.]

Moreover, the traditional opposition to the ants is not found in the serial. La Fontaine's moral fable (La Fontaine is the 'Gallic Homer' quoted above) emphasizes the contrast between the hard-working ant and the lazy cicada. In the novel, the moral is inverted, because the arrival of the cicada compensates for the elimination of the ants. This section draws the reader's attention to the symbolic meaning of the episode. At the same time, the reader is considered to be more able to interpret it than the naive Rubião.

The 'pattern' of the novel (to use a term coined by E. M. Forster) and, consequently, its universalizing meaning, are conveyed by the characters' trajectories and by those symbolic elements which appear throughout the narrative. As such, they are raised above the characters and the romantic plot, thereby becoming the principle on which the narrative is structured in the second version.[37] We see that not only the focusing of attention on Rubião but also the elaboration of the theory of *Humanitismo* play a role in redefining the plot and, consequently, the form in which we read the second version, which is based on the creation of a new reading pattern for the single-volume novel. In this respect, *Humanitismo* is the finishing touch applied to the creation of the overall vision of the novel and, at the same time, one of the solutions found to the creative impasse.

In the second version, the new doctrine is presented allegorically in the form of a theory: *Humanitismo*. As it is associated with Quincas Borba, however, a character whom the narrator considers to be eccentric and mad, the reader does not take the doctrine seriously at the start of the novel. The reader is not compelled to realize that all of the characters' trajectories, including that of Rubião, actually provide proof of Quincas Borba's lucidity and the relevance of his theory. This is the fictional rhetoric used by Machado de Assis in *Quincas Borba*. He uses the narrator to distract the reader's attention (from passing moral judgement on the characters) while the implicit author constructs a story which can ultimately be classed as an exemplification of the theory of *Humanitismo*.

Remembering the words of Alfred Bosi, we find in *Quincas Borba* not only 'o intervalo social menor' [the smallest social distance] in the depiction of the relations between the characters, but also 'a violência real das interações mal dissimulada pela distância aparentemente diminuída' [interactions characterized by real violence, which is poorly dissimulated by the seemingly small distance].[38] The clash between Rubião and Palha could be classed as an example of the stronger/weaker pair described in Darwin's theory of the struggle for life, or, more specifically, as a struggle between those who are more, or less, suited to the new code prevailing in society, which is dominated by commerce and not by the 'velhas relações da burguesia e nobreza terratenentes' [old relations of the bourgeois and landowning nobility].[39] As Darwin writes, '[the] struggle almost invariably will be most severe between the individuals of the same species, for they frequent the same districts, require the same food, and are exposed to the same dangers'.[40]

It is not my intention to explain all the complexity of the novel, or to limit the writer's artistic intentions to the verification of a theory. But as an artist, Machado de Assis needed to find structural solutions to a work whose composition and publication were already in progress. These solutions were provided by *Humanitismo*, the elimination of episodes which verged on the melodramatic, the arranging of the plot into long narrative links, and the focusing of attention on Rubião. Nothing had to be started from scratch since these elements were already present in the first version, either in embryonic form or as fully developed ideas.

We therefore see that, despite not being aware of the existence of any manuscript arising from the creative process of *Quincas Borba*, we are able to investigate the genesis of Machado de Assis's artistic visualization of the novel thanks to be thematic and structural legacy left by the serial to the book form, which, ultimately, is the version to which the reader has had access since 1891 and which we continue to read today.

Notes to Chapter 7

1. Gledson, *Machado de Assis: ficção e história*, pp. 73–133.
2. Wayne C. Booth, *The Rhetoric of Fiction* (Chicago: University of Chicago Press, 1961), p. 151.
3. José Veríssimo, 'Novo livro do Sr. Machado de Assis', *Jornal do Comércio*, 19 March 1900, in Guimarães, pp. 408–14, p. 410.
4. Gledson, *Machado de Assis: ficção e história*, pp. 21–35; and 'Machado de Assis' View of Brazilian History', *The Historical Novel in Latin America*, ed. by Daniel Balderston (New Orleans: Ediciones Hispamérica, 1986), pp. 97–105.
5. Gledson, *Deceptive Realism*, p. 90. This is not the only possible reading of the novel. Other readings exist, including a Freudian reading which posits the view that *Dom Casmurro* is an unwitting homosexual with a great fear of women. Whether he is seen from a sociological or a Freudian perspective, the protagonist cannot decipher the meaning of his own life — this task falls to the reader, who must eventually find meaning in the novel for him/herself. The intrigued reader may believe that the key to the door which will lead to the answer(s) could be in the hands of the implicit author; the implicit author, though, does not carry a key ring by which to open all of the novel's interpretive doors. Another way of looking for meaning in the novel is to study the context in which it was published. As we have already seen in this book, the irony of the novel was easier to understand when we examined the context in which the first version was published before turning to the relationship established in the text between the narrator and the implicit author. For a psychoanalytical reading of *Dom Casmurro*, see Luiz Alberto Pinheiro de Freitas, *Freud e Machado de Assis: uma interseção entre psicanálise e literatura* (Rio de Janeiro: Mauad, 2001).
6. Roberto Schwarz, *Um mestre na periferia do capitalismo: Machado de Assis* (São Paulo: Duas Cidades, 1990).
7. Moema de Resende Vergara, 'A Revista Brasileira: a vulgarização científica e construção da identidade nacional na passagem da Monarquia para a República' (unpublished doctoral thesis, Pontifícia Universidade Católica do Rio de Janeiro, 2003), p. 74.
8. Ibid.
9. N. Midosi, Editorial, *Revista Brasileira*, 1879, p. 6, quoted by Vergara, p. 74.
10. A comparison of the *Revista Brasileira* and *Revue des Deux Mondes* has been carried out by Ana Luíza Martins: 'Seu formato de livro [da *Revue des Deux Mondes*], a sequência exclusiva de artigos, textos densos de temática selecionada, sem ilustração, sem propaganda, permaneceram como modelo de revista cultural, diferenciada da ilustrada e do *magazine* [...] Não seria improvável que parte das revistas brasileiras de cultura da virada do século a tivessem como referência visual, da *Revista Brasileira*, na fase Midosi, à *Revista do Brasil* em sua primeira fase, de 1916' [The book format [of the *Revue des Deux Mondes*], the exclusive sequence of articles, and its dense texts on selected themes, which contain neither illustrations nor advertising, remained a model for the cultural magazine and was distinct from illustrated magazines and periodicals [...] It was probably used as a visual reference by some of the Brazilian cultural magazines published around the turn of the century, from the *Revista Brasileira*, in the Midosi phase, to the *Revista do Brasil* in its first phase in 1916]. See Ana Luíza Martins, *Revistas em revista: imprensa e práticas culturais em tempos de República, São Paulo (1890–1922)* (São Paulo: FAPESP, EdUSP, 2001), p. 77.
11. For the history of the *Revista Brasileira* see also Moema Vergara's article, 'La Vulgarisation scientifique au Brésil: la cas de la Revista Brasileira', *Colloque international pluridisciplinaire 'Sciences et écritures'*, Besançon, Maison des Sciences de l'Homme Claude Nicolas Ledoux, 13–14 Mai 2004. <http://msh.univ-fcomte.fr/programmation/colo4/documents/preactes/Vergara.pdf> [accessed 10 October 2004].
12. Gledson, *Deceptive Realism*, p. 15.
13. José Veríssimo, apud Guimarães, p. 410.
14. Ivan Teixeira, *Apresentação de Machado de Assis* (São Paulo: Martins Fontes, 1987), p. 109.
15. José Murilo de Carvalho, *Os bestializados: o Rio de Janeiro e a República que não foi* (São Paulo: Companhia das Letras, 1987), p. 27. It cannot be overlooked that 1891 was the year when Machado finished the serialization of *Quincas Borba* in *A Estação*, and when the rewritten novel was published as a book.

16. Carvalho, *Os bestializados*, pp. 28–29.
17. Kátia Muricy, 'O legado da desrazão', *A razão cética: Machado de Assis e as questões do seu tempo* (São Paulo: Companhia das Letras, 1988), p. 88. In a further study of the novel from the sociological perspective, Flávio Loureiro Chaves develops a similar argument: he sees Rubião as a problematic protagonist who lives out the drama of 'adaptação individual ao mundo reificado, orientando-se por essa tendência irrefreável para confundir o verdadeiro e o falso, que termina fragmentando a personalidade' [adapting to the reified world, orienting himself by his unrestrainable tendency to confuse the true and the false, which ends up fragmenting his personality]. See Chaves, *O mundo social de Quincas Borba*, p. 65.
18. Mikhail Bakhtin, *Problems of Dostoevsky's Poetics* (London and Minneapolis: University of Minnesota Press, 1984), p. 73.
19. Bakhtin, p. 73.
20. *Quincas Borba*, chap. 18, p. 126. In the serial, the expression only appears in chapter 194. This shows that the philosophy of *Humanitismo* was elaborated during the writing of the second version, as we shall see in this chapter.
21. *Philosopher or Dog?*, p. 26
22. *Quincas Borba*, chap. 18, p. 126. Section absent from *A*.
23. *Quincas Borba*, chap. 68, p. 190; *A Estação*, 15 June 1887; *Quincas Borba apêndice*, chap. 68, p. 67.
24. *Philosopher or Dog?*, p. 000.
25. *Quincas Borba*, 1975, chap. 108, p. 240; *A Estação*, 30 November 1889, chap. 108; *Quincas Borba apêndice*, p. 140.
26. *Philosopher or Dog?*, p. 154.
27. See Chapter 3, p. 95 above.
28. Guilhermino César, 'Dona Fernanda, a gaúcha do Quincas Borba', *O Instituto: revista científica e literária*, 127, 1 (1965), 75–87; John Kinnear, 'The Role of Dona Fernanda in Machado de Assis' novel Quincas Borba', *Aufzätze zur portugiesischen Kulturgeschichte*, 14 (1977), 118–30; and Ingrid Stein, *As figuras femininas nos romances de Machado de Assis* (published doctoral thesis, Philosophischen Fakultät der Rheinischen Friedrich-Wilhelms-Universität zu Bonn, 1983), pp. 115–18. The title of Stein's book is *Figuras femininas em Machado de Assis* (Rio de Janeiro: Paz e Terra, 1984).
29. *Quincas Borba*, p. 60.
30. *Quincas Borba*, p. 126. Section absent from *A*.
31. *Philosopher or Dog?*, p. 25.
32. In her study of the novel from a semiotic point of view, Teresa Pires Vara sees *Humanitismo* as a reduced form of the novel as a whole. See *A mascarada sublime: estudo de Quincas Borba* (São Paulo: Duas Cidades, 1976).
33. *Quincas Borba*, chap. 3, p. 108. Marta de Senna, *Alusão e zombaria: considerações sobre citações e referências na ficção de Machado de Assis* (Rio de Janeiro: Fundação Casa de Rui Barbosa, 2003), p. 45.
34. *Quincas Borba*, p. 219.
35. *Philosopher or Dog?*, p. 130.
36. *A Estação*, 31 May 1888, chap. 94; *Quincas Borba apêndice*, p. 107.
37. E. M. Forster, *Aspects of the Novel* (London: E. Arnold, 1949).
38. See Chapter 4, p. 110 n. 21.
39. Passos, *O Napoleão de Botafogo*, p. 65.
40. Charles Darwin, *On Natural Selection* (London: Penguin Books, 2004), pp. 15–16.

CONCLUSION

❖

Philosopher or Dog?
The Beginning of the End of the Serial?

I have examined and compared the two versions of *Quincas Borba* from a bibliographical point of view, i.e., by considering them as records of a literary production process which manifested itself in two different print media: the newspaper and the book. First, I analysed the role played by the editorial leanings of *A Estação* in the imaginary construction of the novel. Starting from a detailed study of the history of the magazine, I was able to identify that its themes are echoed in the two central axes of the novel. The theme of social climbing lies behind not only the European fashion publicized in the pages of *A Estação*, but also the individual trajectory of the characters in *Quincas Borba*. Second, Rubião's imperial megalomania maintains a dialogue with the imperial leanings of this international magazine, which exalts the institution of empire in its imported German illustrations. The manner in which Machado de Assis treats these two themes in the novel is, however, very ironic, as on the one hand the novel hints at the risks to which subscribers expose themselves when they join the game of social climbing and, on the other hand, it establishes a relationship between the decadent state of the Brazilian Monarchy before the proclamation of the Republic and the imported imperial pomp which the magazine displayed in its illustrations.

The present book therefore arose from the impressions which the first version of *Quincas Borba* caused in me, a modern reader, far removed in time and space from the original context in which the serials were published. It may at times suggest the experience of reading the novel in a format from which the writer later distanced himself, and which he certainly wanted to be replaced by the experience of reading the book, for reasons which were at once aesthetic and commercial. Besides the historic study of the magazine, the attempt to recreate the original environment in which the novel was published and read also proved to be of great help in understanding the second version, mainly because the two central axes of the novel are maintained from one version to the next. The definitive version, which continues to be read today, is therefore entirely dependent on its appearance in a nineteenth century international fashion magazine. Failure to bear in mind the original format and context in which the novel was published limits the interpretive possibilities which can be applied to *Quincas Borba* and the perception that the writer possessed a profound knowledge of his readers and took their expectations into consideration, to the extent that the transgressive effect of the novel was made more subtle and at the same time more effective.

Conclusion

My analysis was not limited to the thematic relations between *Quincas Borba* and the magazine *A Estação*. I also attempted to make explicit the narrative formula found by Machado de Assis to represent, in fiction, a changing society, which, it may be said in passing, was the target readership of the magazine. We have seen that he opted to assemble a plot from the points of view of several characters, which are generated by a third-person narrator. Together, they form what I call a narrative kaleidoscope, which reflects not the events as they happened but rather the impressions that each character retains of them — that is to say, the events which are narrated are not those which have occurred, but rather those which have been deduced or even imagined. It is a mechanism which certainly makes us reflect on Machado de Assis's position within the realist movement, as in this novel the writer tests and subverts fiction's ability to represent the unadulterated truth. In this respect, this book could serve as a starting point for a deeper study into the evolution of the writer's realism from *Memórias póstumas de Brás Cubas* to *Dom Casmurro*.

With regard to the structure of the novel, I attempted to discover whether or not a relation existed between the use of the kaleidoscopic narrative structure and the creative crisis through which the writing passed, which is revealed by the interruptions in the serialization during the five years in which it was published. Machado de Assis used the kaleidoscope narrative to assemble the plot. However, once the plot had been assembled, the author needed to search for another narrative solution to disassemble it, which did not occur to him immediately. It was at this moment of crisis that the novel came closest to the serial. The writer resorted to melodrama and added a large number of episodes which were irrelevant to the plot until he found a narrative resource which resolved the impasse.

It must not be forgotten that one of the consequences of using multiple viewpoints is that time is dilated and meaning is constructed in very long narrative units. While, in the first narrative unit, the passage of time in the story was in step with the real time in which the instalments were published, from the second narrative unit onwards the action is concentrated into one day. When the various events, ideas and dreams which make up this single day are divided into instalments, the reader's perception that they form part of a single temporal unit is adversely affected. As such, while Machado de Assis begins his narrative in the manner of a serial writer, with Rubião's move to the capital (in other words, when he begins representing a changing society), he also changes his way of writing, appearing to focus more on a single volume than a serial. In fact, every time he most obviously employs metalanguage, the narrator of the novel always refers to the text as being a book.[1] The readers will also need to change the way that they read the novel, as they are brought closer to the experience of reading a book. As such, two reading patterns coexist in the first version: the serial form and the single volume.

What makes the creation of Quincas Borba even more interesting is that Machado de Assis began preparing the book before its publication in *A Estação* had finished. As such, the same resources which the author used to finish off the serial, such as the introduction of Dona Fernanda and her social group, are used to transform the text into book form. It therefore becomes almost impossible to analyse each version independently, as each version is born from the other and both benefited from the same tardy solutions to the outcome of the plot.

However, what is exclusive to the second version is the presence of the global vision of the novel, which the writer achieves by overlaying the vision of the narrator with that of the implicit author, who is responsible for conveying the totalizing sense that *Humanitismo* grants to the sum of the individual fates of each character. This only takes effect in the second version, because it owed much to the rewriting of the first chapters of the novel after they had been published. Two other elements which acquire more prominence in the second version are, as we have seen, Rubião's trajectory (through the more marked stages of his progressive madness) and the dilatation of time resulting from the reorganization of the first two narrative units of the novel, which in the book form a temporal unit of one day, distributed across fifty chapters. In fact, this was a consequence of the writer's view that it is impossible to reconstruct faithfully even a single day in the lives of a group of characters. In order to depict it, it is necessary to bear in mind not only the events which take place from morning to night but also the thoughts of the future, memories of the past, deliriums and dreams. Where the events are concerned, these can only be seen through the biased eyes of this or that character.

Comparing *Quincas Borba* with the other novels that Machado de Assis published in serial format, I was able to confirm that the writer's relation with the serial entered a period of crisis during its composition. Firstly, *Quincas Borba* was the novel that suffered the greatest number of interruptions during its serialization. Secondly, it is the novel whose publication was extended over the greatest period of time. Thirdly, it was the most revised, and was therefore the only one to exist in two versions. And, as we have seen, it was the last novel to be published originally in serial form.

The publishing history of the novels which Machado de Assis brought out in serial form, ending with *Quincas Borba*, might provide a good example of the route taken by Brazilian literary fiction in its move from serial to book publication at that period. To date, though, there has been no systematic study of the overall evolution of the serial in Brazil, from the point when it was imported from Europe to the moment when it began to give way to the book as the main means of publishing novels.[2] We do know, however, that in other countries the serial went into decline in the late nineteenth century — in England, for example, it began to lose ground as the original means of publishing literary fiction, and came to be used, above all, for popular fiction.[3] The same might have occurred in Brazil. At least this is what can be concluded from José Ramos Tinhorão's survey of novels published in Brazil in serial form between 1830 and 1994. Although his list is not exhaustive, Tinhorão shows us that the format was, without doubt, very popular until the 1930s.

At the time that Machado de Assis was finalizing the serialization of *Quincas Borba*, Aluísio Azevedo was publishing *A mortalha de Alzira* and *Paula Matos ou O Monte de Socorro*, and Júlia Lopes de Almeida *A família Medeiros*, in the *Gazeta de Notícias*.[4] In the 1890s and the first two decades of the twentieth century, besides Júlia Lopez de Almeida, pre-modernist authors such as Domingos Olímpio, Lima Barreto, João do Rio, Godofredo Rangel, Coelho Neto, and modernists such as Menotti del Picchia and Afonso Schmidt, were still publishing novels in serial form. In the 1930s, for example, we find works by Afonso Schmidt and Jorge Amado. Tinhorão also records the names of Nelson Rodrigues, Raquel de Queiroz, José

Lins do Rego, Marcos Rey, Orígines Lessa and Janete Clair, among the serial writers working in the second half of the twentieth century. In fact, authors who were adept at this format could be found until the 1990s. The last serial mentioned in Tinhorão's survey is by Mário Prata, and was published in *O Estado de São Paulo*, between 21 November 1993 and 20 February 1994.[5]

In numerical terms, Tinhorão's survey shows us that the serial was also very popular in nineteenth century Brazil and was gradually abandoned throughout the twentieth century: between 1839 and 1999, he records 198 serials; while between 1900 and 1949 there were 74; and between 1950 and 1994, only 36. Moreover, the presence of Janete Clair on the list of Brazilian serial writers of the second half of the twentieth century is an indication that, in Brazil, the techniques used in the serialized novel migrated from one format to the next with the development of the mass media: from the newspaper to the radio, and then to television. In other words, fiction published in instalments also survived in Brazil as a popular format, with media other than printing being used to convey it.

For the argument advanced in this book, it was in fact more important to locate *Quincas Borba* within the context in which Machado de Assis's novels were published than to define the position of the novel in the context of the history of the development of the genre in Brazil. Although it may not have been a conscious decision, it was after *Quincas Borba* that he abandoned the format as the medium in which his novels were first published. It therefore fell outside the scope of this work to provide a panorama of the development of the genre in Brazil and England. Nor have I aimed to compare *Quincas Borba* with any foreign serials, such as *The Woodlanders* by Thomas Hardy or *Lord Jim* by Joseph Conrad, which reveal that the nineteenth-century novel was undergoing the same transformative process elsewhere.[6]

My main aim has been to analyse *Quincas Borba* by comparing its two versions. However, we must not overlook the fact that *Quincas Borba* might represent the beginning of the end of the genre in Brazil. In fact, if we recall that the serial had been imported from Europe at the start of the nineteenth century, it is always useful to bear in mind that the composition of *Quincas Borba* forms part of the historic process of transformation undergone by the novel in the West. *Quincas Borba* might therefore prove that Machado de Assis's artistic sensibility perceived the transformations through which the novel was passing in the late nineteenth century and that he courageously confronted them when he rewrote the novel.

Notes to the Conclusion

1. *A Estação*, 15 March 1887, chap. 57; 31 January 1888, chap. 86; 15 November 1888, chap. 102; 30 April 1889, chap. 115; 30 November 1889, chap. 106 [sic]; 15 December 1889, chaps 112 and 113; 15 January 1890, chap. 117; 15 September 1891, chap. 201. *Quincas Borba apêndice*, pp. 57, 96, 113, 127, 138, 144, 150, 248. *Quincas Borba*, chap. 56, p. 173; chap. 106, p. 237; chap. 112, p. 245; chaps 112 and 113, p. 245; chap. 102, p. 246.
2. Various studies exist of the serial in Brazil, including studies of the techniques used in the serialized novel, analyses of foreign influences on it, and even studies of some specific works or authors. However, no study traces the *evolution* of the genre in Brazil during the nineteenth century. See, for example, Brito Broca, 'O romance-folhetim no Brasil', *Românticos, pré-românticos, ultra-românticos: vida literária e romantismo brasileiro* (São Paulo: Polis; Brasília: Ministério

da Educação e Cultura, Instituto Nacional do Livro, 1974), pp. 174–81; Vera Maria Chalmers, 'A literatura fora da lei; um estudo do folhetim', *Remate de males* (UNICAMP) 5 (1985), 136–45; Pina Maria Arnoldi Coco, 'O triunfo do bastardo: uma leitura dos folhetins cariocas do século XIX', *Anais do II Congresso da Abralic*, vol. 3 (Belo Horizonte: Abralic, 1991), pp. 19–24 ; Maria Helena Werneck, 'Uma produção para o esquecimento', *Anais do II Congresso da Abralic*, pp. 13–18; Marlyse Meyer, *Folhetim: uma história* (São Paulo: Companhia das Letras, 1996); José Ramos Tinhorão, *Os romances em folhetins no Brasil: 1830 à atualidade* (São Paulo: Duas Cidades, 1994); Tania Rebelo Costa Serra, *Antologia do romance-folhetim, 1839 a 1870* (Brasília: Editora da UNB, 1997); Marcus Vinícius Nogueira Soares, 'Literatura e imprensa no Brasil do século XIX' (unpublished doctoral thesis, Universidade do Estado do Rio de Janeiro, 1999); and by the same author 'O folhetinista José de Alencar e *O guarani*', in *Literatura brasileira em foco*, ed. by Fátima Cristina Dias Rocha (Rio de Janeiro: EDUERJ, 2003), pp. 107–14.
3. See, for example, Linda K. Hughes and Michael Lund, *The Victorian Serial* (Charlottesville: University Press of Virginia, 1991); N. N. Feltes, *Modes of Production of Victorian Novels* (Chicago: University of Chicago, 1986); Graham Law, *Serializing Fiction in the Victorian Press* (Basingstoke: Palgrave, 2000).
4. Aluísio Azevedo, *A mortalha de Alzira*, under the pseudonym Victor Leal, *Gazeta de Notícias*, Rio de Janeiro, 18 February to 24 March 1891, and *Paula Matos ou O Monte de Socorro*, with Coelho Neto, Olavo Bilac and Pardal Mallet, under the single pseudonym Victor Leal, *Gazeta de Notícias*, 30 June to 14 August 1891; Júlia Lopes de Almeida, *A família Medeiros*, *Gazeta de Notícias*, 16 October to 17 December 1891. See Tinhorão, pp. 77–78.
5. *James Lins, 51 (O playboy que não deu certo)* contains a total of forty chapters. Tinhorão notes that, having been 'published twice a week as a newspaper supplement, which could be folded into a tabloid format, the novel was classified as a 'mini series' by the author, indicating that he was a scriptwriter of stories which are divided into chapters for television' (Tinhorão, p. 95).
6. For more on this subject, see the aforementioned book by Hughes and Lund.

BIBLIOGRAPHY

❖

Primary sources

1. Periodicals

A Estação, Rio de Janeiro and Porto, 1879–94
Die Modenwelt, Berlin, 1865–67, 1886–91
Illustrirte Frauen-Zeitung, Berlin, 1874, 1886–91
La Estación, Madrid and Buenos Aires, 1886
La Stagione, Milan, 1892.
La Saison, Paris, 1868–73, 1887–91
Les Modes de la Saison, Paris, 1881–85
O Cruzeiro, Rio de Janeiro, 1878
O Globo, Rio de Janeiro, 1874–76
Revista Brasileira, Rio de Janeiro, 1880
The Season, London, 1886
The Young Ladies' Journal, London, 1864, 1886–91

2. Others

BALZAC, HONORÉ DE, *La muse du département*, electronic edition <http://fr.wikisource.org/wiki/La_Muse_du_Departement> [accessed 15 July 2006]
DICKENS, CHARLES, *David Copperfield*, edited with an introduction and notes by Nina Burgis, Oxford : Oxford University Press, 1983
—— *Great Expectations*, with twenty-one illustrations by F. W. Pailthorpe and an introduction by Frederick Page, Oxford: Oxford University Press, 1953, repr. 1987
Exposição comemorativa do sexagésimo aniversário do falecimento de Joaquim Maria Machado de Assis (20/IX/1908–29/IX/1968), Rio de Janeiro: Biblioteca Nacional, 1968
GOGOL, NIKOLAS, *Altväterische Leute und andere Erzählungen von Nikolas W. Gogol*, Deutsch von Julius Meixner, Collection Spemann, Stuttgart, Verlag von W. Spemann, [n.d.]
—— *Nouvelles choisies*, Paris, Hachette, 1853
MACHADO DE ASSIS, *A mão e a luva*, Rio de Janeiro: Editores Gomes de Oliveira & Cia, 1874
—— *Bons dias! Crônicas (1888–1889)*, edition, introduction and notes by John Gledson (São Paulo: Editora da UNICAMP, Editora Hucitec, 1990)
—— *Casa velha*, São Paulo: Livraria Martins Editora, 1944
—— *Edições críticas de obras de Machado de Assis*, Rio de Janeiro: Civilização Brasileira, INL, 1975
—— *Helena*, Rio de Janeiro: B. L. Garnier, 1876
—— *Iaiá Garcia*, Rio de Janeiro: G. Vianna & C., Editores, 1878
—— *Memórias póstumas de Brás Cubas*, Rio de Janeiro: Tipografia Nacional, 1881
—— *Obra completa*, 3 vols, Rio de Janeiro: Editora Nova Aguilar, 1992
—— *Philosopher or Dog?*, translated by Clotilde Wilson, New York: Noonday Press, 1954 (as *Heritage of Quincas Borba: A Novel*); reissued New York: Farrar, Straus and Giroux, 1992, and London: Bloomsbury, 1997

―― *Quincas Borba apêndice*, Rio de Janeiro: Civilização Brasileira, INL, 1975
―― *Quincas Borba*, Rio de Janeiro: B. L. Garnier, 1891
―― *Quincas Borba*, Rio de Janeiro: Civilização Brasileira, INL, 1975.
―― *Ressurreição*, Rio de Janeiro: B. L. Garnier, 1872.
MENDONÇA, SALVADOR DE, *Marabá*, Rio de Janeiro: Editores Gomes de Oliveira & Cia, Tipografia do Globo, 1875

Secondary sources

BAKHTIN, MIKHAIL, *Problems of Dostoevsky's Poetics*, London and Minneapolis: University of Minnesota Press, 1984
BARBIERI, IVO (org.), *Ler e reescrever Quincas Borba*, Rio de Janeiro: EdUERJ, 2003
BELGUM, KRISTEN, *Popularizing the Nation: Audience, Representation, and the Production of Identity in 'Die Gartenlaube', 1853–1900*, Lincoln: University of Nebraska Press, 1998
BOOTH, WAYNE C., *The Rhetoric of Fiction*, Chicago: University of Chicago Press, 1961
BOSI, ALFREDO, *Machado de Assis: o enigma do olhar*, São Paulo: Ática, 1999
BRAITHWAITE, BRIAN, *Women's Magazines*, London: Peter Owen, 1995
BRAMSTED, ERNEST K., *Aristocracy and the Middle-Classes in Germany*, rev. edn, Chicago and London: University of Chicago Press, 1964
BROCA, BRITO, *Românticos, pré-românticos, ultra-românticos: vida literária e romantismo brasileiro*, São Paulo: Polis; Brasília: Ministério da Educação e Cultura, Instituto Nacional do Livro, 1974
BROOKS, PETER, *Reading for the Plot: Design and Intention in Narrative*, Cambridge, MA: Harvard University Press, 2003
BUITONI, DULCILIA, *Mulher de papel*, São Paulo: Editora Loyola, 1981
CAMARA JR., MATTOSO, *Ensaios machadianos*, Rio de Janeiro: Livraria Acadêmica, 1962
CÂNDIDO, ANTÔNIO, 'Esquema de Machado de Assis', in *Vários escritos*, 3ª edição revista e ampliada (São Paulo: Duas Cidades, 1995), pp. 17–39
CARVALHO, JOSÉ MURILO DE, *A construção da ordem: a elite política brasileira*, Rio de Janeiro: Civilização Brasileira, 2003
―― *Os bestializados: o Rio de Janeiro e a República que não foi*, São Paulo: Companhia das Letras, 1987
CÉSAR, GUILHERMINO CÉSAR, 'Dona Fernanda, a gaúcha do Quincas Borba', *O Instituto: revista científica e literária*, 127, 1 (1965), 75–87
CHALMERS, VERA MARIA, 'A literatura fora da lei: um estudo do folhetim', *Remate de males*, 5 (1985), 136–45
CHAVES, FLÁVIO LOUREIRO, *O mundo social do Quincas Borba*, Porto Alegre: Movimento, 1974
COCO, PINA MARIA ARNOLDI, 'O triunfo do bastardo: uma leitura dos folhetins cariocas do século XIX', *Anais do II Congresso da Abralic*, vol. 3, Belo Horizonte: Abralic, 1991, pp. 19–24
CORDEIRO, FRANCISCA DE BASTO, *Machado de Assis na intimidade*, 2nd edn, rev. by the author (Rio de Janeiro: Pongetti, 1965)
COUTINHO, AFRÂNIO, *A literatura no Brasil*, vol. 3, Rio de Janeiro: José Olympio e UFF, 1986
DARNTON, ROBERT, *The Kiss of Lamourette*, London: Faber and Faber, 1990
DARWIN, CHARLES, *On Natural Selection*, London: Penguin, 2004
EL FAR, ALESSANDRA, *Páginas de sensação: literatura popular e pornográfica no Rio de Janeiro, 1870–1924*, São Paulo: Companhia das Letras, 2004.
FELTES, N. N., *Modes of Production of Victorian Novels*, Chicago: The University of Chicago, 1986

Forster, E. M., *Aspects of the Novel*, London: E. Arnold, 1949
Freitas, Luiz Alberto Pinheiro de, *Freud e Machado de Assis: uma interseção entre psicanálise e literatura*, 2nd edn, Rio de Janeiro: Mauad, 2001
Garland, Henry & Mary, *The Oxford Companion to German Literature* (Oxford: OUP, 1976)
Genette, Gérard, *Narrative Discourse: An Essay in Method*, trans. by Jane E. Lewin, Ithaca, NY: Cornell University Press, 1980
Gledson, John, 'Machado de Assis' View of Brazilian History', in *The Historical Novel in Latin America*, ed. by Daniel Balderston, New Orleans: Ediciones Hispamérica, 1986, pp. 97–105
—— *Machado de Assis: ficção e história*, 2nd rev. edn, São Paulo: Paz e Terra, 2003
—— *The Deceptive Realism of Machado de Assis*, Liverpool: Francis Cairns, 1984
Gomes, Eugênio, *Machado de Assis*, Rio de Janeiro: Livraria São José, 1958
Gross, Robert, 'Books, Nationalism, and History', *Papers of the Bibliographical Society of Canada*, 36, 2 (1998), 107–23
Guimarães, Hélio de Seixas, *Os leitores de Machado de Assis: o romance machadiano e o público de literatura no século XIX*, São Paulo: Nankin Editorial e Editora da Universidade de São Paulo, 2004
Hallewell, Laurence, *Books in Brazil*, London and Metuchen, NJ: Scarecrow Press, 1982
Hughes, Linda K., and Michael Lund, *The Victorian Serial*, Charlottesville: University Press of Virginia, 1991
Jobim, José Luís (org.), *A biblioteca de Machado de Assis*, Rio de Janeiro: Topbooks, Academia Brasileira de Letras, 2001
Kinnear, J. C., 'Machado de Assis: To Believe or Not to Believe?', *Modern Language Review*, 71, 1 (1976), 54–60
—— 'The Role of Dona Fernanda in Machado de Assis' novel *Quincas Borba*', *Aufzätze zur portugiesischen Kulturgeschichte*, 14 (1977), 118–30
Koseritz, Karl von, *Bilder aus Brasilien*, Leipzig and Berlin: W. Friedrich, 1885
—— *Imagens do Brasil*, tradução, prefácio e notas de Afonso Arinos de Melo Franco, São Paulo: Martins, 1972
Laver, James, *Taste and Fashion: From the French Revolution to the Present Day*, London: George G. Harrap, 1945
Law, Graham, *Serializing Fiction in the Victorian Press*, Basingstoke: Palgrave, 2000
Lima, Luiz Costa, *Dispersa demanda: ensaios sobre literatura e teoria*, Rio de Janeiro: Francisco Alves, 1981
Martins, Ana Luíza, *Revistas em revista: imprensa e práticas culturais em tempos de República, São Paulo (1890–1922)*, São Paulo: FAPESP, EdUSP, 2001
McKenzie, D. F., *Bibliography and the Sociology of Texts*, Cambridge: Cambridge University Press, 1999
Melford, Friedrich, intro., *Zum fünfundzwangzigjährigen Bestehen der Modenwelt, 1865–1890*, Berlin: Lipperheide, 1890
Merquior, José Guilherme, 'Género e Estilo das *Memórias póstumas de Brás Cubas*', *Colóquio/Letras*, 8 (1972), 12–20
Mérimée, Prosper, 'La Littérature de Russie. Nicolas Gogol', *La Revue des Deux Mondes*, nouvelle période, 12 (1851), 631
Meyer, Augusto, *A chave e a máscara*, Rio de Janeiro: Edições Cruzeiro, 1964
Meyer, Marlyse, *As mil faces de um herói canalha e outros ensaios*, Rio de Janeiro: Editora da UFRJ, 1998
—— *Caminhos do imaginário no Brasil*, São Paulo: Edusp, 1993.
—— *Folhetim: uma história*, São Paulo: Companhia das Letras, 1996
Miguel-Pereira, Lucia, *Machado de Assis: estudo crítico e biográfico*, 5th edn, Rio de Janeiro: J. Olympio, 1955

MURICY, KÁTIA, *A razão cética: Machado de Assis e as questões do seu tempo*, São Paulo: Companhia das Letras, 1988

NEEDELL, JEFFREY D., *A Tropical Belle Époque: Elite Culture and Society in Turn-of-the Century Rio de Janeiro* (Cambridge: Cambridge University Press, 1987)

—— *Belle Époque tropical: sociedade e cultura de elite no Rio de Janeiro na virada do século*, trans. by Celso Nogueira, São Paulo: Companhia das Letras, 1993

QUEFFÉLEC, LISA, *Le Romain-feuilleton français*, Paris: Presses Universitaire de France, 1989

PASSOS, GILBERTO PINHEIRO, *O Napoleão de Botafogo: presença francesa em Quincas Borba de Machado de Assis*, São Paulo: Annablume, 2000

PEREIRA, LEONARNO AFFONSO DE MIRANDA, *O carnaval das letras: literatura e folia no Rio de Janeiro do século XIX*, Campinas: Ed. da UNICAMP, 2004.

RASCHE, ADELHEID, *Frieda Lipperheide: 1840–1896*, Berlin: SMPK, Kunstbibliothek, 1999

REGO, ENYLTON DE SÁ, *O calundu e a panaceia: Machado de Assis, a sátira menipeia e a tradição luciânica*, Rio de Janeiro: Forense Universitária, 1989

RIDLEY, JASPER, *Napoléon III and Eugénie*, London: Constable, 1979

ROUANET, SERGIO PAULO, 'The Shandean Form: Laurence Sterne and Machado de Assis', in *The Author as Plagiarist: The Case of Machado de Assis*, ed. by João Cezar de Castro Rocha, Dartmouth: University of Massachusetts, 2006, pp. 81–103

SAINTE-BEUVE, 'Revue littéraire: *Nouvelles russes*, par M. Nicolas Gogol', *La Revue des Deux Mondes*, nouvelle série, 12 (1845), 883–89

SAINT-JULIEN, CHARLES DE, 'La littérature en Russie. Le comte W. Solohoupe', *La Revue des Deux Mondes*, Nouvelle Périodc, 12 (1851), 70–74

SCHWARCZ, LÍLIA, *The Emperor's Beard: Dom Pedro II and the Tropical Monarchy of Brazil*, translated by John Gledson (NY: Hill and Wang, 2004)

SCHWARZ, ROBERTO, *Ao vencedor as batatas*, 4th edn, São Paulo: Duas Cidades, 1992

—— *Um mestre na periferia do capitalismo: Machado de Assis*, São Paulo: Duas Cidades, 1990

SENNA, MARTA DE, *Alusão e zombaria: considerações sobre citações e referências na ficção de Machado de Assis*, Rio de Janeiro: Fundação Casa de Rui Barbosa, 2003

SERRA, TANIA REBELO COSTA, *Antologia do romance-folhetim, 1839 a 1870*, Brasília: Editora da UNB, 1997

SOARES, MARCUS VINÍCIUS NOGUEIRA, 'Literatura e imprensa no Brasil do século XIX' (unpublished doctoral thesis, Universidade do Estado do Rio de Janeiro, 1999)

—— 'O folhetinista José de Alencar e *O guarani*', in *Literatura brasileira em foco*, ed. by Fátima Cristina Dias Rocha, Rio de Janeiro: EDUERJ, 2003, pp. 107–14

SOUSA, GALANTE DE, *Bibliografia de Machado de Assis*, Rio de Janeiro: INL, 1955

SOUZA, GILDA DE MELLO E, 'Macedo, Alencar, Machado e as roupas', *Novos Estudos Cebrap*, 41 (1995), 111–19

—— *O espírito das roupas: a moda no século XIX*, São Paulo: Companhia das Letras, 1987

STEIN, INGRID, *As figuras femininas nos romances de Machado de Assis* (doctoral thesis, Philosophischen Fakultät der Rheinischen Friedrich-Wilhelms-Universität zu Bonn, 1983)

—— *Figuras femininas em Machado de Assis* (Rio de Janeiro: Paz e Terra, 1984)

STOLZE, HELMUT, *Die Französiche Gogolrezeption*, Vienna and Cologne: Böhlau Verlag, 1974

SULLEROT, EVELYNE, *La presse féminine*, Paris: A. Colin, 1963

TARDE, GABRIEL, *Les lois de l'imitation*, Paris: Feliz Alcan, 1895

TEIXEIRA, IVAN, *Apresentação de Machado de Assis*, São Paulo: Martins Fontes, 1987

TINHORÃO, JOSÉ RAMOS, *Os romances em folhetins no Brasil: 1830 à atualidade*, São Paulo: Duas Cidades, 1994

TODOROV, TZVETAN, *Introduction to Poetics*, trans. by Richard Howard, Brighton: Harvester, 1981

TRINDADE, DIAMANTINO FERNANDES, and LAÍS DOS SANTOS PINTO TRINDADE, 'As telecomunicações no Brasil: do Segundo Império até o regime militar' <http://www.oswaldocruz.br/download/artigos/social14.pdf> [accessed 12 December 2009]

VARA, TERESA PIRES, *A mascadara sublime: estudo de Quincas Borba*, São Paulo: Duas Cidades, 1976

VERGARA, MOEMA DE RESENDE, 'A Revista Brasileira: a vulgarização científica e construção da identidade nacional na passagem da Monarquia para a República' (unpublished doctoral thesis, Pontifícia Universidade Católica do Rio de Janeiro, 2003)

——'La vulgarisation scientifique au Brésil: la cas de la *Revista Brasileira*', *Colloque international pluridisciplinaire 'Sciences et écritures'*, Besançon: Maison des Sciences de l'Homme Claude Nicolas Ledoux, 13–14 de maio de 2004, <http: msh.univ-fcomte.fr/programmation/colo4/documents/preactes/Vergara.pdf> [accessed 10 October 2004]

WAUGH, NORAH, *Corsets and Crinolines*, London: Batsford, 1954

WERNECK, MARIA HELENA, 'Uma produção para o esquecimento', *Anais do II Congresso da Abralic*, vol. 3, Belo Horizonte: Abralic, 1991, pp. 13–18

INDEX

❖

Abreu, Capistrano de 95
Aesop 172
Alencar, José de 20, 29, 59, 123, 165
Almanaque do Globo 21
Almeida, Júlia Lopes de 58, 59, 63, 126, 179
Amado, Jorge 179
Andersen, Hans Christian 89
Azevedo, Aluísio 179
Azevedo, Artur 37, 60, 68 n. 56, 80, 81, 115, 117, 126, 127, 166, 167
Azevedo, Manuel Duarte Moreira de 29

Barreto, Afonso Henriques de Lima 179
Barreto (de Meneses), Tobias 164
Beeton, Samuel 66 n. 24
Biblioteca de Algibeira 20
Biblioteca do Globo 19
Biblioteca Universal 20, 21, 29
Bilac, Olavo 126
Bismarck, Otto von 96, 158

Cahn, Joaquim 126
Cervantes, Miguel de 96
Clair, Janete (artistic name of Jenete Stocco Emmer Dias Gomes) 180
Coelho, Carlos 126
Coelho Neto, Henrique Maximiano 179
Conrad, Joseph 180
Cordeiro, Francisca de Basto 95
Correia, Raimundo 37, 126

Darwin, Charles Robert 63, 172, 174
Dinarte, Sylvio (pseudonym of Alfredo d'Escragnolle Taunay) 19, 21
Delfino (dos Santos), Luís 126
Dostoevsky, Fyodor Mikhaylovich 10, 167, 168

Ebner-Eschenbach, Marie 72

Feuillet, Octave 60, 157

Gautier, Théophile 29
Goethe, Johann Wolfgang von 156
Gogol, Nikolai Vasilievich 94–100, 102, 159
Guimarães, Bernardo 29
Gutenberg, Johannes 42

Hardy, Thomas 180
Hees, Otto 73
Heine, Christian Johann Heinrich 96
Heuer and Kirmse, Gustav 52

Princesa Isabel 72, 73, 82, 83, 89

Kallmorgen, Friedrich 73
Klaar, Alfred 96
Keil, Ernest 73
Knötel, Richard 73
Koseritz, Karl von 84

La Fontaine, Jean de 173
Leite, Alfredo 81, 112, 126, 127
Lermontov, Mikhail 97, 98
Lessa, Orígenes 180

Macedo, Joaquim Manuel de 29, 61
Machado de Assis, Joaquim Maria de:
  'O alienista' 14
  Americanas 33 n. 8
  Bons Dias! 95
  Casa velha 15, 60, 102
  Contos fluminenses 33 n. 8
  contracts 16, 18, 21, 27, 29, 65 n. 1
  Crisálidas 33 n. 8
  Dom Casmurro 9, 15, 29, 30, 33 n. 8, 102, 105, 108, 109, 161–67, 178
  Esaú e Jacó 15, 29
  Falenas 33 n. 8
  Helena 5, 15, 18, 19, 21, 22, 24, 27–29, 31, 32
  História de 15 dias 34 n. 26
  Histórias da meia noite 18, 21, 29, 33 n. 8
  Histórias sem data 33 n. 8
  Humanitismo 4, 139, 144, 152, 154, 161, 168, 169, 171, 172, 174, 179
  Iaiá Garcia 5, 15, 18–20, 24, 25, 29, 31, 33 n. 8
  O manuscrito do licenciado Gaspar 18
  A mão e a luva 5, 15, 18, 19, 21–24, 26, 29, 31–33
  Memorial de Aires 15, 29
  Memórias póstumas de Brás Cubas 5, 9, 15, 18, 19, 29–32, 60, 101, 102, 105, 116, 161–67, 178
  Páginas recolhidas 33 n. 8
  Papéis avulsos 33 n. 8
  'A parasita azul' 14
  Ressurreição 5, 15, 17, 18, 33 n. 8

'O segredo de Augusta' 14
Várias histórias 16, 17, 19
Machado de Assis Committee 6–8, 81, 122, 144
Magalhães, Benjamin Constant Botelho de 158
Magalhães, Valentim 58
Melford, Friedrich 54, 74
Mendonça, Lúcio de 126
Mendonca, Salvador de 19, 21, 26
Menzel, Adolph von 72, 82
Mérimée, Prosper 98
Montépin, Xavier de 28
Musset, Alfred de 20

Nabuco, Joaquim 20
Noel, Eugène 19

Oertel, Kaspar Erhardt 52
Olímpio (Braga Cavalcanti), Domingos 179
Oliveira, Alberto de 126

Dom Pedro II 73, 82, 89
periodicals:
  Allgemeine Musterzeitung 69
  De Bazar 48
  O Besouro 85
  Budapesti Bazár 48
  Burda 42
  Correio das Modas 40
  O Cruzeiro 14, 15, 18–21, 25, 29, 31
  Dagmar 48
  The Englishwoman's Domestic Magazine 66 n. 24
  A Época 55
  A Estação, Jornal Ilustrado para a Família. Edição para os Estados Unidos do Brasil 1–4, 6–8, 10, 14, 15, 32, 35–90
  La Estación, Periódico para Senhoras 47, 48, 75
  Focus 55
  Freja 48
  Die Gartenlaube 73, 74
  Gazeta de Notícias 14, 16, 65 n. 1, 179
  Gazeta Ilustrada dos Dous Mundos 50
  O Globo 14, 15, 18–22, 24, 26–28, 31, 50, 51
  Hamburger Zeitschriften Jahrzeiten 69
  Hello! 72
  Hola! 72
  L'Illustrateur des Dames 42
  L'Illustration 79, 81
  Ilustração da Moda 50
  Illustrirte Frauen-Zeitung 38, 48, 53, 70–75, 78, 83, 86, 127
  Jornal das Famílias 14, 50
  Marie Claire 42, 55
  Die Modenwelt 10, 35, 38, 39, 42, 44, 47, 48, 51–55, 57, 65, 69, 70, 72–75, 81
  Les Modes de la Saison 47
  Modni Svet 48
  Модный Свет и Модный Магазинъ 48
  O Mosquito 19, 85
  O Paiz 65 n. 1
  Pariser Damenkleider-Magazin 40, 41, 42
  Revista Brasileira 14, 15, 18, 19, 30, 31, 164, 165
  Revista Ilustrada 85
  Revue des Deux Mondes 54, 60, 97, 98, 164
  Rio Post 95
  La Saison 42, 45, 47, 48, 50, 51, 53, 54
  La Saison. Edição para o Brasil 50, 58
  The Season: Lady's Illustrated Magazine 46, 47, 48
  Souvenir 66 n. 24
  La Stagione. Giornale delle Mode 48
  Tygonik Mód I Powiésci 48
  Vogue 42, 55
  The Young Ladies' Journal 42, 47, 48, 75
Picchia, Paulo Menotti Del 179
Ponson du Terrail, Pierre Alexis 28
publishers and publishing houses:
  Alves, Francisco 39
  A/V Edelmann 53, 54
  Brandão, A. J. Gomes 20, 21
  Carls Otto's Nachfolger 48
  Chardron, Ernesto 48
  CM Joly y Cia 48
  Dürr, Otto 49, 53, 54
  Figuier, L. 50
  G. Vianna & C. 18
  Garnier, B. L. 1, 6, 15, 65 n. 1, 18, 20–22, 27, 29, 37
  Garnier, H. 6, 16–19
  Gebr. Belinfante 48, 49
  Gomes e Oliveira e Cia. 18
  H. Lombaerts & Comp 6, 35, 36, 38, 39, 42, 47, 48, 50–52, 57, 60, 75, 79–81, 124, 126, 12
  Hedberg, J. G. 48
  Hoppe, Eduard 49
  Hoppe, Herman 48
  Imprensa Nacional 18
  The International News Company 48
  Johann von Király 48
  Klinhardt, Jules 53
  Koehler, K. F. 53
  Laemmert 16, 17, 40
  Lebègue et Cie., A. N. 54
  Lebègue et Cie, J. 48, 54
  Librería Gutenberg 48
  Lipperheide, Franz Joseph 38, 39, 40, 42, 43, 47, 48, 52, 54, 70, 71, 73, 74
  Lipperheide, Frieda (Wilhelmine Amalie Friederike) 38, 39, 40, 53, 72, 74
  Littré 50
  Lugan C. Genelioux, sucessores 48
  Nydegger & Baumgart 48
  Oliveira, J. D. De 18
  Skiwskiin, E. 48
  Ufficio della Stagione (U. Hoepli) 48
  Vačlera, Karl 48
  Verlag von W. Spemann 95, 96

Prata, Mário 180
Pushkin, Aleksandr Sergeyevich 97, 98

Queiroz, Raquel de 179

Rangel, Godofredo 179
Rego, José Lins do 179
Rey, Marcos 180
Ribeiro, João 95
Rio, João do 179
Rodrigues, Nelson 179

Sabino, Inês (Maria Inês Sabino Pinho Maia) 126
Sainte-Beuve, Charles Augustin 97
Saint-Julien, Charles de 97, 98
Sand, George 29
Schiller, Johann Christoph Friedrich von 96
Schmidt, Afonso 179

Shakespeare, William 31, 158
Simões, José 126
Skarbina, Franz 73
Solohoupe, Count W. 97
Sterne, Laurence 1, 31, 105, 163

Taunay, Alfredo d'Escragnolle (Visconde de) 19, 29
Thiel, Ewald 73, 82
Turgenev, Ivan Sergeyevich 96

Vasconcellos, Miguel A. de 80, 81
Veríssimo, José 95, 162, 165
Verne, Jules 29
Viardot, Louis 96, 97

Zaluar, Augusto Emilio 19, 21
Zola, Emile 65

Quarterly Essay

---

1   ENEMY WITHIN
       American Politics in the Time of Trump
       Don Watson

---

75   CORRESPONDENCE
       James Curran, Henry Reynolds, Peter Leahy, Kim Beazley, Peter Whish-Wilson, Judy Betts, Malcolm Garcia, Rory Medcalf, James Brown

---

115   Contributors

Quarterly Essay is published four times a year by Black Inc., an imprint of Schwartz Publishing Pty Ltd. Publisher: Morry Schwartz.

ISBN 978-1-86395-867-7 ISSN 1832-0953

ALL RIGHTS RESERVED.
No part of this publication may be reproduced, stored in a retrieval system, or transmitted in any form by any means electronic, mechanical, photocopying, recording or otherwise without the prior consent of the publishers.

Essay & correspondence © retained by the authors.

Subscriptions – 1 year print & digital
(4 issues): $79.95 within Australia incl. GST.
Outside Australia $119.95. 2 years print & digital (8 issues): $129.95 within Australia incl. GST.
1 year digital only: $39.95.

Payment may be made by Mastercard or Visa, or by cheque made out to Schwartz Publishing. Payment includes postage and handling.

To subscribe, fill out and post the subscription card or form inside this issue, or subscribe online:

www.quarterlyessay.com
subscribe@blackincbooks.com
Phone: 61 3 9486 0288

Correspondence should be addressed to:

The Editor, Quarterly Essay
Level 1, 221 Drummond Street
Carlton VIC 3053 Australia
Phone: 61 3 9486 0288 / Fax: 61 3 9011 6106
Email: quarterlyessay@blackincbooks.com

Editor: Chris Feik. Management: Caitlin Yates. Publicity: Anna Lensky. Design: Guy Mirabella. Assistant Editor: Kirstie Innes-Will. Production Coordinator: Siân Scott-Clash. Typesetting: Tristan Main.

ENEMY WITHIN | American Politics in the Time of Trump

Don Watson

1. I am proposing, as it were, that the nations should with one accord adopt the doctrine of President Monroe as the doctrine of the world . . .
    These are American principles, American policies. We could stand for no others. And they are also the principles and policies of forward-looking men and women everywhere, of every modern nation, of every enlightened community. They are principles of mankind and must prevail.
    — Woodrow Wilson, 1917

    US policy is thus definitively approaching a stage of madness . . .
    — Slavoj Žižek, *Living in the End Times*

Every four years the people of the United States of America choose the person they think most likely to keep them free and safe; and best placed to decide what their country's interests are and how they should be pursued. Among those interests are the interests of national security, which means they are in effect choosing the person who will decide who should be spied upon, selectively bombed or invaded, and who left alone; who should live and who should die; if life on the planet should continue or pretty much cease. Well, if they don't do it, who will? Actual voting is for American citizens only: while recognised as people by the US Supreme Court, corporations wholly or partly owned by foreigners cannot vote, but may contribute as much money as they like to the candidate of their choice. On election day, across the country about 130 million of the 230 million who are eligible turn out to vote, some of them with marvellous knowledge of affairs, and some in bottomless ignorance of everything; some with the tiny part of the brain that enables them to reason and judge, and some with the evolutionary accumulations of instinct and fear that lurk in the other 98 per cent of it.

"We have never been just a collection of individuals or a collection of red states and blue states," Barack Obama told the crowd in Chicago the night he was elected in 2008. The words were just the thing for the occasion, of course, but every day since has given the lie to them. Obama was doing in this speech what all the best American speeches do: laying the stress on the egalitarian and the communitarian, as if the qualities recommended by the Reverend John Winthrop for his Christian colony of Massachusetts 400 years ago remain the qualities that set the United States apart. But, of course, if any country is a collection of individuals it is the United States. Otherwise all that talk about rugged individualism and the American Dream and doing it "my way" would be so much hogwash. It has to be a collection of individuals or advertising wouldn't work.

Americans are divided on party lines as never before. The lines between red and blue states, counties and communities have never been so clearly drawn. Of course, there are purple states as well as red and blue ones: "battleground" states, meaning states where the contest is tight, where the ducks are; the ducks being the ones hunted by the candidates, the relative handful of people who decide those questions that a presidential election decides for the world. In purple states the differences that divide one state from another divide the state itself. Check the electoral map of

Pennsylvania: in 2012 Obama won in just 12 of that state's 67 counties, but he took the state and its 20 electoral votes because he took Philadelphia and Pittsburgh. Since 2008, the whole country has come to resemble a battleground, albeit one, like the Somme for long periods, in stalemate. And 2008 was another age: back then there was only one red party and one blue party. Now there are two of each.

The United States is a miracle of an ever-evolving pluralist democracy and, in the absence of any other candidates for the role, still the last great hope of humankind. It is a wonderland of invention, a marvel of freedom and tolerance, and by most measures the greatest country on earth. "We are, and always will be, the United States of America," Obama said. He surfed on the cheering, and in that moment some of us almost joined in. God bless them, we almost said.

But to think of the United States as a place, or even as a state, is probably the first mistake. While their political leaders will forever say there is more to unite than divide them, in fact the citizenry is divided by cultural, historical, racial, ethnic and ideological differences that every day – every minute in the media – make the platitudes laughable. Democrats say there is more to unite them – as they divide them with identity politics. Republicans chide the Democrats for their identity politics while they dog-whistle to bigotry and preach nostrums they learned at the feet of Ayn Rand.

Some of these tears are visible and categorical: in the suburbs and the cities, for instance, where the dividing lines are so abrupt you can find yourself in a different world in the space of a few absent-minded steps. Some are invisible or subterranean: on the highways you cross them, like songlines, without knowing. There are fractures going back to the Civil War and beyond, forces for good and ill generated in now forgotten times that nevertheless impose themselves, even as the politicians declare their "boundless confidence in America's promise" and implore the people to think of tomorrow. The state has been so deeply fractured for so long that only national crises, real or imagined, and their associated eruptions of fear and loathing of an external enemy can bring it together. We talk of Americans wrapping themselves in the flag: they *bandage* themselves in it. The yard signs of the election season are polite disguises for the underlying truth: the United States is a concatenation of sulky tribes, provincial, ignorant and seething with ambition, frustration and resentment.

The first days of June were great days for Hillary Clinton. She had just won the California and New Jersey primaries. In a prerecorded video released by the Democratic Party, Barack Obama had endorsed her as the most qualified candidate for president ever. Elizabeth Warren was busy endorsing her all over the place, including on Twitter. And at last she'd driven off the old wolf who had appeared on the landscape out of nowhere and dogged her wagons every day for months. True, Bernie Sanders was holding out, and Hillary's supporters were unbecomingly narky and impatient with him. But Sanders was thinking of his own supporters: how to keep them believing and wanting to vote, and, before her election platform was agreed, how to bargain as much radical Bernie into routine Hillary as he could. Bernie's crew were going to take some convincing. "Hillary is a bad aunt," an eighteen-year-old girl told me. "What's Bernie?" I asked. "A cool uncle," she said. She was *very* cool, a cool millennial. "Bernie *represents* millennials," she said. "Hillary tries to be *like* them." There was more in that observation than symptoms of a first political crush.

On 10 June Hillary Clinton spoke to the Planned Parenthood Action Fund in Washington, DC. Planned Parenthood had endorsed her way back in January. These were her people. We expected her to be exultant. She was brilliantly not so. As the cheering died down, she offered a history lesson. When Planned Parenthood was founded, in 1921, as the American Birth Control League, women could not vote. In most states they could not sit on juries. It was a crime to offer information about birth control, let alone provide it. Today half of all US college graduates are women and women make up nearly half of the paid workforce. There are twenty women in the Senate. There are women on the Supreme Court and women in leadership positions in Congress. Three women, including Hillary Clinton, have been Secretary of State. And now, the last pane in the glass ceiling, a woman was the Democratic nominee for President of the United States. She resists the applause.

In a steady conversational tone she reminded her audience of the part that Planned Parenthood played in this progress. She thanked them. It was in large measure a result of their efforts, she said, that fifty-one years ago the Supreme Court legalised birth control – for married couples – and soon after, in *Roe v. Wade*, recognised the right of women to have abortions. Planned Parenthood can take credit for the dramatic drop in maternal mortality in the United States, and for the fact that there are fewer unintended pregnancies than ever before, fewer teen pregnancies and fewer abortions.

Clinton drew the links between the work of the organisation and broader realms of public health, economic growth and opportunity, the strength of families. In thanking them, she was doing more than acknowledging the advances they have made for women; more than thanking them for endorsing her. She was also demonstrating that whatever the bitter and often bizarre state of current US politics, the country can change, and not only through technology, or start-ups, or economics of any description. Her paean to Planned Parenthood was to recognise progressive thought as a defining element of American politics, and to acknowledge the grassroots battlegrounds where politicians – Clinton, Obama and Sanders included – earn their chops. Organising around an idea or a cause, networking, lobbying, educating, publicising, protesting and pushing into representative politics to change the world from within – these are American democratic traditions. Hillary Clinton wrote her senior thesis on the subject. Denied the higher offices, grassroots organisations have long been women's political arenas. This was true of both major parties until the election of Ronald Reagan (in the words of a Republican woman) "buried the rights of a hundred million American women under a heap of platitudes" and handed the women's vote to the Democrats.

Planned Parenthood occupies deeply contested territory. In the most recent physical attack, in November 2015, a religious maniac shot dead three people, including a police officer, at a Planned Parenthood office in Colorado Springs. Nine others were wounded. A lot of people who are not religious fanatics also dislike Planned Parenthood. Jeb Bush wants to defund it. So does the Heritage Foundation, and the largest Protestant body in the country, the Southern Baptist Convention. And of course for most of the 95 million evangelical Christians in the United States, some of whom might be called fanatics, Planned Parenthood is an anathema.

Donald Trump has called women fat pigs, dogs, slobs and disgusting animals. He says Elizabeth Warren has a "fresh mouth"; in the old B movies that was usually followed by a whack in the kisser. For asking him difficult questions, he said of the Fox journalist Megyn Kelly, "You could see there was blood coming out of her eyes. Blood coming out of her wherever." Pregnant women he called an "inconvenience" for employers; he has said women who have abortions should be punished; that if women want equal pay, they should "do just as good a job as men." When Clinton says Trump will defund Planned Parenthood and appoint justices who will overturn *Roe v. Wade*, she is telling the truth.

One would expect Clinton to shine in this forum, and she did. It was a gem of a speech, and Clinton herself was compelling. One watched thinking she should never leave the conversational lower register in which her intelligence and knowledge are palpable. She's at her best when she speaks as if at Bible study or a Methodist camp meeting. "We love eloquence for its own sake, not for any truth it may utter, or any heroism it may inspire," Thoreau wrote. With Clinton talking, truth seems at least in prospect; when she orates, it is more distant. But then, is this what she's up against? Men can hector and bellow as much as they like, but women never? Women must not be shrill?

That's the thing about modern news channels: you can tune out and examine your thoughts, even order another beer, knowing that whatever you just saw or heard will be replayed constantly for the next hour or so, and if it's important, half a dozen pundits – including one or two ideological thugs – will be there to tell you why. And if you can't hear it over the din in the bar or the gym, you can follow it on the supers at the bottom. Though the image might remain, as quickly as the words enter the mind they fade from it, and are replaced by something else. *Is that what Sean Hannity looks like? What's that gorilla doing with a toddler in a pond? Which one is Megyn Kelly? Looks like Muhammad Ali is about to die.* The stupefying loop in which we trap ourselves on news channels might owe something to P.T. Barnum's circus: just inside his crowded tents Barnum had a sign saying, "This Way to the Egress." Thinking they were going to see a curious animal, customers found themselves outside the tent and had to pay to get back in again. And while we're outside, consider what an American election is worth to the networks: for the political advertising that super PACs can finance so abundantly, and from advertising around coverage of the circus itself.

Switch to CNN – it's Hillary. To Fox – Hillary's on half the screen and four heads are waiting to talk on the other half. History is not news. The substantive points of policy, the links she's making, the implications for the country – not news. The news is part of what over fifty years ago Daniel Boorstin, writing about American culture in general, called the "thicket of unreality which stands between us and the facts of life." News is making what he called "a pseudo-event" – or rather a series of them – out of a real one. Elections are news made in the same way. The pundits are not there to judge the quality of thought or action, any more than the candidates are there as authentic, spontaneous beings. An election is a horse race and no one cares what horses are thinking. The pundits are there to judge the quality of a thought or the truth of a remark by the political measure only. It may be a shallow thought or an outright lie, but will it work?

Donald Trump understands the news channels better than they understand themselves. He is a walking, talking pseudo-event, a compilation of them. His "outrageous" tweets push people toward the media and the media towards him. He dominates the news. He wins every day. Even when he loses, he wins. He's turned the whole thing inside out and made the media his lackey. Most people see the news rather than watch it. They see it as they move around: in subways, bars and cafés, the back of taxis, in gyms and hotels. Trump doesn't need to be saying anything much. The shallower the better: his *best* thoughts are shallow ones, he says. He doesn't say the people are shallow, or their perceptions are shallow, though he knows they are. Just as long as he's there. The more he's there, the more people might think he's worth a shot.

As Clinton was speaking to her natural constituency, Donald Trump was about to address one that he needs to make his own. Trump having knocked Ted Cruz out of the race, who else can the Faith and Freedom Coalition turn to? The Faith and Freedom Coalition, one more lobby group that man has made of God, is pro-life, pro-marriage, pro-family, pro-economic growth. "Restoring America's greatness and founding principles" is the banner under which the members march. They like to quote Tocqueville: "The safeguard of morality is religion, and morality is the best security of law as well as the surest pledge of freedom. The Americans combine the notions of Christianity and of liberty so intimately in their minds, that it is impossible to make them conceive the one without the other." It remains hard to decide which is the more remarkable: the way Tocqueville saw into the American mind, or how, after nearly 200 years, the American mind is so little changed.

Faith and Freedom is run by Ralph E. Reed, a political associate of the corrupt lobbyist Jack Abramoff. In 1983, while Reed was drinking in the Bullfeathers pub in Washington, DC, the Holy Spirit approached him and demanded he come to Jesus. He did: he joined the Assembly of God by public phone that very night. It was not an agreement that required him to break off the relationship with Abramoff. According to Reed, the Faith and Freedom Coalition is the 21st-century version of the Christian Coalition of America, the creature of Pat Robertson, an evangelical media mogul who numbered among his many business associates the Liberian dictator, war criminal and harbourer of al-Qaeda terrorists Charles Taylor. To Trump's audience, the story of Planned Parenthood that Clinton so admired was an outrage to God and a disgrace to their country. She might call it "giving women control of their own reproductive cycles": they call it denying "the ['God-given and unalienable'] right to life of all innocent persons, from fertilization to natural death." (The threat is contained in the "innocent.") Faith and Freedom asks members and visitors to its website to sign a pledge calling on Congress to "defund Planned Parenthood immediately."

A week earlier, speaking in San Jose, Clinton had attacked Trump as "temperamentally unfit" to be president. The pundits judged it a significant move, possibly a good one. Trump tweeted: "Bad performance by Crooked Hillary Clinton! Reading poorly from the teleprompter! She doesn't even look presidential!" Every day, he tweets something about "Crooked Hillary." For half the country it's her name.

In 1999 Donald Trump gave an interview in which he said he hated abortion, but was – and he was emphatic about it – pro-choice. There was a time when the first President George Bush and Mitt Romney were pro-choice too. They changed their views in time to run for the White House. Who can blame them when more than one in four of the population are evangelical Christians? The evangelicals can't: what's the point of evangelising if not to bring about a change of heart? The religious right hates Planned Parenthood and Donald Trump needs their votes, so now he hates them too. That's okay with the religious right.

Trump's enemies can't help but mock the way he looks. But they mocked Ronald Reagan too: his face, "in repose, suggests the work of a skilful embalmer," Gore Vidal said. But as with Reagan, so with Trump: what about his appearance is not American? The improbably perfect, pearl-white teeth? The glowing skin? The invisible nips and tucks? The coif: I have been told that his hair seems to lead such a mesmerisingly independent existence because science has contrived to attach it to his head by what amounts to a system of guy ropes: each strand actually fixed to his scalp has another six grafted onto it. So Donald Trump has worked on his appearance. What American who wants to succeed has not?

He doesn't have the family with him today. Sometimes he lines his blonde women up like prisoners stolen from a rival beauty pageant. He has a teleprompter, and he looks awkward with it. But he begins with just a few notes, and his pitch is impeccable, if a little ingratiating to some tastes. Some tastes might be to violently gag, but this audience is used to ingratiating. They take his imitation of a God-fearing Christian as the sincerest form of flattery. He thanks Ralph Reed: "He's been just an amazing – just an amazing guy, an amazing support, a terrific man." "I happen to be Presbyterian," he says with a demure smile, and draws applause: "There's about three of you out there," he says, coyly again. Calvin and Knox gave rise to this? Droll Donald.

Yet Trump is speaking to Tocqueville's observation: Christians, evangelicals in particular, but others as well, demand presidents who believe in God for the assurance it gives them that the covenant will be observed. "It is you yourselves who have called us to this office," John Winthrop said; "and, being called by you, we have authority from God." In Winthrop's hands, at least, it's not an entirely nutty proposition, even if it takes nutty forms and nutcases often proclaim it. As much as it is the people's will to elect their governors, it is God's will to have them do so: a guarantee of obedience, up to a point. But there can be no covenant with a non-believer, and no assurance of God's favour, if the office has not "the image of God eminently stamped upon it." The essentially Calvinist notion gathered force in an elemental union with patriotism, which developed through the nineteenth-century revivals and declared the meaning and purpose of the United States to be God's meaning and purpose. "Patriotism should constrain us to evangelise this nation," the Home Missionary Society insisted in 1842, when they were a force.

Americans want a president through whom God can act. But as well as the right president, it must be the right god. Trump understands this too. Lacking a little in the way of theology and bereft of the faith that "electrifies the whole man," he electrifies them instead with a burst of popular cant: "Radical Islamic terrorism is . . . taking over and we can't let that happen. We cannot let that happen!" He is yet to refer to the "Islamo-progressive axis of evil" or declare that the Muslim Brotherhood has infiltrated every reach of government and is "weaponizing political correctness to shield themselves from criticism and keep us blinded to their ultimate objectives": perhaps his speechwriter missed it on the Faith and Freedom website. "It's happening all the time," he says.

Now he's back talking as if he has the wafer on his tongue and is wondering when he should swallow it. How good the Christian community has been, he says. What wonderful support he's had from the "wonderful Christian leaders and Christian voters." How wonderful faith is. "For not he that commendeth himself is approved, but whom the Lord commendeth." He didn't say this, but he might have. How wonderful. How wonderful that anyone can believe he's sincere. But they do.

"Okay," he says and looks towards the prompter. "It's an honour to speak here today and discuss our shared values." "Here are the goals. And I . . . put some of these together . . . just the other night, because of this [meeting]. I wanted them to come from *me*, from my heart." Of course we were not expecting one of those revivalist sermons that took the American soul (and the American language) to heights of the sublime, but his goals came across sounding less heartfelt than talking points some management-trained campaign hack had written out and Trump was seeing for the first time. "We want to uphold the sanctity and dignity of life." Cheers. "Marriage and family as the building block of happiness and success." More cheers. He reads carefully and emphatically, but the words are peculiar: "The people who go to church, who work, and work in religious charities, these are the foundations of our society. We must continue to forge our partnership with Israel and work to ensure Israel's security."

Cheers and whistles. He makes a mess of whatever he was meant to say about the freedom of religion and race and the colour of people's skin, maybe because he choked when he got to the bit about freedom of religion and remembered what he'd just been saying about Muslims. He escapes into cliché: the country is divided and "we're going to bring our nation together."

Then he's into "Crooked Hillary." He tells them that she wants a 500 per cent increase in Syrian refugees. Boos. A young woman stands and shouts, "Refugees are welcome here," and goes on shouting while three giant bull-necked bouncers haul her out of the room, and the faithful chant, "USA! USA! USA!" Then two more young women stand and shout over the chant, "Build bridges not walls!" They too are dragged out as Trump says, "What's happened in our country is so sad. We are so divided . . . By the way, these are professional agitators, folks. They're sent here by the other party."

Now, with his Mussolini pouts and grimaces, he escorts them round the panoply of Hillary's base intentions: federal funding of abortion on demand, up to birth; "ObamaCare" – bureaucrats making decisions about your health; abolition of the Second Amendment (the NRA, he reminds the crowd, has just endorsed him – "Wonderful people"); her "Wall Street agenda will crush working families"; she'll put bureaucrats, not parents, in charge of our lives; she'll destroy our inner cities, trap children in poverty, "raise your taxes tremendously," "plunge our poor African American and Hispanic communities into turmoil and even worse despair. Believe me. You look at what's going on."

And then the emails: "Hillary Clinton jeopardised national security by putting her emails on a private server, all to hide her corrupt dealings. This is the reason she did it, folks." "Bill and Hillary made $153 million giving speeches to special interest groups since 2001." (Fact check: it was $153,669.661.00.) Hillary's donors "own her." "Bernie Sanders was right about that." Trump spent $55 million of his own money to win the primaries, and he did it for you. Yep. He's going to put America first . . .

But the networks have to cut him short because down in Dallas shots have been fired at Love Field, a domestic airport. All the networks have now gone to Dallas. A video has been posted on Instagram. There's a voice — presumably a policeman's — shouting, "Get down! Get down!" The policeman seems to be backing out of the terminal with his gun aimed at something on the floor. He seems to fire at whatever it is. Nine shots. The networks put the video on loop and it rolls for the next hour while their experts speculate. Is it a terrorist attack that's "unfolding"? It doesn't look like it. But if you have the technology to be there and bring it to us as it breaks, what else can you do but speculate aloud? Just wait and see?

It turns out the man being shot at was armed, but only with a rock. He was African American. He'd been trying to smash the windows of his girlfriend's car, first with a traffic cone he'd picked up off the road, and then with rocks from the verge. She had dropped him off at the airport and dumped his luggage on the pavement — you can see it all on the CCTV footage the airport released later. Love gone wrong is all it is. They shot him when he made for the airport door. They shot him again when he was half inside.

But that's not what people see when it's "breaking news." They see an unseen menace. A gun extended. Excited shouts. Shots. People hurrying out of harm's way. "Oh, my God!" they say. The anchors listen in their earpieces for new developments. Is it a terrorist attack? "It's happening every day," didn't Donald Trump just say?

2.   There is always a philosophy for lack of courage.

— Albert Camus

> I became far better at arguing my point of view and far more satisfied with my political positions once I became a conservative, because I realized I was correct. It's the same thing a lot of people have when they convert to Christianity. They suddenly become very committed and dedicated to it, as opposed to the ambivalence they had about their former atheism.
>
> — Mark Belling

It is easy enough to find the east and west coast liberals, and the southern and Appalachian rednecks, and the battered and embittered working class of the rust belt. Just follow the money, the assault weapons or the electoral maps. I was looking for a place that was not one thing or the other, a normal sort of place. I thought the Midwest, the farming states, the heartland. Wisconsin is the state of big dairy farming – the most "normal" farming of all. Wisconsin combines farming, industry and a great university. It's a model of American moral seriousness, Yankee patriotism, political pragmatism and steadfast values. The "nation's ballast," one writer called it. In other places it's called "America's Dairy" and "Cheeseland," for Pete's sake. That sealed it.

It is possible to conceive of American national identity as consisting of two dominant affects: one communitarian, the other individualistic; one surrendering to church, community or state, the other masterless; the steady farming family and the restless wanderer; the town lawyer or teacher and person of ideas, and the rancher, the man of action; the easterner (James Stewart) who thought he shot the devil Liberty Valance, and the man of the west who actually did (John Wayne). Wisconsin, like the rest of the Midwest, is a product of both ideal types. The wild and hairy trappers gave way in the mid-nineteenth century to respectable homesteaders, many of whom had given up their stony blocks in upstate New York and New

England for the 160 stone-free acres on offer further west. The settlers craved independence and saw it offered in the land. In his 1860 election campaign Abraham Lincoln adopted a slogan that had been doing the rounds with radical reformers – "Vote Yourself a Farm." The people did and the *Homestead Act* passed two years later.

In Wisconsin these people of gumption and courage repeated the community-building patterns of the places they had left. They dominated Wisconsin's commercial and political institutions long after they created them. The same morally upright, improving values of the non-conformist churches came with the next wave of settlers, from northern Europe and the British Isles, and laid the foundations for a century of progressive politics.

But you can't fly anywhere – not even to Cheeseland – without going through security. You arrive in the United States and they tell you to put your hands up – that's after they've told you to stand in a glass booth. In Los Angeles a week earlier I made it to the queue for security an hour after joining the queue for customs – with an "express" card. It's the same at LaGuardia. Getting to the other side without screaming, barefoot and possibly with your trousers round your knees, is mainly in the breathing. Once you're through you can sit down and chill out watching Fox, and marvel that the fear is now so universal you never hear a word of complaint.

We fly in over ice-blue Lake Michigan. Squatting on the southwest shore, Milwaukee's gleaming skyline looks brave and prosperous. The inhabitants endure one of the country's toughest winters, but the cold gives them character. Milwaukee is a byword for hardiness, as it is for industry. Many of the city's residents are descendants of nineteenth-century European migrants who came looking for land and wound up in factories and breweries – Milwaukee used to be one of the biggest beer-making cities in the world. Germans and Poles gave Milwaukee brewing, bratwurst, precision engineering and socialism (in days past it elected socialist mayors), and their traditions, although a little faded now, continue in religion, festivals and food. Most of Europe is represented in the white population: Italy, Ireland, Serbia, Sweden, Norway, Greece, Russia; Catholics, Lutherans, Christian Orthodox and Jews. Milwaukee was for a long time the "most foreign city" in the United States.

Milwaukee is both a model 21st-century economy and an echo from the days when industrial enterprise went a long way to defining the United States and its heroic, well-paid, hardworking citizenry. The same citizenry were immortalised after a fashion in *Happy Days* and *Laverne & Shirley*. The city's manufacturing tradition continues, even though professional and service industries now create more wealth and employment, and give the renovated downtown modern ambience. Briggs & Stratton and Harley-Davidson still have their headquarters there. Milwaukee still makes high-quality power tools, mining and agricultural machinery and X-ray equipment. They still have Rockwell Automation and one or two other Fortune 500 companies. Given that jobs in US manufacturing fell by 29 per cent in the first nine years of the twenty-first century, on the surface Milwaukee has not done so badly.

But look closer and you see one of those subterranean divides. Milwaukee is rust-belt USA: surviving, but much changed. In 1960 it was a city of 740,000 people: now it's less than 600,000. The white proportion of the city's 2010 population was just 37 per cent, about half what it was in the mid-twentieth century. Seventeen per cent now identify as Hispanic or Latino, more than four times the number of fifty years ago. African Americans make up 40 per cent. In a state with an abolitionist, Underground Railroad history, it is the most segregated city in the country. The almost exclusively white surrounding suburbs hived off from what a Republican official in 2014 called "the colored section."

When African Americans came to Milwaukee in the 1960s the city had begun to decline. There were no jobs that could not be filled by white workers drifting down from the fading lumber industry in the north. No black middle class arose, and no leaders. They began as an underclass and remained so. Now four out of five black children in Milwaukee live in poverty. In a country with more people in prison than anywhere else on earth (China possibly excepted), Milwaukee has the highest rate of incarceration of any city. Forty per cent of the Milwaukee male prison population are there for low-level drug offences: mandatory "three strikes and you're out" sentencing tripled the Wisconsin prison population between 2000 and 2008. The state now spends more on its correctional system than it does on its education system. In public schools, the "achievement gap" between white and black students is the widest in the country.

That noble skyline is a lie. Milwaukee is one of the four or five poorest cities in the United States. Among many other signs of what that means, 16,000 adults and children are evicted from their rental properties each year. The *New Yorker* reported on "sheriff squads whose full-time job is to carry out eviction and foreclosure orders . . . moving companies [that] specialize in evictions, their crews working all day long, five days a week." That's what a model 21st-century economy can do for you.

Milwaukee votes Democrat: 67 per cent of them voted for Obama in 2008, 15 per cent more than the state as a whole, and in 2012 the figures were exactly the same. But leaving the city on the I94, you pass through the suburbs of Waukesha County, a creation in the main of "white flight" and a Republican voting bloc without equal in the US. Waukesha is the seat of Wisconsin's governor, Scott Walker.

The son of a Baptist preacher and educated at Marquette, a Jesuit college, Walker believes he was called by God to politics. "God has told me I'm chosen to cut taxes and stop killing babies," he once said. He is backed by business, the religious right and, crucially, by two right-wing radio jocks, Charlie Sykes and Mark Belling. Sykes and Belling have shows on the same station that combine into a conservative "SykesBelling" force. Their audience, the exurban blue-collar "septic tank belt," "married women at home with kids" and "old white men," form the base of the Republican Party.

Both Sykes and Belling started out as liberals and converted to what they call conservatism. Both are zealous supporters of Scott Walker and, by most definitions of the term, racist. This from Belling concerning a black Congresswoman, for instance:

> What do you think the chances are she was sitting on the toilet? . . . Maybe Gwen was sitting there on the crapper and this was one that was not working out too well for her or something. "Blew-ee!" "Congresswoman, you've got to vote." "I am sittin' on de toilet!"

Walker and his Republican-controlled state legislature have cut budgets for programs that might help the African American population, pushed for private-school vouchers that undermine public education, with great thoroughness and finesse gerrymandered the electorate for the next decade, stripped collective bargaining rights from unions and introduced voter ID laws that are calculated to disfranchise anything between 200,000 and 350,000 underprivileged voters.

Wisconsin Democrats will tell you that Walker has divided the state to an unprecedented extent, and overturned a tradition of cooperation between the major parties. With the prolonged civil upheaval that his labour laws provoked in 2010–11, the old divides became polar opposites, "different planets" which Republicans characterise as "makers versus takers." Reading a racial dimension into the phrase is optional. It is not just a matter of different parties: social researchers find entirely different worldviews. As a consequence, they say, the will to find answers to big problems dies on the ideological battlefield. Wisconsin, the nation's ballast, is now a fair measure of its predicament.

In a Buick, courtesy of a splendidly successful government bailout of General Motors, I drove the sixty miles west to Madison. Madison is a progressive, liberal, Democrat university town. I read that someone once said Madison was "thirty square miles surrounded by reality." So I was driving through the reality: looking for it in the green and fallow fields and the homey-gothic farmhouses of purest white with their porches and verandas, on immaculate oak-shaded lawns. They perch their homes on low rises, as if to memorialise their triumph over the land and human weakness. Something in their pristine ethereality whispers God or an uneasy element contesting with Him.

Flags flew in the towns, but rarely on the farmhouses: was some Puritan horror of icons at work? The Holstein cows did not graze in pasture but milled round the regulation red barns of the American Midwest, waiting to give up their milk, quite possibly to undocumented Mexican workers, thence to one of the mighty conglomerates of a consumer market that grows ever more concentrated. And ever more irksome to Senator Elizabeth Warren: "It was one of the basic founding principles of our nation," she says, "concentrated power anywhere was a threat to liberty everywhere." Even cows are tethered to the dictums of the founding fathers.

The shock jocks seemed not to be broadcasting. The rental car was tuned to a Christian evangelical station and I left it there. In fact it was not so much a Christian station as an anti-Muslim one. The preacher's solemn exegesis of Paul's Second Letter to the Corinthians seemed but an excuse for the denunciations of Islam that every five minutes interrupted it. Paul's letter could be taken to recommend a little tolerance and humility: "But we will not glory beyond our measure, but according to the measure of the province which God apportioned to us as a measure . . ." The station announcer was having none of it. Love thy neighbour as thyself – phooey! The Christian god and the god of Islam are not the same, and it is a dangerous liberal fallacy to think otherwise. Islam exists to destroy Christianity. Christians are engaged in a war for survival. The US government has been infiltrated. So VCY America waged war in the bucolic calm while the Holsteins (each one generating $34,000 in economic activity, according to a Scott Walker press statement) moped and the green grass swayed and glistened in the sun. "The media, our schools and even our financial institutions are being infiltrated through covert tactics designed by Muslim leaders years ago. Their goal is simply to create an America dominated by Islam," the station website says. Substitute "communist" for "Islam" and "Muslims," and every word could have been uttered by Joe McCarthy in the '50s.

In his famous book published on the heels of the McCarthy era, Richard Hofstadter discerned a "paranoid style in American politics." McCarthy might have been the main target of his investigation, but he found in US history examples of the same "style" among left-wing populists, including the early twentieth-century trust-busters. At other times, paranoid waves have been fed by imagined Masonic conspiracies, Protestant conspiracies and Catholic conspiracies; Jacobin conspiracies, slave-owner conspiracies and international banker conspiracies. Today Hofstadter might find elements of the same style in Bernie Sanders' insistence that the country is being run for the all-but-exclusive benefit of Wall Street's billionaires and millionaires. But he would find the paranoia is deepest where he found it in his own day, on the right wing of American politics among the Tea Party people, the birthers, the Trump supporters. In 1964 he wrote:

> But the modern right wing ... feels dispossessed: America has been largely taken away from them and their kind, though they are determined to try to repossess it and to prevent the final destructive act of subversion. The old American virtues have already been eaten away by cosmopolitans and intellectuals; the old competitive capitalism has been gradually undermined by socialistic and communistic schemers; the old national security and independence have been destroyed by treasonous plots, having as their most powerful agents not merely outsiders and foreigners as of old but major statesmen who are at the very centers of American power. Their predecessors had discovered conspiracies; the modern radical right finds conspiracy to be betrayal from on high.

It's a generally accepted theory that the modern American right came out of the south in the '60s after the passing of the Civil Rights Bill. There's another theory that its origins lie in California in the '30s, when big business jacked up against Roosevelt for empowering unions. Roosevelt had the quaint idea that by raising wages and living standards, unions might help the economy revive. The theories no doubt are good ones. Yet when you're among the grassroots right they don't talk about unions or civil rights for African Americans. They talk about freedom. At the Tea Party rally I went to in 2009, the local republican baritone sang, "I'm proud to be an American / Where at least I know I'm free," and everyone who took the microphone talked about the people "on high" who were eroding their freedom by taking away their assault weapons or imposing Affordable Care on them. They talked too of the people who had died defending freedom. Their banners read: "I'll keep my guns and my liberty. You can keep the Change." "Less taxes. Less government. More freedom." The Kochs might have written them. *Really*, they might have – they finance the Tea Party, including their advertising.

Of course, they will also talk about the threats from *Roe v. Wade*, the federal deficit, Islam, atheism, evolution, homosexuality, the United Nations, trade deals, the military-industrial complex, and Hillary Clinton and other politicians from both sides who have sold them out and want to take their guns. At some point they will put their hands on their hearts and look up at the flag as someone sings "The Star-Spangled Banner."

But freedom is the thing: they speak of it as God-given and guaranteed by the Constitution, and therefore as if it exists only in the United States. It must be a tic passed down from the Revolutionary War. They think that nothing's changed in Europe since 1778. It's useless to tell them that people are free in many other countries as well, and free from worrying about freedom so much, many of them. In America, the rest of the world drops out of sight.

American political analysts have written millions of words in explanation of the Tea Party phenomenon. But the novelist and Christian essayist Marilynne Robinson might come as close to truth as any of them. In an interview this year, Robinson spoke about "a glacier of fear creeping toward the culture." In an earlier essay she wrote: "First, contemporary America is full of fear. And, second, fear is not a Christian habit of mind." She sees fear in the way the right talks about immigration, for instance; on Fox News, in the "commodification of anxiety and hostility through media"; in attempts like Scott Walker's to reduce voting rolls in Wisconsin; in "Americans . . . now buying Kalashnikovs in numbers sufficient to help subsidise Russian rearmament"; in the snake's nest of conspiracy theories, be it that the president is a radical Muslim born in Kenya, or the United Nations has a plan to conquer the whole world, including Texas. She would see fear now in the bizarre dehumanised riot gear in which phalanxes of police confront Black Lives Matter protesters on suburban streets.

By way of explaining how a self-professed Christian country could be gripped by fear, Robinson offers the example of a sixteenth-century French citizen on his way to slaughter Calvinists: he "would no doubt have said that he was taking back his city, taking back his culture, taking back his country, fighting for the soul of France." The ghastly massacres of that era were incited by fear: "by the thought that someone really might destroy one's soul, plunge one into eternal fire by corrupting true belief even inadvertently."

To "fear hobbyists," Robinson says, fear is addictive, a stimulus, and an incitement very often to violent and terrible acts. For Robinson this marks a change in American values and aesthetics. Fear has never been an admirable human trait, particularly in a country that draws much of its self-image from the frontier, and much of the remainder from the example of Jesus. Yet Americans, who once admired courage above all human qualities, now seem to get high on fear. Not that we see them trembling; but we see and hear fear's most common disguise, belligerence. From the very beginning that was the Bush administration's response to 9/11, and it is what we have heard from the Republican Party ever since. It was the mood of the Tea Party. Not the quiet courage once personified on the screen by Gary Cooper or Spencer Tracy, or the real-life self-effacement of General George Marshall, but the belligerence whipped up and exploited by Donald Trump, and the preening self-aggrandisement (and self-enrichment) of General David Petraeus.

Robinson makes a point familiar to viewers of old Hollywood films, that much of the far west and the Midwest was settled not by gunslingers but by communities, very often *religious* communities, descended in spirit from the Puritans. Communities much like the ones through which this highway I was travelling passed: where people once lived out their winters in sod huts, where courage was a close relation of humility and grace, of turning the other cheek, of generosity and sacrifice, and – Native Americans aside – of a mutual obligation to provide liberally for all. Something of the same order is implied in the preamble to the Constitution.

Yet for every dozen Hollywood westerns in which a good community was terrorised by a dreadful individual, there was one in which a community gone to the bad was put right by a good individual. Communities have within them the seeds of horror, as Robinson knows very well. Perhaps her fellow Americans are less inclined to burn witches. Very likely, fewer of today's fearful believe in the eternal fire, but listen to swathes of them and you could be forgiven for thinking they feel their very souls are threatened. And why not, when so many of them continue to believe that their country, no less than the early religious communities, is ordained by God, has "His image stamped upon it" and, when it is not betrayed by government or threatened by axes of evil, walks the path He has chosen. No other nation so relentlessly pores over its founding documents as if, like the Scripture they also pore over, they contain the sacred and inviolable truth and any breach of their tenets is a blasphemy and a threat to existence. While it might recede from time to time, the fear – and the anger and aggression – will remain as long as this exceptionalism is the nation's creed.

Noble and creative as it has often been, provider of an essential thread in the best of the American ideal and source of a rare grace one encounters only in the United States, American Christianity also disguises fear and feeds ignorance, paranoia and prejudice, along with a readiness to smite enemies with weapons of unspeakable destructive force. This too is American exceptionalism.

3. On, Wisconsin! On, Wisconsin!
    Champion of the right.
    "Forward," our motto
    God will give thee might!

    — Anthem of Wisconsin, verse 2

    Corporations and individuals allied with corporations were invited to come in and take what they would . . . I determined that the power of this corrupt influence, which was undermining and destroying every semblance of representative government in Wisconsin, should be broken.

    — Robert La Follette, 1897

One feels the might of the ice sheets in Wisconsin much as one senses the vanished sea in the Australian inland. The Wisconsin Glacial Episode, which ended 11,000 years ago, left not only the lakes and the landforms, but a spectre. The frontier is long gone but you sense it. Even in summer you sense the winter, and find yourself wondering at the qualities men and women brought to bear to make the wild landscape into seeming gentleness. Glaciers made Wisconsin's rich and porous soils. They made the flatlands, the wetlands, the low rounded hills and the lakes. Their retreat created the rivers in which beavers flourished, with pelts adapted to the glacial cold. The European beavers having been hunted to near extinction, from the mid-seventeenth century, French, Dutch and English trappers came to Wisconsin to catch and skin the American beavers to make hats for European heads, both secular and clerical, meanwhile corrupting and blighting with disease and alcohol the indigenous Ho-Chunk as a prelude to dispossessing them entirely.

Downtown Madison was a marsh when the Sauk warrior Black Hawk crossed it with his starving band in 1832. Seven hundred and fifty US soldiers were hot on his heels, among them Abraham Lincoln, Jefferson Davis and several men who later became congressmen, senators, governors and the like: the marriage of military service and politics is as old as the country itself. The war ended with the Battle of Bad Axe on the banks of the Mississippi, where a gunboat cut down Black Hawk's people "like a scythe through grass." Many of those who escaped were later killed by rival tribes who had thrown in their lot with the US troops. That was the end of not only the Black Hawk War, but of resistance east of the Mississippi. Black Hawk was captured, given a celebrity tour of the east coast and died in 1838, by which time the land around Madison was being cut up and sold to eastern speculators, and 200 Europeans had begun to build a city.

At one end of downtown Madison today stands the Capitol, a splendid Beaux-Arts rendition of the familiar sight in US capital cities; a gilded bronze nearly five metres tall stands atop a mighty sixty-metre white granite dome. From the ground it might be Athena, but she's actually "Wisconsin": in robes, an eagle perched on a globe in one of her hands, the other raised as if urging all below to live up to the state motto – "Forward." On her head is a helmet topped with a badger.

Not a mile from the Capitol, at the other end of the city, is the 370-hectare campus of the University of Wisconsin–Madison. With more than 40,000 students and colossal research endowments, UW is one of the great public universities in the United States. (It places ahead of every Australian university except Melbourne in the *Times Higher Education World University Rankings*, and above Melbourne in other surveys.) Charles Lindberg, Frank Lloyd Wright and Joyce Carol Oates went there. So did Dick Cheney.

In the clear, crisp air of the evening, a pretty girl sang country music in a little amphitheatre. Young people promenaded, rode bicycles, ate empanadas and ice-cream and sipped chai lattes at sidewalk tables outside cafés, bars and bookshops. A smart set had assembled in the new art gallery. It was a short walk to the shores of Lake Mendota, where university students were frolicking and drinking beer as the sun set gloriously over the water. A Republican governor named Lee Sherman Dreyfus said

Madison was not reality. He was right. A visitor can't walk around the city without thinking how unlikely the whole thing is. A quarter of a million people living in sparkling amenity; one end dedicated to learning and research ("continual and fearless sifting and winnowing by which alone the truth can be found"), and the other to democracy and justice. In between them, an opera company, a symphony orchestra, a ballet company, a theatre company and a chamber orchestra that plays in the evenings on the lawns of the Capitol. It has a museum of art, a museum of contemporary art, half a dozen community theatres, a historical museum, a children's museum, a veterans' museum and a Centre for Film and Theatre Research. It has music festivals, film festivals and beer festivals. It is regularly named the best city to live in in the USA; the best for college sports, and the healthiest. It has buildings by Louis Sullivan, Frank Lloyd Wright and Cesar Pelli. On Saturdays it stages the biggest farmers' market in the country.

So why, in a country as rich as the United States, are there not more cities like Madison? The link between UW's research and entrepreneurial businesses, together with the assured skills base and the city's general amenity, virtually guarantees Madison's prosperity. Anyone tired of Silicon Valley and wanting to see the sort of city an American future might hold would do well to see Madison.

It didn't happen by accident. The city – and the state of Wisconsin, for that matter – has a long history of progressive politics. The communitarian values of the foundation settlers, centred on church and school, local cooperatives, and traditions of mutual aid laid the foundations, as they did in much of the rural United States. The pattern of boom and bust culminating in the bruising depression of the 1890s, the human costs of industrialisation, the corruption that came with the railways and the corporations, the inequality and abuses of power, generated popular resistance across the country. That old canard, satisfying to many Protestants and Social Darwinists alike, that poverty was the fault of the victim and wealth a reward for virtue, and that both were the natural order of things, lost purchase on the public mind. In Wisconsin it was overthrown. Progressivism became the dominant political ideology and progressives the dominant politicians.

There is a bust of Robert Marion La Follette in the Capitol's rotunda. He has a prodigious head of hair swept back, a broad and resolute jaw, eyes that gaze beyond the general ruck. Born poor in (truly) a log cabin, a teenage farm labourer supporting his fatherless family, La Follette took himself to the University of Wisconsin, thence to the law, Congress, the state governorship and the Senate. According to a 1982 survey of historians, with Henry Clay he was the most effective and influential senator in US history. At UW in the 1870s, La Follette was influenced by the president of the university, John Bascom, a New England Protestant theologian and sociologist. Much less troubled by Darwin and evolution than he was by the "gospel of wealth" and the inequality and corruption of morals to which it gave rise, Bascom believed the state had to take on the social duties once left to the churches. "Fighting Bob" La Follette gave his life to that cause. In 2011, when thousands rallied at the Capitol to protest Scott Walker's anti-union legislation, La Follette's bust was draped with the sign: "Fighting Bob would fight the bill" and "Long Live La Follette."

In his early years in politics, as much as La Follette brought ideas of social reform to the people, the people brought them to him. He found them everywhere, not least among dairymen and other farmers, especially the Norwegians, whose language he spoke, and the professional classes, many of them emerging from the university. A brilliant and tireless speaker and a campaigner of astonishing energy and stamina, he turned latent grievances into political force: which is to say, he was the definitive populist. The word is often a pejorative, especially in this country: we have "shameless" populists, and people who "resort" to populism, as if it's about as low as a politician can go. Despite the triumph of "meritocratic" ideology, which is neoliberalism's specific antidote for the disease, in the US populism on both the left and right remains legitimate.

In the US there are articulate liberal commentators who actually recommend populism. In theory, after all, there can hardly be a purer interpretation of democracy: the uncorrupted people's voice against the self-serving elites. Michael Young, the English sociologist who coined the term "meritocracy," despised the fashion for it: first, because it is largely a smug fantasy perpetuated by those who sit at the top of the social pyramid; and second, because it bestows on those at the bottom the slur that they are there because they have no merit. Even feudalism spared the poor that insult: their lowly station was an accident of birth. While the underclasses in an alleged meritocracy might be reluctant to acknowledge the wound to their dignity, the elites should not be surprised if it adds a savage streak to popular resentment.

Robert La Follette took on the elites for forty years. He took on the railroad trusts, the lumber bosses, the corporations, the party bosses, Woodrow Wilson and the political tide that swept the US into World War I. He allied himself with farmers and trade unions alike, Democrats and Republicans according to their worth; he pursued war profiteers and defended persecuted dissidents. He blasted the Versailles treaty and the League of Nations as a high-sounding farce erected on the same fatal mix of imperialism, nationalism, racism, exploitation and greed that, he said, led to World War I. He stood for an expanded democracy, guarantees of civil liberties, state ownership of the railways and utilities, the rights of workers to form unions, farm credit and plebiscites before any declaration of war. He stood against monopolists, imperialists and "any discrimination between races, classes and creeds." In his run for president, he won a sixth of the vote nationwide.

Wisconsin was the most progressive state in the union. It went into the statutes of the university and became known everywhere as the "Wisconsin Idea": the university would seek wisdom from all the people of the state, and share its knowledge with them. It was "a poem of faith in mankind," a member of the UW Board of Regents said in 2013 when Governor Walker tried to do away with it.

While no single initiative defines the Wisconsin Idea, an abbreviated list of legislation passed in Madison in the first fourteen years of the twentieth century gives a sense of what it meant: women and children's labour laws; laws regarding industrial safety, public health and food standards; conservation laws; workers' compensation. Laws governing campaign spending and lobbying; direct primaries and referendums on citizen initiatives. A tax commission, an inheritance tax, insurance and banking laws, a trade practices act. In addition a first-class education system was established. Progressives came up with what became known as the "Madison Compromise." Concerned that their city lagged in industrial assets and production, but just as worried that industrial growth would have destructive social and environmental consequences, they decided that Madison would have only "high-grade" industries that hired skilled and well-paid workers. In the ten years from 1910 to 1920, both industrial output and factory employment increased by 280 per cent.

This is ancient history, of course: or rather, it would be if La Follette's influence stopped with his death in 1925. It didn't. His program was taken up in other states, and by Upton Sinclair when he ran for governor in California in 1934. Fiorello La Guardia brought his ideas to New York City. More significantly, much of Roosevelt's New Deal can be traced to La Follette: Harold Ickes was an adviser to both men and an architect of the New Deal, which made the United States more socially progressive than any country in Europe. For half a century after Roosevelt's election, tax on incomes over a million dollars averaged 82 per cent. US estate taxes of 70 to 80 per cent were twice those in Germany and France. Wisconsin was a state as progressive as any in the world, and the South aside, the US did not lag so far behind. Yet by the mid-1980s it had been decided that these rates and a federal minimum wage, which had coexisted with the most sustained era of prosperity and social mobility in US history, were an unbearable burden on free enterprise and the American way.

The mayor of Madison these days is Paul Soglin, a Democrat. In the '60s at the University of Wisconsin–Madison he was a campus radical. He appears in a photo taken during a student occupation at UW in 1967. The hood of his sheepskin coat is pulled up over his head, and it neatly frames his young face and the "impishness and charisma" a girlfriend of the time described. All the other students in the front line are caught in a moment of elemental fear, because just behind the photographer the police are advancing with tear gas and truncheons. In what otherwise could be a still from a 1950s horror movie, Soglin looks almost serene: calm enough to have pulled the hood up to protect his head and neck, and to gaze at the advancing cops as if trying to find their historical context. A minute later, he was getting belted on the floor with the others. The Madison police were not progressive. Six months after the occupation Soglin was a Madison city councillor. Six years later, aged twenty-seven, he was mayor. Not long ago he suggested making "Madison – seventy-seven square miles surrounded by reality" the city's motto.

Paul Soglin agreed to meet me on a Sunday morning. Now seventy-one, with greying hair swept back like La Follette's and a matching moustache, he long ago converted his university activism into progressive municipal politics conducted by orthodox democratic means. He was radicalised by the war, by the counter-culture and by a heavyweight history department that included William Appleman Williams, the critic of American exceptionalism; the legendary lecturer and left-wing activist Harvey Goldberg; and the "spellbinding" liberal George L. Mosse. For transforming young minds there is probably nothing more powerful than history in the hands of a charismatic teacher. Soglin also found inspiration in the semi-sacred texts of American thought: William Lloyd Garrison, the abolitionist; and Henry David Thoreau, whose *Resistance to Civil Government* has been a thousand times quoted in support of causes on both the right and left of politics. Brutal police actions can also have a powerful effect in the formation of ideology.

Mayor Soglin hasn't forgotten the old slogans. Long ago Mao Zedong said, "Whoever controls the countryside controls the cities." The mayor says these days, "Whoever controls the sewers controls everything." Because in Madison the left used more intelligence than is often the case, and took control of traditional politics, Ronald Reagan never took hold, he says. The city has held true to its progressive traditions. After his 2008 campaign visit was a massive success, Obama came back in 2012 for the biggest rally of the campaign.

Nine times Soglin has been elected mayor, the last in 2015 with more than 70 per cent of the vote. He can take a lot of the credit for Madison being the good city that it is. The mayoral biographical note, however, describes his philosophy in decidedly modest and unromantic terms: "balanced investment in human capital and appropriate municipal infrastructure" and a "focus . . . on equity and developing a tax base that can support human services." A rough translation from the managerial would be: "Madison is no accident." The city is the result of a much assailed and greatly debilitated, but unbroken American tradition of democratic socialism.

Paul Soglin supports Bernie Sanders. When I spoke to him, Sanders was still in the race and rated an outside chance to win the nomination. That prospect passed soon after, but Sanders' supporters were sustained by the belief that the strength of his campaign would leave Clinton with no choice but to head in their direction, and the party establishment would have to follow suit. On the face of it they were right. Soglin has known Sanders since the late 1970s, when they worked together on reforms to state and local government. Although it is a much smaller city than Madison, Burlington in Vermont has the same combination of a post-industrial service economy, a university and an airport, and as mayor in the early '80s Sanders steered it in much the same direction as Soglin in Madison, and with the same lasting effect. They are two of a handful of radical progressive mayors who have confronted the prevailing pattern of development and established highly liveable alternatives to high-rise ugliness and social decay. Soglin introduced Sanders to a crowd of 8000 when the senator came to Madison in 2016. He came twice more and eventually won the Democratic primary with 56.6 per cent of the vote.

In Paul Soglin's view the modern Republicans are not a true conservative party, but are merely manipulating the angry dispossessed – an assessment to go with that of the former Republican congressional staffer who said they were "becoming less and less like a traditional political party in a representative democracy and becoming more like an apocalyptic cult, or one of the intensely ideological authoritarian parties of 20th century Europe." In the contest with this dark force, Soglin believes Sanders has done most of the heavy lifting and offers a chance for the Democrats to pick up the old populist thread. Millions of young voters can re-energise the party, so long as the party moves with them. There have been three lasting realignments in US politics: after the Civil War, with FDR and with Reagan. Soglin says there is now the prospect of a fourth, and it rests with Sanders and Clinton.

4.   We come back to the magic words and they all depend upon community.

                              – Perry Miller, *The Life of the Mind in America*

Let's drop the domestic stuff altogether . . . I mean, who gives a shit if the minimum wage is $1.15 or $1.20 compared to something like [Cuba]?

                              – President Kennedy to his speechwriter,
                              before his inaugural address, 1961

It is one of the curious things about Bernie Sanders' campaign that, both here and in the US, commentators have characterised his ideology and objectives as, in some way, exotic: if he calls himself a democratic socialist, he must be doing something Scandinavian. In fact, the roots of Sanders' philosophy are firmly in the United States. They reach back as far as the reality to which they are opposed – namely, social inequality and the corruption of politics consequent on the ruthless and unrestrained pursuit of self-interest known as capitalism, or sometimes as greed. They go back to the War on Poverty in the '60s, the GI Bill of the '40s, to the New Deal of the '30s, to the trust-busters, progressives and Eugene V. Debs socialists of the early years of last century. In fact, they go back to the Founding Fathers. Thomas Jefferson wanted primogeniture done away with. Tom Paine wanted a pension for people over fifty, funded by an estate tax, and a leg-up payment to people trapped in poverty. John Adams favoured property qualifications for voters, but believed pretty well everyone should own property. Those freedoms that Americans are forever insisting are guaranteed in the founding documents were, according to the authors of the documents, dependent upon equality.

Given the shape of the US economy, the deep failures of the social system and the unwillingness of Barack Obama and the Congress to make anyone pay for the delinquencies that led to the Great Recession, it would have been much more surprising – and disquieting – if no one had come forth. And yet, with the fading of the Occupy movement, that seemed likely. Imagine, a First World country founded on egalitarian principles in which the top 20 per cent of households have 84 per cent of the wealth, while the bottom 40 per cent have 0.3 per cent; and one family, the Waltons, owns more than the bottom 40 per cent of US families combined; and the ratio of CEO salary to unskilled worker is 354 to 1 (fifty years ago it was 20 to 1). A minimum wage of $7.25 per hour, which is 34 per cent less than workers on the minimum were getting in 1968. More than 20 per cent of children in the United States live in poverty, more than twice the rate of any European country. With a quarter of totalitarian China's population, democratic America has about the same number of people in jail.

These are a few bare facts of modern US capitalism: inequality is worse than in any other Western democracy, and there is less social mobility than in the others. And, as Thomas Piketty argues, with growth unlikely to get beyond 1 to 1.5 per cent in the foreseeable future, the return to (those with) capital will continue to outstrip it by 4 per cent or more and compound the inequality. Piketty is surely right to say that this is "incompatible with the meritocratic values on which our democratic societies are based"; though of course it may not be incompatible with ever-deeper belief in those values among the people with the capital. The task that Piketty set for governments three years ago was to "go beyond growth and help democracy retake control of capitalism."

So what was the appeal of Bernie Sanders? Watch the ovation as he stepped onto the stage in Philadelphia, and the faces in the crowd as he spoke to them. What absence in their souls does the old codger fill that makes twenty-somethings cheer and weep? It's mainly his message, but there's more to it. Could it be that before Bernie Sanders they had only seen "pseudo-events" and never an authentic one on their political screens, much less an authentic Jewish working-class socialist? Sanders never had to worry about an "image problem," because he didn't have an image. When he appeared on television he did not look like a man in search of a camera; more like one who had been teaching school for fifty years and, having just retired, stumbled in on a talkshow. But he was not without stage presence. You can try to manufacture charisma with a haircut and a face-lift, or you've just got it. Sanders was stooped, his face wore every one of his seventy-four years, but he could talk! His beliefs came forth not as mere words, but as unbridled urges. He sweated. His face turned red. He spoke in short concrete sentences with anger not far beneath the surface of them. No epic Lincolnian flourishes, none of Obama's rhetorical music, no cant, no jingoism, no echoes of the preachers. Instead – the facts. And – "We can do better than this." For once the word "passion" fits.

People say he's a grouch; that he's "abrasive" and "combative," and has little or no sense of humour. But politicians don't need humour anymore. There are professional comedians to do it for them. Probably the burden of this responsibility is what has made the comedians by now so very good at it, and some of them outstrip the politicians – and the pundits – for popularity and influence. For politicians who have decided that in worldly matters "one sinks by levity and rises by gravity" (as Lewis Lapham said), there is a twofold risk to this: first, that the comedians begin to be taken more seriously than the politicians; and second, that the politicians forfeit entirely this dimension of their humanity through failing to exercise it, and become ever less attractive to voters looking for a person of ordinary human complexity.

Sanders has escaped that fate. Let Larry David do the humour. At the Democratic convention he offered reassurance. Thanks to his supporters, Hillary Clinton will go to the election on the most progressive platform in the party's history, he said. Thanks to them, the radical work can continue through a new grassroots outfit called "Our Revolution." Not every diehard was satisfied, some no doubt because they hate Hillary, or just don't trust her, or think the Clintons have long been part of the problem, or because they believe Trump will beat her. But even those who saw him swallow the awful pill of capitulation and accepted his reasons for doing so will forever mourn the fact that Bernie Sanders won't be president. It has a lot do with what he said, but it is also the *symbolic* weight of the office he failed to win. He offered something grounded and authentic, and if he promised to do no more or less than give meaning to that part of the preamble to the Constitution that says "promote the general welfare," this was much more than his rivals could be relied on to do. The son of Jewish immigrants seemed to be not only the most genuine of the candidates, but also the one most genuinely descended from the nation's moral and intellectual ancestors.

"I infer that the sovereign, original and foundation of civil power lies in the people," Roger Williams wrote in 1644. In the first half of the seventeenth century Williams, who founded the settlement at Providence, Rhode Island, endured banishment and risked execution by advocating the separation of church and state. He believed in free thought, the abolition of slavery and generous treatment of Native Americans. That was the first time the ideal of the civil power was uttered in America. You do not have to believe it could ever be made wholly real to wish for someone to wholly embody the ambition. Sanders would ennoble the country as well as improve it. That's why he was so hard to give up. He would represent their power, not steal it from them by pretending to be like them.

Surveys taken over the years since the global financial crisis suggest that most of the citizenry don't see it Sanders' way. The American Dream and political supineness go together. Ground that should be good for progressive politicians turns out to be fertile for regressive ones. If only objective self-interest was the sole motivation. But instead we find these people who depend on government loathing government on principle; people who would applaud the view that their country must not become "a politically correct neo-feudal fiefdom of monolithic, paternalistic government" (or other modern Republican formulations of Burkean thought) and boo anyone who tries to tell them what side their bread is buttered.

Just about everyone, including Republicans and the wealthy, favours more equal distribution of wealth, but one study also found that only 5 per cent of them think inequality is a major problem. The average American does think the gap between CEO salaries and average workers is too great: they think a ratio of 7 to 1 is about right. They guess it's about 30 to 1 just now, which is not a tenth of the real figure. Asked to guess how much the richest fifth owned, they reckoned around 60 per cent. Would it were so. Pew found that while six out of ten Americans think the system favours the wealthy, six out of ten also believe that hard work will take you to the top. When the primatologist Frans de Waal put two capuchin monkeys in adjacent cages and gave each of them a piece of cucumber, they were content. When he gave one of them a piece of cucumber and the other a bunch of grapes, the one that got the cucumber threw it at de Waal. Every time he repeated the experiment the victim of unequal treatment got wilder. Capuchin monkeys have no faith in America; they hold to no dream.

America has "never been a nation of haves and have-nots," this year's failed Republican candidate Marco Rubio declared in 2011. "We are a nation of haves and soon-to-haves, of people who have made it and people who will make it." The young Republican may be less inclined to believe it since Donald Trump shattered his dream in this year's primaries. In any event it was not merely because he believed it that Rubio made this apparently puerile claim: it was also because he knew Americans believe it, or at least want to believe it. Late in 2013 Barack Obama said, "the combined trends of increased inequality and decreased mobility are a fundamental threat to the American Dream, our way of life and what we stand for around the globe." Then he went a little quiet on the subject and started talking instead about raising the middle class. Commentators thought he changed tack because stressing inequality is too pessimistic a view and offends the faith of a lot of ordinary folk whose votes the Democrats need. The Republicans are happy to take what the *Economist* called a "semi-Burkean" position: to treat inequality as inevitable and concentrate on the opportunity to rise. It might be an illusion, but it's a "pleasing" one, and "pleasing illusions," Burke believed, make "power gentle and obedience liberal."

All things are forgiven those who prove the Dream's alive. Bernie Sanders won a lot of people with his talk about the power of billionaires and the favours they buy, but another lot of struggling people prefer to believe in the billionaire. So they believe Donald Trump's credentials as an "economic manager" despite his record of bankruptcy, failure, fraud and non-payment of bills and wages – and despite what most economists think of his economic policies. Spend some time talking to folk in rust-belt USA, and you will find they don't speak much of inequality. Hardship a little, unfair treatment a little, Washington elites, yes; but to speak of inequality comes too close to heresy. Believing in America is not optional. If the times should test your faith, then believe in *other* times – times when America was great – and vote for the guy who vows to make it great again.

It might be what they're taught to think. You cannot know what ignorance or dogma, your *perspective* – patriotic, religious, racial or any other – does not permit you to see. You might not see, for instance, that up to the time of LBJ, and even into the Nixon presidency, the United States could accommodate its fanatical attachment to individual freedom with progressive social legislation. Equally, miserable as your circumstances are, you might not know *how* miserable relative to other Western countries. There is that miserable minimum wage, for instance, and average hourly earnings for 80 per cent of the population are not much better. No statutory minimum annual leave. Minimal job security. No equal pay for women. Millions still without health cover. Even when they're angry, the Tea Party people only know the half of it. If they knew the whole of it – if they let themselves know – *then* they might be angry. Still, as the *New York Times* panjandrum David Brooks said in 2010, the American system "leads to more exciting lives." He said this near the end of a recession that saw nine million jobs lost, five million houses foreclosed on and $13 trillion in family wealth wiped out. Between 2007 and 2010 alone,

Latino wealth fell by 40 per cent and African-American wealth by 36 per cent; and according to a Harvard study, 45,000 Americans died each year for want of health insurance.

5.   Squealing over the possibility that the military may call him up, Cassius makes as sorry a spectacle as those unwashed punks who picket and demonstrate against the war.

                                                                   — Red Smith, on Cassius Clay

      He simply refused to be afraid. And being that way, he gave other people courage.

                                                   — Bryant Gumbel, on Muhammad Ali

On a Saturday morning I drove north up to Green Bay as the tributes to Ali flowed in. One station devoted the whole morning to this radical Muslim. Well, he was radical when he started. In the '60s he was the greatest radical in the United States. George Foreman spoke for a while. He said he knew he was in trouble at the end of the third round of the fight in the Kinshasa. He had hit him with everything and Ali was still standing. Early in the seventh round, he hit him hard on the jaw: Ali drew him in and whispered in his ear, "That the best you got, George?" Foreman loved him. Was he the greatest? Well, he didn't have the biggest punch, or the best jab, and he wasn't the quickest – but, yes, he was the greatest. "He was like an eclipse of the sun," said Foreman. He was the greatest human being he ever met. "And, dammit, he was pretty!"

    This was the early '60s: it's hard to imagine the courage a black kid needed to change his name and declare he was a Muslim; and demand to be called by his new name and have his belief respected. Then he stood up to the United States army, to the United States itself, and in doing this gave up what would have been the prime of his career. At an age when the rest of us were struggling with history and sociology essays, a black boxer had seen through the whole edifice, and knew just where the answer lay. At first, when he said he was the greatest, Red Smith and pretty well everybody else thought he was only talking about boxing. But being the greatest boxer was not even half of it: he was also saying he was greater than segregation and discrimination, greater than

America itself and every myth and platitude then sustaining it.

Many of the people who had known Ali talked about his ability to "transcend": to transcend boxing, to transcend race, politics, religion. Listening to George Foreman, and remembering that fight and the one with Joe Frazier in Manila, we might decide that what Ali transcended above all was fear. As a boxer Ali never got much credit for courage. Perhaps it was the pretty way he fought, or because no one could see behind his boasting – "I've handcuffed lightning, thrown thunder into jail" – to the fear his courage overcame. If every boxer who gets in the ring has to overcome his fear, getting into the ring with Foreman and Frazier was surely to know terror. The violence would be terrible, the pain terrible. And even when it's at its worst – especially then – the boxer has to hold his form; keep boxing, not flailing; maintain his self-possession, be who he is, not what the other guy is trying to make him, which is wreckage.

It seemed possible that, being Christians, the people in Wisconsin's farmhouses might have seen something familiar in this interpretation of Ali. To overcome one's fear, endure suffering, speak truth to power. But it's unlikely they were listening. Did they hold Ali up as a model of courage and proof that the Dream was alive? Was he one of their great Americans? Not likely. Not across that wide canyon. The American mind is segregated; broken into facets of belief, culture and identity. Most of them you can enter by turning the knob on your radio, but you can't listen to two at the same time.

I turned into Ripon (pop. 7700 or so) for fuel and came across the Little White Schoolhouse nestled among trees. In 1854 a local man, Alvan Earle Bovay, called a meeting in the schoolhouse to rally opposition to a bill that proposed extending slavery beyond the limits of the Missouri Compromise. Fifty-three people turned up. "We went into the little meeting, Whigs, Free Soilers, and Democrats. We came out Republicans and we were the first Republicans in the union," Bovay recalled. The Republican Party – the anti-slavery party – was formally constituted at a meeting attended by Abraham Lincoln and Horace Greeley in Pittsburgh two years later, but the Little White Schoolhouse in Ripon is called the birthplace of the party.

A Republican think-tank called the Ripon Society was established in 1964 with the intention of turning the party away from its disastrous Goldwater diversion and towards moderation. On Saturday afternoon, Ripon was moderation itself: a quiet and pervasive seriousness that a lot of Midwest towns have. The modest churches and public buildings and the lawns all impeccably kept. And there is Ripon College, established in 1851 and now providing 1000 "high-achieving" students from nearly every state and countries around the world with a "rigorous liberal arts and sciences curriculum and an active residential campus [that] prepares students of diverse interests for lives of productive, socially responsible citizenship." The prose bears little resemblance to hers, but it might have been a scene in one of Marilynne Robinson's novels. In the sunshine by the school in the good little town out on the grassy plain there was scarcely a sound, and not a soul in sight. Nothing to fear. Or is there? "An horrid stillness first invades the ear / And in that silence we the tempest fear."

Oscar Wilde thought socialism was a nice idea, but he could not see it working because he doubted people would be prepared to give up their evenings. Out near the Green Bay airport, in the foyer of the Radisson, the Wisconsin Democrats were at least giving up their Saturday morning. They could have been in the casino, just a step away, through the sliding glass doors. The casino is owned and operated by the Oneida Nation, a New York tribe, some of whom took up land in Wisconsin when it was offered to them in the 1820s and 1830s. At ten in the morning in the dark, smoky nowhere, hundreds were playing the machines. Nothing beats gambling when you want to push life aside. Politics, which is just as addictive, is gambling's reverse: politics buries you alive in life, other peoples in the main, until their lives become yours. The Democrats of Wisconsin sat behind tables ready to push an idea, or a book or a badge, to anyone who ventured near. The speeches were being given in the auditorium, to which I was refused entry until a guest accreditation could be arranged, by which time the speeches were over. So instead I bought a "Forward with Bernie" badge as a memento, and spoke to former state senator, Tim Cullen, who was selling a book he'd written.

Governor Scott Walker had described Cullen as "kind of one of those guys who, he really doesn't care, he's not there for political reasons, he's just trying to get something done . . . but he's not a conservative. He's just a pragmatist." Tim Cullen had made a name for himself as a man who, in keeping with Wisconsin tradition, could cross the party divide. Walker, he reckoned, is the very model of the toxic modern Republican: the base tribal politician. He found that Walker tried to use him; that he didn't want the divide crossed, but widened and intensified. He took a "happy and united state" and set out to "angrily divide its citizens in order to advance his own political career." It might not be all down to Walker, but the state is certainly divided: not so long ago pollsters found 20 per cent were in the "persuadable middle", but now it's 5 to 6 per cent. Cullen quoted Jefferson – most do at some stage – "Great innovations should not be forced by a slender majority." That, he said, had been the guiding philosophy of Wisconsin politics: negotiate compromises, find common cause, keep the people informed and consult with them. But Walker, the conservative, has broken with tradition.

Tim Cullen comes from Janesville (pop. 63,000), on the Rock River 50 minutes south of Madison. Paul Ryan, the Speaker of the House of Representatives and the man most likely to be the next Republican president, comes from the same small city.

I drove into Janesville on a weekday morning. It was the usual long strip mall ending in a missing downtown. Paul Ryan's office was easy enough to find. Directly opposite, a plaque commemorates the spot where Abraham Lincoln made a speech in October 1859. We do not know if the Speaker of the House draws inspiration from it; does he wonder, for instance, if Lincoln would have endorsed Donald Trump? Ryan has a bit of the dark and gloomy look of Lincoln. He endorsed Trump, but the pundits say it is only to protect the Republican position in Congress and take some of the heat out of the party's divisions. I went to Janesville on the rough chance that, if not Ryan himself, someone in his office might be able to explain his thinking. His office, tucked into a sort of arcade, was closed and the lights were off.

Janesville's public buildings, both the old and the relatively new, are massive. In the quietness of the place their grandness looks a bit like collective overreach. Like so many old downtowns, downtown Janesville is not entirely deserted but it feels that way. The commercial buildings that once housed bustling businesses are now tired homes to law firms, barber shops, old wares shops and dimly lit bars that no one seems to go to. The Sons of Norway Lodge. Grafft Investments: property developers. There's a dreamlike sense of life no longer lived. No doubt all the action is in a mall somewhere. The rules of commerce ate the heart out of the heartland cities. Who can say that abandoning all that shared public space was good for American democracy? That it didn't make the polis that much more divided and neurotic? Who can say that this wasn't one of the ideas behind it?

Janesville had a General Motors plant but it closed in the Great Recession and the town is still recovering from the shock. George Parker invented his pen in Janesville around 1910 and they were made in the town for seventy years, until the company went to Gillette in a leveraged buyout and vanished. At eleven in a small café where I was the only customer, a blind man and his dog and a lady who looked like she might have been a vicar sang and played a kind of country dance on a ukulele and another stringed instrument. I was reading an article I'd copied from *Collide* magazine. It referred to "late capitalist services that turn the patterns of our world into information that can be sold back to us." Los Angeles, it said, is for "people who are comfortable with a certain level of cultural chaos and mixing and ambiguity and lack of boundary . . . In LA there's no real right way to be." "You bet," as they say in Wisconsin.

"That was a nice biscuit, thank you," I said to the proprietor.

"You bet," she said.

"Did you make it?" I asked.

"You bet."

Across a deserted street I took a snap of a mural illustrating Janesville's heroic pioneering history and noticed a lady had stopped her car twenty yards back so as not to spoil it. For this extravagant act of civility I waved and called out, "Thank you." I didn't quite catch it as she drove past with a radiant smile, but probably she said, "You bet."

In a bar – I was killing time in the hope that someone would live up to the message on the answering machine and turn up at Paul Ryan's office – the three big news stories were rolling on the television. I was the only customer again and the barmaid was on her phone, so there was no choice but to watch Muhammad Ali lighting the flame at the Atlanta Olympics and knocking out Foreman in the Congo for the hundredth time in three days. It was all happening elsewhere. In other news, Trump had declared a judge could not fairly try a case against him because his parents were born in Mexico. Paul Ryan, among many others, had been appalled. They were still showing the gorilla towing the four-year-old boy wildly through the water – before television we went to bars to escape the trials of existence. Bernie Sanders came on and said that after all these years of people fighting racism and bigotry in America, Donald Trump being the Republican nominee for President was "incomprehensible." He said "incomprehensible" several more times, and one began to wonder if the word was comprehensible to people who leaned towards voting for Trump. Not that they would not know what it means, but rather that they would not use it. They might say "Beats me" instead. An election processes reality into platitudes. Even the images become platitudes. It grinds all the tendons and marrow and flesh of history, and all the cultural overlays of Los Angeles, and the ukuleles and "You bets" of Janesville, into something universally digestible. Hearing a word like "incomprehensible" in the middle of it is like finding a bone in a fish finger.

Janesville has its Tea Party. You can watch the early demonstrations on YouTube. The boards say things like "Defending our Constitution and Taking Back Our Government" and "Honk if You Love Freedom." The Janesville Tea Party endorsed both Paul Ryan and Scott Walker.

A few years ago, in the woods bordering a town in Ohio, I saw men building what I thought were tree houses. I learned from their fellow townspeople that they were "hides," and when the season opens the hunters get inside them and skewer any deer that moseys past within range of their bows and arrows. A former Republican Congressman, Scott L. Klug, told me Paul Ryan hunts deer this way. While it might not strictly qualify as ancestor worship, it seems likely that these men imagine they are connecting to something deeply American in their being.

Scott Klug has the assurance, good looks and glow of a TV presenter, and it turns out that's what he was before he became a Republican congressman. He went to Washington in 1991. Newt Gingrich drafted him into presenting the resolution that ultimately led to the federal government shutdown of 1995 and 1996. It's the general view that the shutdown got Bill Clinton a second term. Klug stepped down in 1999, and in the years since he's gone into the publishing business, written a thriller, and co-chaired Rudy Giuliani's unsuccessful bid for the Republican nomination in 2007–08. As of early June he would be voting for Trump.

With that record, people like me, who struggle with the complexity of US politics, might take Klug for a right-wing Republican. In fact he sits on the centre-right, the "sensible" conservative side. I met him over lunch in a room at the Nakoma Golf Club, which is out in the leafy suburbs of Madison's west. There were six others there: two of them, the editor of the *Wisconsin State Journal* and the past president of the Greater Madison Chamber of Commerce, were centre-right; two others, the managing editor of the *Capital Times* and the founder of a public affairs firm with long experience managing election campaigns, were centre-left; and the remaining two, a former Chancellor of UW and his wife, a retired Government Affairs Vice President at the university, were described to me as "centrist" in their politics.

To me, the remarkable thing about the meeting was that it was held. The former publisher of the *State Journal*, Phil Blake, whom I had only met a day before the lunch, arranged it for me without my asking. He seemed to have no difficulty persuading these people to give up two hours of their Sunday for some blow-in from another country, albeit a most dutiful ally. And even if their natural hospitality inclined them to come, there are few less enticing prospects than sitting round a table with one's political opponents in the middle of an election campaign.

One did not expect plates or food to be thrown, of course. All the same, the bitter political struggles of the past quarter-century have not been fought between the recognised radicals of either side, but people of this civilized stripe. It did not take far-right Republicans or far-left Democrats to shut down the government and impeach a president, or to give the centre-right reasons to do it. It was surely an extreme measure to invade Iraq, but those who decided on it were not political extremists. So moderate is the president who made that decision, he and his entire family boycotted this year's Republican convention, and as of today one of the Democrats who voted for the war is reckoned a "safe option" for the presidency, with a 92 per cent near-certainty to win. The long-running deadlock in Washington has its origins in Tea Party extremists, but they haven't done it on their own. A centrist administration used taxpayer money to bail out the banks that brought about the Great Recession and chose not to prosecute a single person. "Too big to fail" is the radical doctrine of moderates. There are no Tea Partiers on the Supreme Court, but the Citizens United decision, which granted corporations untrammelled rights to fund political campaigns through political action committees, could be judged extremist – or certainly *contributing* to extremism, whether through the potentially corrupting activities of the corporations, or through the disenchantment with regular politics that the appearance of corruption occasions. Paul Ryan is rarely counted on the extreme right of American politics, but he is — or was until recently — a neoliberal devotee of Ayn Rand's *Atlas Shrugged*, and a statistical analysis of Ryan's record when he was Romney's running mate found him substantially to the right of every vice-presidential candidate since the Civil War. It does not take extremists, just tribal politics and the view that beyond declaring war and recruiting young men to fight them, nothing government does can make for better lives and better places.

Four years ago, two experienced Washington analysts gave up pretending that the failures of US politics could be sheeted home in equal measure to both parties. The Republicans had to take most of the blame:

> The GOP has become an insurgent outlier in American politics. It is ideologically extreme; scornful of compromise; unmoved by conventional understanding of facts, evidence and science; and dismissive of the legitimacy of its political opposition. When one party moves this far from the mainstream, it makes it nearly impossible for the political system to deal constructively with the country's challenges.

Yet in the American worldview, individualism and communitarianism, conservatism and liberalism, have long coexisted, in politics and in individuals, and we can presume that, in one combination or another, all are present in any room at any time. Maybe that was what Jim Wood (of the Democrat PR firm) was talking about when, before we started on our Waldorf salads, he said slowly and emphatically, as if to make sure I understood a fundamental truth about his country, "America's genius lies in solving problems, and that's what the Democrats and Republicans will do." His words might be taken to reflect that same *Weltanschauung* — a belief, of an almost mystical character and amounting to a faith, in the unique ability of the United States to find the answers to any problem.

Not for a moment could anyone deny the genius. But if applied only to domestic "problems," the claim is contestable: the problem of racial segregation and discrimination, for instance, Milwaukee's problem, remains manifestly unsolved. And while to list them might be un-American in its negativity, there *is* the problem of inequality, the corruption of politics by money and rent-seeking, poverty, mass incarceration, gun violence and the general malaise that finds expression in one statistic: more than six out of ten Americans think the country is heading in the wrong direction. Or what might be a bigger problem: the unwillingness or inability of the powerful to approach these problems with anything more useful than a bucket of money and re-statements of the faith. If applied to the projection of US power abroad, the faith is even less convincing. The Middle East comes to mind.

6.   I love leverage.

                                        – Donald Trump

Fascism, it should be unnecessary to add, was no ideology in the traditional meaning of that term, but a faith that could not be explained solely in rational terms.
           – George L. Mosse, *The Fascist Revolution*

The dominant semiotic weight of a Star of David over a pile of money is not a sheriff.
        – Rick Wilson, Republican media strategist, 6 July 2016

Michele Bachmann says Donald Trump has been "handpicked by God." But saying he has "1950s sensibilities" is the more telling of her judgments. Looking for dog whistles is a sure route to madness, but this could be one. The 1950s was a time when no white male needed to doubt his predominant place in America. For black Americans, then one in eight of the population, the 1950s was living with discrimination, persecution, poverty and terror. If you were a woman you were almost certainly living at a serious disadvantage, and if you were gay the only safe course was to hide the fact. That left white heterosexual males in charge. Of course, by "1950s sensibilities" Bachmann might have meant beauty pageants, political incorrectness, being the world's tough guy, Billy Graham and family television. Who knows what she meant? But it is true that one of the big changes since the '50s has been, as Hendrik Hertzberg puts it, that "the default position is not middle-aged white male."

Trump does outstandingly well with this group, and he pitches straight at them. It's not just the poor white male and the uneducated white male: two polls, one by Pew, one by *Washington Post–ABC News*, found male college graduates support Trump over Clinton 49 to 42 and 49 to 44, respectively. Graduate women back Clinton 57 to 35, a six-point lead overall that in most polls hides the attitude of the men.

This might have something to do with the changing nature of college education: graduates of the increasingly numerous bottom-tier colleges may not be doing any better than non-graduates and may share their white working-class resentments. There are two ways of discovering what these resentments are: we can look at the polls or we can look at what Trump has been saying. Trump knows that in the last half-century redistributive policies have brought about a substantial shift in income, power and status from the formerly impregnable white males to women and minorities. Everywhere they look they see women and African Americans, Latinos, lesbians and gays with wealth, celebrity and influence. He also knows that when the Reagan years handed the women's vote to the Democrats, the Republicans got the men's to about the same degree. So Trump insults women and Mexicans and singles out black men in his audiences and (while promising, after Orlando, to be the best defender the LBGT community ever had) opposes gay marriage.

Poll numbers among Republican men – graduates and non-graduates – provide a compelling picture of Trump's rusted-on base: for instance, 64 per cent of college-educated white Republicans and 75 per cent of those without a college education support Trump's idea of a fence along the entire border with Mexico. The reason is simple: they believe immigrants are a threat to both American jobs and "American values." A majority of Americans believe the increase in imports is "taking away US jobs" and a majority (among whites 59 per cent) believe that "trade with other countries" causes a net loss of jobs.

It is not, as they say, rocket science. Millions of Americans feel they have been robbed of their birthright. The country's wealth, history and traditions have been subverted or gifted to others. The American future is not theirs. They were losing long before the Great Recession, and since it hit they've lost even more. The greatest country on earth is becoming someone else's: that's if it still is the greatest country. Hell, when did they last win a war? An actual shooting war? Grenada?

Democrats should look to themselves for the answers. This is what happens with identity politics. It's also what happens when you "embrace globalisation", as all good liberals have done for the past thirty years. Liberals – the well-off ones at least – love globalisation for all the excitement and sophistication of it: and, loving that about it, they love immigration, multiculturalism and social inclusiveness. They can truly say these things enrich their lives. But what enriches one tribe impoverishes and threatens another. Globalisation has swallowed jobs, communities, unions and pride. It even takes patriotism: and sends it back relabelled as bigotry and racism. Ordinary prejudices are "inappropriate"; old forms of speech are "inappropriate." Common understanding of the differences between men and women is inappropriate. Political correctness is an attempt by the Puritan communitarian affect to crush the Jacksonian individualist one. Clint Eastwood says Trump gained support because "secretly everybody's getting tired of political correctness, kissing up. That's the kiss-ass generation we're in right now." You don't have to like Clint Eastwood to acknowledge that he has a political point, at least. You can loathe Bret Easton Ellis, and everything he says about feminists, objectified breasts and the male gaze, and still recognise that they're probably not a first-order issue for people who have lost their jobs or their roots in the country, or grew up thinking that gazing was harmless.

In an era when the New Left used the term loosely, George L. Mosse was at pains to find and preserve what the word "fascism" meant. Not much he saw in Madison in the 1960s would qualify. But Donald Trump might be different. Reactionary politics lives off "normative threats." Reactionary politicians instinctively know how to exploit them. European fascism is a case in point. Nationalism and xenophobia; a stress on law and order; the glorification of war and violence; anti-intellectualism; anomie and alienation; impatience tending to disdain for democratic politics; ditto for corrupt big cities (even while practising corruption and dealing with the corrupt): these dispositions Trump's core followers share with fascism. Some of them are as old the United States itself, and some would describe the outlook of millions who could never be called fascist.

That does not mean Trump cannot call them up to his cause and "leverage" them.

George L. Mosse found the fascist temperament was at the heart of communitarianism. Fascism was a "scavenger doctrine" that pulled together old threads of community, picked up on prejudices and affections that people scarcely knew they had. Fascism posits a heroic, even mythic, past that portends the true destiny of the people and the nation. Often it sees the values of that past and the prospect of that destiny as betrayed, and promises a return to greatness. It values nationalism and militarism above all other virtues. Fascism rejects individualism, but absorbs its power in the collective, "each through the power of his own will." Mosse described fascism as a "civic religion," or the "people worshipping themselves."

Little here is inconsistent with the politics of Trump. Watch the Tea Partiers performing the rituals of their religion: in the uniforms of the disfranchised, the non-elites; hands on hearts gazing up to the flag, joining in the anthems, repeating the oaths and the nationalistic platitudes; calling out the treacherous enemies. Mosse found an occult thread in fascist ideology. It might be stretching a point to call some varieties of the born-again churches "occult," or even the near-worship of the tendentiously read Founding Fathers, but it's possible that they serve the same psychological purpose. If fascism makes scapegoats, Trumpism has them in abundance. If it advances a story of betrayal, manipulates the truth with lies and exaggeration, plays to the emotions more than the intellect, bullies and struts, promises to eliminate the nation's enemies at home and abroad, sets up "counter-types" to the national (or racial) aesthetic, plays on fear (Bolshevism in the 1930s case, Islam now), artfully uses the media as an instrument of mass persuasion while avoiding all serious scrutiny and indulges in spectacular display, Trumpism does that too. If, as Mosse insisted, with all fascisms there is a unifying aesthetic, watch the Republican convention.

According to Gwynn Guildford, who went as an ethnographer to Trump rallies in Ohio this year, in each case, in the long wait before

Trump arrives, the crowds are told over loudspeakers to look out for protestors in their midst, but not to touch them. Instead they are to chant "Trump! Trump! Trump!" until security arrives. "This happens repeatedly . . ." Until Trump turns up, they are constantly reminded that their community is threatened by saboteurs and non-believers, which means that when he finally arrives their devotion is at emotional breaking point. The press, meanwhile, have been corralled in a "cattle pen" at the back of the room. At various points in the speech Trump "scowls" at them and calls them the "most disgusting" and "most dishonest" people he's ever seen, pantomiming his disdain with an elaborate sneer before goading his supporters to turn and glare too. On cue, the crowd turns and boos. The orchestrated hate-filled rally was the primary grass-roots weapon of European fascisms.

"I alone," he said in his convention speech. If fascism pivots on the concept of the great leader with uncanny, almost supernatural instincts who alone can lead the nation from its existential crisis into greatness, Trump qualifies here as well. His hair qualifies him: it attracts attention, renders him singular, the one, the lone visionary. The choreography of his arrival at the RNC in the Trump helicopter, with the music from *Air Force One* booming out over the whirring of the blades, as the "Aryan" wife and children rushed forward to meet him, was fascist theatre, and it is hard to believe the performance was unconscious – unless it was unconscious self-satire. When the family are lined up behind him, you could think he was making a point about racial purity, and that the reified women are there to signify the duty their gender must perform – but it's probably more about the 1950s.

Yet, were he to win the presidency in ways resembling Hitler's or Mussolini's, it's inconceivable that Trump's next steps would resemble theirs. His brutish and ingenious destruction of the country club Republicans, and the capitulation of most of the remainder, are shameful and concerning, but even if this meant the end of the Republican Party, that is not the same as the end of US democracy. The Germans of

1933 had had a decade of democracy. The Americans have had a lot more than that.

The one condition on which fascism depends is a nation in deep economic crisis with nowhere else to turn. The US is not in that condition. Far from going backwards, much of the US is doing very well. Consider *The Martian*, a western for the globalised American elites. In keeping with the old western genre, it is an artistic expression of the Monroe Doctrine. The exceptional American in this case is played by Matt Damon, but it could have been James Stewart. Left alone on the frontier of space, our hero, having no instinct for philosophy, survives by combining traditional American can-do and the boundless possibility of American diversity. In the end he is saved not by his own dauntless courage and the help of, say, Walter Brennan or a big-hearted Lutheran dirt farmer, but by dauntless courage and a Silicon Valley hipster nerd, a number of scientists from the Indian subcontinent, a charitable act by the Chinese government, and a valiant, self-sacrificing female mission leader. And there was Trump saying he could not trust a judge because his father was born in Mexico.

Still, there is that unyielding poll figure: over 60 per cent of the population believe the country is heading in the wrong direction. Even as Obama's popularity has risen, and the economy has slowly recovered, the number has stayed the same. For this and many other reasons, Trump could win. If he does, it will not prove Mosse was wrong when he said European fascisms were unlikely to recur; rather, that he was right to say, "the fragments of our Western cultural and ideological past which fascism used for its own purposes still lie ready to be formed into a new synthesis, even if in a different way." Communitarianism, revivalism, populism, racism, messianic Christian faith, paranoia, provincial ignorance, patriotism, war, exceptionalism – the traditional forces in American life and politics combined with the deep divisions and the fear make that synthesis possible.

And if Trump doesn't win, will he walk away? Will his followers? He is telling them if he loses it means the vote was rigged. He doesn't need to be an actual fascist for the day after election day to be a worrying prospect.

7. "Look, Walter," Dulles told him, "I've got to get some real fighting men into the south of Asia. The only Asians who can really fight are the Pakistanis. That's why we need them in the alliance. We could never get along without the Gurkhas."

    "But Foster," Lippman replied, "the Gurkhas aren't Pakistanis."

    "Well, they may not be Pakistanis, but they're Moslems."

    "No, I'm afraid they're not Moslems, either. They're Hindus."

    "No matter!" Foster replied, and launched into a half-hour lecture about the dangers of Communism in Asia.

    — Stephen Kinzer, The Brothers

The issue can be stated as a very direct proposition. If the United States cannot accept the existence of such limits without giving up democracy and cannot proceed to enhance and extend democracy within such limits, then the traditional effort to sustain democracy by expansion will lead to the destruction of democracy.

— William Appleman Williams,
The Tragedy of American Diplomacy

If any of this year's candidates ever read William Appleman Williams, there has been no sign of his influence. Hillary Clinton might have once been seduced by his theories, but as secretary of state and now as the Democratic candidate, she belongs firmly with the Arthur Schlesinger school of triumphalists. Williams liked his history to make people "think otherwise." That is to say he was a revisionist: "one who sees basic facts in a different way and as interconnected in new relationships," to use his own definition. The revisionist upends the *Weltanshauung* (how you see the world and how you think it works). Though a radical thinker and sympathetic to the social revolutions of his time, he was quick to add that his argument was neither categorical nor treasonous. His readers should not "mistake a candid and searching re-examination of their own mythology for a tirade of useless self-damnation," he said. Nearly sixty years on, that mollifying line on the first page of *The Tragedy of American Diplomacy* is as telling as any in the book. Re-examining American mythology is the one thing that American democracy – and American foreign policy – has not been able to do.

For Williams, US foreign policy was an extension of US commercial need and ambition; more than that, it was governed by the same thinking and the same myths as governed the country's worldview. The myths were these, he said: the United States was isolationist until power was thrust upon it; except for a brief adventure around the end of the nineteenth century it was anti-imperialist; by "a unique combination of economic power, intellectual and practical genius, and moral rigor" the US could be the world's beneficent policeman, without an empire to taint it. But the truth was, he said, the US had been bent on expansion since Benjamin Franklin declared it necessary for the democracy. Half a century later, the country declared the Western hemisphere its natural domain. The problem of reconciling a republic with an empire was solved by deciding expansion was essential to the strength and virtue of the republic. There could be no freedom, no democracy – and no fulfilment of God's will – without expansion; be it west of the Appalachians, west of the Mississippi or west of the California coast. Freedom and the other great virtues of the republic were rendered inseparable from commercial interest. To "extend the sphere," in James Madison's words, was the only way the public could be good *and* wealthy.

The genius of US imperial policy was to expand American corporate and national interests without acting or looking like an imperial power, or feeling any need to confess it to anyone, least of all the American people. The so-called Open Door Policy meant an "informal" empire: doors that didn't open readily to American business interests were kicked in, but sheer economic power and muscular application of various inducements reliably forced the issue without the need for occupying armies. Unlike Rome, the republic remained, as did the old anti-colonialist strain, and there was just enough truth in the idea that American trade and influence was good for the underdeveloped world for Americans to feel that theirs was a "virtuous omnipotence."

But an empire it was and has remained. Anyone who doubts the proposition need only read Williams; and anyone who likes a good imperial yarn (in an American vein) should go to the story of those two great door-kickers John Foster Dulles and his brother Allen. Both sides of the Presbyterian character (or the two human responses to the doctrine of election) that are often found in one individual were here found discretely in two: Foster Dulles was a dire moralist and his brother Allen a rake and adventurer. The seventeenth-century Puritan and the frontier individualist joined in the glue of American exceptionalism. Both were hitmen for the cause of US world supremacy. There is astonishing venality, bastardry, deceit and hypocrisy in their story, along with the pitiless exercise of power. But what is more alarming is their misjudgment. In the 1930s, as evangelists for Wilsonian "liberal internationalism," the brothers led a crusade against "Bolshevism" of any stripe and for American business – including business that was crucial to German industrial strength. In March 1939, a week after German troops occupied Czechoslovakia, Foster told the Economic Club of New York, "Only hysteria entertains the idea that Germany, Italy or Japan contemplates war upon us." Two months after the invasion of Poland he had not changed his mind.

On the other side of the war, as Eisenhower's secretary of state and "global attack dog" for the wonderfully Puritan doctrine of containment, he did his best to make sure that the Russians were as paranoid as it was possible to make them, and Americans just as fearful. He took a collapsible lectern whenever he travelled and kept the people thoroughly abreast of his opinions, all of which reinforced their fears, assured them of their country's righteousness and persuaded them that the American Way should be the way of the world. A few doors away in the same street, Allen Dulles ran the CIA in lock step with his brother. They "turned the State Department and the CIA into a reverberating echo chamber for their shared certainties."

There were alternatives to the perilous course that post-war history took. Even if we believe that the United States was never the party that made it perilous, and that the alternatives were worse than the path taken, it remains deeply disturbing to think that on decisions taken by the Dulles brothers the fate of nations and all our lives depended.

Half a century on from the days of the Dulles brothers, observers noticed the same pattern of mutual reinforcement among the people gathered around President George W. Bush. These days it's called "groupthink." Groupthink means everyone pretty much agrees on everything and ignores evidence or logic that might point in another direction. The only thing this group was thinking was invading Iraq. A "slam dunk," one of them said. As the groupthinking went on around him, Bush took up the banner of American exceptionalism with the eloquence of old – the "untamed fire of freedom will reach the darkest corners of the world." Here was groupthink for the masses.

If all America could do was reassert the ideology and policies of the past, rather than accept the limits of its freedom of action, it was doomed, William Appleman Williams said. In 1979, just before the seemingly endless Middle East wars got underway, President Jimmy Carter made a speech that asked US citizens to re-examine their thinking, to "think otherwise." For a millisecond he opened a different door.

The chief subject of the speech was the energy crisis, but Carter addressed something "deeper." "In a nation that was proud of hard work, strong families, close-knit communities, and our faith in God, too many of us now tend to worship self-indulgence and consumption," he said. Boiled down, Carter was asking Americans to change the way they lived and the way they thought about the world. The country had drifted into a "national malaise." He "invited Americans to rethink, in the most fundamental way, what it means to be a free human being."

Carter always subscribed to exceptionalism, and still does. He was not asking the country to renounce the creed, but to look again at its meaning. He was a devout Southern Baptist, an evangelical; the speech, said Hendrik Hertzberg, who was then his speechwriter, was "an exercise in national pastorship." It was a renewal speech, straight from Jimmy Carter's communitarian heart. Carter was speaking of something like another Great Awakening.

The "American malaise" speech might have caused William Appleman Williams to hope the *Weltanschauung* was up for reappraisal. Instead, Carter learned that no president was going to question the national mythology and get away with it. "He has said the malaise is ours, in the tones of a man who knows that it is his own," wrote Eugene Kennedy in the *New York Times*. How dare he "sermonize" to this "big muscular nation," wrote George Will. Self-interest, not self-sacrifice, was the nation's "bedrock," said Irving Kristol. Soon after the speech, the Soviet Union invaded Afghanistan. Then Iranian revolutionaries made hostages of fifty-three embassy staff in the uprising that overthrew the Shah installed by the United States twenty-five years earlier and the moment of self-examination gave way to fear and loathing again. It was as if Americans could not imagine freedom and equality in their own community without "perpetual outrage against the faults of other societies."

In a State of the Union address notably free of agonising, Jimmy Carter proclaimed the Carter Doctrine. In future, any attempt by any country to seize control of the Persian Gulf would be "repelled by any means necessary, including military force." It was very like the Truman Doctrine. Diplomacy was out and the military was in. In no time Carter had signed off on support for Afghans resisting the Soviet occupation. What Andrew Bacevich calls "America's War for the Greater Middle East" began.

Looking back on the military academy he attended, the former career soldier, now historian, Bacevich realised that in such places people are not educated but "socialized" into a particular worldview. When he went to work in Washington, he discovered that everyone seemed to be "a prisoner of an outlook" and thought on the same "predictable" and "banal" lines. As a historian, he finds that pattern of non-thinking underlying US policy in the Middle East, which he treats as one continuous thirty-year war against the Islamic world. And one continuous failure: a catastrophe, in fact, and more far-reaching in its implications week by week. His book on the topic is a gruelling saga of miscalculation, fantasy, deceit, cliché and waste. At one point he reproduces four bullet points a journalist came across in Afghanistan in 2011. They were headed "Key Tenets of the Afghan Narrative":

- 2011/12 Notice what is different
- 2012/13 Change has begun
- 2013/14 Growing confidence
- 2015 A new chance, a new beginning

There is no bleaker moment in the book. "Not for the first time," Bacevich says, "in America's War for the Greater Middle East, narrative was displacing reality." That's the thing about spin — or what goes under the banner today of "communications" — you begin to believe your own bullshit. Spin is the stuff that myths are made of.

He sees no reason to believe this will change, only reasons why it won't. One is America's preponderance of military power and its proportionate lack of wisdom and historical understanding. Another is a fondness for fantasies: of "shaping" the Middle East when it cannot be shaped; of controlling events that can't be controlled; of a narrative in which America always prevails; and assumptions about American arms and the rightness of America's purpose that are not based in fact and not shared by other countries.

Hubris is an incurable American disease. As incurable as the military-industrial machine that keeps coming up with the armaments that make wars seem like slam dunks, but which last for decades; wars that are fought by a very small percentage of the population and, regular effusive acknowledgment of veterans notwithstanding, can be ignored for years. Depending on how you count it, the annual US national security budget is somewhere between $600 billion and $1 trillion. The figure is at least twice what it was before 9/11.

Then there is the persistence of the dogma of exceptionalism that no politician dares to challenge. When Barack Obama said, "I believe in American exceptionalism, just as I suspect that the Brits believe in British exceptionalism and the Greeks believe in Greek exceptionalism," he was charged with a lack of patriotism. Mike Huckabee said, "To deny American exceptionalism is in essence to deny the heart and soul of this nation." Soon after, Obama was saying that the US was indeed "exceptional." Probably, he would prefer to say "indispensable," which it is beyond doubt. And possibly he counts his decision to draw back from his ultimatum to the Syrian regime and to weather the rage from all about him, including Hillary Clinton, as his Great Awakening, if not America's.

When Obama offered "Don't do stupid shit" as a first principle in foreign policy making, Clinton said Bah! It wasn't "an organizing principle." "Great nations need organizing principles." It's just possible the grassroots progressive that lies beneath shares some of Carter's angst, but she's the candidate, she has been for years, and she knows angst will not do. Meanwhile, we are still waiting to see how her organising principle differs from any of those that have been applied to the Middle East for the past thirty years, and elsewhere for a hundred. "Peace, progress and prosperity. This worked for a very long time," she told Jeffrey Goldberg. Goldberg did not ask her where and when it had worked. On Libya it came down to: "We came, we saw, he died." It might have been Dubya speaking. "I will be listening to our admirals and generals", she tells the crowds on the campaign trail – the admirals and generals of the "world's greatest military." With Trump as her opponent, Clinton is doubtless the "safe" option: but she is also a fully fledged, and some would say dangerous, foreign policy hawk with no demonstrated ability to think beyond the doctrine of exceptionalism to which she subscribes as a matter of faith.

But of course, in an election, where foreign policy is concerned every political speech descends (or rises, if bombast's your measure) into the same crowing, self-glorifying cant. Every political debate tends to come down to one side saying the country is the greatest on earth, and the other saying it used to be.

8. You know what you did? You embraced the insanity you were telling us about.

– Don DeLillo, *Great Jones Street*

In the wake of the spectacular Democratic convention it seems unreasonable even to hint at the possibility, but if Trump were to win in November, Hillary Clinton might be the deciding factor. Such speeches! Such enthusiasm! Such ideals! Such drama and emotion! Such a pseudo-event! But a woman nominee – such a moment. And one to make Trumpland look ridiculous. Even that old lizard Bill Clinton was poignant in his way.

But Bill Clinton is the author of NAFTA and the president who ended Glass–Steagall. Hillary Clinton is going to the fight with Trump on a promise to at least look again at NAFTA and reintroduce an equivalent to Glass–Steagall to keep the banks in line. Thanks to Bernie Sanders, that's in the platform. So is a resolution to break up the banks that Congress bailed out – and didn't punish for their sins. Hillary is also now committed to scuttling the Trans-Pacific Partnership, which her new pal President Obama badly wants because it's a big part of his geopolitics. Hillary Clinton has a platform that really isn't hers. The Democrats are proceeding as one party, but in truth there are now two – one subscribes to neoliberalism and the other foreshadows its demise – and she has to represent both of them. Philadelphia was a beautiful and moving thing, and Democrats can only hope that all those tears of joy and love were enough to wash away the contradictions.

This might be unfair. Whether she was driven there by Bernie Sanders or has chosen to renew her old Methodist vows to the poor and meek, Clinton is running on a progressive ticket now, and she might decide to make that the colour of her presidency. She promises to invest heavily in the cities to lift people out of poverty; to invest in infrastructure, create jobs, revive manufacturing and raise the minimum wage. The platform promises comprehensive immigration reform, an end to student debt, paid family leave and much else. It is very likely what Sanders said it was — the most progressive platform in the party's history.

Listening to her now, you might think that after years as a member of the supply-side economics church, Hillary Clinton's joined the revived and steadily expanding demand-side one. Could she in eight years reverse the engines of inequality and corruption, bridge the divides and enliven the democracy? Could she desegregate the cities? Could she get her country leading the world by example to save the planet from global warming? Could she do something about the lobbyists, the power of money in Washington that is destroying American democracy from within? Take on Wall Street? Make the effort on behalf of public decency and ordinary justice that was not made after the financial collapse? Could she get the public interest represented in Washington again? Could she do something about guns? In Chicago on the Memorial Day weekend, sixty-nine people were shot. Six died. As of 1 August, 401 people had been murdered in that one city in 2016, 90 per cent of them with guns.

Are *any* of these things open to remedy? Probably not: the problems run too deep, but the effort would be uplifting and a more productive way to prove her country is exceptional than anything she might have in mind for bloodying foreign noses.

Could she get American troops out of Afghanistan, the fifteen-year war she mentioned not once in her acceptance speech in Philadelphia? That might be the most unlikely of all.

Nothing she says, old or new, will much impress voters who don't trust the Clintons, or think they reek of entitlement, lies and money. The hole she's punched in the glass ceiling won't impress them. But the prospect of Hillary and Bill back in the White House might lift their loathing into realms of mania. It will feel like the ultimate corruption, the ultimate insult, the ultimate proof that the system stinks. You don't have to share this point of view to understand it. At the very least, her supporters could ask themselves what *they* would be making of the $153 million in speaking fees or the $1.8 million she collected from speeches to the banks, if they were pinned to Donald Trump – or to Mitt Romney or John McCain. Ditto the emails. The reasonable fear is that Hillary Clinton will be tempted to pacify the haters by the military expression of exceptionalism.

Clinton just *has* to win. If she loses, not only does the world get Donald Trump (and the US Supreme Court his appointments): the Democrats will have to live forever with their decision to make their nominee the most qualified presidential candidate in history, but also the person most disliked by the American public and possibly the only one that Trump could beat. And with the email business forever hanging about, it might get worse.

We can hope that from her example great numbers of American women will draw inspiration, and believe that both wisdom and opportunity will deepen with their influence on public life. It should have been a moment of pure celebration, seeing Elizabeth Warren on the hustings with Clinton early in June. But you could feel the hackles rising on every neck in every bar in every swing state across the country. Warren mocking Trump, trading insults – and the guys in the bar think she's mocking *them* and make a little resolution and write it inside their hats – "Vote this time." The triumph of one identity is the violation of another.

Trump says, Hand your fear over to me. Hand your loathing over too. I will deal with your enemies as I have dealt with mine. I will give you back your freedom, and your country. Your old lives will be yours to live again. I will halt the terminal decline. American exceptionalism, in which you all hold shares, will be underwritten by an exceptional American.

The Democrats scoff at Trump for wanting to take the country back to the past. But for many of the people whose votes will count in November, Trump's imaginary past is a more concrete thing to contemplate than the Democrats' imaginary present. Trump's also contains more hope, and it serves as a more believable American tomorrow. If, as seems likely, Clinton wins, it will not be out of love, or even hope, but rather out of fear. She can win by simply letting her deplorable opponent lose. On the other hand, she's nothing if not adaptable, and she could yet see in these very favourable circumstances (the Republicans falling apart, negligible interest rates, a public appetite for radical reform) the chance to lead the nation's social and economic regeneration through, for a start, massive investment in education, renewable energy and infrastructure, and an equally massive legislative attack on inequality and political corruption. Call it a New Great Awakening or a New New Deal; it would owe something to both, and to Bernie Sanders as well, but also to her need to be more than the first woman president. Reawakening the old grassroots reformer deep inside could not only heap manifold blessings on the nation and consolidate a liberal Democratic ascendancy; it is surely also the best antidote to the dark forces now feeding on the country's malaise.

In the Branded Steer men and women sat round the bar drinking beer and eating hamburgers. It's out near the Milwaukee airport, on a junction of two eight-lane roads, the only eating house within walking distance of the airport hotels. Sitting there among these people of prodigious girth, I was thinking of *The Deer Hunter*. The food was much as you'd expect in a place called the Branded Steer. The barmaid called me "darling" and wanted to know how my hamburger was. I thought if I sat there for more than half an hour I'd get maudlin. There was a malaise in the Branded Steer that I didn't want to catch.

But too late, I began to feel sorry for myself, and it wasn't just the hamburger. I would have to walk back across those absurdly wide roads, past those miserable chain "accommodations," to my own dark dogbox in the bar-less, café-less Holiday Inn. There to surf the never-ending news. "Shall I kill myself, or have a cup of coffee?" was how Camus put it. But the only coffee in the Holiday Inn was what you could get from a slot machine.

It happens in the US. You can be feeling terribly alive and then you fall into a pit. What were they thinking when they built that Holiday Inn? From what concept of humanity, what manner of philosophy, what thousand-year tradition of hospitality did it derive? How did it come about that humanity's snug little bars and street cafés have ended up in the Branded Steer? And downtown Janesville now lives in an eerie silence. The answer is from no philosophy; no thought at all, except the thought of profit. Commerce "has no principle that can withstand a strong temptation to her insatiable cupidity," as the preacher said.

Ten years after Jimmy Carter talked about an American malaise, John Updike wrote an essay about the state of the union. He found dozens of things that made Americans feel bad: poverty (one in four children), homelessness, crime, industrial decline, racial and generational discrimination, lawyers, bankers, doctors, foreign takeovers, AIDS, environmental squalor and destruction, stalemate in the Middle East, obesity – it was a long list. He called it a "malaise."

The malaise would seem to be, if not permanent, certainly recurrent. In a recent piece on Donald Trump, the American writer Richard Ford used the term again. But Ford's take is slightly different. It's not contemplating the country's failings that brings it on, but something lacking in oneself. To be sure, Donald Trump seems inauthentic, phoney, less than actual; but "it's really we who're threatened with not quite fully existing. It's we who're guilty of not having something better on our minds. It's our national malaise with life that's become the problem."

The TVs flicker half-watched in the Branded Steer. They flicker in the foyer of the Holiday Inn and in the room to which I take myself. Clinton, Trump, the shooting in Dallas, Muhammad Ali's funeral in Louisville's Kentucky Fried Chicken Yum! Center. How do they turn it off? All those flickering impulses that the Donald Trumps can prey on? By taking up the Democratic slogan "America is already great"?

They need an Ali, a hundred million of them, or a president like him brave enough to think otherwise, or at least to think again.

18 August 2016

SOURCES

My thanks to Derek Shearer for his ever generous and expert assistance, and to Phil Blake, who could not have been more helpful, even by American standards of hospitality. The essay is the better for conversations with many people in the United States who kindly gave me their time. The flaws, like the opinions, are entirely down to me.

3   "Obama said": James Fallows notes a dispute between Obama and John Kerry's speechwriters before Obama made his career-defining speech at the 2004 Democrat convention. Obama intended to say "something like, 'We're not red states and blue states; we're all Americans, standing up together for the red, white, and blue,'" but Kerry stole it. James Fallows, "Why Obama Never Said 'Not Red States or Blue States but the United States . . .'", The Atlantic, 17 February 2013.

4   "When Planned Parenthood was founded": By Margaret Sanger, a eugenicist with some vicious opinions.

5   "her senior thesis": A study of the radical activist Saul Alinsky, who wrote a book on grassroots tactics, Rules for Radicals. A Pragmatic Primer for Realistic Radicals, Random House, New York, 1971. Her association with Alinsky caused problems for the Clintons, especially when she refused to make the thesis public. At one point in Alinsky's book he says Lucifer was "the very first activist." At the recent Republican convention, the failed candidate Ben Carson bellowed: "Are we willing to elect someone as President who has as their role model somebody who acknowledges Lucifer?!"

6   "buried the rights": Mary Crisp, quoted in Jill Lepore, "The Women Card", New Yorker, 27 July 2016.

7   "thicket of unreality": Daniel Boorstin, The Image: A Guide to Pseudo-Events, Vintage Books, 1992, p. xiii.

10   "the image of god": "The covenant between you and us is the oath you have taken of us, which is to this purpose: that we shall you govern you and judge your causes by the rules of God's laws and our own . . ." John Winthrop, "On Liberty", speech, 1645.

11   "weaponizing political correctness": The words are Rich Higgins', a self-described former defence department official with "a deep, first-hand knowledge of Muslim Brotherhood infiltration of our government." Faith and Freedom Foundation website.

14   "nation's ballast": Daphne Beal, in Matt Weiland and Sean Wilsey (eds), State by State: A panoramic Portrait of America, Harper Collins, New York, 2008.

14 "two dominant affects": For this discussion I am indebted to a conversation with Patrick Lawrence Smith early in June this year.

16 "the colored section": Gary Legum, "The Quiet, Vicious Racism of Scott Walker's Wisconsin", *Salon*, 6 April 2016.

17 "achievement gap": Kenya Downs, "Why is Milwaukee So Bad for Black People?" *Code Switch*, NPR, 5 March 2015.

17 "sheriff squads": Matthew Desmond, "Letter from Milwaukee," *New Yorker*, Feb.8&15, 2016.

17–18 "septic tank belt", "What do you think", "different planets", etc.: Craig Gilbert, "Dividing Lines", *Milwaukee Journal Sentinel*, 4 Parts, May 2014.

18 "Walker and his Republican-led state legislature": Suevon Lee and Sarah Smith, *Pro Publica*, 9 March 2016.

19 "undocumented Mexican workers": More than 40 per cent of people working in Wisconsin dairies are illegal immigrants, according to a University of Wisconsin study.

20 "But the modern right wing": Richard Hofstadter, "The Paranoid Style in American Politics", *Harper's*, November 1964.

21 "glacier of fear", "commodification of anxiety": Marilynne Robinson, *Salon*, 3 January 2016.

21–2 "First, contemporary America", "Americans . . .", "would no doubt" and "by the thought": Marilynne Robinson, "Fear" in *The Givenness of Things*, Virago, London, 2015.

27 For Robert La Follette, see Peter Dreir, "La Follette's Wisconsin Idea", *Dissent*, 11 April 2011.

27 "The word is often a perjorative": For the local attitude, look no further than Scott Morrison, 7 August 2016: calls for a Royal Commission into Australian banks are "nothing more than a populist whinge."

28 "a poem of faith in mankind": Tim Cullen, *Ringside Seat: Wisconsin Politics, the 1970s to Scott Walker*, Little Creek Press, Mineral Point Wisconsin, 2016, pp. 140–2.

29 For progressives and Madison, see Allen Ruff and Tracy Will, *Forward! A History of Dane: the Capital County*, Woodhenge Press, Cambridge, Wisconsin, 2000.

29 "In the ten years from 1910 to 1920": Ruff and Will, 2000.

30 "Soglin looks almost serene": The photo, from the Madison Daily Cardinal, is reproduced in David Maraniss, *They Marched Into Sunlight: War and Peace, Vietnam and American October 1967*, Simon & Schuster, New York, NY, 2003.

31 "with the same lasting effect": Russell Banks, "Bernie Sanders, The Socialist Mayor", *Atlantic*, 15 October 2015.

32 "becoming less and less": Mike Lofgren, "Goodbye to All That", *Truthout*, 3 December 2011.

34 "Imagine, a First World country": Nicholas Fitz, "Economic Inequality: It's Far Worse Than You Think", *Scientific American*, 31 March 2015.

34 "A minimum wage": David Cooper, "Economic Snapshot", *Economic Policy Institute*, 25 July 2016.

34 "as Thomas Piketty argues": Thomas Piketty, "Can Growth Save Us?" 24 March 2013, *Chronicles on Our Troubled Times*, Viking, UK, 2016.

35 "one sinks by levity and rises by gravity": Lewis Lapham, *Waiting for the Barbarians*, Verso, 1998, p. 129.

35 "Let Larry David do the humour": And Sanders goes off to the Senate to protest the *Puerto Rico Oversight Management and Economic Stability Act*, which, he says, is a "horrific" piece of legislation that curtails the rights of the people and imposes trickle-down economics on them for the benefit of no one except the hedge fund involved. The United States is acting like a "colonial master," he says; and he might have said, according to one half of its nature.

37 "Pew found that": Fitz, 2015.

37 "semi-Burkean": "Illusions of Grandeur", *Economist*, 17 July 2014.

37 "one study also found": Nicholas Fitz, 'Economic Inequality: It's Far Worse Than You Think', *Scientific American*, 31 March 2015;

38 "leads to more exciting lives": *Harvard Gazette*, 17 September 2009; David Brooks, "America vs. Europe", *New York Times*, 13 January 2010.

40 "George Foreman spoke for a while": In another interview, Foreman said he hit Ali a lot on the neck, which was wrong, and he shouldn't have done it, and he worried later it might have caused his Parkinson's disease, and he wished Ali had never got in the ring with him.

42 "A Republican think-tank": In reaction to Goldwater, the 1964 manifesto read: "The moderate course offers the Republican Party the best chance to build a durable majority position in American politics. This is the direction the party must take if it is to win the confidence of the 'new Americans' who are not at home in the politics of another generation: the new middle classes of the suburbs of the North and West – who have left the Democratic cities but who have not yet found a home in the Republican party; the young college graduates and professional men and women of our great university centers – more concerned with 'opportunity' than 'security,' the moderates of the new South – who represent the hope for peaceful racial adjustment and who are insulted by a racist appeal more fitting another generation. These and others like them hold the key to the future of our politics."

43   "kind of one of those guys": Cullen, pp. 178–89. Walker said this in a telephone conversation with a blogger who had persuaded him he was the billionaire Republican donor David Koch. The call ended thus: "David Koch" (Ian Murphy): Well, I tell you what, Scott: once you crush these bastards [the Democrats, unions, liberals, academics, etc.] I'll fly you out to Cali and really show you a good time. Walker: All right, that would be outstanding. Thanks, thanks for all the support and helping us move the cause forward, and we appreciate it. We're, uh, we're doing the just and the right thing for the right reasons, and it's all about getting our freedoms back. "Koch": Absolutely. And, you know, we have a little bit of a vested interest as well. [Laughs] Walker: Well, that's just it … "Koch": All right then. Walker: Thanks a million.

43   "5 to 6 per cent": Alex MacGillis, "The Unelectable Whiteness of Scott Walker", *New Republic*, 16 June 2014.

48   "statistical analysis of Ryan's record": DW-Nominate quoted in Nate Silver, *FiveThirtyEight*, 11 August 2012. Cheney was the next most right-wing, Henry Cabot Lodge and Richard Nixon the least.

48   "The GOP has become and insurgent outlier": Thomas E. Mann and Norman J. Ornstein, "Let's Just Say It: The Republics Are the Problem". *Washington Post*, 27 April 2012.

50   "the default position": Hertzberg, 2009.

51   "A majority of Americans believe": These figures from Thomas B. Edsall, *New York Times*, 14 July 2016.

54   "the crowd turns and boos": Gwynn Guilford, "Inside the Trump Machine", *Quartz online*, 1 April 2016.

58   "turned the State Department": Kinzer, p. 314 and passim.

59   "invited Americans to rethink": Bacevich, esp. pp. 18–22. The quote is from the Smith interview.

60   "an exercise in national pastorship": Hendrik Hertzberg, "A Very Merry Malaise", *New Yorker*, 17 July 2009.

60   "He has said the malaise is ours": Eugene Kennedy, "Carter Agonis", *New York Times*, 5 August 1979.

60   "perpetual outrage": Williams ,1973. Quoted in Henry W. Berger (ed.), *A William Appleman Williams Reader*, Ivan R. Dee, Chicago, 1992, p. 31.

60   "Andrew Bacevich calls": Andrew J. Bacevich, *America's War for the Greater Middle East: A Military History*, Random House, New York, 2016. See also, "The scope of our failure", a two-part interview with Bacevich by Patrick L. Smith, *Salon*, 15 May 2016.

65 "destroying American democracy": See, for example, Lawrence Lessig, *Republic Lost, Version 2.0*, New York, 2015. His TED talk is a riveting twenty-minute summary.

65 "Could she get the public interest": See Packer, p. 288 ff.

68 "Updike wrote an essay": John Updike, *More Matter: Essays and Criticism*, Penguin, 2000.

68 "it's really we who're threatened": Richard Ford, "Anatomy of Donald J. Trump", *Times Literary Supplement*, 13 July 2016.

FIRING LINE | Correspondence

James Curran

James Brown's essay poses a number of important questions for Australia's strategic future and how the country thinks about going to war. He asks on what issues a government would not fight, whether the nation's political leaders have learnt the lessons from the 2003 decision to join the US-led Coalition of the Willing in Iraq, and if there is sufficient debate about the foundations of closer Australia–US military integration. We are, he notes, at the point of a "more sophisticated and pragmatic" alliance with America – one that can handle a greater degree of disagreement and divergence – although Brown worries about its prospects in a Trump White House. The essay sketches the rise of China, calls for deeper thinking on defence and strategic policy and is pessimistic about whether the bureaucracy and the political executive have the right skills to navigate the fractious world ahead.

But there are a number of problems with the argument and its execution. The first and most critical is the claim that an "Iraq template" hovers above the country's political elites, a spectre haunting the corridors of power. Brown is right to join what is virtually a chorus line of lament concerning the lack of planning for the post-invasion phase. But it is passing strange that he devotes precious little analytical energy to unravelling this "template." We are told that it amounts, in essence, to a "government coy to discuss the strategic environment, its alliance activities and its objectives," and one where the "national interest" case was insufficiently made.

Since the claim here is that Canberra remains in thrall to it, this "template" requires closer scrutiny. While it is broadly accepted that the flawed arguments and faulty intelligence marshalled by the Howard government did not differ from those used by George W. Bush and Tony Blair, it does not necessarily follow that the Australian government was "coy" about either the strategic environment or its objectives, especially regarding the implications of the commitment for the US alliance. One can disagree with Howard's analysis of the strategic environment: after all, the tried and tested policy of containing Saddam Hussein was, in essence, working. But on the relevance of the American alliance, Howard was clear. Indeed, the only distinctive argument he used to justify Australia's participation in the Iraq War was the relationship with the United States. This tapped deep wellsprings in John Howard's worldview, his understanding of war and its connection to Australia's history, and his memory of the alliance as it functioned during World War II and the Cold War. Howard often referred to the relationship with the United States as a "two-way street," believed it would get "more, not less" important as the years went by, and argued that Americans would not quickly forget Australia's contribution in Iraq.

Brown's unwillingness to examine the motivations of the key figures in that decision is curious. The explanation for this lacuna? As he states in this essay and during a recent interview on ABC radio, he is a "personal friend" of the former prime minister and therefore feels unable to discuss the political context of the decision. This analytical free pass means that an opportunity is missed to account for the tectonic forces that help to explain why Howard took Australia to war in 2003. As historian David McLean has recently argued, only by looking at the "sense of cultural and ideological affinity" that Howard felt with the United States, by exploring his "quest for personal and political recognition and standing through close association with America," can we start to understand the totality of that crucial decision. These cultural values and beliefs will continue to be part of the calculus in debates over Australia's foreign and defence policy – and indeed in any decision to take the country to war – in the years ahead.

Brown wants instead to focus on the mistakes at the operational level in Iraq. That's fair enough, but to divorce this aspect of the war from the strategic mindset that put Australia in Iraq in the first place represents a major weakness in the argument. Ironically, far more attention is devoted to Tony Abbott's role as a national security leader, with Brown focusing on the sensational claims that the former prime minister suggested the dispatch of 1000 Australian troops to Ukraine in the wake of the shooting down of MH17, and that he wanted to send 3500 diggers into Iraq to combat ISIS. The most respected political journalists in the country have debunked both claims. On Ukraine, the *Australian*'s Paul Kelly argued that the option for troops was "never going to be viable" and that Abbott was "talked around and decided it was too dangerous and inappropriate." And on Iraq, the ABC's Chris Uhlmann was unable to find anyone in the defence department to give the claim a shred of credibility. Even if these ideas were floated or gamed out at some of the countless meetings held to discuss these crises, surely the key point is that the system of checks and balances in Canberra's current national security framework actually performed its function. After all, only a small number of special-forces soldiers were sent to support police investigators in Ukraine, and 200 were sent to Iraq.

This conceptual confusion becomes even more acute when Brown applies the "Iraq template" to the rise of China, and in particular Beijing's growing assertiveness in the South China Sea. The argument here is tenuous, to say the least. Brown does not venture a position, much less an opinion, on how the Australian government should respond to the increasing calls – privately from Washington, publicly from past and present Labor luminaries – for Australia to emulate the United States by conducting freedom-of-navigation operations through the disputed twelve-nautical-mile zone around the contested territories. How, too, does Brown deal with the point that the architect of his Iraq template, John Howard, is now advocating moderation, caution and prudence on the question of possible conflict with China? Brown does not wish the freedom-of-navigation issue to be seen as "emblematic" of the entire US–China relationship, but he surely cannot ignore that the issue is becoming the focal point for what China's rise means for the region and American staying power. Neither Washington nor any of its regional allies has been able thus far to impose any kind of serious cost on Chinese activity.

Closer to home, Brown claims that there was a "degree of blowback" to the announcement in November 2011 of US marine rotations through Darwin. Yet the decision was notable for the broad political consensus it attracted. While there were colourful expressions of outrage from some seemingly aggrieved members of the business community, the only voices of political dissent came from the then leader of the Greens, and former Labor prime minister Paul Keating. Brown argues that the presence of US troops here was first raised in 2003 – but the option of offering the American military training facilities in Australia and even the pre-positioning of equipment was part of the platform the Coalition took to the 1996 federal election.

Perhaps the more notable aspect of the essay, however, is its overwhelming concentration on recent events. It brings to mind Tony Judt's observation that "the twentieth century is hardly behind us but already its quarrels and its achievements, its ideals and its fears are slipping into the obscurity of mismemory." There remains a "perverse contemporary insistence," Judt added, "on not understanding the context of our present dilemmas, at home and abroad; on not listening . . . to some of the wiser heads of earlier decades; on seeking actively to forget rather than remember, to deny continuity and proclaim novelty on every possible occasion."

It is therefore striking that in an essay devoted to the study of how a government makes the decision to go to war, Brown barely glances at how national leaders in the past have acted or spoken when confronted with similar dilemmas. While the first Gulf War is mentioned briefly, the examination of the Hawke government's decision-making processes and, indeed, the case made by the prime minister to justify Australian participation is cursory. Vietnam rates no mention at all, and Australia's involvement in World Wars I and II attracts a solitary sentence. Even then, it is only to make the point that the "thresholds for war" in those conflicts "were set beyond our shores," as if Australia had no distinctive interests of its own in joining those conflicts. The colonies and later the Australian Commonwealth, Brown contends, "did not have the authority to decide on war," since that was "vested . . . in the hands of the colonial redcoat governors and successive British governments."

Such a view is reminiscent of an old-left "radical nationalist" reading of Australia's military past, namely that we fight "other people's wars." But it is a long time since anyone with genuine standing on Australian military history has made that argument. And it fails to take into account the best recent scholarship in the field, which shows Australia's Pacific-centred interests were paramount in the actions and decisions of leaders in both major conflicts of the twentieth century.

To oversee a more rigorous preparation for the future and the kinds of conflicts it might engender, Brown has several recommendations. The first is the creation of a stand-alone, American-style national security council, staffed with the "best and brightest" – a phrase of which he is particularly fond. But in the United States that has often meant the marginalising of the state department and the Pentagon – sometimes with disastrous consequences – and there is no reason to think that the same will not happen here. Whatever Brown's reservations concerning the prime minister's department, Defence and DFAT, they are nevertheless the custodians of the official memory of all the problems the government of the day is called upon to address. And it is their job to warn the government dispassionately about the possible adverse consequences of politically preferred policies. One potential problem with a national security council is that it risks becoming an echo chamber for the incumbent prime minister.

In addition, Brown wants the freshly elected parliament to create a whole suite of committees – four in total – to keep watch on the conduct of Australia's defence, strategic and foreign policy. A new parliamentary defence office would "improve the security debate," although it is not clear how. And he advocates for the federal parliament to be given new powers to subject any military deployment to a "national interest" test – and that it should be given the extraordinary period of ninety days to do so. Such proposals, while earnest and well intentioned, do not take into account the way decisions are made about committing soldiers to war. Brown recognises that the requirement for "full parliamentary approval" would hamper any "effective response to a crisis," but he still wants to give both houses almost three months to "review" whether any military commitment is in the national interest. Yet typically it is the executive leadership of the day that shapes the content and character of the national interest. What point, then, a debate in the parliament on this question when the decision to commit has already been taken? If a vote was taken that chose not to support the government's definition of the national interest, how would that alter tactics or strategy? Many of the questions Brown wants discussed before troops are committed – on costs, public support, the position of the Opposition, new dangers arising from military action – are by their very nature fluid and uncertain. It is asking the impossible. For all its occasional theatrics and vaudeville, Question Time and Senate Estimates remain probably the best forums in which governments can be tested and held to account.

Furthermore, Brown presents no evidence to show how these new layers of oversight – others would call them red tape – would have averted the decision to invade Iraq. Nor, crucially, how they might deal with a scenario in which the United States is pressing Australia to do more in Asia to counter the rise of China – especially if a crisis broke out unexpectedly. Nor, in this dark new world of which Brown speaks – in which "warfare is rapidly evolving" and where "technology is fast running ahead of policy" – is it entirely clear that an avalanche of cumbersome new process is what the national security system needs.

Brown would do well to recall that, thanks to David Halberstam, the phrase "best and brightest" has come to have something of a pejorative connotation in the annals of American national security. These "wise men and whiz kids," as historian Neville Meaney once observed, did not prevent America from sinking into the quagmire of Vietnam: the documents which emerged from the Pentagon papers made a mockery of the Kennedy men's professed claims to "cool realism and liberal humanism." Brown worries that the current generation of strategic analysts in Canberra may not be equipped to think through the complex and complicated challenges ahead. But whence this new generation of Australia's "best and brightest" might emerge is not altogether clear. Certainly not from the universities, as Brown believes they "still view war as a morally tainted activity," a sweeping generalisation that ignores the many courses on campuses that drill deeply into Australia's defence and strategic past.

It is not simply the bureaucracy that is being challenged here: Brown believes that Australian prime ministers over the past few decades have not been well grounded in military matters or well prepared for the art of foreign policy decision-making. Again, however, this is highly debatable. Even if it were conceded that neither Julia Gillard nor Tony Abbott brought to office a depth of experience in strategic policy or foreign affairs, the evidence suggests both learnt quickly on the job. More to the point, both leaders notched up significant wins on the diplomatic stage: Gillard in cementing Australia's place in the US "pivot" and launching the Asian Century White Paper; Abbott in securing a number of free-trade agreements in the region.

Going back further, there is even less to support Brown's claim that the national leaders have been inadequately prepared for this aspect of the job. Gough Whitlam came to office perhaps the most well-informed on international relations of all Australian prime ministers; Malcolm Fraser had been Minister for the Army and indeed defence minister before moving into the Lodge; Bob Hawke had extensive experience abroad as a trade union leader (particularly with the International Labour Organization) and gave thoughtful and reflective speeches on foreign policy in the 1970s, including in his Boyer Lectures of 1979; Paul Keating was the engineer of Australia's embrace of globalisation; John Howard spoke regularly on foreign affairs as Opposition leader in the 1980s and arguably came of age as a national-security leader during the 1999 East Timor crisis; and Kevin Rudd was a former diplomat and China specialist. It can hardly be said, therefore, that these leaders did not bring a depth of experience of the wider world and Australia's role in it to the top job.

Closer attention to the past, of course, will not provide all the solutions, and historians themselves must beware the trap of claiming pompous omniscience in a kaleidoscopic present. But if Brown is looking for a skill set that might help the discussion of these critical issues in the years ahead, he could do far worse than start with a greater sense of history.

James Curran

FIRING LINE | Correspondence

Henry Reynolds

We should welcome the appearance of James Brown's thoughtful assessment of recent developments in Australia's defence and foreign policies. His dual roles as retired army officer and director of research at Sydney's US Studies Centre add to both the interest and cogency of his analysis. *Firing Line* is also a reminder of the alarming deficiency in our communal discourse about war and peace, about national interest and international obligations.

It was symptomatic that defence was never discussed during the recent prolonged election campaign. Neither the major nor minor parties raised the situation of our current engagements overseas. Nor have they shown any desire to examine Australia's past military involvements in the wake of the release of the United Kingdom's Chilcot Inquiry report. The Labor Party stays in lock step with the government, fearing any deviation would lead to damaging accusations of being suspect on security. The American alliance is kept beyond the reach of doubt, or even debate.

We have, then, a strange paradox. We find ourselves in the middle of a seemingly endless cavalcade of commemoration. War is placed in the centre of communal consciousness. We are incessantly told it has been the defining national experience. Yet we are unable to assess whether all our overseas engagements have been worth the loss of life and treasure. The apotheosis of the warrior, the focus on sacrifice and heroism, lifts war above the normal scrutiny given to every other activity of government. Questions as to why Australia has engaged in so many conflicts are judged, at best, imprudent – even unpatriotic and un-Australian.

So James Brown has made a significant contribution to the faltering public debate about what are, by any measure, matters of great national importance. The central question of why and how Australia goes to war has to involve a consideration of the American alliance. *Firing Line* is in part a riposte to recent criticism of the alliance by, among others, Paul Keating and the late Malcolm Fraser. Brown offers a robust, albeit nuanced, defence of the alliance. He characterises it as "a distinctively close relationship – closer to a marriage" than America's many other alliances. This seems a strange and troubling description. Whatever sort of marriage does Brown have in mind, I wonder? Given the vast difference in power between the partners, the metaphor must relate to marriage as it was understood in the middle of the nineteenth century, when wives were the property of their husbands. Another unsettling aspect of this characterisation is the confusion of personal relations with the behaviour of states. Julia Gillard's talk of "mates" was another example of this conceptual slippage. It might be seen as mild sentimental hyperbole. But it's a habit with a disturbing history. For a century, Australians thought of the Empire as family and Britain as a benign and caring mother. It was a delusion that led directly to the disasters of 1942.

One of the troubles is that Australians who engage professionally with American defence and diplomatic personnel overestimate their influence in Washington, just as their forebears did with the mandarins in Whitehall. But that is the whole point. Successful great powers perfect the means of flattering their dependents and leaving them with the impression that they matter much more than they actually do. Brown's argument that the "marriage" with America gives us the capacity to influence decision-making in Washington is surely overdrawn. And there remains the inescapable reality that the alliance means war – and wars that Australia would otherwise have avoided. To suppose that this pattern will not be replicated endlessly is doubtless wishful thinking. Even if "a more sophisticated and pragmatic alliance is developing," as Brown argues, there is little to suggest that Australia will ever be able to turn down an American request for military collaboration, regardless of the location or the nature of the conflict. The greatest danger we face is that we will be drawn into any future conflict with China. The Americans clearly expect our support and no doubt have war plans based on that premise. Such a war may have pressing and legitimate objectives. But the overriding cause may be America's need to assert a slipping hegemony. The really big question is whether the country can ever accept a decline in relative power. The present election campaign is not encouraging, with one side demanding power to make America great again and the other insisting that they are still a nation without peers or rivals.

The danger is that Australia will repeat the great and portentous mistakes of the early twentieth century. The new federation bound itself to a great power in decline and did so with what contemporaries thought were the silken ties of kinship which only the disloyal would dare question. And so we plunged heedlessly into the great conflict which shaped the whole century. It is both instructive and sobering to resurrect the ideas of the colonial critics who had the foresight to see where Imperial loyalty would lead. Their central argument was that the Empire was by definition prone to war and would eventually be involved in a great European conflict. The most dangerous place to be was "married" to a great power which would drag Australia into wars against enemies who presented no threat to the continent. And they were likely to be wars fought faraway against people about whom Australians knew little. This was why the Boer War of 1899 to 1902 was so important. It established an overpowering precedent. If we go to war this time, the critics declared, how will we be able to avoid future wars? The expectation of our great and powerful friend will in itself predispose the country to become involved in whatever future conflicts arise.

It is not clear whether Brown appreciates that the arguments in favour of neutrality reach back deep into Australian history and are not a recent and ephemeral reaction to involvement in the disastrous war in Iraq. And his response to the present generation of imperial sceptics is unsatisfactory for other reasons as well. To understand those people he obviously sees as his intellectual opponents, he reaches unconvincingly for psychological theory about what he calls "the bystander effect." The implication is that those who seek to avoid the path of incessant military engagement are driven by forces of which they themselves are not fully aware. All of the so-called "bystanders," the argument runs, are making the "same unconscious decision: to turn away from the problems of the world, to make them someone else's responsibility." The argument, clearly implicit in much of this, is that the "bystanders" are not only driven by hidden subliminal forces which Brown alone is able to see, but are, as a result, morally deficient as well.

The question arises whether Brown the retired military officer is also a militarist. This is a fair question, which must arise from a reading of *Firing Line*. In particular, it relates to both his treatment of the "bystanders" and his assessment of the role of nation-states. I may not be fair in my reading, but it seems that he believes the many countries which are not constantly at war are turning away from the problems of the world. In response to his assumed intellectual opponents, he writes: "I don't think Australia wants to be, can or should be a bystander to the complexities playing out around us. I don't think we want to be a lonely island, removed from the world and indifferent to its course. We are not a people that can live in splendid isolation." But this is parody rather than a respectful assessment of conflicting opinion. Who is actually arguing in favour of splendid isolation?

And surely there are many small- and medium-sized states which engage fully and fruitfully with the world without going to war, which are not bystanders, have not turned aside from the world and do not live in splendid isolation. Indeed, it could be argued that many of them add more to the wellbeing of humanity than our belligerent homeland.

Henry Reynolds

FIRING LINE | Correspondence

Peter Leahy

As a veteran, James Brown knows the consequences of war and the impact it can have on individuals and communities. He is correct to write, in his Quarterly Essay, that today, in Australia, we rarely think about war. He is also correct to say that we need to think more closely about decisions to go to war. With Australian forces deployed to Afghanistan since 2001 and Iraq since 2003, and now operating in the sky over Syria, we should also deliberate on the decision made every day to remain at war.

The Roman philosopher Cicero told us that we go to war so that we may live in peace. Today conflict seems to be everywhere and it is hard to distinguish between war and peace. The wars in Iraq and Afghanistan have lasted longer than the two world wars combined. Yet our troops continue to go, many of them for multiple deployments, with the ever-present risk of being killed or wounded, both physically and psychologically. But we have not declared war on anyone and we hear precious little about what the troops are doing in our name. Do we even have an answer to the question, what does victory look like?

As a nation, we let our troops down if we don't think about how they are equipped, trained and led, and how well prepared they are for today's wars and the contingencies of the future. Other important questions include: what national interests are served by our involvement? is it legal? what is our strategy? what is our mission? and what tasks do we give deployed forces? At the moment, in both Afghanistan and Iraq, the answers to nearly all of these questions are unclear. As tensions in the South China Sea mount, we need to ask such questions as we contemplate what to do there.

There have been no recent debates in parliament about our war aims and how we are going to achieve them. One obvious problem is that the political parties have decided defence and security matters are to be handled on a bipartisan basis. While comfortable for politicians, this serves to stifle debate on the most important responsibility of the parliament: sending our sons and daughters to war.

There is nothing in the Australian constitution or legislation that requires the government to gain parliamentary approval before deploying military forces or declaring war. This leaves Australia very much on its own in reserving to the prime minister the decision to commit armed forces. Both President Obama and Prime Minister David Cameron saw fit to engage their legislatures over recent deployments to Iraq and Syria. Their subsequent deployments were constrained by the response they received. Even President Putin is obliged by Russian law to seek approval to use military force abroad. It has been granted twice in recent years – for Ukraine and Syria. Not so in Australia.

Following the UK's Chilcot Inquiry, there are suggestions to introduce a bill proposing that the decision to deploy members of the Australian Defence Force be made not by the executive alone, but by the Australian parliament. An earlier version of this bill was rejected in 2010. However, in its consideration of that bill the relevant senate committee stated that it was not against the involvement of both houses of parliament in open and public debate about the deployment of Australian service personnel to warlike operations or potential hostilities. The committee further stated that it agreed with the views of most submitters that the Australian people, through their elected representatives, have a right to be informed and heard on these important matters. The committee saw the 2010 bill as a step along the way to a more mature debate in Australia. It is time for that debate and it is time for a bill to be enacted requiring parliamentary approval before the ADF is deployed.

While addressing a group of retired parliamentarians, I came across a deeply concerning reason why some are reluctant to open the matter to debate and decision in parliament. One retired politician strongly suggested the responsibility must remain with the prime minister as we could not trust the parliament to make such an important decision. We trust it with a whole range of important economic, health and social policy issues – why not the decision to go to war?

Wisely, James Brown discusses the current ill-preparedness of politicians to make important decisions involving defence and security. He notes that few prime ministers and members of the National Security Committee come to the role with an understanding of military matters. He also notes that there are few trained strategic analysts and all of them are distracted by short-term issues at the expense of longer-term policy development. His proposals to reinvigorate the country's national security apparatus are sensible, as are the proposals to expand the range of supervisory committees within the parliament.

He could also have added the need to prepare parliamentarians and their staff, at all levels, to meet the weighty responsibilities they face in considering the path to war. Strategic thinking does not come naturally to many, and given the often catastrophic results of strategic miscalculation, a better way of preparing parliamentarians for their duties is warranted. In Canberra there are two excellent national institutions that could be brought into play to prepare parliamentarians and then support them through their careers. They are the National Security College at the Australian National University and the Centre for Defence and Strategic Studies at the Australian Defence College. Both could arrange an introductory course of around two weeks, which would help equip our parliamentarians to discharge their duties properly. All parliamentarians should attend these courses early in their careers.

War is no longer exclusively large and episodic. Instead it tends to be small, persistent and pervasive. Of the major armed conflicts in the world today, few are between states. In this environment it is difficult for governments to understand the implications of their decisions on the path to war and build a narrative that engages the people and convinces them of the need for war and then for its continuation over an extended period of time. War has become confused. Some wars are seen as wars of choice, others as wars of necessity. Often what starts out as something other than a war ends up looking a lot like a war. Events can quickly change and escalate, so that we are at war before we realise it and unable to extricate ourselves.

Peter Leahy

FIRING LINE | *Correspondence*

Kim Beazley

On my desk sits a photo that was a departure gift from David Shear, then the Assistant Secretary of Defense for Asian and Pacific Security Affairs in the Pentagon. It is of a Chinese warship, snapped from behind a group of waving American sailors on the deck of an American destroyer. The Chinese ship is shadowing the American one as it undertakes a freedom-of-navigation operation in the South China Sea. A note reads: "Kim – hope to see your guys doing this soon. With great respect and appreciation. Dave Shear." Good-natured but pointed humour. It reflects the American expectation that Australians will emerge from calculation of our own interests, in the region of most vital importance to us, and where we are a substantial player, with a determination to demonstrate the validity of the rules governing the global commons. It would help if the United States not only upheld the rules established by the United Nations Convention on the Law of the Sea, but also ratified them. We have done so. In our most recent defence white paper, these rules influence how we equip our armed forces and how we see our responsibilities in the region.

Our ally knows we struggle with decisions to utilise our military forces in support of political objectives in parts of Southeast Asia. If longevity of engagement confers legitimacy on operations, history affirms our right to be a participant in upholding the Law of the Sea in the region. Under the command of General Douglas MacArthur, and with the help of the US Navy, Australian forces conducted the last two amphibious operations of World War II in the zone, at Tarakan and Balikpapan. These operations preceded the Chinese territorial sea claim of the nine-dash line. As that claim incubated in the bowels of the Chinese government, having originated with its nationalist predecessor, Australia was routinely engaged in British struggles with a communist insurgency in Malaya and later in confrontation with Indonesia on behalf of the emerging Malaysian government. As the British withdrew east of Suez, Australia assumed the primary external role in the most longstanding, non-American-involved military alliance in the zone, the Five Power Defence Arrangement, covering Malaysia and Singapore. A RAAF officer still commands the air defence of the Malay Peninsula. Pursuant to this agreement, since the early 1970s Australia has conducted routine air and naval patrols in the South China Sea. The Five Power arrangement also sees permanent rotation of elements of Australian ground forces. These activities have the overt support of two of the South China Sea's littoral states, Malaysia and Singapore, and the implicit support of most of the others. That included China at the time it was in intense disagreement with its Soviet neighbour. Less extensively supported, yet still by some, was Australian involvement in the war in Vietnam (our largest engagement in the zone after World War II).

Today, Australian officials are frequently told by their Chinese counterparts that we have no rights in the game of claim settlement in the zone and no business inserting ourselves in its processes. Our response is that our interest is not in a claim, but in the peaceful legal settlement of claims. Our history and commitments give us at least as much right to engage as anyone else. That we will is regionally acceptable.

From the American point of view, when it comes to external powers we are all there is. This is thoroughly understood by Australia's political leaders. There is no question in their minds that militarising reefs and rocks in the South China Sea is not lawful and produces regional tensions. At the same time, they are aware that the complexities are little understood by the Australian public. They see the danger of accidental clashes. Moreover, there is a constant drumroll from semi-official Chinese media threatening action against Australian units. In one of the latest, on 30 July 2016, the *Global Times* argued, "If Australia steps into the South China Sea waters, it will be an ideal target for China to warn and strike." Maybe. Were that to occur, it would be a real test of ANZUS. This would be an attack on the forces of one of the signatories going about its legitimate business in the Pacific. A substantial response would be required, although Chinese writers seem little concerned by, or else ignorant of, that fact. When it comes to balancing friendships and alliances, this is where the rubber hits the road. The issue is what is sufficient to maintain our position, how we advise our allies and friends on our response, and what theirs ought to be. The question arises: is our decision-making structured in a way that most effectively processes decisions about conflict? James Brown, in his eloquent essay, seeks to answer that.

Firing Line lifts the debate about our military strategy and planning as we contemplate how we will spend the $450 billion the white paper outlaid for future defence spending. And, more importantly, how we will use the force structure created. How we should contemplate and organise for the possibility of war. How we should calculate interests and possibilities. When engaged, how we will assess the relevant force levels, identify desirable outcomes and conclusions. We have got out of the habit of this thinking. In the 1980s, with the Vietnam experience behind us and the Nixon Doctrine with us, these issues were more on the table. Concepts of warning time were worked through at length. Levels of threat were identified, and decisions about force structure made accordingly. Command arrangements were adjusted to ensure effective planning. At the time, mobilisation studies of our national assets in pursuit of self-reliant strategies were all the go. This level of detail featured in none of the succeeding white papers.

The problem was the dominant focus on a single scenario: the defence of our approaches at a time when no regional power was likely to be able to mount a substantial challenge any time soon. Activities further afield were seen principally in the context of a political contribution to allies or UN-based missions. Our experience since then is that although tasks have been manifold, and successfully accomplished, they have not been subject to the same disciplined thinking. Where we have been in the lead, as with East Timor and the Solomon Islands, James Brown's strictures on planning have been reasonably well met. Where we have not been in the lead, our decision-makers have been challenged. He has put forward a set of proposals which are certainly worth detailed thought. Central to that is how we advise our principal ally on how we match our interests with theirs and how we calculate costs and benefits in our region and more broadly. The Americans perceive us now as a highly valuable interlocutor, particularly on regional matters. This was made clear in US Secretary of Defense Ashton Carter's speech to the recent Shangri-La Dialogue, where he said: "The US–Australia alliance is, more and more, a global one. As our two nations work together to uphold freedom of navigation and overflight across this region, we are also accelerating the defeat of ISIL together in Iraq and Syria."

Our ally views us very differently than was anticipated back in 1987. We are not just seen as a willing provider of another flag. We are perceived as adding real capability. Ours may be niche contributions, but they have real military value. In the Iraq War, we were assigned the task of preventing missile launches against Israel from Iraq's western desert. In Afghanistan, at the height of the commitment, we had the task of handling the affairs of a difficult province, Oruzgan. That task expanded to assisting in neighbouring, and much more difficult, Kandahar. More recently, our re-engagement in Iraq includes leading in one of three major training bases established for Iraqi forces. We have had distinct views on how that struggle is pursued, some of it captured in what appeared to be a well-sourced article in the *Weekend Australian* of 23–24 July, although I think the headline "Obama 'Too Soft' in Fight against ISIS" overstated. It is a complex struggle fraught with internal political difficulties in Baghdad. The Pentagon, more than Obama – though he as well – has been sensitive to the Iraqi view that it is their fight and that excessive reliance on foreign forces is domestically, politically, counter-productive. We have been alert to this sensitivity. Differing perspectives have been nuanced rather than absolute, with Iraqi government views respected at all times. As appropriate, our position has been determined by our own analysis of what needs to be done in the struggle with ISIS. We should be under no illusion: our troops are in harm's way. We are taking that responsibility seriously, with senior decision-makers deeply engaged. It is a fight not yet won. If and when James Brown's suggested structure is considered, it will be a core case study.

Most Australian commentators write without a full appreciation of how deep our defence involvement is with the United States. In a sense, our public commentary reflects something of the "frog in boiling water" phenomenon. To use another analogy, we miss the wood for the trees. The last two decades has seen an accumulation of actions and judgment which has brought this about. This is not the place to look at that in detail. However, some points can be made.

On the intelligence side, there have been regular visits by the most senior American officials. They do not occur unannounced, and they reflect what one expert told me: that the volume of exchange with Australia is now the most extensive of the United States' many exchanges. (I hasten to add I can't directly verify this, but it wouldn't surprise me.) The joint facilities, increased in number in recent years, with new facilities related to space awareness, are now of genuinely mutual significance. In my day in Defence, it was a matter of ensuring the Australian government had full knowledge of, and was in a position to concur with, how the facilities were used and how they operated. Now they form a critical element of our own intelligence order of battle and our operation in the field.

Our defence acquisitions have likewise ensured compatibility with the forces of our ally. We spend about A$13 million each working day in the US defence industry. Over 400 military sales and related activities are managed in the Australian embassy in Washington. The result of this can be seen most strikingly in our air defence – arguably the best we have ever had and decisive in our approaches. Full situational awareness comes from our access to satellite product and our over-the-horizon radar system. (The latter is an Australian product, but it started as a joint process and is maintained with American companies.)

Our surveillance aircraft and early warning capabilities are American-sourced, along with our in-flight refuelling. Our strike and interdiction aircraft – Classic Hornets, Super Hornets and Growlers – are likewise all American, as are the F-35s on which we are now training. As to the future, members of our Defence Science and Technology Group are engaged in work on technologies identified in the so-called Third Offset Strategy that is the next phase in the American military's technological revolution.

Finally, it should not be assumed that we have been passive recipients of instructions as the Americans have "pivoted" to Asia. The Americans are thoroughly aware that we have long been advocates of their reorientation. I was tasked, after then Secretary of State Hillary Clinton's mid-2010 announcement of their intention to join the East Asia Summit, to report on how the Americans arrived at their conclusion. "Why, because of you, of course," was the genial response of the first American official approached. He was referring to Prime Minister Kevin Rudd's advocacy of an Asian community. That Australian position is much in mind as we discuss with them activities in the South China Sea. James Brown's essay is timely indeed.

Kim Beazley

FIRING LINE | Correspondence

Peter Whish-Wilson

A government faces few bigger decisions than whether to commit young Australians to war. So it is striking how rarely questions about defence spending and national security policy figure in Australia's public and political discourse, especially in parliament.

Firing Line is an important contribution to what passes as debate on Australia's security interests and priorities. As in Anzac's Long Shadow, James Brown isn't afraid to challenge taboos. It is always encouraging when insight and critique are provided by someone of Brown's military and professional standing, as they are less easy to dismiss.

There is much to respond to in Firing Line, but I will limit my comments to two areas. First, James Brown notes that our country's national security apparatus is "entirely underscrutinised, and it shows." Based on my experience as a senator, I agree. "It is extraordinary," Brown writes, "that so little infrastructure is dedicated to parsing the issues of war." In the last parliament, I sat on both the Joint Standing Committee on Treaties and the Senate Standing Committee on Foreign Affairs, Defence and Trade. I understand full well what Brown means when he says that our oversight of defence matters is both "underdone and weak."

Following the release of the 2016 Defence White Paper in February, I bantered with a few well-known journalists at Aussies Café in Parliament House. "What's wrong with you, Whish-Wilson, are you un-Australian? Where's your patriotism?" they chided, smiling.

As the Greens spokesperson for Defence, I had been outspoken that week, questioning the need to increase defence spending to an arbitrary 2 per cent of GDP when there had been no escalation in Australia's overall security threat, and when such an increase ran the risk of dragging the nation into an arms race in the Asia-Pacific region. I also noted that the white paper had been repeatedly delayed, seemingly to coincide with an election year. This risked politicising defence procurement programs and dressing up industry policy as defence policy.

I also warned that without scrutiny and oversight, this increase in defence spending, the biggest outside wartime, brought with it enormous opportunity costs and risk of waste. Every extra dollar spent on defence equipment could potentially be better spent on foreign aid, infrastructure or climate change adaptation, without detracting from both the overt and implicit aims of the white paper.

These seemed reasonable concerns. But my Greens colleagues and I were the only ones in the Senate to raise them, and among very few in the wider parliamentary circles to do so publicly.

It is the job of a parliamentarian, especially in Opposition, to ask hard questions and scrutinise government decisions. But in recent years, Liberal and Labor have been in on virtually all matters of defence and national security – in furious agreement on recent Iraqi and Syrian deployments, draconian new intelligence laws, the machinations of the secretive Operation Sovereign Borders, and now the decision to ramp up defence spending with record-breaking procurement programs.

To many Australians, this unity ticket seems odd. Parliament dedicates an inordinate amount of time to scrutinising the details of where and how defence money is being spent. This gives the appearance of an Opposition doing its job and occupies a lot of time in Senate Estimates. In reality there is little scrutiny of substance on the public record. Next to no time is given to examining whether this spending serves a particular strategy, let alone whether the strategy is the right one in the first place.

In politics, decisions are based on both party policy and the political realities and practicalities of the day. The reality in this country is that we have an aggressive and belligerent right-wing media promoting conservative agendas, especially in defence and national security. Some elements of the Murdoch press, first and foremost, are only too keen to attack and ridicule politicians who don't support certain agendas. I have been on the receiving end of such attacks. They are designed to belittle the individual, and to undermine or silence proper debate. And they work. I know from conversations with parliamentarians across the political spectrum that there is deep fear of repercussions for speaking out on defence procurement, national security or our participation in foreign conflicts.

The risk of losing political skin is a disincentive to asking too many questions or rocking the boat. Politicians fear being seen to be not "across your brief" – in what are often highly detailed and complex matters. At a more basic level, they fear being accused of not supporting the troops or undermining a strong national defence. This "silent running" acts as a significant and dangerous barrier to transparency and scrutiny.

I'm glad that James Brown has highlighted particular issues that arose during Tony Abbott's time as prime minister and the pressure Abbott put on our national security apparatus and defence personnel. But Captain Brown was being diplomatic. As I see it, Abbott repeatedly politicised national security issues – especially the threat of violent extremism within Australian borders – for political gain. While instances of extremism are real and need to be taken seriously, the politicisation of this issue was both counter-productive and dangerous. This has noticeably cooled since Malcolm Turnbull became prime minister, although the popular and divisive political rhetoric of One Nation threatens to revive the national security dog-whistle.

Given the recent social media frenzy on the national security threat posed by Islamic extremism, I am inclined to disagree with Brown's assertion that "for much of the Australian public, Australia's strategic environment has become somewhat safer" and that "war has largely ceased to be a threat." In an age of global media providing saturation coverage of acts of violence and terror, I believe that we have rarely felt more unsafe or more under siege. In recent surveys such as the Lowy Institute Poll, the threat of violent extremism ranks as this nation's biggest insecurity.

This brings me to my second issue with Firing Line: the idea that we need to move beyond the legacy of the Iraq War and seek new "templates" under which to consider the path to war – or its avoidance.

This is unlikely while the conflict in Iraq remains ongoing and unexamined. Only a full and independent inquiry into Australia's contribution to the 2003 invasion of Iraq and its aftermath will suffice if we are to learn from our mistakes and recast the debate. This examination is long overdue.

We are also unlikely to move on from the Iraq War while the larger political and media context of this conflict is what journalist Peter Greste calls the "appallingly named War on Terror."

When discussing the changing nature of war and how Australians perceive conflict, Brown acknowledges "that mental line has moved further and further outwards, pushed by myriad factors since 1945." Brown suggests that following the invasion of Iraq, there has been public confusion over current or future paths to war, and consequently disengagement. This is perfectly understandable, reflecting the fact that many Australians feel they are in a perpetual state of war – the "long war" promised by Dick Cheney.

I would argue that as a nation we perceive ourselves to be – and in reality *are* – less safe now because of the so-called "War on Terror." Australians rightly question the necessity of foreign deployments and are sceptical of the need to ramp up military spending.

However, this will not be enough to prevent future catastrophes such as Australia's participation in the unilateral invasion of Iraq as it doesn't address the core issue that this decision was not made by the entire parliament, but rather by one or a handful of politicians within the executive.

The Chilcot Inquiry has provided us with a chilling indictment of the flawed processes that allowed a few ideologically motivated individuals to lead us into a catastrophic war in Iraq. James Brown also acknowledges that "the way a country prepares for war, the assessment it makes of possible threats, is a deeply human process, prone to bias and instinct." It is therefore surprising that he doesn't support giving war powers to parliament, rather than to members of our nation's executive, who are more often than not motivated by their own narrow political and ideological objectives.

I disagree with Brown that giving parliament war powers would inhibit any "effective response to a crisis." Any legislation would be structured so that parliament makes the initial decision to go to war, but does not make the operating decisions during the conduct of any conflict. Most importantly, participation must be decided by a conscience vote. Given the gravity of war and the risks posed to the lives and wellbeing of those who serve, each and every parliamentarian should have this decision on their conscience.

Brown feels that Australians are making broader national security decisions based on "instincts, not insights." That may be true, but when the available insights are often heavily politicised by the Murdoch tabloids, and the bipartisan political interests of the two major parties and other vested interests, the public's tendency to be deceived, to fail to trust or to disengage entirely, is perfectly understandable.

It is critical that trust be restored. At a recent lecture I attended during the Tamar Peace Festival, Julian Burnside QC stated that "the path to peace starts with honesty." We can start being honest by holding an open and independent inquiry into Australia's role in the Iraq War, introducing new legislation to give parliament a conscience vote on future deployments, and adopting new ways to scrutinise defence spending and matters of national security.

Peter Whish-Wilson

FIRING LINE | *Correspondence*

Judy Betts

James Brown's Firing Line was well timed: it was released as the Chilcot Inquiry report was handed down in the United Kingdom. In a sad reminder of how devastating the invasion of Iraq has been, the release of the report coincided with the deadliest attack in Iraq since the 2003 invasion. Brown's essay is in part a personal account of wartime experiences in both Iraq and Afghanistan, which puts a human face on the consequences of decisions made by people far removed from the dust and danger of war.

Brown makes a number of suggestions for improving the decision-making process for going to war, a process that is currently flawed by the domination of one person (the prime minister). With the benefit of hindsight, and lessons learnt from the Chilcot Inquiry, would Brown's measures have saved Australia from its decision to join the Coalition of the Willing in what has variously been described as "the worst foreign policy disaster in US history" and "the worst British foreign policy blunder since the Suez"?

First, would a national security council have made a difference? As John Howard himself has pointed out, it is not intelligence agencies that make decisions about going to war. Going to war is a policy decision and such decisions are made on the basis of policy advice, not intelligence advice. Intelligence advice is just one input to considerations which need to be more strategic and holistic.

There is little on the public record about the nature and content of the policy advice provided to government about sending Australian troops to Iraq. Such advice was excluded from the terms of reference of the 2003 *Inquiry into Intelligence on Iraq's Weapons of Mass Destruction* by a parliamentary joint committee (Jull Inquiry) and the 2004 *Inquiry into Australian Intelligence Agencies* by Philip Flood.

However, Paul Kelly, on page 260 of *The March of Patriots*, paints a picture of a public service far removed from the "mythical age of 'frank and fearless' advice much romanticised by the media."

None of the three critical policy departments – Prime Minister and Cabinet, Foreign Affairs and Trade, and Defence – offered advice which questioned the wisdom of going to war. This was confirmed in interviews with a number of senior public servants. Apart from the final submission when cabinet decided to go to war, on 17 March 2003, there was no formal advice from the bureaucracy which examined the merits of such an action. Submissions to the National Security Committee of Cabinet addressed issues of military capability and logistics: implementation, rather than any consideration of the decision itself.

For a national security council to be effective, the government of the day would need to be willing to listen to advice and the staff of the organisation would have to be willing to be "apolitical" and provide "the Government with advice that is frank, honest, timely and based on the best available evidence" in accordance with Australian Public Service values.

Would increased parliamentary oversight, as Brown recommends, have improved accountability? In the case of the Iraq war, the Jull committee's findings were potentially quite damaging, but clever media management by the Howard government (including the selective leaking of parts of the report) dissipated the public and political will to take matters further. The Jull Inquiry found that:

> The case made by the government was that Iraq possessed WMD in large quantities and posed a grave and unacceptable threat to the region and the world, particularly as there was a danger that Iraq's WMD might be passed to terrorist organisations . . . This is not the picture that emerges from an examination of all the assessments provided to the Committee by Australia's two analytical agencies . . . The statements by the Prime Minister and Ministers are more strongly worded than most of the AIC [Australian Intelligence Community] judgements.

A leak to the media, two weeks before the report's official release, primed journalists to see the key issue as politicisation of advice from the Office of National Assessments. As a result, many journalists missed the significance of the most critical finding in the report: namely that, on the basis of the advice of Australia's own intelligence agencies, there was no compelling case for war.

There are many parallels with the Chilcot findings. The UK (read "Australia") chose to join the invasion of Iraq before the peaceful options for disarmament had been exhausted. Military action was not a last resort. The judgments (read "statements by Prime Minister Howard and Minister for Foreign Affairs Alexander Downer") about the severity of the threat posed by Iraq's weapons of mass destruction were presented with a certainty that was not justified. Despite explicit warnings (read "from Mick Keelty, head of the Australian Federal Police"), the consequences of the invasion were underestimated.

Finally, James Brown argues that there is a compelling case for parliament to be given the power to review "within a period of, say, ninety days" whether a military response is "in the strategic national interest." Would this – or any other parliamentary requirement – have made a difference in the case of going to war in Iraq in 2003?

In the three countries that formed the Coalition of the Willing – the US, UK and Australia – there were parliamentary/congressional debates over going to war. In Australia, the parliamentary debate was held on 20 March 2003, after the prime minister and his cabinet had formally decided, on 17 March, to join the Coalition. In the UK, while the executive has the power to declare war without going to parliament, Blair sought parliamentary approval because he did not have the endorsement of cabinet or the support of his party. Chilcot found that almost all of the substantive war-related decisions had been made without reference to the full cabinet. In the United States it is a constitutional requirement that Congress approve any decision to go to war. Military action was authorised in October 2002, on the (flawed) advice that Saddam Hussein continued to possess and develop a significant chemical and biological weapons capability and was actively seeking a nuclear weapons capability.

It would seem that a parliamentary vote or power of veto, especially where the prime minister's party has the numbers in the House, would not have prevented Australia's participation in the disastrous Iraq venture.

Brown's essay is a valuable piece which offers a unique perspective. His proposals have merit and are worth exploring, but of themselves would not necessarily have prevented a determined and skilled political leader from getting his way, as Howard did on Iraq.

There are checks on power. Nothing substitutes for public servants who give frank and fearless advice; media outlets with the time and tenacity to do detailed investigative journalism; principled Opposition politicians with the energy and determination to keep governments accountable; a vigilant public; and whistleblowers with the courage to speak out. Given that Australia's next military involvement is likely to require a more nuanced approach to the US alliance, it is terrifying to contemplate that we may not have learnt from our mistakes.

Judy Betts

FIRING LINE | Correspondence

Malcolm Garcia

In his timely and important Quarterly Essay, James Brown states that there are few things more important for a nation to decide than what it is willing to fight for. I would contend that in Australia, in the absence of public interest in the study of conflict (due to a combination of Anzac-fixated neglect and a peculiar concern, identified by Brown, that to talk about war is somehow to make it more likely), our national security establishment has made a determination on our behalf. In their minds, what we are willing to fight for is maintenance of the Australia–America alliance.

Freed from the need to explain to a largely uninterested Australian public why the government has, since 1999, almost continuously been sending soldiers, sailors and airmen into harm's way, the Canberra establishment has been able to act more deftly than its foreign equivalents. Through skill and intelligence, and some luck, it has contributed to American-led military operations, demonstrating a desire to shoulder some of the burden of the Australia–America alliance. It has also been able to minimise the likelihood of casualties which would cause public questioning of what our military is doing, and, by extension, of the value of the alliance.

Like Brown, I find it difficult to place my experience of the Iraq War in the national political discourse. In mid-2003, I had the first of several deployments to the Middle East as part of an RAAF AP-3C Orion detachment. Soon after my arrival, the mission of this detachment experienced a major change. Until then the Orions had almost exclusively been conducting patrols of the Arabian Gulf and the Arabian Sea. But now the detachment was to conduct missions over Iraq. The Orion crews were largely untrained for these overland flights and the aircraft themselves had only recently been fitted with new equipment to conduct the task. Each with their complement of ten aircrew, the Orions proceeded to inspect the electricity powerlines of Iraq. The reason for the task was that former regime elements (FREs, just one of the acronyms used over the years to describe enemies of the Coalition) were powerlines to cripple the country.

Each sortie lasted upwards of eight hours, and the video collected was painstakingly examined by analysts for evidence of damaged powerlines. Reports and images were then dispatched to military headquarters in Bahrain, Qatar and Baghdad. After several weeks, staff from the Orion detachment inquired about the result of the missions and the usefulness of the reporting. The response from headquarters was that while the information produced was greatly appreciated, this task should ideally have been assigned to unmanned aerial vehicles, not to the Orions. Subsequently, the powerline reconnaissance task stopped.

To the national security establishment the Orion detachment was a neat response to American requests for a contribution. The aircraft and crews had trained with their American counterparts; the air threat environment was relatively benign; and the missions conducted provided a possibly useful, but not critical, contribution – they showed we were "doing something." But the "set-and-forget" nature of Australian military contributions, as discussed by Brown, raises the question: if Orion detachment staff had not inquired about the result, how much longer would these aircraft and crews have been conducting the mission?

It was not only in the Iraq War that we made low-risk, nominal contributions to the Australia–America alliance. Canberra's response to Iraq's invasion of Kuwait in 1990 – which was only repulsed after a massive campaign of air strikes and assault by armoured vehicles – was to send three RAN ships. And in the aftermath of 9/11, a detachment of RAAF F/A-18 Hornets was sent not to the battlefields of Afghanistan, but to the isolated atoll of Diego Garcia, 1800 kilometres south of the subcontinent, to conduct uneventful patrols over the American base there for six months. Both of these contributions fit the template of a cost-effective alliance, even though they were unlikely to fit public perceptions of contributing in a valuable way to something Australia has decided it is willing to fight for.

Brown also highlights the difference between Australia and the United States when it comes to open discussion of military matters, pointing out the Australian government's desire to portray the basing of American marines in Darwin as nothing special and its reflexive denial of possible deployment of American bombers to Australia. This difference is also seen in the ways America and Australia have publicised their military presence in the South China Sea. While a US Navy Poseidon aircraft invited a CNN news crew aboard for a sortie (accompanied by the commander of American maritime patrol aircraft in the Pacific) to show the encroach of China, an Australian Orion patrol was only accidentally discovered to be in the area by a news crew from the BBC. The response from

Canberra to this was that the Orion patrol was routine and that challenges from the Chinese military were not unique.

It is because military decision-making is in the hands of our national security establishment that there is an instinctive culture of secrecy. The members of this establishment have dealt with classified material for hours of every day over several years of their careers, with little requirement to explain what they do to the public, or even to the country's elected representatives. The longevity of tenure in the national security establishment probably also helps explain why there is not the same tradition of selected leaking as in America, as well as why there is a dearth of retired senior officers offering opinions on military issues.

What can be done to improve the situation? I disagree with Brown's suggestion to establish a national security council with a new national security adviser (NSA). Such an organisation would almost certainly be filled with longstanding members of the national security establishment, with an NSA who would likely have senior officer experience in the SASR (Special Air Services Regiment), which is coincidentally one of the most secretive parts of the ADF.

Brown points out that compared to other nations the decision to go to war in Australia lacks substantial political oversight. Perhaps if prime ministers were required to secure the approval of both houses of parliament before deploying troops overseas – for any deployment longer than ninety days, so as to allow for rapid response to a crisis – the public would be better informed about the goal of the mission and when it will likely end. Parliamentarians from both sides of the aisle should be considered mature enough to be entrusted with information that can make our elected representatives part of the important discussion of determining what our nation is willing to fight for.

Malcolm Garcia

FIRING LINE | Correspondence

Rory Medcalf

James Brown's *Firing Line* fills a real gap in Australian public debate. He draws attention compellingly to the poor state of understanding of how and why Australia decides to use force to protect and advance its interests. Brown brings home to us the realities of international security, in a fitting sequel to his book *Anzac's Long Shadow*, which identified the contradiction between many Australians' obsession with a stylised military history and their relative indifference to today's defence force. He warns that our nation has barely begun to think hard about the war-and-peace decisions that loom in the difficult decades ahead. War is not obsolete and, in an uncertain, complex and connected world, no island is an island. Australia cannot and should not be a bystander.

On all these counts Brown is right, and has done Australia a service. But what is also needed is a set of guidelines to help us make the best decisions in the national interest. How much danger and responsibility should Australia be willing to countenance when contributing to the international struggle against jihadist terrorism, which attacks the trust and tolerance underpinning our society? How important, by comparison, are inter-state security challenges (which are almost entirely posed by the rise of China and the resurgence of Russia)? Ultimately, what risks and costs should Australia be willing to incur to discourage armed coercion in the Asian strategic order, including in the South China Sea? In an Australia where political views and perceptions of national interest are becoming increasingly fragmented – an Australia that is a mosaic of more people from more places and backgrounds than ever before – it is becoming ever harder for a government to find effective policy answers to these questions, or to mobilise and maintain public support when it does.

To be fair, to address these questions fully would require a longer format – after all, a signature quality of the Quarterly Essay is its capacity to make us ask the difficult questions, rather than to claim to have all the answers.

Two other observations: one about the education of our political class, the other about the nature of conflict. A theme of the essay – and, indeed, of some of Brown's previous work, including reports he and I co-authored for the Lowy Institute – is the often troublingly low awareness of security issues among parliamentarians. Brown commendably proposes a much more comprehensive range of parliamentary committees on security matters, but our political representatives would not want to go into them cold.

Thus, he also notes that institutions such as the Australian National University can help equip our political class to think about security – and certainly I would be happy for my own part of ANU, the National Security College, to step up in that regard. This means more than briefings and courses for parliamentarians (as rightly recommended by Peter Leahy). Equally important is the need to ground the procession of political staffers in the realities of defence, security and the national interest.

Brown sensibly points out that the nature of conflict is changing rapidly. While the threat of force has resurfaced in international affairs – in truth, it never went away – it would be a mistake to expend great effort to prepare the Australian public and political elite only for conflicts that echo those of the past. Brown focuses especially on the astounding changes in technology which should alert us against investing overwhelmingly in, say, submarines and warships: space, cyber, "swarming weaponised drones," shape-changing objects from 4D (yes, 4D) printing, changes in biologics and nanoscience.

What is also changing profoundly is the nature of conflict and the scenarios in which Australia may need to use its security capabilities – and not only the armed forces. Put simply, the barriers between international and domestic security, and between security and economics, are breaking down. We are seeing a nexus of domestic and international threats; of risks that simultaneously confront government, private and community interests. These challenges – from terrorism to cyber infiltration to potentially harmful geo-economic influence – place a new premium on partnerships. And some of those problems will need to be met on Australian soil, involving new roles for the Australian Defence Force.

Australia's security is no longer a problem for the Commonwealth government alone: it will necessitate cooperation with the states and territories, with business, with the many cultures of the Australian community, and with international partners. These are all reasons for a broader national conversation about security, to which Firing Line is a valuable contribution.

Rory Medcalf

FIRING LINE | Response to Correspondence

James Brown

By the start of the next decade Australia will commence acquiring armed drones. That fact alone is prompting a rethink of how we might go to war, and the systems required to ensure elected representatives exercise effective control over the military. Imagine, if you will, Helen Mirren's *Eye in the Sky* played out with Australian faces around the table. We have, I am sure, considerable work yet to do on the institutions that might support such real-time decision-making.

I wrote *Firing Line* intending it to be the first word, rather than the last, in a new conversation. If the correspondence on the essay is indicative of the prospects for reinvigorating the national conversation on Australia's place in the world, the role of our military and the essential elements of national security, then I am very pleased and look forward to the conversation yet to unfold. There is much more to say. I said little on the role of international law in making decisions to go to war — a topic I think already receives a rare degree of nuanced coverage in our public debates. Nor, as several correspondents elsewhere have pointed out, did I discuss at all the ethics of going to war. I made almost no mention of terrorism and a range of other national security threats, such as cybersecurity. Discussing a topic as expansive as war in 25,000 words means moving quickly and making hard decisions on what to leave out. I wanted the essay to range broadly from the personal and tactical, through the military and political, all the way to grand and regional strategy, because all of these considerations are necessary to inform a decision to go to war. As Andrew Carr said to me, "What the ordinary soldier goes through and what Xi Jinping wants both matter in this discussion."

The responses to *Firing Line* show a consensus that our public debate on defence and national security is underdone. Henry Reynolds notes we have just passed through a federal election in which defence and national security policy barely rated a mention. Indeed, the most prominent defence discussion during the campaign was on whether retired military officers running for office should be allowed to post photos of their previous uniformed career or not (for the record, they should, and I would be surprised if the defence department's judgment on this passes legal review). Senator Whish-Wilson sees bipartisan consensus on defence as the major problem here, as well as misplaced parliamentary priorities: "Parliament dedicates an inordinate amount of time to scrutinising the details of where defence money is being spent," he writes, but "Next to no time is given to examining whether this spending serves the aims of a particular strategy." He worries, too, about "silent running" politicians who are "fearful of speaking out on defence issues" lest they be seen as uninformed. Rory Medcalf, head of the National Security College in Canberra, confirms this impression of a "troubling lack of awareness of security issues among politicians." Malcolm Garcia identifies one impediment to a more informed public and parliamentary debate: the instinctively secretive culture of the Australian Defence Organisation. Let me note another, articulated by Michael Ware during a discussion of the essay in Brisbane: there will only be a better public debate on security issues when the public demands one.

In the meantime, though, plenty of steps can be taken to improve the capacity of parliament to debate these matters. In addition to the measures I have suggested, Peter Leahy suggests a two-week course on strategic thinking for all parliamentarians. Given the newly elected parliament only gets two days to grapple with a century of parliamentary history and systems, two weeks is a big ask. But the idea of shorter sessions aimed at lifting strategic and defence knowledge among parliamentary staffers is worth pursuing.

Three weeks after *Firing Line* was published, the Chilcot Inquiry handed down its report. From predictable Australian corners came calls for our own round of war-crimes trials: witch-hunts which would neither help Australia make decisions on war, nor for that matter be likely to succeed in their cause of putting decision-makers in jail. As the Chilcot report makes clear in its 2.6 million words, mistakes were made, rather than deliberate deceptions contrived. Senator Whish-Wilson would like a full and independent inquiry to be held in Australia, but I don't think that's likely. I would like to see more on the public record, though, particularly on two issues considered in depth by Chilcot. The first is the effectiveness of Australia's military strategy in Iraq between 2003 and 2008–09. It was chilling to read of the lack of clarity about the United Kingdom's military objectives for the Basra-based Multinational Division Southeast, whose headquarters controlled the movements of my unit deployed there in 2005. It was useful to read the analysis of the impact on the British Armed Forces of splitting focus between Afghanistan and Iraq from 2005–06. I have not yet seen a good analysis of how Australia managed the interaction of these two proximate but distinct military theatres. And finally, the examination of the United Kingdom's ability to influence the United States during a time of crisis is the most illuminating part of the Chilcot report, in my view, with echoes for Australia then and now.

I grappled with how best to incorporate Iraq into my essay, not wanting simply to rehash the debates of the last decade, but keen to acknowledge how large the decision to go to Baghdad looms in the Australian psyche, and also wanting to be upfront about the personal biases inherent in the way I look at that conflict. My shorthand for the impact of Iraq on Australian thinking about war – the Iraq template – clearly needs further elucidation. James Curran's critique of this is like so many winter mornings spent at the Singleton military range: bracing, but useful. He rightly points out that the Australian government was not "'coy' about either the strategic environment or its objectives, especially regarding the implications of the commitment for the US alliance." I have acknowledged elsewhere the extent of John Howard's efforts to make the public case for war in Iraq, in the parliament and outside it, including an extensive speech with questions at the National Press Club. I was thinking more of the period after 2003, particularly the difficulty the Rudd and Gillard governments had in discussing Australian deployments to the Middle East, and the deferment of commissioning official histories of recent conflicts. And I acknowledge that alliance considerations were to the fore in calculations then of national interest. In 2016 we run the risk of forgetting the immense pressure that was brought to bear on alliance interests in 2003, and it is important to recall that such considerations led the Japanese prime minister, Junichiro Koizumi, and the Japanese parliament to vote to deploy troops to Iraq – overturning seven decades of pacifism.

Chilcot has led to renewed calls here for parliament to take a greater role in decisions on war, and the Greens have committed to reintroduce their War Powers Bill when the new parliament convenes. I remain unconvinced that a vote before any military deployment is the right course of action, for reasons of both principle and practicality. The executive must preserve the freedom to respond to events, or shape events, with the mandate handed to it by the electorate and should not be excessively hobbled from doing so. Some security crises require a response within days, if not hours – recalling parliament and briefing it on the case for and against deployments would often prove impractical. Judy Betts usefully points out that greater parliamentary involvement in 2003 would not have changed Australia's response to Iraq, given that the government controlled the lower house of parliament. A joint sitting of the House and Senate, beyond increasing the logistical complexity of a vote on military deployments, would also seem to contravene an elected government's mandate, and is only to be used on rare occasions to resolve impasse and deadlock.

But the trend in New Zealand, Canada and particularly the United Kingdom is towards greater involvement of parliament in military deployments. There remains a need for a greater systemic role for parliament in decisions to go to war. James Curran asks what point a ninety-day parliamentary committee review of military deployments would serve, given the decision to send troops has already been made. It is a "cumbersome new process" full of red tape, he suggests. Parliamentary review would serve four purposes. First, it would make the review of military deployment automatic and certain: regularising close consideration of military issues and the alignment of military objectives with political strategy. Second, it would increase transparency of decision-making and likely increase confidence and trust among the public. Third, it would allow consideration of views on the deployment from experts and members of the public outside parliament. Last, there is the purpose of broadening an appreciation of what's at stake in any deployment, and potentially sharpening military strategy through more extensive parliamentary consideration. In arguing for congressional approval of military action in the United States, the Democratic vice-presidential nominee, Senator Tim Kaine, goes further: "It would be the height of public immorality to order service members to risk their lives when the nation's political leadership has not done the work to reach a consensus about the value of a mission." Australia is out of step with other democracies on this issue. As Peter Leahy notes, even President Putin is required by law to consult the State Duma when he wishes to deploy the military overseas (though presumably not when little green men are deployed).

The idea of a more integrated national security secretariat, in the form of a national security council (or office of national strategy, as some have suggested), has received a surprising degree of support in my discussions since *Firing Line* was published. Naturally, there has been some pushback in Canberra, with concerns voiced that current coordination efforts are not being appreciated, or that a new organisation might marginalise existing departments and agencies. Recent developments in Australia's relationship with China, including the blocked sale of Ausgrid, make even more apparent the need for a better-coordinated approach to national security. It is odd that the necessarily reactive Foreign Investment Review Board has become the default body to meld security and economic assessments of the national interest. James Curran is concerned that a national security secretariat might become an echo chamber for the prime minister. Perhaps, but it is no more or less likely to become an echo chamber than a prime ministerial intelligence agency like the Office of National Assessments. Far more pressing is the question of where the strategists to staff this new office might come from: Malcolm Garcia suspects from the military, others have concluded from DFAT. For the most part, we will have to train them anew: policy expertise runs deep within government, strategy expertise less so. As Kim Beazley notes, "we have got out of the habit of this thinking." The need to get back in the habit is pressing.

It is a ticklish matter for me to assess the national security leadership of Tony Abbott, who was replaced as prime minister by my father-in-law. But I think the Abbott example is an important one and worth examining in detail. James Curran criticises my "sensational claims" that "the former prime minister suggested the dispatch of 1000 Australian troops to Ukraine in the wake of the shooting down of MH17, and that he wanted to send 3500 diggers into Iraq to combat ISIS," and concludes that, "The most respected political journalists in the country have debunked both claims."

That is wrong. On the Ukraine deployment, Paul Kelly wrote: "Abbott's every instinct is to deploy Australian military and police assets and he needs to be persuaded by his advisers from such options . . . In the early days of the crisis several weeks ago Abbott wanted to put 1000 Australian troops onto the crash site in conjunction with 1000 Dutch troops. Nothing better testifies to his outrage at the event and his keenness to deploy Australian assets in a cause that affected Australians. This option remained on the table for a few days."

Chris Uhlmann wrote: "Last August no one in the hierarchy rushed to deny a report in the *Australian* that said Mr Abbott wanted to put 1,000 troops into Ukraine, following the shooting down of Malaysia Airlines flight MH17. That was because everyone agreed it was true."

Abbott himself confirmed this in parliament in February 2015: "There was talk with the Dutch about a joint operation . . . This arose out of the most important and the most necessary discussions between the Dutch military and our own to uphold and defend our vital national interests and to do the right thing by the people of our country."

The Iraq report is more contested. Prime Minister Abbott, along with defence chiefs, carefully refuted the notion that Australia was informally or formally planning unilateral action in Iraq, and reiterated that there were "no plans to put Australian combat troops on the ground." Notably, though, the *Australian* did not issue a retraction of the story and Chris Uhlmann concluded that the possibility remained that "the idea of sending troops to Iraq was raised inside the bunker of the Prime Minister's office."

Since Firing Line was published, the *Australian*'s Cameron Stewart and Paul Maley have published a series of articles illuminating the Abbott cabinet's deliberations on deploying the military to fight against ISIS in Iraq and Syria. One of their insights is that in the latter half of 2014, just before the above refutations were being issued, Abbott was actively exploring military options to send further teams of special forces into Iraq. Stewart and Maley report:

> Attorney-General George Brandis said Abbott was "almost visibly frustrated" at the limits of Australian power . . . Abbott's defence minister David Johnston said the prime minister's frustration sometimes bordered on a desire for unilateralism. "He was quite unilateral in his proposition of what we could do and what we should do," Johnston said. "I just kept right away from it. Whenever we had an NSC meeting I used to say, 'We need to be very careful about doing things unilaterally.'"

The substantive issue here is what these episodes reveal about our national decision-making when it comes to military force, in particular the role of the prime minister. Curran concludes that this period shows the system works: the checks and balances of the national security committee of cabinet kept Abbott's eagerness in check. I instead see this as the equivalent of an aviation near-miss. The conclusion Abbott voiced in parliament that Ukraine was a "vital national interest" of Australia is concerning, and the quantity of military (as well as intelligence) resources devoted was problematic. Curran is more sanguine about this than me: "After all, only a small number of special forces soldiers were sent to support police investigators in the Ukraine, and 200 were sent to Iraq." But this misses the point. When you have only a small defence force, deploying such numbers is a risky overcommitment that leaves you exposed elsewhere. Roughly a third of Australia's special forces were deployed to Iraq. Considering the numbers in training or on standby for domestic counter-terrorism, this left precious few to respond to any other crises. It's one thing for a prime minister privately to canvass a range of military options behind doors; it's another for the options canvassed to be outside the realms of reasonableness. And these crises unfolded over months in countries in which our vital national interests were not engaged. What would it have looked like were the issues to have played out over days, in parts of the world where our national interests were vitally engaged? Or in a strategic environment involving newer and more complex forms of warfare? Curran is satisfied that prime ministers and the national security system are up to the challenge. I hope he is right.

There is another important factor here. Kim Beazley refers to Australia as having conducted "demonstrations" with its military. That's an important military term; a demonstration does not rely on having a detailed plan – mission success is just showing up. There is an element of this in Australia's deployments to the Middle East that Malcolm Garcia charts. It is intrinsic in the set-and-forget political culture around some of the ADF's missions in the past decade. Operational and strategic considerations converge in Australian military decision-making: indeed, in a military of the size of Australia's, it is debatable whether you can have an operational level where politics doesn't matter and military commanders are left to make decisions freely. But it is clear that the Australian Defence Force being built right now is intended to do more than just conduct military demonstrations, and that is a step-change our political leaders will need to adjust to.

The Permanent Court of Arbitration ruling of early July has brought some of the security issues in Australia's region to the fore with more force than expected. As I travelled around Australia speaking to audiences about this Quarterly Essay, I was surprised at how many were completely unaware of developments in the South China Sea before the PCA's judgment. Kim Beazley has made, as you would expect, a sophisticated argument about how Australia should decide what to do next in the South China Sea, and has reminded us of our longstanding interests and presence in maritime Southeast Asia. Freedom-of-navigation operations in the South China Sea are certainly an option to be kept in our security toolkit, but it is hard to see how an Australian frigate steaming within twelve nautical miles of Fiery Cross Reef would change the Chinese calculus on the costs of island-building and militarisation right now. It seems likely that these regional issues of maritime assertiveness will increasingly leach into the US–China strategic relationship, although in the long term both China and the United States are motivated to stabilise the relationship and avoid conflict. Australia has a part to play in resisting any move to assert an air defence identification zone in the South China Sea, and in encouraging peaceful resolution of overlapping territorial claims. But this is about more than freedom-of-navigation operations. The Australian public is getting wise to the issues at play in the South China Sea, and the wider strategic competition in Asia. The responses to Olympian Mack Horton's comments, and to the Chinese newspaper *Global Times* urging "revenge" on Australia ("an ideal target for China to warn and strike"), have sharpened appreciated of some of the less palatable trends apparent in China's rise. "Australia's power means nothing compared to the security of China," the *Global Times* warned.

Henry Reynolds is more concerned with the power imbalance between the United States and Australia, and considers my reference to the alliance as a marriage as "a strange and troubling description." He needn't be concerned that I am a soppy alliance sentimentalist, but it is important to acknowledge that beyond the general alignment of Australian and American national interests, our two countries share social capital that should not be underestimated and which remains important to our foreign and defence policy. I am realistic about our ability to influence the course of affairs in Washington. I reject Reynolds' slippery syllogism that "alliance means war – and wars that Australia would otherwise have avoided." It's true that one of Australia's chief talking points in the alliance to date has been our reliability when it comes to fighting with America around the globe, but the path forward for Australia and America's alliance involves more than "incessant military engagement." I'm struck by the fact that Reynolds deems me a militarist too dismissive of the "other people's wars" thesis, while James Curran suggests I'm an old-left radical nationalist who is embracing this notion. The contrast suggests *Firing Line* is on the right path to what Rory Medcalf has suggested could be a more inclusive conversation about security.

James Brown

Kim Beazley was Deputy Prime Minister of Australia from 1995 to 1996 and Leader of the Opposition from 1996 to 2001 and from 2005 to 2006. He served as Ambassador of Australia to the United States from 2010 to 2016.

Judy Betts has recently completed a PhD on the Australian media and the Iraq war.

James Brown is a former Australian Army officer, who commanded a cavalry troop in southern Iraq, served at the Australian taskforce headquarters in Baghdad and was attached to Special Forces in Afghanistan. He is the research director and an adjunct associate professor at the US Studies Centre, University of Sydney. He is the author of Anzac's Long Shadow.

James Curran is Professor of History at the University of Sydney and a research associate at the US Studies Centre. His most recent book is Unholy Fury: Whitlam and Nixon at War.

Malcolm Garcia is a former officer in the Royal Australian Air Force who served in tactical, operational and strategic positions. He is the author of several novels, the latest being Kill-Capture.

Peter Leahy is Director of the National Security Institute at the University of Canberra. He was Chief of Army from 2002 to 2008.

Rory Medcalf is Head of the National Security College at the Australian National University. Formerly, he led the international security program for the Lowy Institute. He was on the independent expert panel for the 2016 Defence White Paper.

Henry Reynolds' groundbreaking histories include The Other Side of the Frontier, Dispossession, The Law of the Land and Why Weren't We Told? His most recent books are Forgotten War and Unnecessary Wars. In 2000 he took up a professorial fellowship at the University of Tasmania.

Don Watson is the author of many acclaimed books, including Caledonia Australis, Recollections of a Bleeding Heart, American Journeys and The Bush. His previous Quarterly Essay was Rabbit Syndrome.

Peter Whish-Wilson was elected a Greens senator for Tasmania in 2012. He is a graduate of the Australian Defence Force Academy and pursued a career in international finance before moving to Tasmania, where he was a lecturer in economics and finance at the University of Tasmania, a wine-maker and an activist.

QUARTERLY ESSAY AUTO-RENEWING SUBSCRIPTIONS NOW AVAILABLE

SUBSCRIBE to Quarterly Essay & SAVE up to 23% on the cover price.

Enjoy free home delivery of the print edition and full digital access on the Quarterly Essay website, iPad, iPhone and Android apps.

FORTHCOMING ISSUES:

Stan Grant on Indigenous Futures
December 2016

David Marr on the Enemies of Change
March 2017

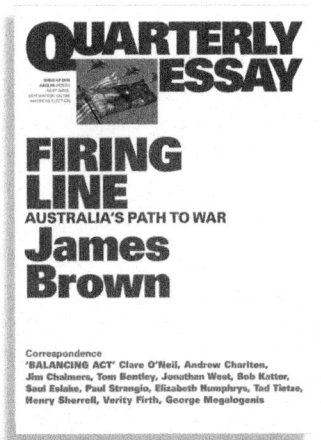

Subscriptions: Receive a discount and never miss an issue. Mailed direct to your door.
- ☐ **1 year auto-renewing print and digital subscription*** (4 issues): $69.95 within Australia. Outside Australia $109.95
- ☐ **1 year print and digital subscription** (4 issues): $79.95 within Australia. Outside Australia $119.95
- ☐ **1 year auto-renewing digital subscription*** (4 issues): $34.95
- ☐ **1 year digital only subscription** (4 issues): $39.95
- ☐ **2 year print and digital subscription** (8 issues): $149.95 within Australia

Gift Subscriptions: Give an inspired gift.
- ☐ **1 year print and digital gift subscription** (4 issues): $79.95 within Australia. Outside Australia $119.95
- ☐ **1 year digital only gift subscription** (4 issues): $39.95
- ☐ **2 year print and digital gift subscription** (8 issues): $149.95 within Australia

All prices include GST, postage and handling. *Your subscription will automatically renew until you notify us to stop. Prior to the end of your subscription period, we will send you a reminder notice.

Please turn over for subscription order form, or subscribe online at **www.quarterlyessay.com**
Alternatively, call 1800 077 514 or 03 9486 0244 or email subscribe@blackincbooks.com

Back Issues: (Prices include GST, postage and handling.)

- ☐ **QE 1** ($15.99) Robert Manne *In Denial*
- ☐ **QE 2** ($15.99) John Birmingham *Appeasing Jakarta*
- ☐ **QE 3** ($15.99) Guy Rundle *The Opportunist*
- ☐ **QE 4** ($15.99) Don Watson *Rabbit Syndrome*
- ☐ **QE 4** ($15.99) Mungo MacCallum *Girt By Sea*
- ☐ **QE 6** ($15.99) John Button *Beyond Belief*
- ☐ **QE 7** ($15.99) John Martinkus *Paradise Betrayed*
- ☐ **QE 8** ($15.99) Amanda Lohrey *Groundswell*
- ☐ **QE 9** ($15.99) Tim Flannery *Beautiful Lies*
- ☐ **QE 10** ($15.99) Gideon Haigh *Bad Company*
- ☐ **QE 11** ($15.99) Germaine Greer *Whitefella Jump Up*
- ☐ **QE 12** ($15.99) David Malouf *Made in England*
- ☐ **QE 13** ($15.99) Robert Manne with David Corlett *Sending Them Home*
- ☐ **QE 14** ($15.99) Paul McGeough *Mission Impossible*
- ☐ **QE 15** ($15.99) Margaret Simons *Latham's World*
- ☐ **QE 16** ($15.99) Raimond Gaita *Breach of Trust*
- ☐ **QE 17** ($15.99) John Hirst *'Kangaroo Court'*
- ☐ **QE 18** ($15.99) Gail Bell *The Worried Well*
- ☐ **QE 19** ($15.99) Judith Brett *Relaxed & Comfortable*
- ☐ **QE 20** ($15.99) John Birmingham *A Time for War*
- ☐ **QE 21** ($15.99) Clive Hamilton *What's Left?*
- ☐ **QE 22** ($15.99) Amanda Lohrey *Voting for Jesus*
- ☐ **QE 23** ($15.99) Inga Clendinnen *The History Question*
- ☐ **QE 24** ($15.99) Robyn Davidson *No Fixed Address*
- ☐ **QE 25** ($15.99) Peter Hartcher *Bipolar Nation*
- ☐ **QE 26** ($15.99) David Marr *His Master's Voice*
- ☐ **QE 27** ($15.99) Ian Lowe *Reaction Time*
- ☐ **QE 28** ($15.99) Judith Brett *Exit Right*
- ☐ **QE 29** ($15.99) Anne Manne *Love & Money*
- ☐ **QE 30** ($15.99) Paul Toohey *Last Drinks*
- ☐ **QE 31** ($15.99) Tim Flannery *Now or Never*
- ☐ **QE 32** ($15.99) Kate Jennings *American Revolution*
- ☐ **QE 33** ($15.99) Guy Pearse *Quarry Vision*
- ☐ **QE 34** ($15.99) Annabel Crabb *Stop at Nothing*
- ☐ **QE 35** ($15.99) Noel Pearson *Radical Hope*
- ☐ **QE 36** ($15.99) Mungo MacCallum *Australian Story*
- ☐ **QE 37** ($15.99) Waleed Aly *What's Right?*
- ☐ **QE 38** ($15.99) David Marr *Power Trip*
- ☐ **QE 39** ($15.99) Hugh White *Power Shift*
- ☐ **QE 40** ($15.99) George Megalogenis *Trivial Pursuit*
- ☐ **QE 41** ($15.99) David Malouf *The Happy Life*
- ☐ **QE 42** ($15.99) Judith Brett *Fair Share*
- ☐ **QE 43** ($15.99) Robert Manne *Bad News*
- ☐ **QE 44** ($15.99) Andrew Charlton *Man-Made World*
- ☐ **QE 45** ($15.99) Anna Krien *Us and Them*
- ☐ **QE 46** ($15.99) Laura Tingle *Great Expectations*
- ☐ **QE 47** ($15.99) David Marr *Political Animal*
- ☐ **QE 48** ($15.99) Tim Flannery *After the Future*
- ☐ **QE 49** ($15.99) Mark Latham *Not Dead Yet*
- ☐ **QE 50** ($15.99) Anna Goldsworthy *Unfinished Business*
- ☐ **QE 51** ($15.99) David Marr *The Prince*
- ☐ **QE 52** ($15.99) Linda Jaivin *Found in Translation*
- ☐ **QE 53** ($15.99) Paul Toohey *That Sinking Feeling*
- ☐ **QE 54** ($15.99) Andrew Charlton *Dragon's Tail*
- ☐ **QE 55** ($15.99) Noel Pearson *A Rightful Place*
- ☐ **QE 56** ($15.99) Guy Rundle *Clivosaurus*
- ☐ **QE 57** ($15.99) Karen Hitchcock *Dear Life*
- ☐ **QE 58** ($19.99) David Kilcullen *Blood Year*
- ☐ **QE 59** ($19.99) David Marr *Faction Man*
- ☐ **QE 60** ($22.99) Laura Tingle *Political Amnesia*
- ☐ **QE 61** ($22.99) George Megalogenis *Balancing Act*
- ☐ **QE 62** ($22.99) James Brown *Firing Line*

☐ I enclose a cheque/money order made out to Schwartz Publishing Pty Ltd.
☐ Please debit my credit card (Mastercard, Visa or Amex accepted).

Card No.

Expiry date / **CCV** **Amount $**

Cardholder's name **Signature**

Name

Address

Email **Phone**

Post or fax this form to: Quarterly Essay, Reply Paid 90094, Carlton VIC 3053 / Freecall: 1800 077 514
Tel: (03) 9486 0288 / Fax: (03) 9011 6104 / Email: subscribe@blackincbooks.com
Subscribe online at **www.quarterlyessay.com**